Language Teacher Psychology

PSYCHOLOGY OF LANGUAGE LEARNING AND TEACHING

Series Editors: **Sarah Mercer**, *Universität Graz, Austria* and **Stephen Ryan**, *Waseda University, Japan*

This international, interdisciplinary book series explores the exciting, emerging field of Psychology of Language Learning and Teaching. It is a series that aims to bring together works which address a diverse range of psychological constructs from a multitude of empirical and theoretical perspectives, but always with a clear focus on their applications within the domain of language learning and teaching. The field is one that integrates various areas of research that have been traditionally discussed as distinct entities, such as motivation, identity, beliefs, strategies and self-regulation, and it also explores other less familiar concepts for a language education audience, such as emotions, the self and positive psychology approaches. In theoretical terms, the new field represents a dynamic interface between psychology and foreign language education, and books in the series draw on work from diverse branches of psychology, while remaining determinedly focused on their pedagogic value. In methodological terms, sociocultural and complexity perspectives have drawn attention to the relationships between individuals and their social worlds, leading to a field now marked by methodological pluralism. In view of this, books encompassing quantitative, qualitative and mixed methods studies are all welcomed.

All books in this series are externally peer-reviewed.

Full details of all the books in this series and of all our other publications can be found on http://www.multilingual-matters.com, or by writing to Multilingual Matters, St Nicholas House, 31–34 High Street, Bristol BS1 2AW, UK.

PSYCHOLOGY OF LANGUAGE LEARNING AND TEACHING: 1

Language Teacher Psychology

Edited by
Sarah Mercer and Achilleas Kostoulas

MULTILINGUAL MATTERS
Bristol • Blue Ridge Summit

DOI https://doi.org/10.21832/MERCER9450
Library of Congress Cataloging in Publication Data
A catalog record for this book is available from the Library of Congress.
Names: Mercer, Sarah, editor. | Kostoulas, Achilleas, 1977- editor.
Title: Language Teacher Psychology/Edited by Sarah Mercer and Achilleas Kostoulas.
Description: Blue Ridge Summit, PA: Multilingual Matters, [2018] | Series: Psychology
   of Language Learning and Teaching: 1 | Includes bibliographical references and
   index.
Identifiers: LCCN 2017038806| ISBN 9781783099443 (softcover : alk. paper) |
   ISBN 9781783099450 (hardcover : alk. paper) | ISBN 9781783099467 (pdf) |
   ISBN 9781783099474 (epub) | ISBN 9781783099481 (kindle)
Subjects: LCSH: Language acquisition—Research—Methodology. | Language
   acquisition—Psychological aspects. | Language and languages—Study and
   teaching—Psychological aspects. | Psycholinguistics.
Classification: LCC P118.5 .L26 2018 | DDC 401/.9—dc23 LC record available at
   https://lccn.loc.gov/2017038806

British Library Cataloguing in Publication Data
A catalogue entry for this book is available from the British Library.

ISBN-13: 978-1-78309-945-0 (hbk)
ISBN-13: 978-1-78309-944-3 (pbk)

Multilingual Matters
UK: St Nicholas House, 31–34 High Street, Bristol BS1 2AW, UK.
USA: NBN, Blue Ridge Summit, PA, USA.

Website: www.multilingual-matters.com
Twitter: Multi_Ling_Mat
Facebook: https://www.facebook.com/multilingualmatters
Blog: www.channelviewpublications.wordpress.com

The policy of Multilingual Matters/Channel View Publications is to use papers that
are natural, renewable and recyclable products, made from wood grown in
sustainable forests. In the manufacturing process of our books, and to further
support our policy, preference is given to printers that have FSC and PEFC Chain of
Custody certification. The FSC and/or PEFC logos will appear on those books
where full certification has been granted to the printer concerned.

Typeset by Nova Techset Private Limited, Bengaluru and Chennai, India.
Printed and bound in the UK by Short Run Press Ltd.
Printed and bound in the US by Edwards Brothers Malloy, Inc.

Contents

Tables and Figures

Figures

Abbreviations

AAAL	American Association of Applied Linguistics
AEIS	Adult Education Interest Section
AILA	*Association Internationale de Linguistique Appliquée*, International Association of Applied Linguistics
APA	American Psychological Association
CALL	Computer Assisted Language Learning
CAS	Complex Adaptive Systems
CASEL	Collaborative for Academic, Social and Emotional Learning
CDS	Complex Dynamic(al) Systems
CITE	Current Issues in Teaching English
CLIL	Content and Language Integrated Learning
CLT	Communicative Language Teaching
DST	Dynamic(al) Systems Theory
ECTS	European Credit Transfer System
EFL	English as a Foreign Language
EI	Emotional Intelligence
ELL	English Language Learners
EMPATHICS	Emotion and Empathy; Meaning and Motivation; Perseverance; Agency and Autonomy; Time; Hardiness and Habits of Mind; Intelligences; Character Strengths; and Self Factors
ESL	English as a Second Language
FTP	Future Time Perspective
GTM	Grammar-translation Method
ICT	Information Communication Technology
ID	Individual Differences
IST	In-service Teachers
JALT	Japanese Association for Language Teaching
L2	Second Language
LexTALE	Lexical Test for Advanced Learners of English
LTC	Language Teacher Cognition
LTI	Language Teacher Identity
LTP	Language Teacher Psychology
LTSE	Language Teacher Self-efficacy

MS	Multiple Sclerosis
MYE	Manage Your Emotions (Questionnaire)
NNS	Non-native Speaker
NS	Native Speaker
PASSS	Post-application of Signature Strength Survey
PERMA	Positive Emotion, Engagement, Positive Relationships, Meaning and Accomplishment (or Achievement)
PLLT	Psychology of Language Learning and Teaching
PST	Pre-service Teachers
PTE	Personal Teaching Efficacy
SCOBA	Scheme of a Complete Orienting Basis of the Action
SCT	Sociocultural Theory
SD	Standard Deviation
SEL	Social and Emotional Learning
SI	Social Intelligence
SLA	Second Language Acquisition
SOC	Selection, Optimisation and Compensation
TATE	Third Age Teacher Educators
TEFL	Teaching English as a Foreign Language
TEI	Trait Emotional Intelligence
TEIques-SF	Trait Emotional Intelligence Questionnaire – Short Form
TESL	Teaching English as a Second Language
TESOL	Teaching English to Speakers of Other Languages
TSE	Teacher Self-efficacy
VIA	Values in Action
WEIS	Wong Emotional Intelligence Scale
ZPD	Zone of Proximal Development

Contributors

Editors

Sarah Mercer is the Head of the ELT Research and Methodology section at the University of Graz. She is interested in all aspects of language learning psychology, in particular self-related constructs, motivation, affect, agency, attributions, mindsets and belief systems. In her research, she prefers to employ qualitatively oriented approaches. Currently, she is engaged in considering aspects of language learner psychology through a complexity lens and exploring a diverse range of methodological approaches for this purpose. Furthermore, she is currently working on projects in the areas of language teacher psychology, socio-emotional intelligences, and mindsets. Some of Sarah's recent publications in the field of language learning psychology include *Exploring Psychology in Language Learning and Teaching* (co-authored with Marion Williams and Stephen Ryan), *Positive Psychology in SLA* (co-edited with Peter D. MacIntyre and Tammy Gregersen), and *Multiple Perspectives of the Self in SLA* (co-edited with Marion Williams).

Achilleas Kostoulas taught English in primary and secondary schools in Greece before moving on to language teacher education. He completed a PhD at the University of Manchester (UK), and now works in the ELT Research and Methodology section of the Department of English Studies at the University of Graz (Austria), where he teaches courses in ELT and applied linguistics. Achilleas' research interests focus on the psychology of language learning and teaching.

Authors

Having taught modern foreign languages and classics in secondary schools in Cleveland and London, **Gary Chambers** joined the School of Education, University of Leeds in 1989. He has published widely on many aspects of modern foreign languages learning and teaching, motivational and attitudinal perspectives in particular. Gary has recently completed a British Academy funded research project on the approach to primary to secondary school transition in modern foreign languages in Saxony-Anhalt, Germany. Between 1996 and 1999 he was Editor of the *Language Learning Journal*.

Andrew D. Cohen (Professor at UCLA, Hebrew University; Professor Emeritus, University of Minnesota) has been an applied linguist for many years, was Secretary General of the International Association of Applied Linguistics (AILA) and Secretary Treasurer of the American Association of Applied Linguistics (AAAL). In addition, he co-edited *Language Learning Strategies* (Oxford University Press, 2008), authored *Strategies in Learning and Using a Second Language* (Routledge, 2014) and co-authored *Teaching and Learning Pragmatics* (Routledge, 2014). Actively retired, Andrew is grandparenting, maintaining a Mandarin blog of his life, playing trumpet in a band and writing a new book on pragmatics.

Dr **Peter I. De Costa** is an Assistant Professor in the Department of Linguistics, Germanic, Slavic, Asian and African Languages at Michigan State University. He is the author of *The Power of Identity and Ideology in Language Learning: Designer Immigrants Learning English in Singapore* (Springer, 2016). Peter also recently edited *Ethics in Applied Linguistics: Language Researcher Narratives* (Routledge, 2016), and guest edited (with Suresh Canagarajah) a special issue of *Linguistics and Education* which focused on scalar approaches to language learning and teaching.

Jean-Marc Dewaele is Professor of Applied Linguistics and Multilingualism at Birkbeck, University of London. He has published widely on individual differences in psycholinguistic, sociolinguistic, pragmatic, psychological and emotional aspects of multilingualism. He is the author of the monograph *Emotions in Multiple Languages* (Palgrave Macmillan, 2010). Jean-Marc is President of the International Association of Multilingualism and former president of the European Second Language Association. He is General Editor of the *International Journal of Bilingual Education and Bilingualism*. He won the Equality and Diversity Research Award from the *British Association for Counselling and Psychotherapy* (2013) and the Robert C. Gardner Award for Excellence in Second Language and Bilingualism Research (2016) from the *International Association of Language and Social Psychology*.

Joseph Falout, Associate Professor at Nihon University (Japan), authored or co-authored over 40 papers and book chapters about language learning psychology. He received awards for publications and presentations from the Japan Association for Language Teaching (JALT). He edits for JALT's *OnCUE Journal* and *Asian EFL Journal*. Collaborations include creating the theoretical and applied foundations of critical participatory looping, present communities of imagining, and ideal classmates. Joseph has taught rhetoric and composition, public speaking and ESL at colleges in the USA.

Anne Feryok is a senior lecturer in the Department of English and Linguistics at the University of Otago (New Zealand). Her main research area is in language teacher cognition and development, mostly conducted within sociocultural theory, and occasionally within complex dynamic systems, both of which reflect her interest in initial genesis or emergence and ongoing development in different contexts. Anne's work has been published in international journals such as *The Modern Language Journal, System, Language Teaching Research* and *Teachers and Teaching: Theory and Practice.*

Christina Gkonou is a lecturer in TESOL and MA TESOL Programme Leader in the Department of Language and Linguistics, University of Essex (UK). She convenes postgraduate modules on teacher training and education and the psychology of language learning and teaching. Her main research interests are in all areas of the psychology of learners and teachers, but more specifically in language anxiety and emotions, teacher identity and agency, and emotion-regulation strategies for language learning. Christina is the co-editor of *New Directions in Language Learning Psychology* (Springer, 2015) and *New Insights into Language Anxiety: Theory, Research and Educational Implications* (Multilingual Matters, 2017), and co-author of the *MYE (Managing Your Emotions) Questionnaire.*

Tammy Gregersen, PhD in linguistics from Valparaiso (Chile), began her teaching and researching career in a university in the Atacama Desert in the North of Chile and is now a Professor of TESOL and teacher educator at the University of Northern Iowa (USA). She is the author, with Peter D. MacIntyre, of *Capitalizing on Language Learners' Individuality: From Premise to Practice* (Multilingual Matters, 2014) and *Optimizing Language Learners' Nonverbal Behavior: From Tenet to Technique* (Multilingual Matters, 2017). She also co-edited *Positive Psychology in SLA* (Multilingual Matters, 2016) and *Innovative Practices in Language Teacher Education: Spanning the Spectrum from Intra- to Inter-personal Teacher Development* (Springer, 2017). She has published extensively on individual differences, teacher education, language teaching methodology and nonverbal communication in language classrooms. Tammy is passionate about travelling and has presented at conferences and graduate programmes across the globe.

Phil Hiver received his PhD in applied linguistics from the University of Nottingham, and is Assistant Professor of Education at Florida State University. His research focuses on the role of social and psychological factors in second language teaching and learning, and the contribution of complexity theory to applied linguistics research. Phil's published work has appeared in journals such as *Applied Linguistics, Learning and Individual Differences, Language Teaching Research* and *The Modern Language Journal.*

Paula Kalaja is Professor Emerita of English (with a PhD degree from Georgetown University, Washington, DC) in the Department of Language and Communication Studies, University of Jyväskylä (Finland). She specialises in L2 learning and teaching and has co-authored and co-edited *Beliefs about SLA: New Research Approaches* (Springer, 2003), *Narratives of Learning and Teaching EFL* (Palgrave Macmillan, 2008) and *Beliefs, Agency and Identity in Foreign Language Learning and Teaching* (Palgrave Macmillan, 2016) and locally published introductory books on research methods in applied linguistics and learning to learn skills, and some EFL textbooks.

Jim King is Lecturer in Applied Linguistics and Psychology of Language Education within the University of Leicester's School of Arts. His research interests centre around situated psychological aspects of foreign language teaching and second language acquisition, with current research projects exploring the issues of silence and nonverbal communication in language learning from an affective (emotions) perspective. Jim's publications include the 2013 monograph *Silence in the Second Language Classroom* and the 2015 edited volume *The Dynamic Interplay Between Context and the Language Learner* (both published by Palgrave Macmillan).

Tae-Young Kim (PhD OISE/University of Toronto) is Full Professor in the Department of English Education at Chung-Ang University, Seoul, South Korea, where he teaches both undergraduate and graduate courses in applied linguistics and TESOL. His research interests include ESL/EFL learning/teaching (de)motivation, sociocultural theory, English education policy and qualitative/mixed methods approaches. He has published over 100 papers on various topics in L2 motivation and L2 learning.

Youngmi Kim is a PhD student in the Department of English Education at Chung-Ang University, Seoul, South Korea. She completed her MA in applied linguistics in 2013 at the University of Nottingham. Her current research interests lie in the areas of L2 learning motivation/demotivation, L2 teacher motivation, L2 teacher autonomy and L2 teacher education.

Martin Lamb joined the School of Education at the University of Leeds in 1999 after 16 years teaching English abroad, mostly in Indonesia and Bulgaria. At Leeds he teaches BA and MA courses in various aspects of applied linguistics. Martin's main research interest is learner/teacher motivation and how it interacts with sociocultural context.

Anita Lämmerer works as a research assistant and language teacher educator at the University of Graz (Austria), where she is pursuing her PhD. She also works as an English language teacher at a secondary school, where in

addition to her teaching duties she coordinates a school–university partnership programme. Part of her current work is focused on teacher psychology and content and language integrated learning (CLIL).

Wendy Li is a PhD student of the second language studies program in the
Department of Linguistics, Germanic, Slavic, Asian and African
Languages at Michigan State University. Before coming to United States,
she taught English as a foreign language in different educational institutions in China. Her research interests include second language acquisition,
language teacher identity and language pedagogy. She holds an MA in
TESOL from Lancaster University (UK).

Peter D. MacIntyre received his PhD in psychology from the University of
Western Ontario (now Western University, Canada) in 1992 with R.C.
Gardner, and is currently a Professor of Psychology at Cape Breton
University (Canada). His research examines emotion, motivation and cog-
nition across a variety of types of behaviour, including interpersonal com-
munication, public speaking and learning. The majority of Peter's research
examines the psychology of communication, with a particular emphasis on
second language acquisition and communication. He is co-author of
*Capitalizing on Language Learners' Individuality: From Premise to
Practice* (Multilingual Matters, 2014) and *Optimizing Language Learners'
Nonverbal Behaviour: From Tenet to Technique* (Multilingual Matters,
2017) with Tammy Gregersen. He co-edited *Motivational Dynamics in
Language Learning* with Zoltán Dörnyei and Alastair Henry (Multilingual
Matters, 2015), *Positive Psychology in SLA* with Tammy Gregersen and
Sarah Mercer (Multilingual Matters, 2016) and *Innovative Practices in
Language Teacher Education: Spanning the Spectrum from Intra- to Inter-
personal Teacher Development* with Tammy Gregersen (Springer, 2017).

Katja Mäntylä, PhD, is Senior Lecturer/Adjunct Professor in the
Department of Language and Communication Studies, University of
Jyväskylä (Finland). She has done research on language awareness of L2
learners, language assessment, vocabulary studies and multilingual learners. Katja has developed several new courses for language students, such
as 'Developing teaching materials' and 'Using popular culture in language
teaching'. In addition to teaching pre-service teachers, she is involved in
developing a training programme for in-service teachers.

Tim Murphey, PhD from Université de Neuchâtel (Switzerland), TESOL's
Professional Development in Language Education series editor, co-author
with Zoltán Dörnyei of *Group Dynamics in the Language Classroom*
(Cambridge University Press, 2003), and author of *Music and Song*
(Oxford University Press, 1992), researches Vygotskian sociocultural
theory with transdisciplinary emphasis at Kanda University, Japan. Tim's

most recent books are *Teaching in Pursuit of Wow!* (Abax, 2012) and *Meaningful Action: Earl Stevick's Influence on Language Teaching* (Cambridge University Press, 2013), co-edited with Jane Arnold.

Ng Kwan Yee Sarah is a lecturer in the English Language Teaching Unit of the Chinese University of Hong Kong. Her current research focuses on the role of emotion, particularly positive emotion, and emotional regulation in second language acquisition. On a broader level, she is interested to know how and where L2 learners' general affective and cognitive attributes, especially those related to emotion and epistemological beliefs, intersect with L2-specific ones.

Rebecca L. Oxford received a Lifetime Achievement Award and is a University of Maryland Distinguished Scholar-Teacher and Professor Emerita. This third-ager presents internationally (40+ countries spanning her lifetime). She has published 14 books, three co-edited book series, eight special issues and over 250 articles/chapters. Rebecca helps care for an advanced third-age mother (93 years) and conducts research on third-agers. Her topics also include learning strategies, culture, transformative education, positive psychology and peace, all united by the thread of compassion.

Taguhi Sahakyan is an early-career researcher working in the field of English language education. She has taught various English language courses in the university context both in the UK and Armenia. She holds a Master's degree in applied linguistics from the University of Nottingham and is currently working towards her doctoral degree in education from the University of Leeds. Taguhi's main research interests involve teacher motivation and teacher development.

Mehvish Saleem is currently reading for a PhD in applied linguistics at the University of Graz (Austria). Her research interests include language teacher psychology, complex systems theory and teaching English in 'difficult circumstances'. Mehvish's research project focuses on the holistic exploration of language teachers' psychology.

Virginia Gill Simmons retired after 50+ years in two states' public school systems. She enjoyed teaching (grade 1–graduate), coordinating local and state programs, leading a high school and directing an award-winning adult education program. She was Technology Educator of the Year, Adult Education Director of the Year, and most recently a US State Department English Language Fellow (Cambodia). She also taught in Russia and Moldova. Ginny is active in international TESOL, Carolina TESOL and related organisations. Her goal is creating 'thinking' ESL classrooms.

Manka Varghese is an Associate Professor at the University of Washington, Seattle (USA). Her main areas of research focus on the topics of language teacher identity and emerging bilingual/immigrant students' college-going selves. She also engages in critical perspectives that involve the exploration of agency in her theoretical frameworks. She was recently the lead editor of a *TESOL Quarterly* Special Issue on Language Teacher Identity. Manka's articles have appeared in *TESOL Quarterly*, *Journal of Language, Identity and Education*, *Critical Inquiry in Language Studies* and *International Journal of Multicultural Education*, along with numerous book chapters in edited volumes.

Cynthia White is Professor of Applied Linguistics, Massey University (New Zealand) and has published widely on affect, identity and agency in distance and online language teaching learning. She is on the editorial boards of eight international journals, including *TESOL Quarterly*, and is Associate Editor for *Language Learning & Technology*. Cynthia has been plenary speaker at international conferences and workshops in Germany, Thailand, Singapore, China, UK, Hawai'i and Malaysia and has completed collaborative research projects with Oxford University, Open University UK and Nottingham University. Her most recent projects include the analysis of teacher narrative accounts of agency and emotion in relation to classroom conflict.

Mark Wyatt is Assistant Professor in Communication at the Petroleum Institute in Abu Dhabi (UAE), supporting project-based learning and practitioner research. He previously worked with in-service Omani and pre-service Malaysian teachers on BA TESOL/TESL programmes for the universities of Leeds and Portsmouth, respectively. His qualitative case study research on language teachers' growth in practical knowledge and teachers' self-efficacy beliefs has appeared in various journals.

Foreword

Applied linguistics is by definition an 'applied' discipline. As such, at the heart of virtually any aspect of applied linguistic research into second language acquisition (SLA) has been a concern to improve the quality of language learning. Accordingly, the 'unit of analysis' of such research has predominantly been the language learner – which, of course, left language teachers somewhat neglected: in most cases, they were seen as little more than one of the many factors affecting learner success. To make matters worse, when comparing the various factors affecting learning outcomes, language teachers have not fared particularly well, largely because it is rather difficult to pin down their individual impact on the success of their learners. This is well illustrated by the following summary concerning one specific area of language teacher psychology, namely, teacher motivation:

> The ultimate aim of motivation research is always to explain student learning, and in order to associate the latter meaningfully with the motivation of teachers, we need to show first that an increase in teacher motivation leads to improved motivational practice on their behalf, which in turn promotes student motivation, which eventually results in enhanced student performance. While the chain is intuitively convincing, it is difficult to get empirical confirmation for it because of the manifold confounding variables at each connection level. (Dörnyei & Ryan, 2015: 101)

What is more, for quantitatively-oriented scholars, it is not only the manifold confounding variables that have hampered research efforts but also the logistical problem of generating a sufficiently large sample size of teachers willing to participate in order to ensure statistically significant results. When planning an ambitious research design for a quantitative study, a sample of at least 100 participants is typically seen as the bare minimum – or else one is likely to run into problems of insufficient normality of the distribution of the data. While this is usually easily achievable when investigating learners, the technicalities of producing a similarly large teacher sample may often be perceived as forbidding.

Finally, not only is it difficult to demonstrate the link between teacher-specific characteristics and student learning outcomes, but it may be equally problematic to identify what exactly good teacher characteristics and practices involve. Different teachers can achieve success in different situations by means of a range of widely divergent strategies, and it is unclear if or how transferrable some of the 'best practices' are from one situation to another. As such, research has struggled to provide exact specifications of the main attributes of a 'good' language teacher. Indeed, in a complex educational and sociocultural situation such as the language classroom, it may prove hard to identify empirically the general significance of even the seemingly most beneficial teacher characteristics, given that there are likely to be scenarios where diverse combinations of factors can result in equally favourable student outcomes.

All these considerations and empirical challenges have tended to work against the feasibility of widespread language teacher research in the past and have thus discouraged many scholars from initiating investigations with the teacher as their focus – after all, it seemed sensible to invest one's limited amount of time and energy into areas that were likely to yield greater insights in the short run. Yet, the irony of the situation is that almost every language learner – and indeed, language researcher – would agree that the teacher is not merely one of the many factors of the educational setup but is one of the single most important factors – if not *the* most important one. This point has been well argued by most studies in this volume, which suggests that the relative absence of sufficient research on language teaching has been contradictory to the very essence of the study of SLA, namely, its applied, practical focus on what really matters. Language teachers *do* matter, and not paying enough attention to them is therefore a shortcoming which can (perhaps) be explained but not excused. It is against this backdrop that the value of the current volume becomes evident: it represents an ambitious attempt to start redressing the balance and giving language teacher research its due significance. And ambitious this attempt is: the 17 chapters by well-known scholars, accompanied by a detailed Introduction and Conclusion, present rich and irrefutable evidence that the area of language teacher psychology is a vibrant field which is hugely relevant to our overall understanding of language education.

In the Introduction, the editors formulate two central aims for the book: to place the subject matter of language teaching psychology on the broader map of the study of SLA, and – by providing a comprehensive overview – to make sure that on this metaphorical map the domain is not merely a small new island but a massive continent. I believe that everybody who embarks on discovering this new land as outlined in this volume will agree that the project has been an unqualified success in both respects. The editors have managed to recruit a stellar cast of contributors, and the variety of concepts, approaches and methodologies represented in the chapters is genuinely impressive and inspiring. Yet, at the same time, the variety of voices does not result in a cacophony but converges in a unified coda proclaiming that the study of language teaching psychology is a highly fruitful research area with considerable practical and theoretical implications. At the very end of the Conclusion, the editors reiterate their hope that this volume will generate a greater interest in and awareness of the subject in the community at large – all I can say is that with the help of their contributors they have done everything within their means to make this happen and have produced a volume that represents applied linguistic scholarship at the highest level.

Zoltán Dörnyei

Reference

Dörnyei, Z. and Ryan, S. (2015) *The Psychology of the Language Learner Revisited.* New York: Routledge.

1 Introduction to Language Teacher Psychology

Sarah Mercer and Achilleas Kostoulas

> There is no system in the world or any school in
> the country that is better than its teachers.
> Teachers are the lifeblood of the success of schools.
> Ken Robinson, 2013

Why a Book on Language Teacher Psychology?

If you think back to your language learning at school, you might remember specific tasks or projects you did, but, even more likely, you will remember your teachers. You will remember the kind of people they were, the atmosphere they created in their classrooms and how you felt in their class and in your relationship with them. Teachers are absolutely defining in terms of a person's educational experience as well as often in terms of their life trajectories after school. Surely these people, who have the privilege and considerable responsibility of crafting learning experiences, are so important that understanding their characteristics, personalities, needs, motivations and well-being should be a priority. And yet, in second language acquisition (SLA) to date, this has not been the case.

Understandably and quite rightly, the learner-centred movement drew attention to individual learners. It raised awareness among educators and researchers of the ways in which learners can vary as individuals and how these differences can impact on how they acquire additional languages. This movement was necessary in light of the dominant focus at the time on the language itself and the technical methods for teaching language to learners, with little or no consideration of their personal characteristics. However, in the field's eagerness to move pedagogically and empirically away from teacher-centred approaches, it has perhaps inadvertently led to a neglect of attention being paid to teachers as a population and as individuals. While the field of individual differences in SLA blossomed in respect of learner characteristics such as motivation, sense of self, beliefs, styles and strategies, attention to the teacher and teacher individual differences all but vanished. Around the 1990s this began to change as researchers started to examine teacher identities and teacher cognition, marking a gradual introduction of a body of work focusing on teachers as individuals, yet still comparatively limited in scope when compared to the body of work which examines learners.

More recently, the field of learner individual differences (ID) research in SLA has also undergone something of a transformation. First, the field has expanded its empirical focus to include research on constructs such as emotions (Dewaele, 2015; MacIntyre & Gregersen, 2012), attributions (Williams *et al.*, 2001), mindsets (Mercer & Ryan, 2010; Ryan & Mercer, 2012), goals (Woodrow, 2012), personality (Dewaele, 2012; Oxford, 1996) and others (Dörnyei, 2009; Ehrman *et al.*, 2003; Gregersen & MacIntyre, 2014). In a parallel development, there has also been a broadening of methodological approaches used to investigate learner diversity, incorporating qualitative and mixed method designs in addition to the more typical quantitative studies which dominated early work in the field (Tatzl *et al.*, 2016). As the field has broadened, there has also been a notable trend towards increased interest in more holistic approaches, which examine interconnections between constructs and also the situated nature of constructs, and these new perspectives have often been influenced by complexity theories (Dörnyei, 2009; Dörnyei & Ryan, 2015). Most recently, the field of ID research has grown to such an extent in content, scope and diversity of approaches that there is increasingly recognition of a community of research that falls under the umbrella of 'psychology of language learning and teaching', as evinced by the series in which this collection is situated. This new emerging field of scholarship extends beyond the traditional ID paradigm and, as such, creates the perfect conditions for broadening the agenda of those working in this area to include teachers, as is our intention with this collection.

There are several reasons why we feel it is especially important to study the psychology of language teachers. One important reason for studying the psychology of teachers is a need to redress the imbalance between studies that have focused on learners and those that have focused on teachers. When compared with the diversity, depth and breadth of research available on learner psychology, there is a notable scarcity of comparable studies examining a wide range of psychological constructs in teachers, teachers at all career stages and from multiple theoretical perspectives. Yet, if we can better understand teacher psychology, we can more easily appreciate the kind of support language teachers need to ensure that they flourish in their professional roles and are able to be the best teachers they can possibly be – for the sake of their own professional well-being as well as for their learners' well-being and ultimate learning. Indeed, understanding teacher psychology is a worthy goal in its own right (Holmes, 2005). As Maslach and Leiter (1999) point out, teachers are the most valuable part of the educational system and so their professional well-being must be a priority.

Yet, teachers are also at the centre of classroom life and their feelings, thoughts, goals and resulting behaviours dictate to a large extent the atmosphere for the whole group as well as individual learners (DeVries & Zan, 1995; Reyes *et al.*, 2012). Essentially, teachers who are in a positive and enabling state of mind when they teach will not only enjoy their jobs more, but research shows that they will do their job better, with more creativity and enhanced pedagogical skills (Albrecht, 2006; Corcoran & Tormey, 2012; Furrer *et al.*, 2014). As Bajorek *et al.* (2014: 6) explain, 'a teacher with high job satisfaction, positive morale and who is healthy should be more likely to teach lessons which are creative, challenging and effective'.

However, it is more than just the atmosphere they create. In many ways, teacher and learner psychologies represent two sides of the same coin. Through the process of contagion, we know that positive teacher emotions are closely connected to the affective states experienced by the learners (Frenzel *et al.*, 2009; Patrick *et al.*, 2000). This means that if teachers are happy and motivated, then it is more likely that their learners will be too. If learners are motivated and engaged, this too is motivating for teachers and so ensures an upward spiral of positivity, which benefits both teachers and learners (Fredrickson, 2013). As Mercer *et al.* (2016: 224) conclude, 'successful language learning depends to a large degree on teachers and, as such, for all concerned, we must make their professional well-being a priority'.

This book represents a plea for the importance of extending our understanding of the psychology of teachers, first, because they represent centrally important stakeholders in the language education process and are worthy of investigation in their own right, and secondly, because understanding language teacher psychology is centrally related to an understanding of the psychology of their learners too.

What We Already Know about Language Teacher Psychology

It is important perhaps to stress here that we are not claiming that there is no work on teacher psychology in SLA. A considerable body of research already exists, although there is a clear imbalance in respect to the work on teacher and learner psychologies (see Mercer, 2016, in press). Perhaps one of the key areas that has developed an extensive body of work concerns teacher cognitions – a term that encompasses teacher knowledge, beliefs and thinking processes. Research on the cognitions of language teachers builds on a well-established body of empirical and theoretical work in mainstream education (e.g. Shulman, 1986). An overview of early research on language teacher cognition has been provided by Borg (2003), who notes that research on teacher cognitions has typically focused on connections to prior language learning, teacher education and classroom practice. Later studies have tended to focus on three additional themes: a possible mismatch between teacher and learner beliefs; the connections between teacher cognitions and classroom practices; and the development of teacher cognitions in the course of the teachers' career trajectory (Kalaja *et al.*, 2016). Within this body of literature there have been notable developments that are relevant for our understandings of the field of teacher psychology as a whole. Recently, a special issue of the *Modern Language Journal* has expanded the scope of research on teacher cognitions by suggesting contemporary understandings of the construct, which reflect their dynamic nature, their embeddedness in contexts, and the related trend towards the use of complex systems theory as a conceptual frame (Kubanyiova & Feryok, 2015). These developments foreground more holistic approaches which examine teacher cognitions in relation to other dimensions of teacher psychology, including teacher emotions in particular (e.g. Aragão, 2011; Barcelos, 2015; Golombek & Doran, 2014).

A second main body of work in language teacher psychology consists of studies conducted in the field of teacher identity, which has been heavily influenced by research on learner identities, following the seminal publication of Norton (2000). Writing 10 years ago, Tsui (2007) identified three salient themes in research, namely the multidimensionality of identity, the relations between social and private identities, and the relations between agency and structure in the way identities are constructed. Work on identity has continued to expand in scope; the vibrancy of the field can be seen in the publication of recent special issues that have appeared in *TESOL Quarterly* (Varghese *et al.*, 2016) and the *Modern Language Journal* (De Costa & Norton, 2017), as well as comprehensive collections of empirical and theoretical papers edited by Cheung *et al.* (2014) and Barkhuizen (2016). The diversity of theoretical perspectives in teacher identity research was outlined by Varghese *et al.* (2005), who argued for an openness to theoretical pluralism, although the vast majority of work has tended to take some form of sociocultural perspective. This sociocultural focus has resulted in increased sensitivity to the situated nature of identity construction, which has proved to be an enduring theme in teacher identity work (e.g. Clarke, 2008, 2009; Hawkins & Norton, 2009; Kanno & Stuart, 2011; Menard-Warwick, 2013).

Another area of research that is beginning to attract empirical and theoretical attention is language teacher motivation, which has drawn on an increasing body of work in teacher motivation research in general education (Richardson *et al.*, 2014). Considering the salience of motivation in SLA research in general, it is perhaps surprising that such interest has been slow to develop. Typically, teachers have been examined in terms of how they can influence learners' motivation but not in terms of the character and quality of their own motivation. One especially notable recent publication is Dörnyei and Kubanyiova (2014), in which the authors describe how the L2 Motivation Self System (Dörnyei, 2005) can also be considered in respect to the psychology of language teachers. Other areas connected to teacher motivation which have been studied more recently include professional development (e.g. Hiver, 2013), professional commitment (e.g. Gao & Xu, 2014), as well as in relation to self-beliefs (e.g. Kubanyiova, 2009).

Finally, there have also been a few isolated studies in areas such as teacher self-efficacy (e.g. Mills & Allen, 2007; Wyatt, 2014, 2016), emotions (e.g. Cowie, 2011; Kalaja *et al.*, 2016; King, 2016), agency and autonomy (e.g. Kalaja *et al.*, 2016; Lamb & Reinders, 2007; Smith, 2003; White, 2016), and also teacher ID as interlocutors (Gurzynski-Weiss, 2013). However, these cannot yet be thought of as representing fully developed fields of research, even when compared with language teacher cognition and identity, which themselves have been relatively limited in their scope, depth and breadth (see also Mercer, 2016, in press). As Kalaja *et al.* (2016) conclude in their overview:

> … compared with research on learner beliefs, research on teacher beliefs has made less progress over the past few decades in opening up new theoretical starting points, or challenging traditional definitions or research methodology. (Kalaja *et al.*, 2016: 12)

One other development in the field that has led to a growth in attention to teachers is the emergence of work inspired by positive psychology in SLA (Gabryś-Barker & Gałajda, 2016; MacIntyre *et al.*, 2016). This has introduced a range of new constructs, many of which lend themselves well to being examined in relation to teachers. For example, recent publications have highlighted the relevance of resilience and related constructs to the professional lives of teachers (Day & Gu, 2014; Howard & Johnson, 2004; Tait, 2008), and this construct has been picked up in respect of language teaching and extended by Hiver and Dörnyei (2017), who proposed the idea of 'teacher immunity'. They see this as being a kind of protection that evolves over time as part of teachers' identities and they caution that it can develop into either productive or also potentially maladaptive immunity. Another strand of positive psychology inspiring work with regard to teachers has examined language teacher emotional and social intelligences. Research in this area is prompted by awareness of the role of emotional and social intelligence in shaping classroom environments which are conducive to learning (Elias & Arnold, 2006; Nizielski *et al.*, 2012), as well as concerns about teacher well-being (Day & Gu, 2009). In a recent publication, Gkonou and Mercer (2017) look specifically at the emotional and social intelligence of language teachers and the ways in which these constructs are enacted in classroom practices.

Therefore, we see positive developments in the field and a contemporary climate that is fertile for investigating teacher psychology in depth and from a range of theoretical and methodological perspectives. Yet, in briefly reviewing the work in the field, we notice that there appears to be another imbalance, namely in the types of teachers who are being studied. The larger focus lies mostly on pre-service or early career stage teachers. There are likely to be pragmatic reasons for this as researchers have easier access to pre-service teachers and they may well represent the populations with which they work and thus are intrinsically of interest to the researchers. Furthermore, pre-service teachers are still most clearly open to development and part of teaching programmes, which means research can more readily have clear implications for practice in terms of suggestions for training courses. In addition, in-service teachers are often under greater time pressures, which could possibly make them more reluctant to be involved in research projects. However, in-service teachers across the career trajectory are a vitally important population to understand in terms of their unique psychological situations and the specific challenges they face (Day *et al.*, 2007). We also note that late career stage teachers approaching retirement remain even more woefully under-researched with no investigation into how they can be supported in flourishing in their jobs all the way up to retirement, ensuring they leave the profession on a positive professional high (see Oxford *et al.*, this volume). Clearly, such research into teachers across the professional lifespan would offer vitally important lessons for policy makers, continual professional development programmes, and educational leaders including school principals as well as for teachers themselves. With this collection, we hope to provide impetus for further research and set an agenda which is open to a range of constructs and teacher populations as well as diverse methodological and theoretical approaches.

What Our Aims Are with the Book

As such, our main aims with the book are twofold. First, we wanted to explicitly name the area of research of language teacher psychology and thereby generate further interest in the field. The field of psychology in language learning and teaching (PLLT) is becoming increasingly well established as a community. It has its own biennial conference, a book series with a major international publisher, several special issues and books in the field, as well as a nascent professional association. However, PLLT remains dominated by a focus on the learner (Mercer, 2016) and, as the field grows, it is necessary to take stock of the balance and profile of work being done under the broad umbrella of PLLT. In doing so, it became apparent that there is a need to 'redress the balance', ensuring that we better understand teacher psychology from a more complex, nuanced and diversified perspective. As such, we hope to see a broadening in the range of constructs being investigated in respect to teachers with a consideration of work already being done in general education as well as positive psychology specifically. We also wanted to draw attention to teachers as valuable individuals across the professional lifespan and encourage a greater understanding of the issues facing language education professionals across the globe and across different career stages. We also believe in the central importance of teachers as key stakeholders and one of the most influential factors in successful learning (Hattie, 2009); understanding them as a population and as individuals must become a priority for the field if we wish to have a comprehensive understanding of processes of language learning and teaching.

A second concern for us was that the existent work on language teachers that is available as outlined above is sometimes seen as disparate and unconnected. In some ways, interconnections in the existent work have been hampered as a result of differing conceptualisations and assumptions about the various areas of research. For example, many scholars in the field of identity research rejected cognitive approaches and assumed all work in the field of psychology took a cognitive approach. Our understanding is that psychology is a domain of enquiry, not a specific theoretical or methodological approach to the study of this. Similarly, many cognitive researchers have only recently started to acknowledge the importance of other psychological dimensions and dynamism, such as affect as well as the role of contexts. Thus, another aim for this book was to show explicitly that psychology represents a broad field of interest, not a specific theoretical perspective or set of constructs. As such, we have tried to ensure that we include a range of perspectives, constructs and contexts in the collection to show where there might be opportunities for interconnections to be made. The umbrella discipline of PLLT will profit most from methodological and theoretical plurality to ensure a more comprehensive and richer set of understandings of the lived lives of teachers. Our hope with this shared publication is that by facilitating a holistic appreciation of the larger field, people new to the field may find inspiration and ideas for related studies bridging conceptual gaps.

This Book

The contributions that make up this edited collection can be read in any order. However, we have loosely arranged them to take readers from aspects of language teacher psychology which have already received somewhat more attention in the literature to the discussion of themes that are only recently beginning to be more widely examined. We begin our exploration of language teacher psychology by looking at somewhat more familiar constructs such as motivation, identities and cognition (Chapters 2–7). Then, in Chapters 8 through 12, we examine specific constructs such as self-efficacy, beliefs, emotions, agency and attitudes; areas in which our understandings in SLA are still in their early stages with respect to teachers. The third loose grouping of chapters (Chapters 13–17) examines constructs from the field of positive psychology such as well-being, resilience and meaning making, which are now increasingly being investigated with regard to various types of language teachers. We conclude the collection with a chapter which suggests how a holistic perspective on teacher psychology might offer fresh insights and potentially be informed by a complexity perspective.

In the first chapter that follows this introduction (Chapter 2), Phil Hiver, Tae-Young Kim and Youngmi Kim reflect on language teacher motivation. A thematic approach is used to present empirical work on language teacher motivation, focusing on the questions of what motivates teachers to enter the profession, what motivates teachers in the classroom, and how teacher motivation is linked to classroom dynamics and professional development. The chapter explores how these aspects of teacher motivation have been described in mainstream educational literature and then examines language teacher motivation specifically. Through the discussion, the authors identify research trends as well as gaps in our current knowledge of language teacher motivation, and conclude by putting forward an agenda for future research which could address these gaps.

The call for language teacher motivation research is picked up in Chapter 3 by Paula Kalaja and Katja Mäntylä, who report on an empirical study that used envisioning and a future selves perspective to the motivation of future language teachers. In the study, 35 pre-service teachers were asked to envision 'an English class of their dreams' – a depiction of a desirable and pragmatically feasible language class that they would like to teach after graduating. The pre-service teachers provided the authors with drawings and verbal commentaries describing these classes, and these multimodal data were then subjected to qualitative content analysis. In the chapter, the authors present six illustrative examples, in order to showcase the diversity of teaching contexts, equipment and materials and activities that formed part of the pre-service teachers' visions of ideal classes, and by extension their envisioned ideal selves as language teachers.

Chapter 4, by Taguhi Sahakyan, Martin Lamb and Gary Chambers, extends the discussion of motivation and possible selves. In their chapter, they report on an empirical investigation that examined how the motivation of tertiary-level English teachers in Armenia changed over the course of their careers. The authors note that, at the beginning of their careers, the language teachers' ideal selves seemed to be predominantly shaped by past learning experiences. However, these early conceptualisations of their future selves were eventually transformed or even abandoned and replaced by more feasible teacher selves, which were derived from the participants' own teaching experiences and adapted to their contexts of work.

In Chapter 5 Manka Varghese introduces the construct of language teacher identity, and explores its connections to teacher education, while showing how conceptual tools from cognitive/cultural anthropology can be used to enhance our understanding of the constructs. The chapter begins by surveying work on teacher education, looking both at the mainstream education literature and at scholarship specific to the education of language teachers. Varghese traces how teacher development has been described in the literature, at times coming across processes of change similar to those described by Sahakyan *et al.* (Chapter 4). Building on these, she puts forward a theorisation of teacher education as a participatory process of identity construction and 'learning about being teachers', which she contrasts to understandings of learning as acquisition of knowledge. She draws on the constructs of *cultural models* (Quinn & Holland, 1987) and *figured worlds* (Vågan, 2011), and shows how these can be used to make sense of processes of identity construction, agency and change in language teacher psychology.

The development of language teachers' professional identity is also the topic of Chapter 6, by Wendy Li and Peter De Costa, which looks into the experiences of two novice teachers in China. The authors draw on the constructs of *community of practice* (Wenger, 1998) and *cultural myths* (Britzman, 1986, 2003), in order to investigate how the novice teachers' professional identity developed in different settings. In a sense, this study parallels both Varghese's conceptually focused contribution (Chapter 5) and the findings reported by Sahakyan *et al.* (Chapter 4), which were framed from a different theoretical perspective. Li and De Costa note that their participants' professional identities as prospective English language teachers initially developed as they were learning about 'being and becoming an English teacher', while attending a UK-based postgraduate TESOL programme. These identities were subsequently negotiated by striking a balance between the Westernised teaching philosophy that they had developed in the UK-based course, and the cultural beliefs that they encountered when faced with local classroom realities, when they started their teaching career in China.

Chapter 7, by Anne Feryok, examines whether the concept of emergence contributes to research on language teacher cognition. Taking a historical approach, Feryok briefly examines the philosophical and psychological origins of emergence to arrive at Vygotsky's work on the nature of psychology and the role of language in mediating human cognitive development, and its relevance to language teacher development and practice. The main focus of the chapter is her examination of how language teacher cognition emerges in three recent research studies. She argues that teachers need tacit and conceptual knowledge which are integrated in praxis, and she concludes with suggestions for researching its emergence.

The second set of chapters look at diverse personal constructs connected to language teacher psychology, which have received comparably less attention to date. In the first of these chapters (Chapter 8), Mark Wyatt looks into the topic of language teacher self-efficacy beliefs. The chapter explores recent developments in the ways language teacher self-efficacy beliefs are theorised, and shows that these are increasingly understood as dynamic constructs which are task- and domain-specific. In addition, Wyatt showcases the diversity of methodological approaches that have been employed in the study of language teacher self-efficacy beliefs by juxtaposing five illustrative studies. The importance of finding ways to help language teachers feel more efficacious in their work is highlighted, in particular in the context of threats that might arise from the marginalisation of languages other than English in the foreign language teaching curricula, as well as critical public discourse that calls into question some teachers' linguistic abilities.

In Chapter 9 Jim King and Sarah Ng consider the role of emotions in the professional life of language teachers. The chapter begins with an overview of existing literature on teacher emotions, noting that research in language teacher emotions has tended to focus on the types of emotions teachers experience and the conditions under which these emotions are experienced. This discussion leads to the presentation of a theoretical framework which brings together the interrelationships between emotions, cognitions, motivation and behaviour (which the authors label the *intra-organismic dimension*) and the experience of emotions at classroom, institutional and societal level (the *inter-organismic dimension*). The ways in which emotions are experienced in the intra- and inter-organismic dimensions are then showcased empirically, with reference to a study that investigated the emotional labour of teachers working in Japan (King, 2016).

In Chapter 10 Christina Gkonou and Sarah Mercer take a focused look into the beliefs and practices of teachers with high levels of social and emotional intelligence. This chapter, which reports on aspects of a larger study (Gkonou & Mercer, 2017), begins by defining the constructs of social and emotional intelligence and arguing for their relevance to language education. Next, using data from observations and stimulated recall interviews with six teachers who had high levels of social and emotional intelligence, the authors discuss the role of interpersonal relationships between teachers and learners, among learners, and between teachers and significant figures in their professional contexts. The chapter concludes by discussing implications for teacher education and further research.

Chapter 11 also aims to shed light on how aspects of teacher-related factors can influence the nature of teacher–student relationships in language classrooms. In this chapter Jean-Marc Dewaele and Sarah Mercer report on the results of a questionnaire survey that was administered to 513 English language teachers from all around the world, which investigated their attitudes towards learners. In the study, a distinction is made between general attitudes towards students and attitudes towards lively students, as the latter might be perceived as more challenging. Relationships are reported between attitudes and Trait Emotional Intelligence (Petrides, 2009), English language proficiency, teaching experience and gender. The findings of this study concerning the connection between emotional intelligence and teacher attitudes complement those reported in Chapter 10. Moreover, the finding that teachers with high self-reported linguistic proficiency tend to have more positive attitudes towards students echoes Wyatt's call for enhancing the teachers' self-efficacy beliefs (Chapter 8).

In Chapter 12 Cynthia White discusses language teacher agency, which she links to teachers' decisions and actions inside and outside the classroom, discussing it from both a theoretical and an empirical perspective. The chapter reviews definitions of teacher agency and associated theoretical approaches, particularly sociocultural theory, ecological approaches, activity theory, dialogical frameworks and complexity theory. Empirical work into teacher agency is critically reviewed in terms of five key studies focusing on the influence of experience outside the classroom on teacher agency, identity negotiations and a teacher candidate's sense of agency, the long-term emergence of teacher agency through CALL practice, the emergence of identity agency among pre-service teachers, and teacher agency in narrative accounts of classroom conflict. To conclude, the chapter argues that alongside recent work on teacher agency in relation to policy changes, there is a need for more fine-grained understanding of agency within the course of everyday demands that teachers face and work with in the ongoing dialectic of person and practice.

From Chapter 13 onwards, our focus shifts to constructs connected to positive psychology, with a more explicit emphasis on language teacher well-being. In Chapter 13 Joseph Falout and Tim Murphey report on a small-scale study that aimed to demonstrate how language teachers actively make their job more meaningful, through a process of *job crafting* (Wrzesniewski & Dutton, 2001) which involves changing the tasks, relationships and roles usually associated with their work. In the first phase of this two-phase study, teachers were asked to report on how they created meaning in their professional roles. These data were then used to define four reconceptualised teacher roles which reflected expanded and more meaningful ways in which teachers conceptualised themselves. In the second phase of the study these roles were then looped back to teachers, who were asked to reflect on the extent to which they identified with them. In doing so, the authors provide an example of how language teachers can exert control on their professional well-being in order to cope with the challenges facing the profession.

Coping with professional challenges is also the topic of the next contribution. In Chapter 14 Phil Hiver discusses language teacher resilience, which he defines as the capacity of language teachers to 'to maintain effective functioning in their practice despite threatening circumstances'. The chapter begins by surveying different conceptualisations of resilience drawn from the literature in mainstream psychology, and then examines how the construct of resilience has informed empirical work in education. This is followed by a discussion of the construct of *teacher immunity*, which is derived from empirical work with language teachers (Hiver & Dörnyei, 2017), and which he argues is more useful analytically. Hiver concludes by proposing a research agenda that aims to enhance our understanding of resilience as a dynamic, holistic construct.

Kostoulas and Lämmerer further extend the discussion of language teacher resilience in Chapter 15, in which they report on a case study that looked into how an experienced language teacher transitioned into a new role as a teacher educator in a university context. The authors put forward a tentative conceptual model of language teacher resilience, which they define as an emergent process of psychological growth that enables practitioners in language education to cope with the challenges associated with their professional roles. This model is then used as a frame to illustrate how their participant drew on diverse psychological resources in order to manage the transition into her new professional role, and also how the transition helped to foster her resilience.

Chapter 16, by Tammy Gregersen and Peter MacIntyre, looks into the ways in which new teachers can be supported in their transition into the profession with appropriate support from experienced mentors. The authors report on an empirical project which aimed to connect new teachers with mentors, by capitalising on their character strengths, including creativity, fairness and kindness. These were identified using the Values in Action (VIA) inventory, a web-based, standardised test that measures 24 strengths. On the basis of similarities in reported strengths, six novice teachers were matched with three more experienced mentors, who advised them on how to use these strengths in new ways. This resulted in uniformly positive outcomes, such as greater relationship satisfaction and increased well-being, confidence, resilience and coping skills among the mentees. The authors conclude by pointing out the potential of identifying the character strengths of emergent teachers, and actively finding new applications for them.

Chapter 17, by Rebecca Oxford, Andrew Cohen and Virginia Simmons, 'discusses aspects of the psychology of third-age teacher educators (TATEs)'. In this chapter the authors report on an in-depth, narrative, multiple-case study that looked into the experiences of the authors, who define themselves as TATEs. Four salient themes are identified in the data, namely the ways in which authors engage with emotions and regulate them, their perspective about the future, their psychological responses to the physical and cognitive changes associated with ageing, and their sense of self-concept, self-esteem and achievement.

Saleem's chapter (Chapter 18) concludes this volume by reporting on a case study that used a holistic perspective in order to describe the psychology of a language teacher in tertiary education. In her study, Saleem uses a thematic approach to describe how an analysis of themes such as emotional control, the inspirational role of teachers, and mentorship roles can illustrate the interactions of the teacher's cognitions, emotions, motivation and behaviours as an integrated whole. Her data also show the intricate interconnections between the teacher's psychology and the social context in which it is embedded, in a way that echoes the interplay between inter- and intra-personal dimensions of emotion described by King and Ng (Chapter 9). Saleem concludes by discussing the potential of complex systems theory to inform empirical work that takes a holistic, situated perspective on language teacher psychology.

The overview of the 17 contributions that make up this volume hints at the vibrancy and multidimensionality of the emerging field of language teacher psychology. As editors, we have been inspired by the breadth of constructs that are beginning to receive attention, both conceptually and empirically, as well as the overlaps and interconnections between the diverse themes that are being explored. While we have included in the collection diverse constructs, theoretical perspectives and methodological outlooks, we are also aware of a range of dimensions of teacher psychology not represented and as such, this collection should not be seen as comprehensive but as an opening up of the field. We have seen how scholars have drawn on a range of theoretical perspectives to inform their work and how language teacher psychology is inherently interdisciplinary in character with rich potential to learn from existent studies in the fields of general education, psychology, as well as related studies into language learner psychology. It is our hope that as you read, you too will share the excitement we have felt while putting together this volume, and draw inspiration for your own work, be that in conceptual, empirical, theoretical or methodological terms. The collection represents an opening discussion, which we hope will be expanded upon in the future, as the field continues to grow and diversify. We are convinced that the work conducted in the field has an important role to play in seeking to ensure that language teacher professional well-being becomes a priority not only for scholarship but in consequence also for policy makers and educational leaders, who must be thus inspired to become more 'teacher centred' in their priorities for effective language education.

References

Albrecht, K. (2006) *Social Intelligence: The New Science of Success.* San Francisco, CA: Jossey-Bass.

Aragão, R. (2011) Beliefs and emotions in foreign language learning. *System* 39 (3), 302–313.

Bajorek, Z., Gulliford, J. and Taskila, T. (2014) *Healthy Teachers, Higher Marks? Establishing a Link between Teacher Health and Wellbeing, and Student Outcomes.* London: The Work Foundation. See https://www.educationsupportpartnership.org.uk/sites/default/files/resources/healthy_teachers_higher_marks_report_0.pdf

Barcelos, A.M.F. (2015) Unveiling the relationship between language learning beliefs, emotions, and identities. *Studies in Second Language Learning and Teaching* 5 (2), 301–325.

Barkhuizen, G. (ed.) (2016) *Reflections on Language Teacher Identity Research.* London: Routledge.

Borg, S. (2003) Teacher cognition in language teaching: A review of research on what teachers think, know, believe and do. *Language Teacher* 36 (2), 81–109.

Britzman, D. (1986) Cultural myths in the making of a teacher: Biography and social structure in teacher education. *Harvard Educational Review* 56 (4), 442–457.

Britzman, D.P. (2003) *Practice Makes Practice: A Critical Study of Learning to Teach* (revised edn). Albany, NY: State University of New York Press.

Cheung, Y.L., Said, S.B. and Park, K. (eds) (2014) *Advances and Current Trends in Language Teacher Identity Research.* London: Routledge.

Clarke, M. (2008) *Language Teacher Identities: Co-constructing Discourse and Community*. Clevedon: Multilingual Matters.

Clarke, M. (2009) The ethico-politics of teacher identity. *Educational Philosophy and Theory* 41 (2), 185–200.

Corcoran, R.P. and Tormey, R. (2012) How emotionally intelligent are pre-service teachers? *Teaching and Teacher Education* 28 (5), 750–759.

Cowie, N. (2011) Emotions that experienced English as a foreign language (EFL) teachers feel about their students, their colleagues and their work. *Teaching and Teacher Education* 27 (1), 235–242.

Day, C. and Gu, Q. (2009) Teacher emotions: Well being and effectiveness. In P.A. Schutz and M. Zembylas (eds) *Advances in Teacher Emotion Research: The Impact on Teachers' Lives* (pp. 15–32). Dordrecht: Springer.

Day, C. and Gu, Q. (2014) *Resilient Teachers, Resilient Schools: Building and Sustaining Quality in Testing Times*. London: Routledge.

Day, C., Sammons, P., Stobart, G., Kington, A. and Gu, Q. (2007) *Teachers Matter: Connecting Lives, Work and Effectiveness*. Maidenhead: Open University Press.

De Costa, P.I. and Norton, B. (eds) (2017) Identity, transdisciplinarity, and the good language teacher (Special Issue) *The Modern Language Journal* 101 (S1).

DeVries, R. and Zan, B. (1995) Creating a constructivist classroom atmosphere. *Young Children* 51 (1), 4–13.

Dewaele, J.-M. (2012) Personality traits as independent and dependent variables. In S. Mercer, S. Ryan and M. Williams (eds) *Psychology for Language Learning: Insights from Research, Theory and Practice* (pp. 42–58). Basingstoke: Palgrave Macmillan.

Dewaele, J.-M. (2015) On emotions in foreign language learning and use. *The Language Teacher* 39 (3), 13–15.

Dörnyei, Z. (2005) *The Psychology of the Language Learner: Individual Differences in Second Language Acquisition*. Mahwah, NJ: Lawrence Erlbaum.

Dörnyei, Z. (2009) Individual differences: Interplay of learner characteristics and learning environment. In N.C. Ellis and D. Larsen-Freeman (eds) *Language as a Complex Adaptive System* (pp. 230–248). Oxford: Wiley-Blackwell.

Dörnyei, Z. and Kubanyiova, M. (2014) *Motivating Learners, Motivating Teachers: Building Vision in the Language Classroom*. Cambridge: Cambridge University Press.

Dörnyei, Z. and Ryan, S. (2015) *The Psychology of the Language Learner Revisited*. New York: Routledge.

Ehrman, M.E., Leaver, B.L. and Oxford, R.L. (2003) Overview of research on individual differences. *System* 31 (3), 313–330.

Elias, M.J. and Arnold, H. (eds) (2006) *The Educator's Guide to Emotional Intelligence and Academic Achievement: Social-emotional Learning in the Classroom*. Thousand Oaks, CA: Corwin.

Fredrickson, B.L. (2013) Positive emotions broaden and build. *Advances in Experimental Social Psychology* 47, 1–53.

Frenzel, A., Goetz, T., Lüdtke, O., Pekrun, R. and Sutton, R. (2009) Emotional transmission in the classroom: Exploring the relationship between teacher and student enjoyment. *Journal of Educational Psychology* 101 (3), 705–716.

Furrer, C.J., Skinner, E.A. and Pitzer, J.R. (2014) The influence of teacher and peer relationships on students' classroom engagement and everyday motivational resilience. *National Society for the Study of Education* 113 (1), 101–123.

Gabryś-Barker, D. and Gałajda, D. (eds) (2016) *Positive Psychology Perspectives on Foreign Language Learning and Teaching*. Cham: Springer.

Gao, X. and Xu, H. (2014) The dilemma of being English language teachers: Interpreting teachers' motivation to teach, and professional commitment in China's hinterland regions. *Language Teaching Research* 18 (2), 152–168.

Gkonou, C. and Mercer, S. (2017) *Understanding Emotional and Social Intelligence among English Language Teachers*. London: British Council.

Golombek, P. and Doran, M. (2014) Unifying cognition, emotion, and activity in language teacher professional development. *Teaching and Teacher Education* 39, 102–111.

Gregersen, T. and MacIntyre, P.D. (2014) *Capitalizing on Language Learners' Individuality: From Premise to Practice*. Bristol: Multilingual Matters.

Gurzynski-Weiss, L. (2013) Interlocutor/instructor individual differences in cognition and second language acquisition. *International Journal of Applied Linguistics* 23 (3), 398–399.

Hattie, J. (2009) *Visible Learning: A Synthesis of Over 800 Meta-Analyses Relating to Achievement*. Abingdon: Routledge.

Hawkins, M. and Norton, B. (2009) Critical language teacher education. In A. Burns and J. Richards (eds) *Cambridge Guide to Second Language Teacher Education* (pp. 30–39). Cambridge: Cambridge University Press.

Hiver, P. (2013) The interplay of possible language teacher selves in professional development choices. *Language Teaching Research* 17 (2), 210–227.

Hiver, P. and Dörnyei, Z. (2017) Language teacher immunity: A double-edged sword. *Applied Linguistics* 38 (3), 405–423.

Holmes, E. (2005) *Teacher Well-being: Looking after Yourself and Your Career in the Classroom*. Abington: Routledge.

Howard, S. and Johnson, B. (2004) Resilient teachers: Resisting stress and burnout. *Social Psychology of Education* 7 (4), 399–420.

Kalaja, P., Barcelos, A.M.F., Aro, M. and Ruohotie-Lyhty, M. (2016) *Beliefs, Agency and Identity in Foreign Language Learning and Teaching*. Basingstoke: Palgrave-Macmillan.

Kanno, Y. and Stuart, C. (2011) Learning to become a second language teacher: Identities-in-practice. *The Modern Language Journal* 95 (2), 236–252.

King, J. (2016) 'It's time, put on the smile, it's time!': The emotional labour of second language teaching within a Japanese university. In C. Gkonou, D. Tatzl and S. Mercer (eds) *New Directions in Language Learning Psychology* (pp. 97–112). Cham: Springer.

Kubanyiova, M. (2009) Possible selves in language teacher development. In Z. Dörnyei and E. Ushioda (eds) *Motivation, Language Identity and the L2 Self* (pp. 314–332). Bristol: Multilingual Matters.

Kubanyiova, M. and Feryok, A. (eds) (2015) Language teacher cognition in applied linguistics research: Revisiting the territory, redrawing the boundaries, reclaiming the relevance (Special Issue). *The Modern Language Journal* 99 (3), 435–601.

Lamb, T.E. and Reinders, H. (eds) (2007) *Learner and Teacher Autonomy: Concepts, Realities and Responses*. Amsterdam: John Benjamins.

MacIntyre, P.D. and Gregersen, T. (2012) Affect: The role of language anxiety and other emotions in language learning. In S. Mercer, S. Ryan and M. Williams (eds) *Psychology for Language Learning: Insights from Research, Theory and Practice* (pp. 103–118). Basingstoke: Palgrave Macmillan.

MacIntyre, P.D., Gregersen, T. and Mercer, S. (eds) (2016) *Positive Psychology in SLA*. Bristol: Multilingual Matters.

Maslach, C. and Leiter, M.P. (1999) Teacher burnout: A research agenda. In R. Vanderberghe and A.M. Huberman (eds) *Understanding and Preventing Teacher Burnout: A Sourcebook of International Research and Practice* (pp. 295–303). Cambridge: Cambridge University Press.

Menard-Warwick, J. (2013) *English Language Teachers on the Discursive Faultlines: Identities, Ideologies and Pedagogies*. Bristol: Multilingual Matters.

Mercer, S. (2016) Psychology for language learning: Spare a thought for the teacher. Plenary presentation delivered at the 'Individuals in Contexts' (Psychology of Language Learning 2) International Conference, University of Jyväskylä, Finland, 22–24 August.

Mercer, S. (in press) Psychology for language learning: Spare a thought for the teacher. Plenary speeches. *Language Teaching*.

Mercer, S. and Ryan, S. (2010) A mindset for EFL: Learners' beliefs about the role of natural talent. *ELT Journal* 64 (4), 436–444.

Mercer, S., Oberdorfer, P. and Saleem, M. (2016) Helping language teachers to thrive: Using positive psychology to promote teachers' professional well-being. In D. Gabryś-Barker and D. Gałajda (eds) *Positive Psychology Perspectives on Foreign Language Learning and Teaching, Second Language Learning and Teaching* (pp. 213–229). Cham: Springer.

Mills, N.A. and Allen, H.W. (2007) Teacher self-efficacy of graduate teaching assistants of French. In H.J. Siskin (ed.) *From Thought to Action: Exploring Beliefs and Outcomes in the Foreign Language* (pp. 213–234). Boston, MA: Thomson-Heinle.

Nizielski, S., Hallum, S., Lopes, P.N. and Schütz, A. (2012) Attention to student needs mediates the relationship between teacher emotional intelligence and student misconduct in the classroom. *Journal of Psychoeducational Assessment* 30 (4), 320–329.

Norton, B. (2000) *Identity and Language Learning: Social Processes and Educational Practice*. London: Longman.

Oxford, R.L. (1996) Personality type in the foreign or second language classroom: Theoretical and empirical perspectives. In A. Horning and R. Sudol (eds) *Understanding Literacy: Personality Preferences in Rhetorical and Psycholinguistic Contexts* (pp. 149–175). Creskill, NJ: Hampton Press.

Patrick, B.C., Hisley, J., Kempler, T. and College, G. (2000) 'What's everybody so excited about?': The effects of teacher enthusiasm on student intrinsic motivation and vitality. *Journal of Experimental Education* 68 (3), 1521–1558.

Petrides, K.V. (2009) Psychometric properties of the Trait Emotional Intelligence Questionnaire. In C. Stough, D.H. Saklofske and J.D. Parker (eds) *Advances in the Assessment of Emotional Intelligence* (pp. 85–101). New York: Springer.

Quinn, N. and Holland, D. (1987) Cognition and culture. In D. Holland and N. Quinn (eds) *Cultural Models in Language and Thought* (pp. 3–40). Cambridge: Cambridge University Press.

Reyes, M.A., Brackett, S.E., Rivers, M.W. and Salovey, P. (2012) Classroom emotional climate, student engagement, and academic achievement. *Journal of Educational Psychology* 104 (3), 700–712.

Richardson, P.W., Karabenick, S.A. and Watt, H.M. (2014) *Teacher Motivation: Theory and Practice*. London: Routledge.

Ryan, S. and Mercer, S. (2012) Implicit theories: Language learning mindsets. In S. Mercer, S. Ryan and M. Williams (eds) *Psychology for Language Learning: Insights from Research, Theory and Practice* (pp. 74–89). Basingstoke: Palgrave Macmillan.

Shulman, L.S. (1986) Those who understand: Knowledge growth in teaching. *Educational Researcher* 15 (2), 4–14.

Smith, R.C. (2003) Pedagogy for autonomy as (becoming-) appropriate methodology. In D. Palfreyman and R. Smith (eds) *Learner Autonomy across Cultures* (pp. 129–146). Basingstoke: Palgrave Macmillan.

Tait, M. (2008) Resilience as a contributor to novice teacher success, commitment, and retention. *Teacher Education Quarterly* 35 (4), 57–75.

Tatzl, D., Gkonou, C. and Mercer, S. (2016) Introduction: New directions in language learning psychology. In C. Gkonou, D. Tatzl and S. Mercer (eds) *New Directions in Language Learning Psychology*. Cham: Springer.

Tsui, A.B.M. (2007) Complexities of identity formation: A narrative inquiry of an EFL teacher. *TESOL Quarterly* 41 (4), 657–680.

Vågan, A. (2011) Towards a sociocultural perspective on identity formation in education. *Mind, Culture, and Activity* 18 (1), 43–57.

Varghese, M., Morgan, B., Johnston, B. and Johnson, K.A. (2005) Theorizing language teacher identity: Three perspectives and beyond. *Journal of Language, Identity & Education* 4 (1), 21–44.

Varghese, M.M., Motha, S., Park, G., Reeves, J. and Trent, J. (eds) (2016) Language teacher identity in (multi)lingual educational contexts (Special Issue). *TESOL Quarterly* 50 (3).

Wenger, E. (1998) *Communities of Practice: Learning, Meaning, and Identity.* New York: Cambridge University Press.

White, C.J. (2016) Agency and emotion in narrative accounts of emergent conflict in an L2 classroom. *Applied Linguistics*, 1–16; doi:10.1093/applin/amw026 amw026.

Williams, M., Burden, R.L. and Al-Baharna, S. (2001) The role of the individual in motivation theory. In Z. Dörnyei and R. Schmidt (eds) *Motivation and Second Language Acquisition* (pp. 171–184). Honolulu, HI: University of Hawai'i Second Language Teaching and Curriculum Center.

Woodrow, L. (2012) Goal orientations: Three perspectives on motivation goal orientations. In S. Mercer, S. Ryan and M. Williams (eds) *Psychology for Language Learning: Insights from Research Theory and Practice* (pp. 188–202). Basingstoke: Palgrave Macmillan.

Wrzesniewski, A. and Dutton, J.E. (2001) Crafting a job: Revisioning employees as active crafters of their work. *Academy of Management Review* 26 (2), 179–201.

Wyatt, M. (2014) Towards a re-conceptualization of teachers' self-efficacy beliefs: Tackling enduring problems with the quantitative research and moving on. *International Journal of Research & Method in Education* 37 (2), 166–189.

Wyatt, M. (2016) 'Are they becoming more reflective and/or efficacious?' A conceptual model mapping how teachers' self-efficacy beliefs might grow. *Educational Review* 68 (1), 114–137.

2 Language Teacher Motivation

Phil Hiver, Tae-Young Kim and Youngmi Kim

This chapter begins with an overview of teacher motivation and how it is theorised in mainstream educational literature. In order to highlight the complementarity of different theories, we have chosen to draw from Pintrich's (2003) integrated perspective of how motivation underpins four key concerns: individuals' choice of activity (i.e. why individuals choose one course of action over another), individuals' level of activity (i.e. how much or how little individuals engage in this activity), individuals' persistence through an activity, and individuals' performance on an activity. These elements guide our review. Regardless of conceptual perspective, there is widespread agreement that teacher motivation is complex with interconnected personal, relational, experiential, affective and contextual layers. Teachers' motivations too, like all human motivations, display both stable tendencies and variability. We continue in the chapter by examining second language (L2) teacher motivation specifically and attempt to draw parallels between it and the larger discourse of mainstream teacher motivation. We review the growing body of L2 teacher motivation research thematically and highlight both trends and gaps in our current knowledge of this domain. Finally, we propose an agenda for research that we hope will help recapture the relevance of L2 teacher motivation for the broader field of applied linguistics.

Conceptualising Teacher Motivation

In comparison to the research on student motivation, some have described the field of teacher motivation research as still 'in its infancy' (Urdan, 2014: 228). However, an increasing volume of scholarship has sought to better understand the dynamics of teacher motivation by reformulating established social cognitive theories of motivation initially applied in the domain of student motivation. The most prominent and productive motivational theories that have been repurposed and adapted to explore the motivation of teachers empirically are self-efficacy (Tschannen-Moran & Woolfolk Hoy, 2001; see also Wyatt, this volume), achievement goal theory (Butler, 2012), self-determination theory (Roth et al., 2007) and expectancy-value theory (Watt et al., 2012).

Self-efficacy has been defined as an individual's beliefs or confidence in their ability to engage in a course of action which is required to accomplish a given task (Bandura, 1997, 2012). Achievement goal theory focuses on the purposes for which individuals perform a task, and their orientations and perceptions of competence while engaged in that activity (Elliot & McGregor, 2001). Self-determination theory is founded on the premise that when basic psychological needs (i.e. autonomy, competence and relatedness) are satisfied as a function of interpersonal dynamics and social settings, individuals develop adaptive, growth-oriented propensities – namely, internalisation and intrinsic motivation (Deci & Ryan, 2000, 2012). Expectancy-value theory emphasises that individuals' investment of effort and persistence in a task depends on their expectancy of success, belief in their ability and the degree to which they value the opportunity to engage in the task (Wigfield & Eccles, 2000).

In order to explore what each theoretical framework sheds light on and where its limitations lie, this chapter will address some broad questions from mainstream teacher education. (1) What motivates individuals to enter the teaching profession? (2) What motivates teachers in the classroom? (3) How is teacher motivation linked to teacher development? (4) How does teacher motivation influence the dynamics of classroom practice? As mentioned previously, these questions borrow from Pintrich's (2003) four suggested concerns and serve as a guide for theoretical development and empirical research about teacher motivation.

What motivates individuals to enter the teaching profession?

Few would dispute the notion that the work of teaching is vital to the advancement of student learning and social achievement (Hanushek, 2011), and the questions of why individuals choose teaching as a career and what they hope to achieve have grown in significance as policy makers and teacher educators worldwide grapple with how to attract and retain the highest quality teachers (Richardson & Watt, 2016). Because teachers' career motivations are central to their professional engagement and commitment, it should not be surprising that research has intensified over the past few years into who chooses to enter the teaching profession, what attracts them to make this decision and how to retain effective professionals – almost across the globe (Zumwalt & Craig, 2008).

From the perspective of self-determination theory, the drive to become a teacher arises from intrinsic (autonomous) or extrinsic (controlled) antecedents thought to exist on a continuum of self-determination (Roth, 2014). Extrinsic motivation ranges from the least self-determined form, external-regulation, to introjected-regulation (i.e. when external forces of control have been internalised to some extent), identified-regulation (i.e.

when an internalised sense of the personal value of an activity is achieved), and integrated-regulation (i.e. when performing an activity becomes a means of expressing core aspects of one's identity). Although it originates externally, integrated-regulation shares several characteristics with intrinsic motivation, given that it stems from values that are fully congruent with aspects of one's self.

In addition to intrinsic and extrinsic categories, it is often the prosocial or altruistic value of teaching that draws individuals to the profession (Richardson & Watt, 2014). This includes factors such as love, passion and dedication to learners, as well as a personal or moral commitment to contribute to society or reduce social inequality. Research from an expectancy-value model posits that, in addition to assigning a value to the task of teaching, individuals appraise the workload and commitment demands prior to entering the profession and weigh these against their expectations of their own ability to be effective teachers (Watt *et al.*, 2012).

There is also growing evidence that sociocultural contexts play a significant role in shaping individuals' initial teaching motivations, and that these teaching motivations impact teachers' performance, effort and persistence in the profession (Alexander *et al.*, 2014). This is evinced by the varying importance of the above factors across cultural and geographical boundaries. While intrinsic factors are the primary movers in many contexts, teachers in other countries reference more extrinsic motives including pay, job security and career status (Visser-Wijnveen *et al.*, 2014). However, even within a single sociocultural context, different teachers will display different motivational profiles, and the context in which a teacher works can influence and change those motivations, regardless of how they are manifested at the outset of a teacher's career (Madni *et al.*, 2015). Thus, in initial teacher motivation, the sociocultural context plays a significant role in who becomes a teacher and why.

What motivates teachers in the classroom?

Social cognitive theory emphasises the importance of agency through which individuals are able to make decisions about and exercise control over what they do, and because teachers are thinking and feeling agentic individuals, a productive way of conceptualising teacher motivation is to look at teachers' levels of confidence in their ability to help students learn (Zee & Koomen, 2016). Teachers' self-efficacy beliefs are the judgements they make about how effectively they are able to engage students and help them to learn (Klassen *et al.*, 2011). Positive appraisals of personal teaching-specific capabilities are important to a teacher's motivation for many reasons. Among other things, these positive self-efficacy beliefs are associated with teacher enthusiasm and confidence, commitment to teaching, job satisfaction, instructional effort and persistence (Klassen & Tze, 2014). In addition to the strong sense of individual self-efficacy that motivated teachers are likely to possess, successful schools are character-ised by teachers' collective beliefs in their capabilities to create a climate of learning for students (Goddard *et al.*, 2000). This collective teacher efficacy, conceptualised as an emergent property of schools, is thought to contribute to the differential effect that schools have on student achieve-ment (Goddard *et al.*, 2004). Additionally, while social cognitive theory sees self-efficacy as relatively stable once established (Bandura, 1997), the temporal nature of a career in teaching affords a dynamic aspect to teach-ers' goals and self-efficacy beliefs. For instance, because there is constant potential for new challenges, obstacles, constraints and difficulties for teachers to overcome, teachers' agency and the expectations they hold of their capacity to accomplish desired teaching-specific outcomes are con-tinuously developing (Skaalvik & Skaalvik, 2010).

The notion of goal pursuit, from achievement goal theory, offers another way of looking at what teachers seek to achieve in the classroom (Retelsdorf *et al.*, 2010). In their teaching, teachers may be spurred by *mas-tery* goals, a desire to develop professionally and to enhance their teaching skills; *performance-approach* goals, a desire to demonstrate superior teaching ability; *performance-avoidance* goals, a desire to avoid displays of failure through poor quality teaching; or *work-avoidance* goals, a desire to get by and do as little as possible. Another unique dimension of teaching concerns the way teachers incorporate others' goals into their own set of professional goals, and this has been explored by Butler (2012) under the rubric of *relational goals*. This programme of research sees relational striv-ings (i.e. to achieve caring relationships with students) and mastery striv-ings (i.e. to develop competence) as two distinct teacher motivational goals, each with different consequences for teacher behaviours (Butler, 2007). A greater focus on relational goals is often associated with teachers' socio-emotional support for students, while teacher mastery goals tend to con-tribute more to cognitively stimulating instruction and higher student interest. However, even relational goals are closely tied to teachers' sense of personal accomplishment and feelings of competence (Butler & Shibaz, 2014). Generally, teachers' dual endorsement of mastery and relational goals is associated with greater enjoyment of teaching and greater invest-ment of effort, and they predict greater use of mastery-oriented instruc-tional practices (e.g. encouraging students' critical thinking) as well as emotional availability and supportiveness (Becker *et al.*, 2014; Soenens *et al.*, 2012). Thus, because teaching is a purposeful endeavour, it is by nature goal directed. At times, these goals may target personal desires, while at others, they may relate to a more interpersonal orientation.

For its part, self-determination theory sees ongoing teacher motivation as emerging out of the satisfaction of psychological needs through the activity of teaching (Roth, 2014). Self-determination theory suggests that people must feel autonomous, be aware of their strengths and weaknesses, understand how their needs can be met, feel capable in their abilities and connect to those around them (Deci & Ryan, 2000, 2012). Autonomous motivation is crucial to motivated teacher behaviour because of educators' inherent tendency to explore and assimilate new knowledge, seek out novelty and challenges and exercise their intellectual capacities. For teachers, this means that if they enjoy the process of teaching and engage enthusiastically in those tasks which make up teaching, they will exercise volition and choice, achieve a sense of personal accomplishment and satisfaction and fully realise their abilities (Roth et al., 2007). Of course, whether teachers experience need satisfaction while teaching – as opposed to need frustration – depends a great deal on the classroom context and broader educational environment. For instance, studies of the antecedents of teachers' autonomous motivation highlight how role ambiguity, emphasis on high-stakes testing, external accountability and coercive school leadership undermine teachers' autonomous motivation because these pressures represent controlling forms of motivation (Reeve & Su, 2014). This underscores the importance of school culture for teachers' own goals for teaching and the classroom climates they create for students.

How is teacher motivation linked to teacher development?

Motivation research has attempted to account for how the level and quality of teachers' motivations change across their lifespans and how this might parallel teachers' career trajectories (Alexander, 2008). This is important because the complex and psychologically demanding task of teaching can span decades over the course of one's career. Longitudinal research from the expectancy-value model has shown that teachers' instructional efforts, planned persistence, professional development, leadership aspirations and career satisfaction are linked positively to particular initial motivational profiles (Richardson & Watt, 2016). This is illustrated by evidence that self-reported and idiosyncratic descriptions of teachers' classroom teaching style differ depending on whether those teachers associate with the more intrinsic values for teaching or extrinsic values such as personal utility and social persuasion (Reeve & Su, 2014). Another common pattern of motivational change relates to pre-service teachers who possess a positive idealistic motivational profile but when confronted by the challenges of reality experience a rapid decline in their self-efficacy, career satisfaction and commitment to the profession (Richardson & Watt, 2010).

Additional insights from self-efficacy research show that the discrepancy between teachers' evaluations of their abilities and the needs of their students is often implicated in how teachers' motivations to address those abilities and needs change as they progress through their careers (Remijan, 2014). Pre-service and early-career teachers often report a higher sense of teaching efficacy than mid- to late-career teachers do (Tang et al., 2014), most likely because they have not faced the mismatch which often occurs between individuals' anticipated experience of classroom processes and interactions and the reality of the experience. Low self-efficacy, as well as feelings of inadequacy and incompetence, can significantly contribute to teacher demotivation (Skaalvik & Skaalvik, 2010). Previously committed teachers often disengage from their work due to self-efficacy doubts, and teachers may even become apathetic, cynical or convinced of their inefficacy.

How does teacher motivation influence the dynamics of classroom practice?

Despite its clearly social objectives, teaching has tended to be regarded 'primarily as a cognitive activity' (Zembylas, 2003: 104). However, a situative perspective challenges this view, and provides evidence that motivation, cognition and emotion are always situated and, furthermore, are fundamentally interdependent (Storbeck & Clore, 2007). The main implication of this notion for teacher motivation is the focus on the co-constitutive nature of classroom settings and teacher motivation (Radel et al., 2010). This reticulated view of teacher motivation is corroborated by evidence that teachers' enthusiasm for teaching, their goals and their sense of professional autonomy, mediated through their classroom practices, shape their students' perceptions and behaviours. Through the actions and responses of students, these contexts provide the necessary conditions for teacher motivation to flourish adaptively and relationally (Frenzel, 2014).

In fact, most of the existing evidence in teacher research consistently highlights the reciprocal links between teachers' work and their motivation. For instance, teachers who are more autonomously motivated report: (a) greater use of autonomy-supportive teaching practices (Reeve & Su, 2014); (b) more mastery-oriented goals, which in turn lead to more adaptive teaching strategies and better teaching performance (Soenens et al., 2012); (c) higher links with feelings of accomplishment (Moller et al., 2006); (d) greater support for students' engagement in learning activities (Butler, 2007); (e) deeper value for the subjects they teach and methods for helping students master those subjects (Garner, 2010); and (f) increased investment in maintaining students' quality of learning (Roth et al., 2007).

Other teacher motivations that impact powerfully on instructional practice again correspond to the teacher's ability to engage, target and strengthen these factors in their students. These include intellectual curiosity, the need for genuine achievement, relational needs for affiliation and the need for social support and approval (Butler, 2012). Although this research does not imply an ideal set of motivations which all teachers should demonstrate throughout their years in the profession, particular combinations of these are undoubtedly the hallmarks of a motivated and effective teacher (Pintrich, 2003).

Thus, the picture that emerges from this overview of the conceptual frameworks used to study mainstream teacher motivation is that there exists a solid foundation for understanding the reasons for teachers entering the profession, how and why they construct their place in the profession and the links between teacher motivation and key processes and outcomes (Kaplan, 2014). We now focus on language (L2) teacher motivation in order to determine how it compares, whether there are equally systematic conclusions and implications to be drawn from recent field-specific research, to ascertain where there are gaps, and to explore what elements may or may not be particular to the domain of L2 teacher motivation.

Language Teacher Motivation

What motivates language teachers to enter the profession?

Studies conducted in recent years indicate equally prominent intrinsic and extrinsic motives for language teachers' career choice. Intrinsic factors relate to satisfaction of needs and interests, emotional payoffs, and the internal desire for personal growth, intellectual fulfilment and meaningfulness often found in educational settings. Within the language teaching profession, these most often refer to individuals' love of the language and of teaching itself, both powerful drives for career choice as a language teacher (Hayes, 2008; Wong et al., 2014). Realising this potential for growth can provide inspiration and motivation for language teachers in their profession of choice (Baleghizadeh & Gordani, 2012). Another source of L2 teachers' intrinsic interest in the language and in teaching is their previous learning experience; when individuals see themselves as possessing a strong language learning aptitude that engenders positive achievement in the process of learning a language, this may also function as a major driving force for those people to enter the language teaching profession (Hayes, 2008). In other instances, early learning experiences play a crucial role in individuals selecting their current job, including observing their own teachers' enjoyment and dedication to teaching; these factors in turn motivate learners later to choose the L2 teaching occupation (Warford & Reeves, 2003). By extension, altruism and the desire to contribute to society in general is another superordinate intrinsic motive regarding professional career choice (e.g. Koran, 2015 for Iranian teachers; Topkaya & Uztosun, 2012 for Turkish teachers), and these studies report that teachers entering the L2 teaching profession considered it important to be able to influence the next generation positively.

Beyond this intrinsic interest, extrinsic factors also influence the job selection of many L2 teachers. Extrinsic factors here concern external incentives such as material benefits, the social status accorded to L2 teachers, and job security (Karavas, 2010; Koran, 2015). There is considerable sociogeographic variation in the occupational prestige and community respect afforded to language teachers, and this is often linked to the perceived competitiveness of entry into, and the exclusivity of the profession

(Erten, 2014). In countries where a teaching job is considered to be a stable profession guaranteeing job security and social status, teachers, particularly female teachers, may be pressured to enter the L2 profession by significant figures such as parents (Kim & Kim, 2015; Koran, 2015). Economically, material rewards such as guaranteed pay and pension plans for educators in many disadvantaged local settings are also strong, attractive reasons for choosing the occupation (Gao & Xu, 2014; Hayes, 2008). Additionally, in districts where educational opportunities are restricted, few choices present themselves, apart from teaching and nursing, as a pathway to continue towards tertiary education. In such cases, teachers may choose this occupation in the absence of any existing interest in the culture or language (Erten, 2014).

The stereotyping of teaching and teachers which is prevalent in certain educational contexts can, of course, have significant effects on the attractiveness of teaching as a career. For example, in the case of teaching English as a foreign language (EFL), in the era of globalisation, English proficiency can be perceived as a measure of affluence and social savviness. Thus, the implicit social values and interest in foreign cultures that accompanies English language use can create EFL teachers' global orientation and function as a source influencing teachers to enter the profession (Baleghizadeh & Gordani, 2012; Kim & Kim, 2015). By contrast, in the case of less commonly taught languages such as Arabic, the perceptions of social value and attitudes of undesirability can exert a strongly negative influence on L2 teachers' motivation to teach the language (Kong *et al.*, under review). To sum up, previous L2 teacher studies have identified various influencing factors in intrinsic and extrinsic motives for language teachers' career decisions. However, these studies are largely descriptive and are less based on the theoretical foundation of studies investigating general teacher career motives.

How is second language teacher motivation linked to teacher development and the dynamics of classroom practice?

Those who choose a career as language teachers often enrol in institutions which prepare L2 educators. Formal pre-service L2 teacher education typically encompasses a range of courses and a teaching practicum typically scheduled in the last year of training. The practicum is arguably one of the more influential elements in a language teacher education programme. During a practicum, pre-service teachers often have the opportunity to observe practising teachers as well as teach classes themselves in order to apply theory and practice from their training programme and experience for themselves what really happens in an L2 classroom. When the teaching practicum unfolds in a supportive atmosphere, this can result in feelings of self-efficacy and self-reflection which are a vital boost to self-confidence and thus create motivation (Atay, 2007; Gan, 2014).

It is apparent that when this input is positively reconstructed through interactions and self-reflection, practicum courses become a meaningful springboard for individuals pursuing their career and development as a language teacher.

After successfully becoming a language teacher, teachers' motivations are undoubtedly shaped at a micro level by their ongoing experiences, as well as the more general developmental patterns of change across their professional lifespan (Kimura, 2014). Beyond their individual developmental process, contextual factors can also influence language teacher motivation on both a macro and micro contextual level (Dörnyei & Ushioda, 2011). Macro contextual factors here refer to the influence of students' parents, the local community and society in general, whereas the micro dimension is more related to the actual institution and school context where the practice of teaching occurs.

At the micro level, novice teachers experience a transformation process from a pre-service L2 teacher to an in-service one, and this is accompanied by cognitive and emotional challenges. Novice L2 teachers may discover that the actual teaching site is different from what they have envisioned, despite having previously learned what and how to teach, and this experience of discrepancy can challenge L2 teachers' motivation. This was the case, for instance, with novice L2 teachers in Japan who reported their primary source of difficulties as being the gap between what they had expected and what they actually experienced in the classroom (Kumazawa, 2013). These teachers indicated their interest in employing more constructivist teaching methods, but encountered difficulty implementing these methods in the classroom due to learners' limited L2 proficiency in interacting in the target language.

As novice teachers gain more hands-on experience of teaching, the enjoyment of teaching and teaching autonomy in the classroom serve as motivating factors for L2 teachers (Hettiarachchi, 2013; Tsutsumi, 2014). A distinctive motivational dimension on the micro level is learners' communicative involvement using the L2 (Tardy & Snyder, 2004). When L2 teachers observe learners' genuine involvement in L2 learning activities and their authentic conversations in the L2, it can motivate teachers. In addition, because L2 teachers function as role models of competent L2 speakers (Chacon, 2005), this can stimulate L2 learners' interactions, which in turn positively impact on L2 teachers' motivation.

Beyond the classroom, the school atmosphere can impact on in-service L2 teachers' motivation. In particular, relationships with colleagues are found to have an important motivational effect (Cowie, 2011). Relationships with other colleagues who are unsupportive, emotionally cold or at best display an ambivalent attitude towards innovative teaching methods can contribute to a sense of futility and isolation which causes negative shifts in the motivation of in-service teachers. With respect to the L2 specifically, a lack of interest among colleagues in developing their

L2 proficiency and an absence of experts such as L2 teaching specialists or qualified teachers who are first language users has also been found to have an adverse effect on L2 teacher motivation (Erkaya, 2012; Hettiarachchi, 2013).

Another dimension to note in respect to in-service L2 teacher motivation on the micro level is the potential effect of oppressive bureaucratic school culture (Crookes, 2009). In many formal instructional settings, language teaching may not even be the L2 teachers' primary duty. In a characteristic pattern reported by Kim *et al.* (2014), Kumazawa (2013), Ruohotie-Lyhty (2013) and Sugino (2010), teachers are often expected to deal with an excessive amount of paperwork and to prepare extracurricular activities. For those who dream of being a teacher dedicated to inspiring learners and helping them to communicate in the target language, such a highly regulated, administrative-heavy environment can hamper teachers' best efforts in teaching (Khani & Mirzaee, 2015).

On the macro level, the influence of parents and society can function as (de)motivating factors among L2 teachers. For example, whether L2 teachers receive recognition for their efforts and success from students' parents is one element which can influence L2 teacher motivation (Zhang, 2017). Further, when parents express doubts regarding teachers' ability and take an excessive interest in what transpires in the classroom, it can be detrimental to teacher autonomy, leading to L2 teacher demotivation (Kim *et al.*, 2014). Besides parents, the wider community itself is another consideration at the macro level. For example, any discrepancy between socially preferred teaching methods and teachers' actual practices can negatively impact L2 teacher motivation (Zhao, 2008). The social status or value of a specific L2 is also a key macro factor that affects broad levels of L2 teacher motivation. When an L2 (e.g. EFL) has high perceived status, it endows a prestigious position on the L2 teaching profession which enhances L2 teacher motivation (Hettiarachchi, 2013). As can be seen, L2 teacher motivation is deeply intertwined with both micro and macro contextual factors and cannot be thought of as solely an internal psychological state.

In this section, we have once again adopted questions from Pintrich's (2003) orienting perspective of how motivation impacts human choice and action, and summarised some of the most recent research with regard to L2 teacher motivation. In contrast to the strong theoretical threads which tie mainstream teacher motivation research together, it is apparent that L2 teacher motivation research tends to be more thematic and descriptive in how it explains phenomena of interest, which may lead casual observers to consider the field as being somewhat under-theorised. However, while this criticism may apply to certain aspects of L2 teacher motivation research, starting from practice and generating theory bottom-up could also be seen as an ecologically valid form of research. In the final section of this chapter we examine what established theories of motivation have to offer for theorising L2 teacher motivation and propose how a pro-gramme of L2 teacher motivation research might advance the field in the years to come.

Research on Teacher Motivation: Future Directions

Over the last decade, the study of teacher motivation in general educa-tion has been revitalised by renewed interest, thus gaining prominence within contemporary educational psychology (Richardson *et al.*, 2014). The field has begun to explore what established theories of learning and motivation have to offer in theorising teacher motivation (Richardson & Watt, 2010). The same challenge is now facing L2 teacher motivation, and researchers will need to explore how established theories could be adopted and adapted to explain L2 language teacher motivation specifically. An empirical programme is now needed to systematically establish the useful-ness and relevance of existing frameworks from more mainstream teacher motivation research (e.g. self-efficacy, achievement goal theory, self-determination theory) for L2 teachers and teaching. However, we must also acknowledge the wealth of evidence from established frameworks for L2 learning motivation (e.g. the L2 motivational self-system) and consider what they have to offer when applied to language teacher motivation (e.g. Dörnyei & Kubanyiova, 2014). The fact is that many language teachers are both educators and language learners, and thus the domain of lan-guage teacher motivation is well positioned to become a richer field of enquiry because of its crossover appeal. Drawing on all sources of insights and incorporating all perspectives from within SLA and beyond might allow L2 teacher motivation to embrace general educational theories as well as those being used specifically in respect to second language learners and their development.

Along with much of the past decade of work on self-related concepts in L2 motivation research (Boo *et al.*, 2015), rapid advances are being made in terms of theoretical frameworks and empirical designs (e.g. Dörnyei *et al.*, 2015). These include, among others: adopting a dynamic, situated perspective of motivation using complexity theory; reaffirming the interdependent nature of emotion and cognition for motivation; expanding research to account for the implicit and unconscious side of motivation; recognising the centrality of identity to motivational devel-opment processes; and reflecting on the role of technology-based L2 pedagogies. We would add, however, that due to the nature of the profes-sion itself there are adequate reasons to suspect that language teacher motivation differs from L2 learning motivation. This warrants careful evaluation and adaptation of conceptual frameworks, models and meth-odologies for teacher motivation from theory and evidence within L2 learner motivation. One example of this is the language teacher motiva-tion research adopting constructs from the L2 motivational self-system which show that, although possible future self-guides may exist for certain practitioners (Hiver, 2013; Kubanyiova, 2012), these may not be the most desirable types of vision and there may even be language teaching contexts in which teachers are neither willing nor able to engage in the critical reflective thought required to construct and elaborate these future self guides (Gao & Xu, 2014; Hwang *et al.*, 2010; Kumazawa, 2013; Wong *et al.*, 2014).

Finally, because 'the two are inextricably linked' (Dörnyei & Kubanyiova, 2014: 3), the link to teacher classroom practice and by extension students' motivation and learning must be made explicit empirically. Teachers undoubtedly deserve to enjoy positive professional well-being and greater motivation, and thus there is a compelling need for future research to reassess its practice-relevant impact for L2 classrooms. One way it might do this is to demonstrate whether and to what extent language teachers' motivation links to desirable external outcomes, such as teachers' instructional practices, student motivation or student achievement. Research in general education has already shown that these links exist (e.g. Butler & Shibaz, 2014; Radel *et al.*, 2010), and it is likely to be the case in the L2 domain as well. Given the complexity of what transpires in L2 classrooms, student and observer reports of teacher behaviour may not be directly associated with teachers' reports of their own motivation. In instances where teacher motivation and practices have been linked to student outcomes such as motivation and achievement (e.g. Bernaus & Gardner, 2008; Maeng & Lee, 2014; Papi & Abdollahzadeh, 2012), the ways in which student behaviour and teacher motivation and practices might be mutually reinforcing remain unclear, partly because much of this research has not taken as its starting point the day-to-day concerns of practising L2 teachers. In order to establish the direction and significance of these links, future research will need to incorporate measures that go beyond teacher self-reports, and while these effects are unlikely to be simple, direct, linear or even unidirectional, our position is that empirical substantiation is essential in order to take the field forward.

References

Alexander, P.A. (2008) Charting the course for the teaching profession: The energizing and sustaining role of motivational forces. *Learning and Instruction* 18, 483–491.
Alexander, P.A., Grossnickle, E.M. and List, A. (2014) Navigating the labyrinth of teacher motivations and emotions. In P.W. Richardson, S.A. Karabenick and H.M. Watt (eds) *Teacher Motivation: Theory and Practice* (pp. 150–163). New York: Routledge.
Atay, D. (2007) Beginning teacher efficacy and the practicum in an EFL context. *Teacher Development* 11 (2), 203–219.
Baleghizadeh, S. and Gordani, Y. (2012) Motivation and quality of work life among secondary school EFL teachers. *Australian Journal of Teacher Education* 37 (7), 30–42.
Bandura, A. (1997) *Self-efficacy: The Exercise of Control*. New York: W.H. Freeman.
Bandura, A. (2012) On the functional properties of perceived self-efficacy revisited. *Journal of Management* 28, 9–44.

Becker, E.S., Goetz, T., Morger, V. and Ranellucci, J. (2014) The importance of teachers' emotions and instructional behavior for their students' emotions – an experience sampling analysis. *Teaching and Teacher Education* 43, 15–26.

Bernaus, M. and Gardner, R.C. (2008) Teacher motivation strategies, student perceptions, student motivation, and English achievement. *The Modern Language Journal* 92, 387–401.

Boo, Z., Dörnyei, Z. and Ryan, S. (2015) L2 motivation research 2005–2014: Understanding a publication surge and a changing landscape. *System* 55, 145–157.

Butler, R. (2007) Teachers' achievement goal orientations and associations with teachers' help seeking: Examination of a novel approach to teacher motivation. *Journal of Educational Psychology* 99, 241–252.

Butler, R. (2012) Striving to connect: Extending an achievement goal approach to teacher motivation to include relational goals for teaching. *Journal of Educational Psychology* 104, 726–742.

Butler, R. and Shibaz, L. (2014) Striving to connect and striving to learn: Influences of relational and mastery goals for teaching on teacher behaviors and student engagement. *International Journal of Educational Research* 65, 41–53.

Chacon, C.T. (2005) Teachers' perceived efficacy among English as a foreign language teachers in middle schools in Venezuela. *Teaching and Teacher Education* 21 (3), 257–272.

Cowie, N. (2011) Emotions that experienced English as a foreign language (EFL) teachers feel about their students, their colleagues and their work. *Teaching and Teacher Education* 27 (1), 235–242.

Crookes, G. (2009) *Values, Philosophies, and Beliefs in TESOL: Making a Statement.* Cambridge: Cambridge University Press.

Deci, E. and Ryan, R. (2000) The 'what' and 'why' of goal pursuit: Human needs and the self-determination of behavior. *Psychological Inquiry* 11, 319–338.

Deci, E. and Ryan, R. (2012) Motivation, personality, and development within embedded social contexts: An overview of self-determination theory. In E. Deci and R. Ryan (eds) *The Oxford Handbook of Human Motivation* (pp. 85–107). New York: Oxford University Press.

Dörnyei, Z. and Kubanyiova, M. (2014) *Motivating Learners, Motivating Teachers: Building Vision in the Language Classroom.* Cambridge: Cambridge University Press.

Dörnyei, Z. and Ushioda, E. (2011) *Teaching and Researching Motivation* (2nd edn). Harlow: Longman.

Dörnyei, Z., MacIntyre, P.D. and Henry, A. (eds) (2015) *Motivational Dynamics in Language Learning.* Bristol: Multilingual Matters.

Elliot, A. and McGregor, H. (2001) A 2 × 2 achievement goal framework. *Journal of Personality and Social Psychology* 80, 501–519.

Erkaya, O.R. (2012) Factors that motivate Turkish EFL teachers. *International Journal of Research Studies in Language Learning* 2 (2), 49–61.

Erten, İ.H. (2014) Understanding the reasons behind choosing to teach English as a foreign language. *Novitas-ROYAL (Research on Youth and Language)* 8, 30–44.

Frenzel, A. (2014) Teacher emotions. In E. Linnenbrink-Garcia and R. Pekrun (eds) *International Handbook of Emotions in Education* (pp. 494–519). New York: Routledge.

Gan, Z. (2014) Learning from interpersonal interactions during the practicum: A case study of non-native ESL student teachers. *Journal of Education for Teaching* 40 (2), 128–139.

Gao, X.A. and Xu, H. (2014) The dilemma of being English language teachers: Interpreting teachers' motivation to teach, and professional commitment in China's hinterland regions. *Language Teaching Research* 18, 152–168.

Garner, P. (2010) Emotional competence and its influences on teaching and learning. *Educational Psychology Review* 22, 297–321.

Goddard, R., Hoy, W. and Woolfolk Hoy, A. (2000) Collective teacher efficacy: Its meaning, measure, and impact on student achievement. *American Education Research Journal* 37 (2), 479–507.

Goddard, R., Hoy, W. and Woolfolk Hoy, A. (2004) Collective efficacy beliefs: Theoretical developments, empirical evidence, and future directions. *Educational Researcher* 33 (3), 3–13.

Hanushek, E.A. (2011) The economic value of higher teacher quality. *Economics of Education Review* 30, 466–479.

Hayes, D. (2008) Becoming a teacher of English in Thailand. *Language Teaching Research* 12 (4), 471–494.

Hettiarachchi, S. (2013) English language teacher motivation in Sri Lankan public schools. *Journal of Language Teaching and Research* 4 (1), 1–11.

Hiver, P. (2013) The interplay of possible language teacher selves in professional development choices. *Language Teaching Research* 17 (2), 210–227.

Hwang, S.-S., Seo, H.-S. and Kim, T.-Y. (2010) Korean English teachers' disempowerment in English-only classes: A case study focusing on Korea-specific cultural aspects. *Sociolinguistic Journal of Korea* 18 (1), 105–133.

Kaplan, A. (2014) Theory and research on teachers' motivation: Mapping an emerging conceptual terrain. In P.W. Richardson, S.A. Karabenick and H.M. Watt (eds) *Teacher Motivation: Theory and Practice* (pp. 52–66). New York: Routledge.

Karavas, E. (2010) How satisfied are Greek EFL teachers with their work? Investigating the motivation and job satisfaction levels of Greek EFL teachers. *Porta Linguarum* 14, 59–78.

Khani, R. and Mirzaee, A. (2015) How do self-efficacy, contextual variables and stressors affect teacher burnout in an EFL context? *Educational Psychology* 35 (1), 93–109.

Kim, T.-Y. and Kim, Y.-K. (2015) Initial career motives and demotivation in teaching English as a foreign language: Cases of Korean EFL teachers. *Porta Linguarum* 24 (2), 77–92.

Kim, T.-Y., Kim, Y.-K. and Zhang, Q.-M. (2014) Differences in demotivation between Chinese and Korean English teachers: A mixed-methods study. *The Asia-Pacific Education Researcher* 23, 299–310.

Kimura, Y. (2014) ELT motivation from a complex dynamic systems theory perspective: A longitudinal case study of L2 teacher motivation in Beijing. In K. Csizér and M. Magid (eds) *The Impact of Self-concept on Language Learning* (pp. 310–332). Bristol: Multilingual Matters.

Klassen, R. and Tze, V.M.C. (2014) Teachers' self-efficacy, personality, and teaching effectiveness: A meta-analysis. *Educational Research Review* 12, 59–76.

Klassen, R., Tze, V.M.C., Betts, S. and Gordon, K. (2011) Teacher efficacy research 1998–2009: Signs of progress or unfulfilled promise? *Educational Psychology Review* 23, 21–43.

Kong, J.-H., Lee, H.-J., Shin, S.-H. and Kim, T.-Y. (under review) Arabic teachers' perception of Arabic learners' L2 learning motivation and demotivation.

Koran, S. (2015) Analyzing EFL teachers' initial job motivation and factors effecting their motivation in Fezalar educational institutions in Iraq. *Advances in Language and Literary Studies* 6 (1), 72–80.

Kubanyiova, M. (2012) *Teacher Development in Action: Understanding Language Teachers' Conceptual Change*. Basingstoke: Palgrave.

Kumazawa, M. (2013) Gaps too large: Four novice EFL teachers' self-concept and motivation. *Teaching and Teacher Education* 33, 45–55.

Madni, A., Baker, E., Chow, K., Delacruz, G. and Griffin, N. (2015) Assessment of teachers from a social psychological perspective. *Review of Research in Education* 39, 54–86.

Maeng, U. and Lee, S.-M. (2014) EFL teachers' behavior of using motivational strategies: The case of teaching in the Korean context. *Teaching and Teacher Education* 46, 25–36.

Moller, A., Deci, E. and Ryan, R. (2006) Choice and ego-depletion: The moderating role of autonomy. *Personality and Social Psychology Bulletin* 32, 1024–1036.

Papi, M. and Abdollahzadeh, E. (2012) L2 teacher motivational practice, student motivation and possible L2 selves: An examination in the Iranian EFL context. *Language Learning* 62, 571–594.

Pintrich, P. (2003) A motivational science perspective on the role of student motivation in learning and teaching contexts. *Journal of Educational Psychology* 95, 667–686.

Radel, R., Sarrazin, P., Legrain, P. and Wild, T.C. (2010) Social contagion of motivation between teacher and student: Analyzing underlying processes. *Journal of Educational Psychology* 102, 577–587.

Reeve, J. and Su, Y.-L. (2014) Teacher motivation. In M. Gagné (ed.) *The Oxford Handbook of Work Engagement, Motivation, and Self-determination Theory* (pp. 349–362). Oxford: Oxford University Press.

Remijan, K.W. (2014) Improving teacher motivation in secondary schools with hybrid positions. *American Secondary Education* 42 (3), 30–38.

Retelsdorf, J., Butler, R., Streblow, L. and Schiefele, U. (2010) Teachers' goal orientations for teaching: Associations with instructional practices and teachers' engagement. *Learning and Instruction* 20, 30–46.

Richardson, P.W. and Watt, H.M. (2010) Current and future directions in teacher motivation research. In T. Urdan and S. Karabenick (eds) *The Decade Ahead: Applications and Contexts of Motivation and Achievement* (pp. 139–173). London: Emerald Group.

Richardson, P.W. and Watt, H.M. (2014) Why people choose teaching as a career: An expectancy-value approach to understanding teacher motivation. In P.W. Richardson, S.A. Karabenick and H.M. Watt (eds) *Teacher Motivation: Theory and Practice* (pp. 3–19). New York: Routledge.

Richardson, P.W. and Watt, H.M. (2016) Factors influencing teaching choice: Why do future teachers choose the career? In J. Loughran and M.L. Hamilton (eds) *International Handbook of Teacher Education* (pp. 275–305). Singapore: Springer.

Richardson, P.W., Karabenick, S.A. and Watt, H.M. (2014) Teacher motivation matters: An introduction. In P.W. Richardson, S.A. Karabenick and H.M. Watt (eds) *Teacher Motivation: Theory and Practice* (pp. xiii–xxii). New York: Routledge.

Roth, G. (2014) Antecedents and outcomes of teachers' autonomous motivation: A self-determination theory analysis. In P.W. Richardson, S.A. Karabenick and H.M. Watt (eds) *Teacher Motivation: Theory and Practice* (pp. 36–51). New York: Routledge.

Roth, G., Assor, A., Kanat-Maymon, Y. and Kaplan, H. (2007) Autonomous motivation for teaching: How self-determined teaching may lead to self-determined learning. *Journal of Educational Psychology* 99, 761–774.

Ruohotie-Lyhty, M. (2013) Struggling for a professional identity: Two newly qualified language teachers' identity narratives during the first years at work. *Teaching and Teacher Education* 30, 120–129.

Skaalvik, E. and Skaalvik, S. (2010) Teacher self-efficacy and teacher burnout: A study of relations. *Teaching and Teacher Education* 26, 1059–1069.

Soenens, B., Sierens, E., Vansteenkiste, M., Dochy, F. and Goossens, L. (2012) Psychologically controlling teaching: Examining outcomes, antecedents, and mediators. *Journal of Educational Psychology* 104, 108–120.

Storbeck, J. and Clore, G. (2007) On the interdependence of cognition and emotion. *Cognition and Emotion* 21, 1212–1237.

Sugino, T. (2010) Teacher demotivational factors in the Japanese language teaching context. *Procedia-Social and Behavioral Sciences* 3, 216–226.

Tang, S., Cheng, M. and Cheng, A. (2014) Shifts in teaching motivation and sense of self-as-teacher in initial teacher education. *Educational Review* 66, 465–481.

Tardy, C.M. and Snyder, B. (2004) 'That's why I do it': Flow and EFL teachers' practices. *ELT Journal* 58 (2), 118–128.

Topkaya, E.Z. and Uztosun, M.S. (2012) Choosing teaching as a career: Motivations of pre-service English teachers in Turkey. *Journal of Language Teaching and Research* 3, 126–134.

Tschannen-Moran, M. and Woolfolk Hoy, A. (2001) Teacher efficacy: Capturing an elusive construct. *Teaching and Teacher Education* 17, 783–805.

Tsutsumi, R. (2014) Exploring Japanese university EFL teacher motivation. *Journal of Pan-Pacific Association of Applied Linguistics* 18 (1), 121–143.

Urdan, T. (2014) Concluding commentary: Understanding teacher motivation. In P.W. Richardson, S.A. Karabenick and H.M. Watt (eds) *Teacher Motivation: Theory and Practice* (pp. 227–246). New York: Routledge.

Visser-Wijnveen, G., Stes, A. and Van Petegem, P. (2014) Clustering teachers' motivations for teaching. *Teaching in Higher Education* 19, 644–656.

Warford, M.K. and Reeves, J. (2003) Falling into it: Novice TESOL teacher thinking. *Teachers and Teaching: Theory and Practice* 9, 47–65.

Watt, H.M., Richardson, P.W., Klusmann, U., Kunter, M., Beyer, B., Trautwein, U. and Baumert, J. (2012) Motivations for choosing teaching as a career: An international comparison using the FIT-Choice scale. *Teaching and Teacher Education* 28, 791–805.

Wigfield, A. and Eccles, J.S. (2000) Expectancy-value theory of achievement motivation. *Contemporary Educational Psychology* 25, 68–81.

Wong, A.K., Tang, S.Y. and Cheng, M.M. (2014) Teaching motivations in Hong Kong: Who will choose teaching as a fallback career in a stringent job market? *Teaching and Teacher Education* 41, 81–91.

Zee, M. and Koomen, H. (2016) Teacher self-efficacy and its effects on classroom processes, student academic adjustment, and teacher well-being: A synthesis of 40 years of research. *Review of Educational Research*; doi:10.3102/0034654315626801.

Zembylas, M. (2003) Caring for teacher emotion: Reflections on teacher self-development. *Studies in Philosophy and Education* 22, 103–125.

Zhao, H. (2008) Why did people become secondary-school English as a foreign language teachers in China? An examination of the pathways, motivations and policy through a life-history narrative approach. *Educational Research for Policy and Practice* 7 (3), 183–195.

Zhang, Q.-M. (2017) Research on second language teacher motivation from a Vygotskian Activity Theory perspective: A case study of two novice English teachers in China. In M.T. Apple, D. Da Silva and T. Fellner (eds) *L2 Selves and Motivations in Asian Contexts* (pp. 172–194). Bristol: Multilingual Matters.

Zumwalt, K. and Craig, E. (2008) Who is teaching? Does it matter? In M. Cochran-Smith, S. Feiman-Nemser and D.J. McIntyre (eds) *Handbook of Research on Teacher Education: Enduring Questions in Changing Contexts* (pp. 404–423). New York: Routledge.

3 'The English Class of My Dreams': Envisioning Teaching a Foreign Language

Paula Kalaja and Katja Mäntylä

The psychology of the second (or foreign) language learner has been extensively researched since the mid-1950s. Unfortunately, the same cannot be said for the psychology of the teacher. For the psychological make-up of the learner, motivation has been found to be one of the key issues affecting not only the outcome but also the process of learning second (or foreign) languages. Much less is known about the motivation of the teachers involved in these efforts.

The teaching of English as a foreign language is faced with new challenges because of the rapid spread of the language in different parts of the world, including Finland. Here, this has meant reconsidering the status of the language, with consequent revisions of the curricula of both schools and teacher education. In this chapter our concern is with university students of English and how they keep up their motivation as future teachers. More specifically, our focus is on the development of their pedagogical knowledge in teaching the language before they start their careers as qualified teachers in Finland and their ability to turn this knowledge into principles and practices that they could imagine applying in their future English classes. Related to their motivation and identities as future professionals, it is their ability to envision, or the *visions* of these students, which the study will look into. For this purpose, a group of pre-service teachers were asked to visualise and draw an image of their ideal class teaching English to be given in the not-so-distant future and elaborate on the picture in writing: where would the class take place, what would be taught and how?

This chapter is organised as follows. First, some background is provided for the present study by reviewing such key issues as teacher motivation, envisioning and narratives, and by summarising some related studies. After this, the study that was carried out is reported in more detail, including its aims, data collection and analysis, and findings. Finally, the implications of the study are discussed.

Background to the Study

Teacher motivation and envisioning

The motivation of learners of foreign languages has been studied extensively and from a number of different theoretical starting points over the past few decades (for a review, see for example Dörnyei & Ushioda, 2010). Recently, it has been suggested that learner motivation be viewed in terms of a *motivational self-system* (e.g. Dörnyei & Ushioda, 2009), consisting of learners' possible selves, including their ideal self and ought-to self, and related to their past experiences of learning a foreign language. This system taps into two major aspects of learning a foreign language: first, the learners' own aspirations, fears and ideals (in comparison to their actual self or selves); and, secondly, the expectations of, or social pressure from, others around them (e.g. teachers, parents, friends, school and society at large), each playing a role in, and having an effect on, the process and outcomes of learning a foreign language.

Even more recently, it has been suggested that the motivational self-system could be applied to teachers of foreign languages too (e.g. Dörnyei & Kubanyiova, 2014): to both pre-service teachers and in-service teachers. Teacher motivation – in all its current complexity – is thus a crucial issue to address in teacher education: in the course of their studies, student teachers acquire pedagogical knowledge of the various aspects involved in learning and teaching foreign languages, while at the same time improving their proficiency in the language they will be teaching. In addition, their identities and ideal or ought-to selves are bound to develop. It is important for student teachers to compare the current reality in schools with their ideals: how do they see themselves and their practices now and in the future, and how far or how close are these from each other? The ability to envision their teaching in the years to come is thus related to their motivation. However, as pointed out by Dörnyei and Kubanyiova (2014), the purpose

> is not to identify some kind of idealised fantasy image of a language class-room that may never exist, but, rather, to develop a personally meaning-ful *possible* vision that is integral to who the teacher is and that is sensitive to the context in which his/her work is located. (Dörnyei & Kubanyiova, 2014: 125, emphasis in original)

The point is to make student teachers aware of their beliefs about their professional future, and to reaffirm or reconsider these, which will possibly have consequences for the principles and practices that they will apply in their teaching once they enter working life as qualified teachers.

Visual narratives looking forward in time

In teacher education, narratives have been acknowledged to be a means for pre- and in-service teachers to make sense of themselves and their profession (e.g. Johnson & Golombek, 2011, 2013), more specifically, in constructing their identities and reflecting on their experiences of teaching English or other foreign languages.

One way of describing *narratives* is to say that they consist of a series of events:

> Briefly, in everyday oral storytelling, a speaker connects events into a sequence that is consequential for later action and for the meanings that the speaker wants listeners to take away from the story. Events perceived by the speaker as important are selected, organized, connected, and evaluated as meaningful for a particular audience ... (Riessman, 2008: 3)

Another way is to define them by function. Narratives can be used not only in looking back but also in looking forward: '[Stories] assist humans to make life experiences meaningful. Stories preserve our memories, prompt our reflections, connect us with our past and present, and assist us to envision our future' (Kramp, 2004: 107, as quoted in Barkhuizen, 2013: 4). Furthermore, narratives can be recounted in more than one mode: they can be verbal (oral or written), visual, or multimodal, e.g. text complemented with pictures, tables, figures, etc. or sound and video-clips. Depending on the mode, narratives have different possibilities and limitations (Kress & van Leeuwen, 2006: 46): what can be described verbally may not be possible to do visually, and vice versa. The present study is an attempt to explore further the possibilities of visual narratives (e.g. Kalaja, 2016; Kalaja *et al.*, 2013), this time in looking forward in time and addressing visions of future teachers of English.

Review of related studies

A small number of studies have been carried out which have focused on visions of teachers or future teachers or made use of narratives. In her studies, Hammerness (e.g. 2003, 2006) asked novice teachers in the United States to imagine their ideal classroom. Data were collected by administering a survey ($n = 80$) and conducting interviews with some of the teachers ($n = 16$) involved, in which they were asked to imagine taking the interviewer round their ideal classroom and to give details in response to a set of questions. Basically, they were asked what they would teach, how and why. The teachers' visions (reported verbally) were analysed along three dimensions: focus, range and distance. In other words, the images or visions of future classrooms were viewed in terms of either being clear or vague in focus; broad or narrow in range; or close to or distant from the teachers' current practices or daily experiences. Although these two studies are interesting in their research topic, design and methodology, they do not focus on language teachers or their ideal visions.

In contrast, a follow-up study to a longitudinal project entitled *From Novice to Expert* (e.g. Kalaja, 2016; Kalaja *et al.*, 2013) asked student teachers of foreign languages, including English ($n = 61$), who were just about to graduate from an MA degree programme in Finland, to envision a future class. This was done not only verbally but also visually, by having the participants draw a picture and comment on it briefly in writing. This study made use of visual narratives to look forward in time and asked the teachers to imagine what would be involved in the teaching of foreign languages in the future.

In another two studies (Borg *et al.*, 2014; Clarke, 2008), student teachers were asked to recollect some positive examples of what it was like to teach English to small children in two very different contexts: in Spain and the United Arab Emirates. In the first study, the students were expected to describe events like this visually in two different ways: first by drawing a picture before and after a teaching methodology course, and then orally, in an interview. In other words, visual narratives were used to look back in time in order to recollect what had happened before, when teaching English. In the second study, data were collected by asking students to submit postings to an internet discussion forum.

The findings of the three studies with student teachers of English or other foreign languages are in fact quite comparable, despite their different foci, type of data or contexts. In all the studies, two discourses could be identified: one was based on the participants' past experiences of learning English; this was in contrast to the other discourse, which was based on their current understanding of what the teaching of English involves. In the latter, such principles and practices were recycled as student-centredness, the teacher as guide, a focus on meanings or oral/real communication, the use of modern IT, and authentic materials. These were complemented with comments on how their classrooms would be organised and what their classrooms would be equipped with. The principles and practices seem to stand in sharp contrast to their past experiences as learners of English, when they were still at school.

The Present Study

The present study is a continuation of previous research carried out in Finland, but with a more recent group of student teachers and some refinements in research methodology. Overall, this is an attempt by us to make this group aware, first, of their ideal teacher selves (i.e. what they would expect of themselves once they enter working life as professionals in a few years' time), and secondly, of their current teaching practices and ideals, and how close or far apart these are at this point in their studies. These issues are closely related to how motivated they feel about entering the profession in the next few years. While the students in the previous study reviewed above (Kalaja, 2016; Kalaja *et al.*, 2013) were about to complete their teacher education, the students in the present study were only half-way through. We used visual narratives to look forward in time, and carried out their collection in a more focused and structured way than in the previous study by using a set of prompt questions.

The study seeks to answer the following research question: What would an ideal class of English be like and, more specifically, where would the class take place, what would be taught there, and how? In order to answer the questions, the pre-service teachers were asked to envision a future class of English, but a class that would still be feasible to give after their graduation, and to describe it in two modes, visually and verbally. The findings of the analysis will be reported in the form of case studies to illustrate the overall variation in the classes of English envisioned.

Context of the study

English is the most popular foreign language studied and taught in the Finnish educational system. Until now, its study started in Year (or Grade) 3, i.e. from the age of nine years, but following the latest revisions to the national curricula, it can be offered even earlier in Years 1 and 2.

The teaching of English or any other foreign language is regulated to varying degrees by a number of guidelines. Some of these are European (*The Common European Framework of Reference for Languages*, Council of Europe, 2001), some national, and others local (e.g. a town, a local authority or a school might have curricula of its own). The Finnish National Core Curricula for compulsory education (Years 1–9) and for post-secondary education (Years 10–12 or Sixth Form), where students take the matriculation examination, a nationally administered high-stakes test, before graduating, have just been revised, and so have the local curricula, all effective as of August 2016.

The previous curricula were drawn up in the early 2000s. In the new curricula, the order of importance of the three main aims for the teaching of foreign languages has been reversed and their emphasis and scope have been revised. Now the first aim is to raise learners' awareness and appreciation of multilingualism and multiculturalism, and of languages in general. The second aim is to provide students with practice in learning-to-learn skills, and the third is to develop their proficiency in English in three skills, namely, in the ability to interact, interpret and produce oral, written and multimodal texts. Importantly, it is now acknowledged that the status of English has changed to a lingua franca or global language, even though the language does not as yet have an official status in Finland. However, young people in Finland learn and use English not only in formal school contexts but also, and increasingly, in a variety of informal contexts such as hobbies, spare time activities, travelling, using modern IT with all its applications, including the internet, and later on in working life as well. The teaching of English in Finland is thus faced with new challenges in terms of its aims, classroom practices, teaching materials, roles of teachers and learners and assessment (for details, see Kalaja *et al.*, in press a).

Participants

Teacher education is a joint effort of two departments on the campus where this study was conducted in Finland. The Department of Teacher Education offers studies in pedagogy, including a teaching practicum in cooperation with local schools. Completing a Bachelor's degree in pedagogy qualifies a student for any teaching post in the Finnish educational system. In contrast, the Department of Language and Communication Studies is responsible for providing all pre-service teachers with two compulsory introductory courses on learning and teaching any foreign language (or Finnish). The English section of the department continues from there by offering a third course called Current Issues in Teaching English (CITE) and some other more advanced courses.

The participants in the study were a group of pre-service teachers of English ($n = 35$), mainly second- or third-year university students. The majority, whether majoring or minoring in English, were studying to become foreign language teachers at the secondary or post-secondary level. However, a few students wanted to become elementary school teachers, getting a qualification to teach in English or offer courses in content and language integrated learning (CLIL). In addition, there were a couple of exchange students taking the course. All the participants had some pedagogical studies behind them. Some had also completed their practical teacher training and/or worked as supply teachers. The participants formed a heterogeneous group in that the amount of studies they had already completed varied, as did their teaching experience.

The students attended CITE, which is a compulsory course for future teachers of English, in the academic year 2015–2016. The data for this study were collected at the end of the course. The course is a five-credit (ECTS) course and part of the BA programme, that is, second- or third-year studies, in English. The students had weekly reading assignments from an introductory textbook by Hummel (2014), and the topics were discussed in class. The course focused on the teaching of English in the context of Finland, and the topics addressed included a review of key issues in research on second language acquisition over the past few decades, contexts of learning, the development of learner language, individual learner differences, teaching methodology, syllabus design, assessment and bi- or multilingualism. Considering that the field is full of controversies, it was interesting to see how this group of student teachers made sense of the pedagogical knowledge they had acquired so far during their studies and how they managed to turn it into a set of principles and practices that they could imagine applying in their teaching of English after entering the profession.

The data and their processing

For the purposes of the study, a task sheet was designed. It drew on ideas from the studies by Hammerness (2003, 2006), and was our attempt to explore further the possibilities of visual narratives for the purpose of envisioning (e.g. Kalaja, 2016; Kalaja *et al.*, 2013). There were two tasks (for details, see Appendix A).

Task 1 asked the participants to produce a picture entitled 'An English class of my dreams', in which they depicted a class that they could imagine giving after graduating from the five-year MA programme. The images could be drawn by hand or done on a computer, or produced by compiling a collage out of magazine clippings. In addition, the participants were asked to comment on the picture, writing a few sentences in response to the question 'What would be taking place in your class – and why?'.

Task 2 (on the reverse side of the task sheet) asked the participants to consider the envisioned English class in greater detail (and in a more systematic way than before, e.g. Kalaja, 2016; Kalaja *et al.*, 2013). This gave the students a chance to elaborate on the target group that they would like to teach, the roles of those involved (i.e. the teacher and students), what they would teach and how, where their teaching would take place and what equipment would be available to them.

The students completed the task sheet in Finnish (with the exception of the few exchange students attending the course) as the last home assignment of the introductory course. The pictures were compared and contrasted in discussions (first in small groups and then as a whole group) in English during the very last session of the course – either in late November 2015 or in April 2016. The pictures as such were not assessed, and they did not count towards the overall grade for the course. Permission was requested from the students (in writing) to use the pictures and descriptions anonymously for research purposes.

The contents of the visual narratives, complemented by their verbal commentaries, were first examined to get an overall idea of what the pool of data contained. In addition, the written explanations and elaborations of the pictures were analysed to gain a more thorough and accurate understanding of their visual narratives. In the written texts, the participants gave, for instance, explanations for their choices or clarified their drawings and their contents. After this, the focus was narrowed down for the purposes of this study, and the visualisations of 'The English class of my dreams' were grouped according to: (1) what the physical environment for the class would be; (2) what roles the future teacher and his or her students would adopt; and (3) what would be taught and how in the future English class. The cases are presented below using pseudonyms to guarantee the anonymity of the participants.

Findings

A total of six contextualised case studies (as defined by Duff, 2007) will be reported below to illustrate the overall variation in the pictures, or in the ways the pre-service teachers envisioned giving a class of English in the years to come. Two cases from each of the three groups, the physical environment, the roles of the teachers and the students, and the contents and means of teaching were selected. The cases per group illustrate the range of visions in the data.

Environment (1): Omnipresent language

In Mikko's picture, the idea was of a language learning environment that was omnipresent (Figure 3.1), and this placed the focus on the learner. There was no classroom and there were no walls, but language could be learnt everywhere. There were books, and the learner's curiosity was emphasised, as was the variety of language learning contexts and, to an extent, also interaction with others.

Figure 3.1 Mikko – teacher training and pedagogical studies completed

Mikko was quite advanced in his studies and had completed his peda-gogical studies and teacher training. In his commentary, he explained that the lessons were designed to meet the interests of the students. The idea of integrating languages with other subjects was strongly present. This mir-rors the ideas of the new National Core Curricula, which emphasise lan-guage awareness and the integration of school subjects. Also, Mikko would like to teach in ways that the students themselves want and need, taking different learners into account. This reflects the ideals of teacher education in Finland in recent years: future teachers have been made aware of the variety of learning styles. He thought it was important, however, that whatever the students learn should be written down, whether the equip-ment is a blackboard or a tablet computer. This urge to write down is perhaps in slight contradiction to his willingness to take teaching to a new level, steering away from the classroom and textbooks and emphasising real language use and communication. Mikko said he was teaching life.

Environment (2): A classroom with sofas

Tiina's picture offered a more traditional view of language learning and its environment (Figure 3.2). There was a classroom with desks for the stu-dents and a chair for the teacher at the front of the classroom. The teacher's

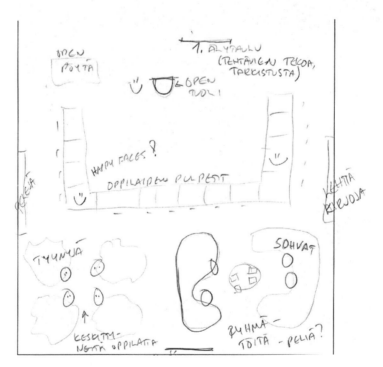

Figure 3.2 Tiina – some pedagogical studies

desk had been placed to the side. There was also a smartboard for doing and checking exercises. What made the setting different from a traditional classroom was that the desks were in a horseshoe arrangement, and there were cushions, sofas, games, books and magazines. Tiina had done some pedagogical studies but not the practical training, and she did not have any teaching experience at that time. Her views are therefore likely to have reflected quite heavily how she herself had been taught languages at school.

What was done in this rather traditional classroom was interesting. Unlike in Mikko's picture, where the focus had been on language usage, culture and interaction, in Tiina's description the emphasis was on practising vocabulary and going through texts, and taking advantage of mnemonics when learning grammar. Tiina regarded games, mnemonics and the like as innovative methods that motivate students to learn. Thus, her view of language is traditional, as to a large extent are also the ways of teaching it. Furthermore, in her commentary Tiina talked about *going through issues*, implying that the teacher has a list of curricular content points to cover and this is then done using games and other activities, employing different learning and teaching strategies.

Roles of the teacher and students (1): Student in the centre

Sanna attempted to present a fairly comprehensive and complex picture of language learning (Figure 3.3), with many different roles for the

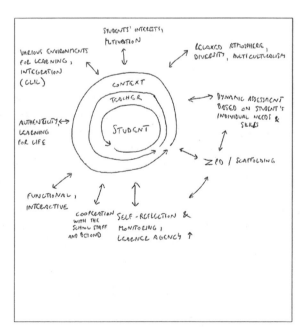

Figure 3.3 Sanna – training for elementary school teachers completed

teacher and student. The students were in the centre, surrounded by the teacher and the context. Different factors affecting language learning and teaching were mentioned, such as the zone of proximal development (ZPD), atmosphere and authenticity. Sanna also mentioned quite a few teacher tasks, from scaffolding and motivating students to dynamic assessment, thus expanding the role of the teacher. Sanna was a second-year student of English but she was about to graduate as an elementary school teacher. She had not done pedagogical studies targeted specifically at language teachers. However, her previous pedagogical studies and work experience as an elementary school teacher showed in the concepts she used. These concepts, such as lifelong learning, learner agency, ZPD and dynamic assessment are at the very core of current thinking in teacher education in Finland. Also, authenticity has been a frequently discussed theme in language teaching in Finland for the past few years. In her verbal commentary Sanna, too, emphasised the central role of the learner as an active participant in learning; the teacher's role was to support learning. On the other hand, the teacher was also claimed to be a transmitter of information, which is a more traditional view and conflicts with the picture and its buzzwords. As for the methods, Sanna mentioned a wide range of options, from the use of a smartboard and the internet to games and using drama. However, in her explanation, she made no reference to the pedagogical opportunities offered by these different methods; they were rather seen as a necessary variation to keep students interested. All in all, interaction and communication were once again highlighted.

Roles of the teacher and students (2): Modern roles

Päivi expressed a similar idea to Sanna's in her picture (Figure 3.4), but worded it more simply or, rather, in layman's terms. This probably reflects the fact that Päivi was at the beginning of her pedagogical studies and as yet had no teaching experience. She mentioned that the classroom could be a traditional one, organised in a traditional way, and that books, games and other traditional means would be useful as equipment. However, her ideas of the roles of the teacher and the learner were following more recent ideas of teaching and learning: the teacher's role is to listen, while students are expected to listen and also speak. The setting, then, was irrelevant: what was more important was what happened in the lesson and the classroom and what kind of roles the teacher and students took. Päivi's picture includes a list of qualities such as being motivated, curious and self-confident, but it is not quite clear whether these apply to the teacher, students or both. Authenticity, equality, visuality, practice, many-sidedness and enthusiasm were also mentioned. In her verbal commentary, Päivi also stressed a pleasant atmosphere in the classroom.

Figure 3.4 Päivi – no pedagogical studies or teaching experience

Ways of teaching and learning (1): Project work in groups

Instead of a traditional classroom, or even the more modern one of the local teacher training school that the students were familiar with, Noora opted for something different (Figure 3.5). In her picture, the lesson was taking place in a grand house, offering ample opportunities for group work, which formed the core of her teaching. Interestingly, the teacher was the only one standing, and she seemed to be keeping an eye on things and being available when needed. The students were shown as working in small groups, using English and working on their projects, related to culture. Also, activities outside the classroom were mentioned. The teacher was seen as a facilitator and guide, and the focus was on the learners. Even though the setting was an old-fashioned mansion, modern technology, including tablet computers, was present. Noora also talked about projects and the integration of different school subjects, for instance, biology and languages. This is very much in accordance with the National Core Curricula, which highlight language awareness and reaching over subject boundaries at school. Noora had completed her pedagogical studies, and as part of her studies she had also acted as a supervisor in a language camp for children, which had relied heavily on action-based learning.

Ways of teaching and learning (2): Each item in the classroom has a purpose

Finally, let us consider Iris's picture (Figure 3.6). Iris was an exchange student, and she had completed some pedagogical studies and teacher

Figure 3.5 Noora – pedagogical studies completed

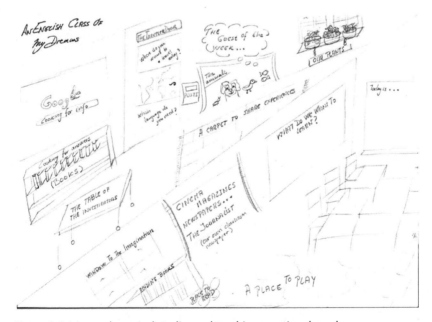

Figure 3.6 Iris – pedagogical studies and teaching practice abroad

training in her home country. Her lesson could have taken place anywhere, but the classroom was organised so that each area in it and each object had a specific function. In Iris's picture, it was irrelevant whether there were chairs or cushions, but the classroom had various items that each served a specific language usage function. A carpet was there to share experiences on, a window was a window to the imagination, etc. The blackboard or smartboard was not used to check the correct answers to exercises but, for instance, to share ideas about what the students wanted to learn. In her commentary, Iris explained that the teacher would give out the theme of the week, and the students could then decide what they wanted to learn about the theme and carry out a small-scale project to that end. The students shared information among themselves, and the teacher was a facilitator in the students' construction of their own knowledge. Hence, the ways of learning were varied but always student centred.

Comparison of cases

As far as the environments of learning are concerned, the cases reviewed above illustrate the student teachers' underlying beliefs that more novel ways of learning are possible even in classroom settings that have been found in schools for centuries, that is, a teacher's desk facing neatly arranged rows of student desks. On the other hand, when given a free rein to depict language learning and teaching settings, the participants were willing to visualise life outside the school building and classroom walls. Languages are not learnt in a vacuum, and not from textbooks. The absence of textbooks was indeed interesting, as a fairly recent survey shows that language teachers in Finland in fact rely heavily on textbooks in their teaching (Luukka et al., 2008). In all the pictures, there was at least an attempt at student-centred learning. The idea of professional selves shows not only in the terminology used by, for instance, Sanna, but also in the ideals in the pictures: students are at the centre of what is going on; the methods of teaching and learning are varied and encourage co-operation and interaction; and authenticity and integrating languages with other school subjects were seen as significant. This seems to be a reflection of what has been highlighted in pedagogical studies, but also in the guidelines of the National Core Curricula.

One common trait in all the pictures and their commentaries was the highlighting of a relaxed, friendly atmosphere in the classroom. Finnish schools have often been criticised for their atmosphere, and even though the learning results may be good internationally speaking, children do not feel comfortable at school (Harinen & Halme, 2012). This is something that has been discussed a lot in Finnish society, and this discussion was also reflected in the pictures: the students were presented as being given a say in what and how they learn, in a positive and relaxed atmosphere.

Discussion

This study set out to discover how a specific group of pre-service teachers would envision future classes of English. Their visions turned out to vary in a number of respects.

First, there was variation in the environments where the teaching and/ or learning of English would take place. More specifically, the English class would take place either in a regular classroom, with some further variation in how the classroom would be furnished or equipped, or outside the classroom. In other words, it is assumed either that the teaching and learning of English is confined within the walls of a traditional classroom or, alternatively, that these activities can take place anywhere, not only in formal but also in informal contexts (for an even more complex account of contexts, see Benson & Reinders, 2011). Some pictures described the classroom in minute detail, indicating that where the teaching or learning of English would take place was important, while others paid little attention to this aspect, even claiming that the environment was of little or no relevance at all.

Secondly, there was variation in the activities and therefore also in the roles of those involved. Some of the visions highlighted some aspects of teaching by a teacher as the main activity in a future class of English; others the learning by learners; and yet others teaching and learning as a joint activity, involving negotiation between two parties, that is, the teacher and students. The role(s) of the teacher varied accordingly: from that of a transmitter of information, in control of what takes place in the classroom, to that of a guide, ensuring learning opportunities for everyone, and as one partner in negotiating what would take place in the class and how. The role(s) of learners varied, too: from passive recipients of information to active seizers of learning opportunities and an equal partner in the negotiations. In other words, there was variation in how teacher- or student-centred the visions were. Similarly, there was variation in the responsibilities the teacher would have in the classroom: not only teaching, but also motivating students, assessing learning outcomes, fostering lifelong learning and ensuring a positive atmosphere.

Thirdly, there was further variation in the focus of teaching and learning of English. On the one hand, the focus could be on the actual teaching *of* English. There was then variation in the aspects addressed in a future English class: was English to be addressed in terms of an abstract system, including vocabulary and grammar, or in terms of its uses in specific contexts, or as a means of communication? On the other hand, the focus could be on teaching *in* English. In other words, English would be used as a medium of instruction in teaching other school subjects (or in CLIL).

The pictures and their explanations reflected both the ideal and ought-to selves of the pre-service teachers. While the participants, for instance, wanted to teach life and saw language and opportunities for its learning everywhere, they at the same time found it necessary to write down important things in the class. Hence, their ideals went hand-in-hand with what they were used to in their own school days and maybe considered to be something expected of them.

Conclusion

To sum up, this study made use of visual narratives and their commentaries, or *multimodal* data, in looking forward in time, that is, asking pre-service teachers to envision an ideal English class to be given in the years to come after they have graduated from their MA programme. Envisioning, in turn, is an aspect of feeling motivated in the profession in the future. In addition, the study was an attempt by us to refine our research methodology, that is, making use of visual data but also collecting data in another mode (written commentaries) to ensure a more systematic comparison of the cases than before (e.g. Kalaja, 2016).

The findings are basically comparable to those of the previous studies reviewed above, despite the partly different contexts and student bodies. There is, however, a clear difference in that in this study there seems to be much greater variation in the pools of data, and so the group of pre-service teachers is much more heterogeneous in their visions of giving a future English class: some classes are envisioned as being not very different from the classes the students themselves attended when they were at school, while other classes have been inspired by more recent developments in the fields of applied linguistics (or foreign/second language learning and teaching) or foreign language education. In addition, they seem to be well informed about the innovations in the new National Core Curricula (effective from August 2016). The awareness of all this is already reflected in some of the principles or practices the students wish to apply in their future teaching, albeit to varying degrees and with some contradictions (of which they themselves appeared to be unaware). It seems that this variation is at least partly dependent on the stage in the MA degree programme at which the students found themselves and, perhaps even more importantly, on their experience of teaching English. As was explained earlier, the group was heterogeneous in this regard, as some students had taught under the supervision of teacher trainers as part of their pedagogical studies and others had worked as supply teachers at some point in their studies – for a shorter or longer period of time. The more advanced the students were in their studies and/or the more teaching experience they had had, the more sophisticated or complex their visions of an ideal English class tended to be.

The set of tasks that we have described here was an attempt to make the students on our course aware of their beliefs about teaching and learning English, to compare and contrast their own beliefs with those of their classmates, and to reflect on possible discrepancies between their current understanding of the issues involved and their ideals. Becoming aware is, however, only the first stage in possible changes in thinking or behaviour or in the professional development of pre- or in-service teachers of foreign languages (e.g. Kalaja *et al.*, in press b; Kubanyiova, 2012). However, our research design was not rigorous enough to make systematic comparisons over a term (that is, before and after CITE, the introductory course as such). For us as teacher educators, the study is – at any rate – an indication of how long and complex for students the process is of acquiring new pedagogical knowledge and turning it into a systematic and justified set of principles and practices to be applied in future English classes. We must still wait some time before we can see whether the students in the present study manage to keep up their motivation and hold onto their ideals or visions, especially if these were very different from their past school experiences, once they start their careers as teachers of English in the Finnish educational system (for a few longitudinal studies on the fate of previous groups of novice teachers of foreign languages in Finland, see, for example, Kalaja, 2017; Nyman, 2009; or Ruohotie-Lyhty, 2011, 2016a, 2016b).

Appendix A: Task Sheet (Main Points) Translated from Finnish into English

Task 1

General instructions

- Create a picture (either by drawing by hand, or by using computer software or cuttings out of newspapers/magazines, etc.): 'An English class of my dreams'. Depict a class that you could imagine giving after graduation.
- Describe what is taking place in your class (in a few sentences).
- Give reasons why your class would be as described above.

Task 2

More specific prompt questions

- Who would be your students?
- What would you be teaching?
- How would you be teaching?
- What would be the role(s) of the teacher in your class?
- What would be the role(s) of the students in your class?
- What would the environment be like?
- What equipment would you have at hand in your class? How would you use them?
- Any further comments?

References

Barkhuizen, G. (2013) Introduction: Narrative research in applied linguistics. In G. Barkhuizen (ed.) *Narrative Research in Applied Linguistics* (pp. 1–16). Cambridge: Cambridge University Press.

Benson, P. and Reinders, H. (eds) (2011) *Beyond the Classroom*. Basingstoke: Palgrave Macmillan.

Borg, S., Birello, M., Civera, I. and Zanatta, T. (2014) *The Impact of Teacher Education on Pre-service Primary English Language Teachers*. London: British Council.

Clarke, M. (2008) *Language Teacher Identities: Co-constructing Discourse and Community*. Clevedon: Multilingual Matters.

Council of Europe (2001) *Common European Framework of Reference for Languages: Learning, Teaching, Assessment*. Cambridge: Cambridge University Press.

Dörnyei, Z. and Kubanyiova, M. (2014) *Motivating Learners, Motivating Teachers: Building Vision in the Classroom*. Cambridge: Cambridge University Press.

Dörnyei, Z. and Ushioda, E. (eds) (2009) *Motivation, Language Identity and the L2 Self*. Bristol: Multilingual Matters.

Dörnyei, Z. and Ushioda, E. (2010) *Teaching and Researching Motivation* (2nd edn). London: Routledge.

Duff, P.A. (2007) *Case Study Research in Applied Linguistics*. New York: Lawrence Erlbaum.

Hammerness, K. (2003) Learning to hope, or hoping to learn? The role of vision in the early professional lives of teachers. *Journal of Teacher Education* 54 (1), 43–53.

Hammerness, K. (2006) *Seeing through the Teachers' Eyes: Professional Ideals and Classroom Practices*. New York: Teachers College Press.

Harinen, P. and Halme, J. (2012) *Hyvä, paha koulu. Kouluhyvinvointia hakemassa* [*Good, Bad School. Seeking for Welfare at School*]. Helsinki: UNICEF/Nuorisotutkimusseura. See http://www.nuorisotutkimusseura.fi/julkaisut/verkko-kauppa/verkkojulkaisut/952-hyva-paha-koulu (accessed 10 August 2016).

Hummel, K.M. (2014) *Introducing Second Language Acquisition: Perspectives and Practices*. Chichester: Wiley-Blackwell.

Johnson, K.E. and Golombek, P.R. (2011) The transformative power of narrative in second language teacher education. *TESOL Quarterly* 45 (3), 486–508.

Johnson, K.E. and Golombek, P.R. (2013) A tale of two mediations: Tracing the dialectics of cognition, emotion, and activity in novice teachers' practicum blogs. In G. Barkhuizen (ed.) *Narrative Research in Applied Linguistics* (pp. 85–104). Cambridge: Cambridge University Press

Kalaja, P. (2016) 'Dreaming is believing': The teaching of foreign languages as envisioned by student teachers. In P. Kalaja, A.M.F. Barcelos, M. Aro and M. Ruohotie-Lyhty (eds) *Beliefs, Agency and Identity in Foreign Language Learning and Teaching* (pp. 124–146). Basingstoke: Palgrave Macmillan.

Kalaja, P. (2017) 'English is a way of travelling, Finnish the station from which you set out...': Reflections on the identities of L2 teachers in the context of Finland. In G. Barkhuizen (ed.) *Reflections on Language Teacher Identity Research* (pp. 196–202). New York: Routledge.

Kalaja, P., Dufva, H. and Alanen, R. (2013) Experimenting with visual narratives. In G. Barkhuizen (ed.) *Narrative Research in Applied Linguistics* (pp. 105–131). Cambridge: Cambridge University Press.

Kalaja, P., Alanen, R. and Dufva, H. (in press a) ELT in Finland (Grades 1 through 12): Currents and cross-currents. In J. Liontas (ed.) *TESOL Encyclopedia of English Language Teaching*. Malden, MA: Wiley.

Kalaja, P., Barcelos, A.M.F. and Aro, M. (in press b) Revisiting research on learner beliefs: Looking back and looking ahead. In P. Garrett and J.M. Cots (eds) *Routledge Handbook on Language Awareness*. New York: Routledge.

Kramp, M.K. (2004) Exploring life and experience through narrative inquiry. In K. deMarrais and S.D. Lapan (eds) *Foundations for Research: Methods of Inquiry in Education and the Social Sciences* (pp. 103–121). Mahwah, NJ: Lawrence Erlbaum.

Kress, G. and van Leeuwen, T. (2006) *Reading Images: The Grammar of Visual Design* (2nd edn). London: Routledge.

Kubanyiova, M. (2012) *Teacher Development in Action: Understanding Language Teachers' Conceptual Change*. Basingstoke: Palgrave Macmillan.

Luukka, M., Pöyhönen, S., Huhta, A., Taalas, P., Tarnanen, M. and Keränen, A. (2008) *Maailma muuttuu – mitä tekee koulu? Äidinkielen ja vieraiden kielten tekstikäytänteet koulussa ja vapaa-ajalla* [*The World is Changing – What about the School? Mother Tongue and Foreign Language Literacy Practices at School and at Leisure*]. Jyväskylä: Centre for Applied Language Studies, University of Jyväskylä.

Nyman, T. (2009) Nuoren vieraan kielen opettajan pedagogisen ajattelun ja ammatillisen asiantuntijuuden kehittyminen [The development of pedagogical thinking and professional expertise of newly qualified language teachers]. Jyväskylä Studies in Education, Psychology and Social Research No. 360, University of Jyväskylä. See https://jyx.jyu.fi/dspace/handle/123456789/21739 (accessed 15 July 2016).

Riessman, C.K. (2008) *Narrative Methods for the Human Sciences*. Thousand Oaks, CA: Sage.

Ruohotie-Lyhty, M. (2011) Opettajuuden alkutaival: Vastavalmistuneen vieraan kielen opettajan toimijuus ja ammatillinen kehittyminen [First steps on the path of teacherhood: Newly qualified foreign language teachers' agency and professional development]. Jyväskylä Studies in Education, Psychology and Social Research No. 410, University of Jyväskylä. See https://jyx.jyu.fi/dspace/handle/123456789/27200 (accessed 15 July 2016).

Ruohotie-Lyhty, M. (2016a) Dependent or independent: The construction of the beliefs of newly qualified foreign language teachers. In P. Kalaja, A.M.F. Barcelos, M. Aro and M. Ruohotie-Lyhty (eds) *Beliefs, Agency and Identity in Foreign Language Learning and Teaching* (pp. 149–171). Basingstoke: Palgrave Macmillan.

Ruohotie-Lyhty, M. (2016b) Stories of change and continuity: Understanding the development of identities of foreign language teachers. In P. Kalaja, A.M.F. Barcelos, M. Aro and M. Ruohotie-Lyhty (eds) *Beliefs, Agency and Identity in Foreign Language Learning and Teaching* (pp. 172–201). Basingstoke: Palgrave Macmillan.

4 Language Teacher Motivation: From the Ideal to the Feasible Self

Taguhi Sahakyan, Martin Lamb and Gary Chambers

In this chapter we consider teachers' motivation for their work: why they chose to do that work, and the intensity and direction of effort that they invest in that work over time. Teacher motivation should be a major issue for education policy makers and researchers for at least three reasons. First, whether conceptualised as passion for teaching (Carbonneau *et al.*, 2008), enthusiasm (Kunter *et al.*, 2011), self-determination (Roth *et al.*, 2007) or self-efficacy (Holzberger *et al.*, 2013), it has been shown to affect teacher behaviour, which in turn impacts on learner motivation and achievement. Enthusiastic teachers can inspire learners to love their subjects (Chambers, 1999; Lamb & Wedell, 2015), while conversely teachers lacking in enthusiasm or self-efficacy may well demotivate their learners (Atkinson, 2000). Secondly, teacher motivation matters in terms of the teachers' own job satisfaction, psychological well-being and ultimately their persistence in the profession (Watt & Richardson, 2008). Thirdly, motivated teachers are far more likely to support progressive educational reform, both because they are constantly looking for ways to improve their practice and because they are more likely to put the necessary effort into implementing change (Jesus & Lens, 2005). As many commentators have pointed out (e.g. Jesus & Lens, 2005; Skaalvik & Skaalvik, 2011), despite the acknowledged importance of motivation, teachers worldwide are among the most motivationally challenged (Bennell & Akyeampong, 2007). The discrepancy is particularly striking in societies under economic or political strain, such as in developing countries where teachers lack basic resources to carry out their work (Bennell & Akyeampong, 2007) or countries going through periods of political transition and social upheaval, where the curriculum content and goals are changing and teacher status is being undermined.

We draw on findings from a study of teacher motivation in one such pressurised context: the university sector in post-Soviet Armenia. This qualitative study aimed to gain an in-depth understanding of how individual tertiary-level English teachers' motivation to teach evolves during their career and how it is socially constructed in their working contexts. We report on one of the most salient findings: the way the lecturers' initial ideals for their work appear to morph into less exalted but more feasible visions for personal and professional satisfaction. We first review the theoretical relevance of future self-guides for teacher motivation, before describing the methodology of the study. Having presented our evidence for an apparent shift in teacher self-conceptions, we discuss its possible implications for our understanding of teacher motivation.

Key Teacher Motivation Theories

The recent surge of research interest in teacher motivation has resulted in diverse conceptualisations of the phenomenon, mainly adaptations of theories of learner motivation. Thus, in achievement goal theory (Butler, 2007, 2012), teacher motivation is connected to their desires to achieve goals in order to succeed at their job. With regard to teacher self-efficacy (Tschannen-Moran & Hoy, 2007), it is argued that teachers' beliefs about their abilities to influence their students' achievements and motivation have an impact on the effort they invest in teaching, their persistence and behaviours. Expectancy value theory (Watt & Richardson, 2008) focuses on the individuals' expectations for success in a task and its perceived value, which will predict their effort and persistence in it. In self-determination theory (Ryan & Deci, 2000), probably the most popular theoretical framework for exploring teacher motivation, teachers who have more internalised motives for their work, or who derive intrinsic pleasure from it, are more likely to invest effort in their work and show resilience in the face of professional challenges, in turn potentially promoting autonomous motivation in their students (Roth *et al.*, 2007; see also Hiver *et al.*, this volume).

Although all these theoretical frameworks make an important contribution to the understanding of the teacher motivation phenomenon, they typically focus on a limited set of mental components (e.g. goals, or self-efficacy, or achievement beliefs). As Kubanyiova (2012: 23) states, 'we have tended to focus on measuring isolated constructs in an isolated manner without setting them in a bigger picture of who the teachers are, what they are striving to accomplish in their interactions with their students, colleagues, and parents and why'. Here we argue that possible selves theory (Richardson & Watt, 2010) offers scope for a more holistic and multifaceted understanding of teacher motivation, since it views teachers' motivated behaviour in and out of class as the potential enactment of their present and future professional identities.

Possible Selves and Motivation

The concept of possible selves was introduced by Markus and Nurius (1986), who argued that they embody the individual's hopes, fantasies and fears based on their particular sociocultural and historical context and experiences. Although they do not technically define various facets of possible selves, they suggest that possible selves can have several dimensions: selves which one would like to become; selves which one feels one should become; and selves which one is afraid of becoming.

Further developing the possible selves concept, Higgins (1987) proposed a self-discrepancy theory where he defines three key self components: the actual self, which represents the attributes one believes one possesses; the ideal self, related to the qualities one ideally would like to have (e.g. aspirations, hopes, wishes); and the ought-to self (which Higgins originally named ought self), representing the qualities one believes one ought to possess (e.g. obligations, responsibilities, duties). When there is a discrepancy between one's actual self and one's ideal or ought selves, one is motivated to engage in actions to reduce that discrepancy.

Although possible selves theory has been criticised for being excessively self-centred and neglecting the social nature of the selves (Andersen & Chen, 2002; Erikson, 2007), it is important to stress that possible selves emerge from representations within one's social environment and experiences because people are 'unlikely to engage in the adoption, modification, maintenance, or abandonment of images in social isolation' (Marshall et al., 2006: 145). Possible selves develop based on one's past successes and failures, which are measured when judged in comparison with the outcomes of the actions of others. Even one's values, ideals and aspirations are socially constructed because they are shaped by social contexts (Korthagen, 2004; Oyserman, 2001).

While possible selves theory has been more broadly used in examining learners' motivation (e.g. Islam et al., 2013; Lamb, 2011; Oyserman et al., 2006), only a few studies have adopted it to gain insights into teacher motivation (e.g. Cardelle-Elawar et al., 2007; Hamman et al., 2010, 2013; Hiver, 2013; Kubanyiova, 2009, 2012). Most of these studies concentrate on novice or pre-service teachers' hoped-for and feared selves (the teacher one avoids becoming) at various stages of their teaching practice. For example, Fletcher (2000) explores how student teachers' possible selves are influenced by their relationships with mentors and how visualisation techniques can help them approach desired and avoid feared selves enhancing their professional development. Hamman and his associates (2013) focus on the changes in the novice teachers' possible self images as a result of gaining experience, of reflection and of the input of mentors, as well as revealing the ways those selves regulate their behaviour.

In language education, two separate studies have examined the relationships between teachers' possible selves and their involvement in professional development. Kubanyiova (2012) has argued on the basis of her work with Slovakian teachers of English that their specific ideal teacher selves lie at the heart of their motivation to teach, profoundly influencing their choice of methodologies and their responsiveness to professional training. Hiver (2013) likewise found that Korean teachers' ideal and ought-to teacher selves, especially in relation to their mastery of English, provided the main motives for voluntary engagement in professional development. An important point to emerge from these studies is the complexity and dynamism of teachers' possible selves – any individual teacher is likely to have multiple, often competing visions of themselves as teachers, and these will change over the course of a career. 'A profitable direction for future studies in this area', Hiver (2013: 221) claims, 'would be to investigate the longitudinal shifts in centrality, strength and combinatory patterns of possible language teacher selves'. Accordingly, a possible selves theoretical perspective was adopted to explore the evolving motivation of Armenian teachers of English.

The decision to focus on tertiary-level teachers was based partly on the fact that, hitherto, teacher motivation studies have mostly been conducted in school settings. As Visser-Wijnveen *et al.* (2012) point out, university staff may have entered the profession with more interest in research than teaching, and so it is particularly important to investigate the nature of their motivation to teach if we are to help them invest optimal levels of effort into that aspect of their jobs.

The Study

According to Steers and Porter (1979, cited in Kleinginna & Kleinginna, 1981), motivation can be defined in terms of what instigates and directs certain behaviour and how that behaviour is maintained. Linking this definition to possible selves theory, we define teacher motivation as a driving force that initiates pedagogic action and guides an individual to fulfil and maintain their desired teacher self. Recognising that these desired selves may be more or less internally significant, and may evolve over the course of a career, the research question addressed in this chapter is as follows:

> In what ways are the participants motivated in their work by their ideal and ought-to self images at different stages of their careers?

The context and participants

Armenia is a country that underwent dramatic political, economic and societal changes after the collapse of the Soviet Union in 1991. These transformations have inevitably affected the educational sector; the state spends only 3% of its Gross National Product on education, which is the third lowest in the Commonwealth of Independent States (UNICEF, 2011). Although teachers are still respected and valued in the society, they hold lower status in comparison to other careers, which negatively affects their enthusiasm and desire to remain in the profession (Perkins & Yemtsov, 2001).

The purposive sampling method was employed to recruit the teachers (Patton, 1990). The main criteria applied were their diverse sociocultural background and an experience of teaching English at university level in Armenia. Recruiting participants with various backgrounds enabled us to gain insights into teachers' behaviours, experiences and beliefs from different angles and capture a wide range of perspectives related to teacher motivation.

The participants were six language teachers of different ages (30–64), chosen deliberately for their diverse teaching experiences (5–40 years) and sociocultural backgrounds (i.e. teachers with Armenian and Russian educational backgrounds as well as a native speaker of English). They were teaching various English courses at three universities in Armenia.

Data collection and analysis

The data were collected in three phases over a period of six months (November 2014–May 2015) using semi-structured interviews, journal writing and unstructured classroom observations followed by post-observation interviews (see Appendix A for the data collection details). In each phase, the first author spent approximately a month at the research site conducting in-depth interviews (20 in total) to understand the participants' perceptions, viewpoints and beliefs, and classroom observations (28 in total) to gain insights into their behaviours and interactions in the classroom, which were followed by the post-observation interviews (26 in total). Throughout the study, the participants were also asked to reflect on what motivated and demotivated them at the end of every week in the journal (62 journal entries in total).

Through the interviews the first author developed a rapport with the participants which enabled us to gain richer data and assure trustworthiness (Pitts & Miller-Day, 2007). With anonymity and confidentiality of the data guaranteed, and full explanations offered about how the data would only be used for the purpose of the research project, it was notable in fact how all the participants seemed to value the opportunity to talk about their working lives to a sympathetic and interested listener.

The data generated from the first two phases were subject to thematic analysis, which facilitated 'identifying, analysing, and reporting patterns (themes) within data' (Braun & Clarke, 2006: 6). Although the analysis was mainly inductive (emerging from the data), occasionally it had certain deductive (influenced by the theory) elements. In order to foster trustworthiness and achieve rigour in data analysis, both manual and electronic analytical tools (NVivo v.10) were combined (Davis & Meyer, 2009).

For each participant, a diagram with themes and sub-themes was developed and in the last phase of data collection this was directly discussed with each participant as a form of member checking, enabling us to construct shared interpretations of the data, clarify particular points and build richer portraits of the individuals which they themselves endorsed (Harvey, 2015).

Findings

As described above, the purpose of this study was to explore the motivational impact of the participants' ideal and ought-to selves. After data analysis, the following key findings were identified:

- When reflecting on their experiences as beginning teachers, the participants reported having vivid ought-to, feared and ideal teacher self images. Their initial ideal self images seemed to derive from their own learning experiences and, in some cases, were based on the images of their own teachers.
- The initial ideal self images were later transformed or abandoned because (a) the image was not internalised as their own, (b) the image was perceived to be unachievable or (c) it conflicted with other self images.
- With increasing experience and having moved on from 'beginning' teacher status, the participants developed a more holistic 'feasible' self, blending components of ideal, ought-to and feared selves.

These findings were based on an analysis of six participants' data (see Appendix B for the participants' biographical data). However, due to word limit constraints, we will illustrate our findings in this chapter with reference to two contrasting cases: Anna, who is a representative of local teachers, and Tom, a native speaker of English (both pseudonyms).

Anna: 'I tried but none of them worked.'

When Anna started her teaching career, she clearly possessed ought-to, ideal and feared teacher selves, which derived from her own learning experiences. As an employee, her ought-to self image was influenced by university rules, responsibilities and requirements which she was obliged to meet:

> I had that book, which actually wasn't even a book. It was just a photo-copy of different materials. I had to (...) cover certain units and if, let's say, they had decided to observe me and noticed that I deviated from that, I brought something else, it could have become a problem because there was a clear curriculum, which we had to follow. (Interview 1, 28 November 2014)

Her ought-to self image was also influenced by the society-shaped representation of a teacher. For more than 70 years, Armenia was a part of the Soviet Union with an educational system where teachers belonged to the intelligentsia and enjoyed respect, prestige and even admiration at all levels of society (Karakhanyan *et al.*, 2011; Zajda, 1980). Teachers had an important function in the process of raising a Soviet individual and this involved being a role model which implied 'knowing everything' in their subject. This image still prevails in society and affected Anna's teacher self representation. Similarly to other participants, she was worried about not living up to the expectations of the teacher image created in the society, especially with regard to language competence:

> I was worried about … what if they [students] asked me a word and I wouldn't know and I would make a mistake and I wouldn't know how to continue the topic because you never know, especially in speaking lessons, you don't know what will be discussed. (Post-observation interview 1, 26 February 2015)

Although Anna maintained that as a non-native speaker it was impossible to be fully proficient in English, she acknowledged that she still felt uncomfortable when facing an unfamiliar expression during lessons and admiringly emphasised her colleague's language competence:

> One of our lecturers … if you ask her the meaning of any [English] word in Armenian, she will answer … I don't even know if she's ever had a situation when she was asked the meaning of something in Armenian and she said, 'I don't know'. (Interview 4, 19 May 2015)

In addition to this ought-to self, Anna possessed ideal and feared self images derived from her own learning experiences. By observing her own teachers, she learnt 'how one shouldn't teach' and later developed an initial ideal self image, which was based on the combination of her two teachers' images. She acknowledged the importance of her own teachers and made every effort to adopt their teaching styles, approaches and manner, to almost become a clone of the classroom practitioners she so admired. However, the initial representation she created was later abandoned because it was not fully internalised and did not evolve into her own teacher self image:

> A: I had this beautiful teacher image … my speaking skills teacher who we weren't listening to when she entered the classroom … we just were admiringly looking at her. And I had an image of my primary school teacher who was an example of a … calm … I don't remember her being angry at anyone, raising her voice …
> T: When you started [teaching], did you try to combine both [ideal images]?
> A: I tried but none of them worked. (Interview 1, 28 November 2014)

After realising that it was not her own representation, Anna started to develop a more personalised teacher self image. Following the new emphasis in language pedagogy on communicative and learner-centred approaches (Richards, 2006), she envisioned her teacher self as a 'facilitator or … perhaps sometimes guide but facilitator mostly'. However, later she acknowledged its limitations and mentioned that this image was not completely achievable in her current context:

> There are some classes ... when you employ student-centred approach ... I mean this student-centeredness is always there, but there are some classes where you try to look at everything through their [students'] lenses, you put them in the centre ... You want them to make decisions ... They ... are simply not mature, not ready in their mentality. I mean they just get confused and don't know what to do ... (Interview 1, 28 November 2014)

Anna continued talking about her immediate context – current classes, ongoing issues she was facing with students and attempts to solve these issues – stressing the unattainability of that image in her current classes:

> Very many things depend on the learners. I mean when I enter the classroom when I see everybody is half sleeping ... I'm trying to do things but I mean that can last something like 20 minutes or 30 minutes or 40 minutes maximum. (Interview 2, 3 March 2015)

It seems that Anna had to compromise on her 'idealistic' principles and develop a context-specific self, attainable in her current classroom – a 'motivator' self:

> I would like to have the ability ... the ability, the tool, kind of a technique to be able not to give up, to keep on trying. Because right now I really give up after maximum 40 minutes, I cannot be dancing all the time, I mean I need some feedback. When I don't get that feedback ... it really becomes awful. (Interview 2, 3 March 2015)

Importantly, Anna's readiness to become a motivating teacher was reinforced by her feared self image of a 'boring' teacher recalled from her own learning experiences. Similarly, it was affected by her ought-to self because she felt she had to cover the curriculum and generate high results. As a result, Anna seemed to develop a balanced self, characterised by components of the ought-to, feared and compromised ideal self images, which were not isolated elements but rather interacting facets of a coherent self that functioned simultaneously, that is, a feasible self.

Tom: 'I'm not sure whether the students ... or administration is ready for that.'

Even though Tom, a native speaker of English who grew up in the UK, had different learning experiences compared to the local participants, his early ideal and feared teacher selves similarly derived from his interpretations of his salient past experiences and were closely linked to his own teacher images:

> I definitely did not want to be like my teachers at school [laughs] ... just what you would expect, you know, a stereotypical teacher. 'Please open your books and read this. Tom, would you please read this paragraph?'

He was a History teacher, he fought in World War II. He was a tank commander. He would sit there and he would talk about his war experiences and things. It was wonderful ... I really enjoyed it and all the kids were like ... we would sit there in awe at this guy. He would tell us his stories ... we would join him and ask him questions and things. So, occasionally he would say, 'OK, open your books on this'. But he would actually bring it all to life which was great. (Interview 1, 26 November 2014)

Recalling that experience, Tom wanted his students to enjoy his lessons and desired to earn similar admiration from his students and initially developed an abstract ideal self image – 'teacher loved by his students'. He did not have a clear vision of how it could be achieved through teaching and, as a result, preferred a route of 'being a showman' and pleasing his students instead of engaging in 'real teaching':

I was doing games for the sake of doing games. There was little reason for doing the game ... I think it's important to be liked but it's not the most important thing. You also have to get them to grasp the language. So, it's great to be liked, they think, 'Oh, great! We like Tom.' But what are they getting from it? So I think you have to be aware that being liked ... doing things just to be liked is not the objective. And I learned that. (Interview 2, 27 February 2015)

However, inevitably, it conflicted with Tom's ought-to self; the students had to pass exams and his supervisor asked him to teach students with lower levels of English proficiency. She stressed that he was not 'very good at explaining grammar' and did not 'really understand it'. Tom felt that his avoidance of teaching grammar negatively affected his students' learning and, in an effort to address what he regarded as his limitations, he shaped a new teacher self representation – a competent teacher. Unlike the local participants for whom competence was largely linked to language proficiency, for Tom, this image was related to his ability to teach grammar, in particular, tenses:

I had a lot of fears about mistakes but it was mostly worries about terminology. If somebody said, 'Oh, that's the infinitive, isn't it?' And I was like, 'What the hell is infinitive? What is that?' – you know. 'Oh, you used the past participle for the present perfect.' 'Really?' Those fears ... So what I did was I would say to my students right in my first lesson, 'Look, I know how to speak English, OK? Trust me. But I may not know the terminology. It doesn't mean I don't know what to teach. You just have to bear with me. Trust me.' And they would trust me because they know my background. (Interview 3, 12 May 2015)

In addition to the image of a competent teacher, Tom perceived his ideal teacher self as someone who was not bound by restrictions and was completely autonomous in his decisions about what to teach, how to teach and where to teach. For Tom, effective teaching involved teaching in real life situations outside the classroom environment, which would make teaching/learning more relevant and context specific as well as help maintain students' motivation. However, after voicing this view, Tom acknowledged that it was not feasible in his current context; he had to compromise and adapt considering both institutional requirements and his students' expectations:

> I would like to be able to go out of the classroom environment. ... We could go to the zoo. I don't know go to a cafe, go to a restaurant, we could go for a walk in the park, look at the plants. ... We could go to the hospital. We could go to a university. If you look at all the units – environment, health, communication – all ... many of these things could be taught in their true environment and not in the classroom. But as a teacher, we don't have that and I'm not sure whether the students are ready for that or whether the administration is ready for that. (Interview 2, 27 February 2015)

Obviously, Tom had to accept the contextual limitations and find other ways of effective teaching and sustaining his students' motivation; he incorporated an element of fun in his lessons (e.g. writing poems, role-play). In contrast to his initial lessons, all his activities aimed to develop certain language skills and were connected to the lesson topic. To conclude, Tom's teacher self evolved from 'teacher loved by his students' to the teacher who simultaneously possessed the components of his ought-to self – a teacher who had to provide sufficient knowledge so that students could successfully complete the course, and his ideal teacher self – a teacher who could teach entertainingly, while simultaneously avoiding being his feared teacher self – a teacher who was unable to teach grammar. Like the other participants, all these selves were interconnected and formed a holistic self, which was feasible in his context.

Discussion

At the beginning of their careers, all the participants had clear ideal self images which mainly originated from their learning experiences. Similarly to the experiences of novice teachers in other studies (e.g. Cardelle-Elawar et al., 2007; Fletcher, 2000; Hamman et al., 2010), the formation of their initial possible teacher selves emerged from their positive and negative experiences as students in their school and university contexts. Research suggests that teachers' experiences as learners have a key impact on their teaching, previously identified as the 'apprenticeship of observation' (Lortie, 1975; Pennington & Richards, 2016). Consequently, their beliefs about teaching start forming from their own learning experiences (Kubanyiova & Feryok, 2015; Murphy et al., 2004) and the fact that these teachers were imitating their own teachers at the early stages of their careers is not surprising.

However, the data show how the participants' initial ideal self images were later abandoned or transformed. Research suggests (Dörnyei & Kubanyiova, 2014; Erikson, 2007; Hamman *et al.*, 2013; Norman & Aron, 2003) that one of the most important prerequisites that instigates motivational behaviours and makes the future self *feasible* is its availability and accessibility. The participants encountered various restrictions, which made their initial ideal selves unattainable. In Tom's case, his ideal self image conflicted with his ought-to self and, consequently, he had to reassess and adapt it. Anna's attempt to match her initial ideal teacher self image was unsuccessful because it was not internalised as her own and her subsequent 'facilitator' ideal self was also not feasible in most of her classes. As a result, like all the participants in our study, they had to make compromises, reconciling their high aspirations with daily constraints.

The notion of feasibility emerges as a key feature in the participants' later formed dynamic and context-specific self images. They all were brought up in particular sociocultural environments with fixed norms, perceptions and societal expectations of a teacher, which inevitably had an impact on their self formation. The sociocultural impact is especially obvious when comparing Tom, who grew up in a Western environment and positioned himself as 'one of the people in the class', with the participants like Anna who grew up in Armenia. As previously discussed, teachers are still placed on a pedestal in the Armenian society, which entails being an authority who is an expert in their subject. This affected all the local participants' self images, especially their feeling of self-efficacy. Similar to non-native speaker teachers in other studies (Hiver, 2013; Jenkins, 2005; Moussu & Llurda, 2008; Reves & Medgyes, 1994), the participants' fears overwhelmingly concerned their English proficiency. Unlike the Korean teachers in Hiver's (2013) study, however, the Armenian participants perceived themselves as proficient language users and gradually acknowledged the fact that they were non-native speakers, living in an environment where English was rarely used in public, and that it was impossible to fully master the language. Consequently, an unreachable representation of teacher perfection was replaced with a feasible image of a 'competent' language user as a part of their teacher selves.

In addition to the sociocultural dimension, feasibility of the teachers' selves was strengthened by their contextual dependency at a micro level. When reflecting on the self images they currently possessed, the participants in this sample were not portraying their abstract distant future representations; instead, they were elaborating on more specific images, linked to their particular courses and classes. Obviously their teacher selves could not develop in isolation but they emerged from their immediate social contexts and experiences with others (Andersen & Chen, 2002;

Mead, 1934; Oyserman & Fryberg, 2006), especially students. The teachers had a genuine concern for their students, were proud of student achievements and were disappointed by student misbehaviour, failures and lack of motivation.

Another factor that affects the feasibility of the teachers' self images is its temporal proximity. Although the motivational force of possible selves is commonly regarded as future-orientated (Higgins, 1987; Markus & Nurius, 1986), the concept of future is diverse – it can be distant (e.g. 10 years) or proximal (e.g. next week, next semester). Based on that variability in the notion of future, possible selves can be distant or proximal (Oyserman & James, 2011), altering over time (Ryff, 1991). Research suggests that the distance of the future possible selves from the current self is age specific (Frazier et al., 2002) and the discrepancy between the ideal and actual selves normally decreases with age (Oyserman & James, 2011). A younger person's future possible self is more remote, triggers more global and abstract descriptions (Pronin & Ross, 2006) and requires dramatic changes in behaviour to achieve (Markus & Nurius, 1986), whereas a proximal possible self elicits a more pragmatic vision of the self and of the actions required to attain that self (Kivetz & Tyler, 2007). With regard to teachers, this suggests that experienced teachers' future selves are positioned closer to their current selves than those of novice teachers. The participants' early career ideal self images were distant, in some cases, too idealistic and unreachable but, as they entered the post-beginning teacher phase, they adjusted their images and developed more proximal and attainable selves, increasing the possibility of their achievement (Oyserman & James, 2011). These selves were frequently linked to the present, which implies that there was a need for specific action plans to attain them (Strahan & Wilson, 2006).

Having discussed feasibility as a central feature of the self images participants currently possessed, it is important to highlight that the participants' possible selves were not distinct isolated self images but were rather coupled with each other, strengthening a motivational effect and increasing the possibility to achieve the desired state. Several researchers point out that various possible selves act in conjunction because frequently one is motivated to simultaneously attain a positive component of the self and avoid its feared component, creating a balance within possible selves (Hiver, 2013; Hoyle & Sherrill, 2006; Oyserman & Fryberg, 2006). Balanced positive and negative selves can be a part of the same domain, having positive effects on achieving goals and maintaining engagement (Oyserman & James, 2011).

To sum up, the findings suggest that feasibility and blending of possible selves are key features of the participants' teacher selves. Therefore, we propose that instead of having distinct ideal, ought-to and feared self images, the participants developed a balanced self-concept – a *feasible teacher self* – as an entity comprising features of various possible selves (e.g. ideal, ought-to, feared selves) which are *realistic* and *achievable* in a particular context. The notion of the self as 'holistic, dynamic, and situated in contexts' is emphasised by Kostoulas and Mercer (2016: 133) as a prevailing theme in contemporary self research. The idea of having a holistic self consisting of several possible components was identified much earlier by Markus and Nurius (1986) when they introduced the possible selves theory; they highlight that possible selves are coherent components of a larger unified self, a notion which is supported by other researchers (Oyserman, 2001; Oyserman & James, 2011), although when referring to the balanced self as an instigator of stronger motivation, researchers tend to stress the concurrent existence of ideal and feared self images (e.g. Hamman *et al.*, 2013; Hoyle & Sherrill, 2006), the ought-to self should not be neglected. As the sample cases have demonstrated, the teachers had to meet both societal expectations and the requirements of the institutions they worked in.

Conclusion

At the outset of their careers, the participants of the study possessed evident ideal and feared teacher selves mainly derived from their past experiences as learners as well as ought-to selves imposed by the institutions they were teaching in. However, their initial ideal self images were later disowned or considered too difficult to achieve. The findings suggest that instead of forming distinct ideal, ought-to and feared selves, the teachers constructed a feasible teacher self which was a synthesis of various possible self components derived from the teachers' previous experiences, which was attainable in a particular context of work. The context-specific nature of the feasible self entailed more motivating power and required specific actions from the teachers to achieve it.

The small scale of the study clearly precludes any generalisable claims about teacher self-development, but we believe the construct of feasible self warrants further investigation. Would retrospective narratives from teachers in other pedagogic contexts also reveal a tendency towards a compromise of the ideal self, and towards the harmonisation of different future selves in an integrated feasible self? If so, is this pattern adaptive for teacher motivation? Is it one part of the ongoing process of 'immunisation' that Hiver and Dörnyei (2017; see also Hiver, this volume) describe, whereby early career teachers gradually build up the necessary resilience to face the daily challenges of classroom teaching, and forge a professional identity that is congruent with both their inner selves and their context? These are questions which we believe are worth pursuing.

Appendix A: Details of the Data Collection

Participants (all names are pseudonyms)	Phases	Interviews	Observations	Post-observation interviews (13 min on average)	Journal entries
Anna	Phase I	Interview 1: 31 min	0	0	10
	Phase II	Interview 2: 37 min	2	2	
	Phase III	Interview 3: 43 min Interview 4: 19 min	2	2	
Tom	Phase I	Interview 1: 62 min	0	0	7
	Phase II	Interview 2: 55 min	3	2	
	Phase III	Interview 3: 98 min	2	2	
Nelly	Phase I	Interview 1: 44 min	1	1	14
	Phase II	Interview 2: 45 min	2	2	
	Phase III	Interview 3: 111 min	2	2	
Lara	Phase I	Interview 1: 65 min	1	1	11
	Phase II	Interview 2: 59 min	2	2	
	Phase III	Interview 3: 98 min	2	2	
Marine	Phase I	Interview 1: 47 min Interview 2: 39 min	0	0	5
	Phase II	Interview 3: 61 min	2	2	
	Phase III	Interview 4: 114 min	2	2	
Shushan	Phase I	Interview 1: 52 min	0	0	15
	Phase II	Interview 2: 49 min	2	2	
	Phase III	Interview 3: 119 min	3	3	

Appendix B: Participants' Background

Participants	Age	Gender	1st and 2nd languages	Origin	Education	Number of years teaching	University and courses taught
Anna	30	Female	L1 – Armenian L2 – Russian	Armenian from Armenia	English school; BA, MA in English and Spanish; Master's degree in communication & administration of cultural affairs; 4th year PhD student	9	University B (EFL/ESP courses)
Tom	55	Male	L1 – English L2 – Armenian	Armenian from the UK; moved to Armenia in 2005	Boarding school in the UK; Bachelor's degree in mechanical engineering; CELTA	5	University A (EFL courses)
Nelly	36	Female	L1 – Armenian L2 – Russian	Armenian from Armenia	Russian school; BA in linguistics; MA TEFL; 2nd year PhD student	10	University A (EFL courses) and C (EFL/ESP courses)
Lara	34	Female	L1 – Armenian L2 – Russian	Armenian from Armenia	Russian school; BA in Roman and German languages; MA TEFL; 2nd year PhD student	8	University C (EFL/ESP/ linguistics courses)
Marine	64	Female	L1 – Russian L1 – Armenian (considers both Russian and Armenian as her L1 but is more confident in Russian)	Armenian from Armenia; moved to Armenia at the age of 10 from Georgia	Russian school, MA in Russian and English languages	40	University C (EFL/ESP/ linguistics courses)
Shushan	31	Female	L1 – Armenian L2 – Russian	Armenian from Armenia	Armenian school, BA, MA in linguistics; PhD (completed in May 2015)	7	University B (EFL/ESP courses)

References

Andersen, S.M. and Chen, S. (2002) The relational self: An interpersonal social-cognitive theory. *Psychological Review* 109 (4), 619–645.

Atkinson, E.S. (2000) An investigation into the relationship between teacher motivation and pupil motivation. *Educational Psychology* 20 (1), 45–57.

Bennell, P. and Akyeampong, K. (2007) *Teacher Motivation in Sub-Saharan Africa and South Asia*. London: Department for International Development (DfID).

Braun, V. and Clarke, V. (2006) Using thematic analysis in psychology. *Qualitative Research in Psychology* 3 (2), 77–101.

Butler, R. (2007) Teachers' achievement goal orientations and associations with teachers' help seeking: Examination of a novel approach to teacher motivation. *Journal of Educational Psychology* 99 (2), 241–252.

Butler, R. (2012) Striving to connect: Extending an achievement goal approach to teacher motivation to include relational goals for teaching. *Journal of Educational Psychology* 104 (3), 726–742.

Carbonneau, N., Vallerand, R.J., Fernet, C. and Guay, F. (2008) The role of passion for teaching in intrapersonal and interpersonal outcomes. *Journal of Educational Psychology* 100 (4), 977–987.

Cardelle-Elawar, M., Irwin, L. and Sanz de Acedo Lizarraga, M.L. (2007) A cross cultural analysis of motivational factors that influence teacher identity. *Electronic Journal of Research in Educational Psychology* 5 (3), 565–592.

Chambers, G.N. (1999) *Motivating Language Learners*. Clevedon: Multilingual Matters.

Davis, N.W. and Meyer, B.B. (2009) Qualitative data analysis: A procedural comparison. *Journal of Applied Sport Psychology* 21 (1), 116–124.

Dörnyei, Z. and Kubanyiova, M. (2014) *Motivating Learners, Motivating Teachers: Building Vision in the Language Classroom*. Cambridge: Cambridge University Press.

Erikson, M.G. (2007) The meaning of the future: Toward a more specific definition of possible selves. *Review of General Psychology* 11 (4), 348–358.

Fletcher, S. (2000) A role for imagery in mentoring. *Career Development International* 5 (4–5), 235–243.

Frazier, L.D., Gonzalez, G.K., Kafka, C.L. and Johnson, P.M. (2002) Psychosocial influences on possible selves: A comparison of three cohorts of older adults. *International Journal of Behavioural Development* 26 (4), 308–317.

Hamman, D., Gosselin, K., Romano, J. and Bunuan, R. (2010) Using possible-selves theory to understand the identity development of new teachers. *Teaching and Teacher Education* 26 (7), 1349–1361.

Hamman, D., Coward, F., Johnson, L., Lambert, M., Zhou, L. and Indiatsi, J. (2013) Teacher possible selves: How thinking about the future contributes to the formation of professional identity. *Self and Identity* 12 (3), 307–336.

Harvey, L. (2015) Beyond member-checking: A dialogic approach to the research interview. *International Journal of Research & Method in Education* 38 (1), 23–38.

Higgins, E.T. (1987) Self-discrepancy: A theory relating self and affect. *Psychological Review* 94 (3), 319–340.

Hiver, P. (2013) The interplay of possible language teacher selves in professional development choices. *Language Teaching Research* 17 (2), 210–227.

Hiver, P. and Dörnyei, Z. (2017) Language teacher immunity: A double-edged sword. *Applied Linguistics* 38 (3), 405–423.

Holzberger, D., Philipp, A. and Kunter, M. (2013) How teachers' self-efficacy is related to instructional quality: A longitudinal analysis. *Journal of Educational Psychology* 105 (3), 774–786.

Hoyle, R.H. and Sherrill, M.R. (2006) Future orientation in the self-system: Possible selves, self-regulation, and behaviour. *Journal of Personality* 74 (6), 1673–1696.

Islam, M., Lamb, M. and Chambers, G. (2013) The L2 motivational self system and national interest: A Pakistani perspective. *System* 41 (2), 231–244.

Jenkins, J. (2005) Implementing an international approach to English pronunciation: The role of teacher attitudes and identity. *TESOL Quarterly* 39 (3), 535–543.

Jesus, N. and Lens, W. (2005) An integrated model for the study of teacher motivation. *Applied Psychology* 54 (1), 119–134.

Karakhanyan, S., van Veen, K. and Bergen, T.C.M. (2011) Teachers' voices in the context of higher education reforms in Armenia. *European Journal of Education* 46 (4), 508–523.

Kivetz, Y. and Tyler, T.R. (2007) Tomorrow I'll be me: The effect of time perspective on the activation of idealistic versus pragmatic selves. *Organizational Behaviour and Human Decision Processes* 102 (2), 193–211.

Kleinginna, P.R. and Kleinginna, A.M. (1981) A categorized list of motivation definitions, with a suggestion for a consensual definition. *Motivation and Emotion* 5 (3), 263–291.

Korthagen, F.A. (2004) In search of the essence of a good teacher: Towards a more holistic approach in teacher education. *Teaching and Teacher Education* 20 (1), 77–97.

Kostoulas, A. and Mercer, S. (2016) Fifteen years of research on self and identity in System. *System* 60, 128–134.

Kubanyiova, M. (2009) Possible selves in language teacher development. In Z. Dörnyei and E. Ushioda (eds) *Motivation, Language Identity and the L2 Self* (pp. 314–332). Bristol: Multilingual Matters.

Kubanyiova, M. (2012) *Teacher Development in Action: Understanding Language Teachers' Conceptual Change.* Basingstoke: Palgrave Macmillan.

Kubanyiova, M. and Feryok, A. (2015) Language teacher cognition in applied linguistics research: Revisiting the territory, redrawing the boundaries, reclaiming the relevance. *The Modern Language Journal* 99 (3), 435–449.

Kunter, M., Frenzel, A., Nagy, G., Baumert, J. and Pekrun, R. (2011) Teacher enthusiasm: Dimensionality and context specificity. *Contemporary Educational Psychology* 36 (4), 289–301.

Lamb, M. (2011) Future selves, motivation and autonomy in long-term EFL learning trajectories. In G. Murray, X. Gao and T. Lamb (eds) *Identity, Motivation and Autonomy in Language Learning* (pp. 177–194). Bristol: Multilingual Matters.

Lamb, M. and Wedell, M. (2015) Cultural contrasts and commonalities in inspiring language teaching. *Language Teaching Research* 19 (2), 207–224.

Lortie, D.C. (1975) *Schoolteacher: A Sociological Study.* Chicago, IL: University of Chicago Press.

Markus, H. and Nurius, P. (1986) Possible selves. *American Psychologist* 41 (9), 954–969.

Marshall, S.K., Young, R.A. and Domene, J.F. (2006) Possible selves as joint projects. In C. Dunkel and J. Kerpelman (eds) *Possible Selves: Theory, Research and Applications* (pp. 141–161). New York: Nova Science.

Mead, G.H. (1934) *Mind, Self and Society.* Chicago, IL: University of Chicago Press.

Moussu, L. and Llurda, E. (2008) Non-native English speaking English language teachers: History and research. *Language Teaching* 41 (3), 315–348.

Murphy, P.K., Delli, L.A.M. and Edwards, M.N. (2004) The good teacher and good teaching: Comparing beliefs of second-grade students, preservice teachers, and in-service teachers. *Journal of Experimental Education* 72 (2), 69–92.

Norman, C.C. and Aron, A. (2003) Aspects of possible self that predict motivation to achieve or avoid it. *Journal of Experimental Social Psychology* 39 (5), 500–507.

Oyserman, D. (2001) Self-concept and identity. In A. Tesser and N. Schwarz (eds) *Blackwell Handbook of Social Psychology: Intraindividual Processes* (pp. 510–666). Oxford: Blackwell.

Oyserman, D. and Fryberg, S. (2006) The possible selves of diverse adolescents: Content and function across gender, race and national origin. In C. Dunkel and J. Kerpelman (eds) *Possible Selves: Theory, Research and Applications* (pp. 17–39). New York: Nova Science.

Oyserman, D. and James, L. (2011) Possible identities. In S.J. Schwartz, K. Luyckx and V.L. Vognoles (eds) *Handbook of Identity Theory and Research* (pp. 117–145). New York: Springer.

Oyserman, D., Bybee, D. and Terry, K. (2006) Possible selves and academic outcomes: How and when possible selves impel action. *Journal of Personality and Social Psychology* 91 (1), 188–204.

Patton, M. (1990) *Qualitative Evaluation and Research Methods* (2nd edn). Thousand Oaks, CA: Sage.

Pennington, M.C. and Richards, J.C. (2016) Teacher identity in language teaching: Integrating personal, contextual, and professional factors. *RELC Journal* 47 (1), 5–23.

Perkins, G. and Yemtsov, R. (2001) *Armenia: Restructuring to Sustain Universal General Education.* Washington, DC: World Bank.

Pitts, M.J. and Miller-Day, M. (2007) Upward turning points and positive rapport-development across time in researcher–participant relationships. *Qualitative Research* 7 (2), 177–201.

Pronin, E. and Ross, L. (2006) Temporal differences in trait self-ascription: When the self is seen as an other. *Journal of Personality and Social Psychology* 90 (2), 197–209.

Reves, T. and Medgyes, P. (1994) The non-native English speaking EFL/ESL teacher's self-image: An international survey. *System* 22 (3), 353–367.

Richards, J.C. (2006) *Communicative Language Teaching Today.* Cambridge: Cambridge University Press.

Richardson, P.W. and Watt, H.M. (2010) Current and future directions in teacher motivation research. In T.C. Urdan and S.A. Karabenick (eds) *The Decade Ahead: Applications and Contexts of Motivation and Achievement* (pp. 139–173). Bingley: Emerald Group.

Roth, G., Assor, A., Kanat-Maymon, Y. and Kaplan, H. (2007) Autonomous motivation for teaching: How self-determined teaching may lead to self-determined learning. *Journal of Educational Psychology* 99 (4), 761–774.

Ryan, R. and Deci, E. (2000) Self-determination theory and the facilitation of intrinsic motivation, social development, and well-being. *American Psychologist* 55 (1), 68–78.

Ryff, C.D. (1991) Possible selves in adulthood and old age: A tale of shifting horizons. *Psychology and Aging* 6 (2), 286–295.

Skaalvik, E.M. and Skaalvik, S. (2011) Teacher job satisfaction and motivation to leave the teaching profession: Relations with school context, feeling of belonging, and emotional exhaustion. *Teaching and Teacher Education* 27 (6), 1029–1038.

Steers, R.M. and Porter, L.W. (1979) *Motivation and Work Behaviour* (2nd edn). New York: McGraw-Hill.

Strahan, E.J. and Wilson, A.E. (2006) Temporal comparisons, identity, and motivation: The relation between past, present, and possible future selves. In C. Dunkel and J. Kerpelman (eds) *Possible Selves: Theory, Research and Applications* (pp. 1–15). New York: Nova Science.

Tschannen-Moran, M. and Hoy, A.W. (2007) The differential antecedents of self-efficacy beliefs of novice and experienced teachers. *Teaching and Teacher Education* 23 (6), 944–956.

UNICEF (2011) *Teachers: A Regional Study on Recruitment, Development and Salaries of Teachers in the CEECIS Region.* Geneva: UNICEF Regional Office for Central and Eastern Europe and the Commonwealth of Independent States (CEECIS).

Visser-Wijnveen, G.J., Stes, A. and Van Petegem, P. (2012) Development and validation of a questionnaire measuring teachers' motivations for teaching in higher education. *Higher Education* 64 (3), 421–436.

Watt, H.M. and Richardson, P.W. (2008) Motivations, perceptions, and aspirations concerning teaching as a career for different types of beginning teachers. *Learning and Instruction* 18 (5), 408–428.

Zajda, J. (1980) Education and social stratification in the Soviet Union. *Comparative Education* 16 (1), 3–11.

5 Drawing on Cultural Models and Figured Worlds to Study Language Teacher Education and Teacher Identity

Manka M. Varghese

> I wanted to be a bilingual teacher because
> I wanted a child's experience to be different than mine.
> Elizabeth (bilingual teacher)

A significant focus of research in language teacher education and language teacher identity remains that of teachers' beliefs and experiences, including why teachers make certain choices about their profession and how these reasons may be connected to their personal experiences, as shown in the quote above by Elizabeth, a bilingual teacher with whom I was working in a research project of mine. One of the reasons why examining language teachers' beliefs and experiences is important is because it provides us with a greater understanding of what shapes teachers' learning and professional identity along with other factors such as their professional development/teacher education experiences. It can also provide an insight into language teachers' professional paths such as what kind of jobs they may seek and why, where they would be seeking such jobs, how long they may stay, and what types of support may assist teachers in staying in and enjoying the particular professional paths they have sought.

Earlier individualistic notions of teaching and learning (Nolen *et al.*, 2015; Vågan, 2011) have been challenged, with many now viewing teaching and learning as a sociocultural phenomenon with an emphasis on processes of participation and becoming rather than on acquisition per se (Vågan, 2011). This chapter also brings sociocultural approaches – specifically, those of *cultural models* and *figured worlds* – to the teaching, learning and identity of language teachers.

In this chapter I take the view that a language teacher's learning and professional identity construction develops relationally between the individual and his/her contexts, highlighting the notion of the process of learning. As mentioned above, the emphasis on learning here is also not on acquisition but rather on participation and identity construction. Although there are a number of conceptual frameworks that support such a view, the overall goal of this chapter is to describe and discuss the usefulness of *cultural models* and show how *figured worlds* have become the next iteration of this kind of work, which can enhance our study of language teacher education and teacher identity construction as contextually and relationally constructed. I focus, in particular, on how these concepts can be used to better make the connections between language teacher learning, education and identity constructions. Before I do this, I provide first a brief summary of the work in mainstream teacher education and then specifically in language teacher education and identity, which has emphasised a sociocultural approach on teaching and learning. This background provides a useful historical context, which helps explain how cultural models and figured worlds are helpful frameworks with which to study language teacher identity and education.

Background

Learning to teach in mainstream teacher education

In its initial years the learning-to-teach literature, which has examined how teachers learn at different career stages, has focused on the internal, individual cognitive beliefs of teachers but then gradually moved into examining how these interact with the professional environments that teachers participate within. Some of the seminal articles representing this movement include those of Carter (1990), Grossman (1992), Kagan (1992) and Richardson (1990). In these articles there are attempts to relate this literature to other bodies of scholarship such as teacher knowledge and that of teacher-change. These attempts exemplify the difficulty of looking solely at one area of teacher education; in fact, very often, in order to understand one area it is also necessary to be cognizant of others as they interconnect. Richardson (1990) tries to define the learning-to-teach field as a separate entity in her article by stating the following:

> The learning-to-teach research, in contrast, focuses more on individual teacher's cognitions, beliefs, and other mental processes than on behaviors. This literature addresses two types of questions: Are there differences in the way teachers think at different stages of their careers? What accounts for how teachers think about what they do? (Richardson, 1990: 12)

As Grossman (1992) points out, there are different dimensions within the learning-to-teach literature, including some studies that try to understand the process through 'life histories' (Bullough, 1991; Bullough & Baughman,

1997; Connelly & Clandinin, 1990) and some through the subject matter (Shulman, 1987). Freeman and Johnson (1998b), in their article on second language teacher education, helpfully summarise the various perspectives under four categories:

> the role of prior knowledge and beliefs in learning to teach (...) the ways in which such teaching knowledge develops over time and throughout teachers' careers (...) the role of context in teacher learning (...) the role of teacher education as a form of intervention in these areas. (Freeman & Johnson, 1998b: 407)

First, the learning-to-teach research emphasises the importance of what teachers come with, their personal biographies as they grow and develop professionally. This seems to include mainly experiences of how they learned and the exemplary teachers they had (Kagan, 1992). Many studies have been personalistic in nature, focusing on teacher life histories and their professional attitudes (Carter, 1990).

Secondly, the learning-to-teach research has increasingly emphasised the conflicts that are inherent in becoming a teacher. Kagan (1992) proposes that teachers progress through developmental stages, suggesting rather fixed stages where novices think first of classroom management and then question the teaching of the subject matter. Grossman (1992), in her response to Kagan's article, states the need to problematise these stages. She argues that in each phase teachers wrestle simultaneously with moral and ethical issues on teaching content and how to balance classroom management with teaching of subject matter. Therefore, the model of novice-apprentice is useful to think of, but we need to be aware of the conflict that resides for teachers in different areas and at different stages. One of the major conflicts that Shulman (1987) found teachers to have is that of pedagogical content knowledge, or how 'blending of content and pedagogy into an understanding of how particular topics, problems, or issues are organised, represented, and adapted to the diverse interests and abilities of learners, and are presented for instruction' (Shulman, 1987: 8). The category of pedagogical content knowledge is an important one to consider in the knowledge base of language teaching because one of the central concerns is how to teach through language(s) and/or possibly content.

Other studies in the area of learning to teach have also focused on conflict in terms of how novice or apprentice teachers are taught. A common finding in many of these studies has been the problems new or future teachers have with university courses, or understanding the relevance of university work in relation to their classrooms and the importance of the school and the classroom to their development as teachers. This is also the focus of Johnson (1996) in her study of an ESL teacher who faces the tension of the 'vision' of her university courses versus the 'reality' of her classroom. An exemplary learning-to-teach study in mainstream education that has tried to look at the interactions of these diverse components on the beliefs and practices of an individual teacher is that of Eisenhart *et al.* (1993). This study found that Ms Daniels, a student teacher of mathematics for procedural and conceptual knowledge, was influenced by tensions in her university methods class, her classroom and schools contexts (cooperating teachers, administrators, students), as well as the beliefs she came in with. Other examples of studies that have looked at such conflicts in language teacher education are Johnston (1997) in his examination of English as a foreign language (EFL) teachers in Poland who demonstrate an unstable professional trajectory, and Varghese's (2006, 2008) study of bilingual teachers, where she found that each of the teachers developed a different sense and embodiment of their professional identity.

To summarise, this section has highlighted how teachers' sense of themselves is a product of their personal histories, what and how they have learned about being teachers, as well as their individual institutional and structural professional environments. It additionally underscores the conflicts that teachers experience during their professional identity forma-tion. As will be seen, these are themes that are relevant to how cultural models and figured worlds are useful concepts to draw on in understand-ing language teachers' beliefs and experiences, their teaching and learning process and their identity construction.

Language teacher education and teacher identity

Three edited volumes (Bailey & Nunan, 1996; Freeman & Richards, 1996; Richards & Nunan, 1990), a special issue of the *TESOL Quarterly* (Freeman & Johnson, 1998a) and the first Language Teacher Education Conference in 1998 all mark a historical beginning of the subdiscipline of language teacher education and the development of second language teach-ers as opposed to other teachers. Freeman and Johnson (1998b) famously proposed a reconceptualisation of language teacher education in a similar interactive and multilevel perspective as proposed by mainstream teacher educators and described above. The three domains of this knowledge base that they proposed were the teacher-learner, the social context and the ped-agogical process. The teacher-learner is connected to the learning-to-teach literature outlined above but focuses in particular on the language teacher as the learner. In including the social context, Freeman and Johnson (1998b: 409) argue 'against approaches that see language teacher education in purely neutral and technicist terms and that do not engage teacher-learners in issues and dynamics of the sociocultural contexts of schools and schooling'. The pedagogical process or the activity of teaching includes not only under-standing how individuals learn languages but also elements of 'successful teaching' (Freeman & Johnson, 1998b: 411). Johnson (2009: 17) describes how the new understandings of second language teacher education increas-ingly became focused on 'how teachers come to know what they know, how certain concepts in teachers' consciousness develop over time, and how their learning processes transform them and the activities of L2 teaching'.

Although there have been a number of studies from the 1990s relating to ESL, bilingual and foreign language teachers' professional lives (Duff & Uchida, 1997; Johnston, 1997; Moran, 1996), they had never been grouped together as a subtopic in the larger field of language teacher education until about a decade ago. This area of research seeks to differentiate the paths of identity formation that, professionally, language teachers as compared to other teachers experience, and to highlight the singular contexts within which language teachers' professional identities play out (Cross, 2010). Duff and Uchida (1997: 452), in their study of EFL teachers' roles, articulate this conceptualisation of teacher identity in the following way: 'the identities and ideologies that become foregrounded depend in large measure upon the institutional and interpersonal contexts in which individuals find themselves, their purposes for being there, and their personal biographies.' In their study, they observed that teacher identities were formed through an interaction between teachers' biographical experiences, their interpretations of the curriculum, and their relationships with colleagues and students. Two recent volumes on language teacher identity (Barkhuizen, 2016; Cheung *et al.*, 2014), and two special issues on the topic in flagship journals (De Costa & Norton, 2017; Varghese *et al.*, 2016) underscore the significant interest this topic has generated in applied linguistics and TESOL.

One way in which teacher professional identities have been defined in past and more recent studies is as an interaction of how individuals see themselves as language teachers and how they enact their profession in their settings. As I have discussed elsewhere recently, such an articulation of teacher identity formation would put it in the category of 'identities in practice' rather than 'identities in discourse' (Varghese, 2016; Varghese *et al.*, 2005):

> By drawing on identities in practice, the definition of language teacher identity rests on a sense of a core professional identity that is created by a set of individual experiences and material resources and that changes and evolves as language teachers go through their teacher preparation program and through their classroom and school settings. (Varghese, 2016: 45–46)

These identities are seen as being mediated by teachers' beliefs, their personal histories, the discourses and influences that characterise them, and their professional/institutional settings. The professional identities the teachers are in the process of producing and enacting are therefore viewed as formed by prior and present (personal, professional, institutional) experiences as well as what meanings they have ascribed to such experiences. Thus, there is a movement away from an individualistic, static approach to role or professional identity to one where identities are viewed as being in constant negotiation intra- and interindividually. Identity in general and professional identity are concerned with 'how people understand their relationship to the world' (Norton, 1997: 410). As such, there is a sense of the relationship between the individual and the collective in identity formation. Norton (1997) usefully states that, 'identity relates to desire – the desire for recognition, the desire for affiliation, and the desire for security and safety' (Norton, 1997: 410).

Both cultural models and figured worlds are useful constructs to understand how language teachers' prior experiences and contexts shape teacher identities; cultural models, as a framework, views this understanding as a culturally formed cognitive schema that is largely shared, while figured worlds looks at identity construction as a narrative or storyline within which social identities and relationships are constructed and individuals with their social identities participate in. The framework of figured worlds grew out of that of cultural models. What is key about both constructs is that they attempt to connect individual identity formation to the learning process and to a larger shared understanding or collective, as I explain more fully in the next sections.

Cultural Models and Figured Worlds

Cultural models

Cultural theories had for a number of years fallen short in terms of including individual agency and identity within an understanding of the social system. Jacob (1997) describes the almost artificial separation that took place in anthropological studies between cognition and context. This is the reason Strauss and Quinn (1994) called for a cognitive/cultural anthropology and proposed the concept of cultural models. In it they ask, 'how can actors invent, negotiate, and contest their cultural worlds unless they have internalised motives for doing so [inventing, negotiating and contesting]' (Strauss & Quinn, 1994: 287). This draws a parallel with Giddens, who states:

> a theory of motivation is crucial because it supplies the conceptual links between the rationalization of action and the framework of convention as embodied in institutions. But a theory of motivation also has to relate to the unacknowledged conditions of action: in respect of unconscious motives, operating or 'outside' the range of self-understanding of the agent. (Giddens, 1979: 58)

For cognitive/cultural anthropologists, the focus has been on schemas as it has been for cognitive anthropology. Schemas are interpretive systems held by all humans, internalised patterns that serve as a guide to action for individuals (D'Andrade, 1992) or, as Mandler (1984) explains, ways of organising experience. The power of the social actor is taken into consideration because the actions and beliefs of individuals are not direct products of experiences but are mediated by these schemas, or learned prototypes (Strauss & Quinn, 1994). When considering teachers, these experiences and the schemas teachers use to make choices about these experiences are considered to be a crucial and motivating aspect of their professional identity, as the quote at the beginning of the chapter suggests.

In the same way as practice theory, schema theory moves away from symbolic anthropology, which tends to see culture as unchanging and monolithic. However, cognitive anthropology attempts to delve deeply into looking at how people evolve into doing what they do (for an excellent review of the history and development of cognitive anthropology, see D'Andrade, 1995).

A set of schemas is defined as a 'cultural model', although these words are very often used interchangeably in the literature. As Quinn and Holland explain in their book, *Cultural Models in Language and Thought* (1987):

> cultural models are pre-supposed, taken-for-granted models of the world that are widely shared by members of a society and play a big role in understandings and behavior in that world ... [they] specify the cognitive organizations and how the way human beings think is linked. (Quinn & Holland, 1987: 3)

Cultural models are a way of linking why people to do what they do, and their agency, to identity construction in a way that connects individual interpretations to a larger collective understanding. They are a useful way to explain sharedness as well as an individual's behaviour, goals, actions and how they see the world. As mentioned earlier, newer currents in cultural anthropology and sociology put the social actor to the forefront, without explaining why the social actor might make certain decisions versus others. Cultural models, therefore, also give the researcher a tool to look at cultural schemas and psychological processes which 'interact to make each other up' (D'Andrade, 1995: 241). They are ways of understanding the world and, as such, they are not only representations but also processors (D'Andrade, 1995: 136). For example, there are schemas of romance, of work, of family, etc., and to interpret the meaning of the word 'father', one must have a schema for family. As practice theory makes clear, structures in the mind interact with structures in the world; physical representations depend on cognitive schemas to give them meaning and schemas need physical representations to convey and interpret meaning (D'Andrade, 1995: 146). D'Andrade continues by stating,

> emotional experience and goals are made up, in part, by cultural schemas (...) a reasonable theory of power needs some psychological theory (...) little research has been done on the degree to which social influences are necessary to maintain the psychological force of cultural schemas ... (D'Andrade, 1995: 241–242)

The missing element in examining the behaviour and actions of social actors in cultural anthropology has been a psychological theory, although practice theory has laid out the essential stepping stones. Explanatory advantages of looking through the lens of cultural/cognitive anthropology abound and include the following: the level of variation between individuals, the importance of context in the variation and in socialisation processes, the value of experience in the process of internalisation, and the level of identification one has with a particular aspect of the schema are important positive contributions of such a conceptual stance. As proposed by cultural/cognitive anthropologists, messages can be transmitted in varying and inconsistent forms, and also interpreted differently, depending on individual experiences and their environments. Strauss (1992) powerfully explains that social messages are difficult to read and interpret, and cultural/cognitive anthropology escapes the fax-like explanations that infused other socially deterministic theories.

If we look at specific studies in this area, such as that of romance among American college women, research has found that although a shared model of romance was globally accessible to the women, there was a range of variation in how salient romance was in their lives (Holland & Eisenhart, 1990). There were some women who had internalised it at a deep level, others who followed it at a cliché level, and still others who rejected it. To understand these findings, it is important to refer to Spiro's (1987) categories of internalised knowledge: at the first level of internalisation, a certain practice is understood but not considered important, or rejected; at the second level, a practice is a cliché, talked about but not carried out; at the third level, a practice is somewhat internalised and enacted; at the fourth level, a practice is deeply internalised and highly salient. For example, the American schema of self-reliance is rejected or just understood by many non-Americans, while many are at the fourth level; they have highly identified with self-reliance and negatively view people who are not self-reliant.

The different levels of internalisation and degree of identification with romance that Holland (1992) and Holland and Eisenhart (1990) observed varied according to the level of expertise of the women. In other words, the more experience women had with romantic activities and romance, the more romance became salient in their lives. Therefore, romantic expertise and identification were observed to be co-constructed with a social process. Another important finding these researchers made is that women pursued romance more if they were successful at it; so, success at the activity motivated the women to continue, while failure made some women only follow romance at a cliché level or reject it. In the same way, when teachers or language teachers pursue a certain methodology and they are successful at it, they will pursue it more, or they might reject it if they are not successful at it.

As mentioned earlier, the individual will differ in his or her interpretations of a certain dominant ideology – a perspective that cultural models take into account. This will depend on the quality and quantity of the experiences they had. For example, as I found in my dissertation work

(Varghese, 2006, 2008) on bilingual teachers, although the teachers may have shared a cultural model of bilingual teaching that is globally accessible, different teachers and administrators had their own interpretations of it and this was related to their experiences with it and the emotions associated with such experiences. Moreover, the confusion over bilingual education greatly enhanced the inconsistency and vagueness of the meanings intended by individual social actors. I found that teachers, administrators and other bilingual educators differed in their experiences, their emotions, motivations and past experiences, which in turn affected how certain events were understood and interpreted.

Using cultural models to understand teachers' beliefs and experiences and their agency and the process of learning takes into account the situation and posits how internalised schemas come into fruition as they interact with social processes (Holland, 1992). This is important for research in that it suggests that, when studying the process of people's internalised beliefs and practices, the social context of the learning has to be taken into account. Moreover, as mentioned earlier, this viewpoint accounts for the individual differing in his or her interpretations of a certain dominant ideology. This variation may depend on many factors, including how and in what context certain things have been learned and put into practice, and how people's success and failures lead to differential levels of investment of their pursuits.

Figured worlds

Although for some, cultural worlds and figured worlds are seen as equivalent and treated in that manner, figured worlds can be described as the next iteration of the concept of cultural models proposed by Holland and colleagues. Cultural models are linked more directly to individuals, although they may be shared as described above, whereas figured worlds are described as larger storylines where it is possible 'to tease out the underlying schemes that actors may use as well as how the same actors simultaneously identify themselves and others as certain social types' (Vågan, 2011: 49). In other words:

> By 'figured world,' then, we mean a socially and culturally constructed realm of interpretation in which particular characters and actors are recognized, significance is assigned to certain acts, and particular outcomes are valued over others. Each is a simplified world populated by a set of agents (in the world of romance: attractive women, boyfriends, lovers, fiancés) who engage in a limited range of meaningful acts or changes of states (flirting with, falling in love with, dumping, having sex with) as moved by a specific set of forces (attractiveness, love, lust). (Holland *et al.*, 1998: 52)

In my dissertation study (Varghese, 2000), I showed how four bilingual teachers shared some aspects of a cultural model of bilingual education but also differed in certain dimensions of it. If I had been using figured worlds as a theoretical framework, I would have been able to articulate bilingual teaching in that particular context as a figured world in and of itself with its actors, outcomes, relationships and activities and with certain conflicts at play. In using cultural models, I was able to articulate each of the teacher's schemas of bilingual education in relationship to a collective cultural model of bilingual education and teaching. On the other hand, if I had used figured worlds, I would have described the whole world of bilingual teaching and education in that particular school district as a figured world and showed how the teachers and other stakeholders were involved in that particular world with the particular actions and decisions they made. Both frameworks attempt to connect an individual/psychological explanation with a cultural and contextual one to understand and demonstrate how people come to believe in a particular schema or set of beliefs as they are engaged in actions that are related to these sets of beliefs. However, figured worlds are more aligned with a framework of identity formation than cultural models, which focus more on explaining how individuals come to a set of beliefs and practices rather than the formation of a whole professional identity.

Urrieta's (2007a) special issue on figured worlds and education is an attempt to show how figured worlds can be 'operationalized for empirical research' (Urrieta, 2007a: 111), as a way to 'study identity production in education' (Urrieta, 2007a: 112). According to Urrieta (2007a), figured worlds are part of the attempt to conceptualise and understand identity and agency in a more sophisticated manner compared to Holland and her colleagues. Urrieta's (2007b) own work on how a group of Mexican Americans became Chicano/a activists and then educators by engaging in figured worlds of Chicano/a activism in postsecondary institutions is featured in the special issue. What is especially useful about this special issue, which also contains a range of studies that take place in different educational settings, is that in addition to showing how figured worlds can be a significantly useful concept to use in educational research, it demonstrates a range of ways that figured worlds can be articulated – from postsecondary institutions, to particular groups of professionals and also as a particular school or classroom – all of these can be characterised as figured worlds.

The notion of figured worlds builds in an understanding of change and agency (although it is of an agency that is shown to be constrained) that was not present in cultural models. Moreover, cultural models can be best described as more similar to schemas and, therefore, associated with individual people. For example, the bilingual teachers in my dissertation study seemed to have individual cultural models around bilingual teaching that was contained within a larger umbrella of bilingual teaching. On the other hand, in figured worlds, people are viewed as enacting a certain way of being, an identity, within a figured world through a social process and 'in historical time' (Holland *et al.*, 1998: 55). At the same time, they create and recreate the figured worlds that they inhabit as they are in engagement with each other and where they ascribe meaning to each other's actions, including status and positions.

Two aspects of teacher identity conceptualisation and construction that are salient in the concept of figured worlds and connected to agency and change are that of relational identities and positional identities (Costley, 2015). Holland *et al.* (1998: 127) differentiate them in the following way: 'Relational identities have to do with behavior as indexical of claims to social relationships with others', while positional identities 'have to do with the day-to-day and on-the-ground relations of power, deference and entitlement, social affiliation and distance-with the social-interactional, social-relational structures of the lived world'. In her chapter on a classroom language assistant in the UK, Costley (2015: 79) uses figured worlds to describe how Maria's 'identity was constructed in and through her practice/s', especially focusing on how she used her space in a particular school to gain particular advantages for herself. As Costley (2015) concludes in her chapter:

> a key feature of the idea of figured worlds and the identities in practice that constitute them, is that they move and shift over time and space. Identities do not remain fixed and/or static. They both respond to and create changes. (Costley, 2015: 84)

Farrell (2011) also used figured worlds based on the work of Holland *et al.* (1998) and Urrieta (2007a) in his study where he facilitated group discussions over the period of two years of experienced ESL teachers in a Canadian intensive English programme. By using this conceptual framework, Farrell (2011) showed how these teachers articulated different dimensions of their identities such as teacher as manager and teacher as professional, and how they talked about these identities as developing as they participated in specific worlds.

In a recent article that draws on figured worlds in conceptualising language teacher identity, Kasun and Saavedra (2016) use it to describe and theorise the ESL pre-service teachers in a study abroad experience in Mexico. They use this framework to understand the students' shifting sense of their identities. Three significant aspects of figured worlds resonated with what Kasun and Saavedra (2016) discovered about their participants – one is the ability of this framework to show how language teachers can be simultaneously part of different figured worlds; the second is the understanding inherent in figured worlds that although teachers have agency, this agency is constrained by circumstances that are often beyond their control (Mills & Gale, 2007); and the third is the usefulness of figured worlds to make salient tensions that are evident in language teachers' sense of themselves. Overall, the authors used the conceptual lens of figured worlds to show the tensions between the different figured worlds of the teachers; these mainly revolved around their roles as classroom teachers in the United States, such as that of managers, which contrasted with the indigenising and decolonising knowledge and practice they had learned about in their study abroad trip to Mexico.

The construct of figured worlds is currently being drawn on more and more to examine the construction of language teacher identity, as the examples above demonstrate – especially how motivation, learning, conflicts and agency play into the construction of a figured world for language teachers according to their contexts and the type of language teachers they are in the process of becoming. In this chapter I showed how cultural models were the first iteration of figured worlds and were an attempt to embed what was considered to be a psychological view of why people (and in this case, teachers) did what they did within a cultural theory. However, even if cultural models provided some important attributes in helping us understand how language teachers came to appropriate certain beliefs and enact certain practices, they were too static to truly represent the evolution and fluidity of language teacher identity construction. On the other hand, figured worlds, as the next iteration of a cognitive/cultural conceptual framework, are able to capture more clearly how language teachers' participation in particular worlds both shape and are shaped by them, leading to particular identities as language teachers, underscoring their agency and the conflicts inherent in their identity formation.

Conclusion

Although the disciplines of language teacher education and language teacher identity within TESOL, applied linguistics, and bilingual/multilingual education have not significantly drawn on cultural models as way of conceptualising, studying and documenting how language teachers come to articulate certain beliefs, figured worlds have been increasingly used as a framework to document how language teachers engage in ways of participating and becoming ESL/EFL/bilingual teachers. The concept of figured worlds is an especially sophisticated sociocultural framework used both to understand and to show identity development and identity production, while articulating the contexts, activities and roles that are at play within a particular professional identity construction. A goal of this chapter was to describe how the concept of cultural models is helpful to understand as a precursor to that of figured worlds but also as distinct from it. The overall aim of this chapter was to demonstrate that cultural models (to some extent) and figured worlds (especially) can serve as extremely helpful frameworks in conceptualising and researching the construction of language teacher identities. Both of these frameworks view the formation of language teacher identity as going beyond the individual and beyond a cognitive understanding of identity; the future of scholarship in language teacher identity will continue to build on frameworks which will allow for a consideration of the interplay of teachers and their relationship to other stakeholders within their particular settings incorporating their agency.

References

Bailey, K.M. and Nunan, D. (eds) (1996) *Voices from the Language Classroom.* New York: Cambridge University Press.

Barkhuizen, G. (ed.) (2016) *Reflections on Language Teacher Identity Research.* New York: Routledge.

Bullough, R.V. Jr. (1991) Exploring personal teaching metaphors in pre-service teacher education. *Journal of Teacher Education* 42 (1), 43–51.

Bullough, R.V. Jr. and Baughman, K. (1997) *'First Year Teacher' Eight Years Later: An Inquiry into Teacher Development.* New York: Teachers College Press.

Carter, K. (1990) Teachers' knowledge and learning to teach. In W.R. Huston (ed.) *The Handbook of Research on Teacher Education* (pp. 291–310). New York: MacMillan.

Cheung, Y.-L., Ben Said, S. and Park, K. (eds) (2014) *Advances and Current Trends in Language Teacher Identity Research.* New York: Routledge

Connelly, F.M. and Clandinin, D.J. (1990) Stories of experience and narrative inquiry. *Educational Researcher* 19 (5), 2–14.

Costley, T. (2015) What's in a name? Power, space, and the negotiation of identities. In Y.-L. Cheung, S. Ben Said and K. Park (eds) *Advances and Current Trends in Language Teacher Identity Research* (pp. 74–85). New York: Routledge.

Cross, R. (2010) Language teaching as sociocultural activity: Rethinking language teacher practice. *The Modern Language Journal* 94 (3), 434–452.

D'Andrade, R. (1992) Schemas and motivation. In R. D'Andrade and C. Strauss (eds) *Human Motives and Cultural Models* (pp. 23–44). Cambridge: Cambridge University Press.

D'Andrade, R. (1995) *The Development of Cognitive Anthropology.* Cambridge: Cambridge University Press.

De Costa, P.I. and Norton, B. (2017) Transdisciplinarity and language teacher identity. *The Modern Language Journal* 101 (S1), 1–105.

Duff, P.A. and Uchida, Y. (1997) The negotiation of teachers' sociocultural identities and practices in postsecondary ESL classrooms. *TESOL Quarterly* 31 (3), 451–486.

Eisenhart, M., Borko, H., Underhill, R., Brown, C.A., Jones, D. and Agard, P. (1993) Conceptual knowledge falls through the cracks: Complexities of learning to teach mathematics for understanding. *Journal for Research in Mathematics Education* 24 (1), 8–40.

Farrell, T. (2011) Exploring the professional role identities of experienced ESL teachers through reflective practice. *System* 39 (1), 54–62.

Freeman, D. and Johnson, K.E. (eds) (1998a) Research and practice in English language teacher education [Special Issue]. *TESOL Quarterly* 32 (3), 393–632.

Freeman, D. and Johnson, K.E. (1998b) Reconceptualizing the knowledge-base of language teacher education. *TESOL Quarterly* 32 (3), 397–417.

Freeman, D. and Richards, J.C. (eds) (1996) *Teacher Learning in Language Teaching.* Cambridge: Cambridge University Press.

Giddens, A. (1979) *Central Problems in Social Theory: Action, Structure and Contradiction in Social Action.* Berkeley, CA: University of California Press.

Grossman, P. (1992) Why models matter: An alternate view on professional growth in teachers. *Review of Educational Research* 62 (2), 171–179.

Holland, D.C. (1992) How cultural systems become desire: A case study of American romance. In R. D'Andrade and C. Strauss (eds) *Human Motives and Cultural Models* (pp. 61–89). Cambridge: Cambridge University Press.

Holland, D.C. and Eisenhart, M. (1990) *Educated in Romance: Women, Achievement, and College Culture.* Chicago, IL: University of Chicago Press.

Holland, D., Lachicotte, W., Skinner, D. and Cain, C. (1998) *Identity and Agency in Cultural Worlds.* Cambridge, MA: Harvard University Press.

Jacob, E. (1997) Context and cognition: Implications for educational innovators and anthropologists. *Anthropology & Education Quarterly* 28 (1), 3–21.

Johnson, K.E. (1996) The vision vs. the reality: The tensions of the TESOL practicum. In D. Freeman and J.C. Richards (eds) *Teacher Learning in Language Teaching* (pp. 30–49). Cambridge: Cambridge University Press.

Johnson, K.E. (2009) *Second Language Teacher Education: A Sociocultural Perspective.* London: Routledge.

Johnston, B. (1997) Do EFL teachers have careers? *TESOL Quarterly* 31 (4), 681–712.

Kagan, D. (1992) Professional growth among preservice and beginning teachers. *Review of Educational Research* 62 (2), 129–169.

Kasun, G.S. and Saavedra, C.M. (2016) Disrupting ELL teacher candidates' identities: Indigenizing teacher education in one study abroad program. *TESOL Quarterly* 50 (3), 684–707.

Mandler, G. (1984) *Mind and Body: The Psychology of Emotion and Stress.* New York: Harper & Row.

Mills, C. and Gale, T. (2007) Researching social inequalities in education: Towards a Bourdieuian methodology. *International Journal of Qualitative Studies in Education* 20, 433–477

Moran, P.R. (1996) 'I'm not typical': Stories of becoming a Spanish teacher. In D. Freeman and J.C. Richards (eds) *Teacher Learning in Language Teaching* (pp. 125–153). Cambridge: Cambridge University Press.

Nolen, S.B., Horn, I.S. and Ward, C.J. (2015) Situating motivation. *Educational Psychologist* 50 (3), 234–247.

Norton, B. (1997) Language, identity, and the ownership of English. *TESOL Quarterly* 31 (3), 419–430.

Quinn, N. and Holland, D. (1987) Cognition and culture. In D. Holland and N. Quinn (eds) *Cultural Models in Language and Thought* (pp. 3–40). Cambridge: Cambridge University Press.

Richards, J.C. and Nunan, D. (eds) (1990) *Second Language Teacher Education.* Cambridge: Cambridge University Press.

Richardson, V. (1990) Significant and worthwhile change in teaching practice. *Educational Researcher* 19 (7), 10–18.

Shulman, L. (1987) Knowledge and teaching: Foundations of the new reform. *Harvard Educational Review* 57 (1), 1–22.

Spiro, M.E. (1987) Collective representations and mental representations in religious symbol systems. In B. Kilborne and L.L. Langness (eds) *Culture and Human Nature: Theoretical Papers of Melford E. Spiro* (pp. 161–184). Chicago, IL: University of Chicago Press.

Strauss, C. (1992) Models and motives. In R. D'Andrade and C. Strauss (eds) *Human Motives and Cultural Models* (pp. 1–20). Cambridge: Cambridge University Press.

Strauss, C. and Quinn, N. (1994) A cognitive/cultural anthropology. In R. Borofsky (ed.) *Assessing Cultural Anthropology* (pp. 284–300). New York: McGraw Hill.

Urrieta, L. (2007a) Figured worlds and education: An introduction to the Special Issue. *Urban Review* 39 (2), 107–117.

Urrieta, L. (2007b) Identity production in figured worlds: How some Mexican Americans become Chicana/o activist educators. *Urban Review* 39 (2), 117–144.

Vågan, A. (2011) Towards a sociocultural perspective on identity formation in education. *Mind, Culture, and Activity* 18 (1), 43–57.

Varghese, M. (2000) Bilingual teachers-in-the-making: Advocates, classroom teachers, and transients. Unpublished PhD thesis, University of Pennsylvania.

Varghese, M. (2006) Bilingual teachers-in-the-making in Urbantown. *Journal of Multilingual and Multicultural Development* 27 (3), 211–224.

Varghese, M. (2008) Using cultural models to unravel how bilingual teachers enact language policies. *Language and Education* 22 (5), 289–306.

Varghese, M. (2016) Thoughts on language teacher educator identity and language teacher identity: Towards a social justice perspective. In G. Barkhuizen (ed.)

Reflections on Language Teacher Identity Research (pp. 43–48). New York: Routledge.

Varghese, M., Morgan, B., Johnston, B. and Johnson, K. (2005) Theorizing language teacher identity: Three perspectives and beyond. *Journal of Language, Identity & Education* 4 (1), 21–44.

Varghese, M., Motha, S., Park, G., Reeves, J. and Trent, J. (eds) (2016) Language teacher identity in (multi)lingual educational contexts (Special Issue). *TESOL Quarterly* 50 (3), 545–571.

6 Exploring Novice EFL Teachers' Identity Development: A Case Study of Two EFL Teachers in China

Wendy Li and Peter I. De Costa

> At beginning, I felt that, we should be like friends,
> and learn from each other. It's not like I should
> be the one from whom they learn new things.
> I can also learn things from them.
> Ella (Interview/before teaching)

> I started to have a sense of myself being their teacher
> when they started to ask me questions and I know
> I am supposed to have the answers.
> Ella (Interview/after teaching)

These two comments were made by one of our participants (Ella) in this study, which focused on her understanding of being an English teacher before and after she started her teaching practice in China. Ella, having completed a one-year MA TEFL (Teaching English as a foreign language) programme in the UK, positioned herself as an English teacher who engaged students in an equal and mutually beneficial relationship. After starting her teaching career at a public high school in China, Ella constructed her teacher identity as an expert and authority in English who should be able to answer any student's questions. A similar identity transformation also occurred for another focal participant – Kate, who later summarised this phenomenon as follows: 'students expect you to be an expert in your profession; otherwise, they won't see you as their teacher and you don't get to teach them' (Interview, Kate).

Ella and Kate are among a growing number of graduates of TESOL or TEFL programmes who transition into their first year English teaching career. Such graduates have attracted increasing attention in the field of

SLA and second/foreign language pedagogy (e.g. Kanno & Stuart, 2011; Liu & Fisher, 2006; Tsui, 2007; Xu, 2012). The language teacher identity (LTI) literature often describes how novice teachers usually go through a critical stage when their imagined perception of teaching conflicts with the realities of the classroom. Similarly, the present study aimed to investigate how two Chinese novice EFL teachers grappled with conflicts in their first year teaching practice through the lens of teacher identity.

Teacher Identity Research

Within language teacher research, many studies have adopted teacher cognition, teacher beliefs and teacher learning as constructs to examine how L2 teachers' thinking processes change and develop over time and in various teaching practice contexts (see Borg, 2012; Burns *et al.*, 2015 for a review). In contrast, LTI research is at an emergent stage because, as Block (2015) pointed out, much identity research has focused on language learner identities. Comparatively, teacher identity has received less attention, although recent years have witnessed an increase in LTI research (e.g. Barkhuizen, 2017; Cheung *et al.*, 2015; De Costa & Norton, 2017; Liu & Fisher, 2006). Situated within the UK, Liu and Fisher (2006), for example, followed three student teachers' conceptions of self over three academic terms and illustrated how they came to identify themselves as English teachers over time. Nevertheless, the teacher identity construction of graduates of Western TESOL programmes who have to navigate stark teaching realities such as large-sized classroom and grammar-centred Chinese high school environments remains under-investigated (for an exception, see Wolff & De Costa, 2017). Furthermore, studies such as Chowdhury and Le Ha (2008) and Ilieva *et al.* (2015) also demonstrated that some TESOL programmes that promote Western-oriented pedagogies (e.g. communicative language teaching) do not necessarily address the issues and difficulties that returning international TESOL graduates encounter when teaching in their home countries. Thus it is of great relevance to language teacher education to examine how teachers (1) reconcile Westernised English instructional practices with their own teaching contexts, and (2) construct their language teacher identities in the process.

Theoretical Framework

In their review of three widely used frameworks that have been used in LTI research, Varghese *et al.* (2005) identified Lave and Wenger's (1991) theory of situated learning as a key framework. In a later conceptualisation of this theory, Wenger (1998) refined the construct of community of practice and developed identity as one of the primary elements in the theory. Responding positively to this theoretical development, Varghese *et al.* (2005), however, noted that Lave and Wenger's (1991) theory failed to demonstrate the power relations and underlying ideologies within the community. According to them, while Lave and Wenger acknowledged that participants who entered a new community needed to learn to become a community member, the issue of how these participants were accepted by the community members was less attended to by the theory. In light of this conceptual gap and for the purpose of our study, we elected to supplement Wenger's (1998) theory with Britzman's (1986, 2003) notion of *cultural myths*.

Wenger's (1998) communities of practice

According to Wenger (1998: 71), a community of practice shares three characteristics: (1) it is a community with a shared interest; (2) members of a community of practice share mutual engagement in activities and discussions; and (3) a community of practice consists of practitioners who develop a repertoire of resources. Crucially, in a community of practice, identity is constructed in the process of negotiating what it means to be a community member (Wenger, 1998). Of relevance to our study on novice teachers' identity construction are the following two observations by Wenger (1998), who viewed identity as negotiated experience and community membership. According to Wenger, negotiated experience refers to the mediation of learners' lived experiences of participation in the practices of the community and social labels that the community reifies for participants to gain community membership. As useful as Wenger's theory has been in explaining how our identity as community members is manifested in an individual's personal choices and actions, and ultimately becomes part of his/her individuality, what is lacking in his theory is a clear description of processes undertaken by new participants within the community as they attempt to develop and demonstrate the 'competence' desired by the community in order to be recognised as a full community member. To address this gap, we turn to Britzman's (1986; see also Britzman, 2003) notion of cultural myths, which is described next.

Britzman's cultural myths

Britzman (1986) developed the concept of cultural myths based on his 1985 study of secondary student teacher socialisation in which he found shared views by the society towards prospective teachers and the professionals. Cultural myths, according to Britzman (1986: 448), 'provide a set of ideal images, definitions, justifications and measures for thought and activity' of the student teachers. These myths, he adds, are empowered by the school structure and 'contribute to the student teacher's taken-for-granted views of power, authority, and knowledge'. The cultural myths construct has served as a valuable theoretical lens when examining the professional development of both pre-service and experienced teachers (e.g. Beeman-Cadwallader *et al.*, 2014; Fenimore-Smith,

2004). For example, in her study of a fourth grade student teacher in a US school, Fenimore-Smith (2004) illustrated how participation in team teaching practices and reflecting on her teaching with the researcher helped a novice teacher re-examine conventional views of teaching and move beyond the cultural myths surrounding teaching. Extending this body of work which has used cultural myths to guide research on language teacher education, we focus on two cultural myths – *everything depends on the teacher* and *the teacher is the expert* – in this present study because of their relevance to our data.

Everything depends on the teacher refers to the power struggle between teachers and students in the classroom. As Britzman (1986: 449) stated, 'unless the teacher establishes control, there will be no learning, and, if the teacher does not control the students, the students will control the teacher'. Put simply, teachers are expected to control the students as well as the learning process. According to this perspective, teaching is constructed as implanting knowledge, which is a strong manifestation of teacher authority, instead of discovering and learning about the unknown with students (Britzman, 1986, 2003). A second cultural myth is *the teacher as expert*. The underlying assumption is that 'teachers must be certain in their knowledge' (Britzman, 1986: 450) and, therefore, any uncertainty about their teaching materials might threaten their authority as experts. Unfortunately, this view of teachers, as explained by Britzman, prevents them from pursuing further knowledge construction. Having explained the theoretical framework that guided our study and before we introduce the methodology that we used in our study, which focused on two novice Chinese EFL teachers, we present a brief overview of English education in China in order to better situate our study.

English Education in China

Two major English teaching methods in Chinese schools and universities have come under pedagogical scrutiny in recent years. The first is communicative language teaching (CLT), which claims that language is better learned in authentic communicative contexts. From a CLT perspective, students are respected as independent individuals who are able to make decisions in terms of using the language (Nunan, 1991). In contrast, the traditional method, which is still widely used in many Chinese high school classrooms, views (1) language as a set of rules that should be systematically learned and taught by rote, and (2) teachers as knowledge transmitters who have absolute authority in the classroom over passive students (Ouyang, 2003).

Admittedly, traditional English instruction in China has been problematic as students develop competence in grammar, but lack speaking and listening skills. This phenomenon prompted Tsui (2007: 662) to disturbingly label this brand of English as 'deaf-and-dumb English'. As a result, the Ministry of Education has sought to reform English instructional practices and promote CLT in schools and universities (Hu, 2002). However, authentic CLT is rarely adopted in Chinese classrooms and some teachers even refer to CLT as 'cruel language teaching' (Tsui, 2007: 666). In fact, Wette and Barkhuizen (2009: 197) list the following challenges associated with implementing CLT in China[1]:

- it conflicts with how Chinese students are accustomed to learning English, that is, to acquire declarative linguistic knowledge systematically;
- it places unusually high demands on teachers, who are forced to conduct their lessons in English and to create authentic situations for their students to use English for communication purposes;
- contextual factors, such as large classes, limited teaching resources and grammar-focused assessment, also constrain the implementation of the communicative approach.

Furthermore, regional differences, unequal access to educational resources and a wide range of teacher competencies also affect the implementation of CLT in China. For example, in his investigation of the language learning experiences of 252 Chinese students from capital cities in coastal places and inland places, Hu (2016) reported that in less developed parts of China, the traditional teaching method has not waned in popularity. Based on the theoretical frameworks discussed in this section, and taking into consideration the realities of contemporary English education in China, this study attempts to address the following three questions: (1) How did two novice English teachers construct their identities in secondary schools in China during their first year of teaching? (2) What role did a foreign graduate language teacher education programme play in the process of their identity construction? (3) How did the different teaching contexts affect their teacher identity development?

Methodology

The data consisted of interviews with our focal participants (Ella and Kate) and with the TEFL programme director, artefacts including the programme introduction materials, participants' teaching materials, and the participants' posts on the Chinese social media platform WeChat (see Table 6.1). The interviews were conducted through an online chat software (i.e. Skype), were audio-recorded and later transcribed. During the interview with the TEFL programme director, English was the language for communication and data collection, as the director is a native speaker of English. For our focal participants, Chinese was used during the interviews and the data were later translated into English. In terms of the data collected from social media, with the two participants' consent, we were allowed to browse all their posts on WeChat and collect posts that were relevant to the purpose of this study.

Table 6.1 Data sources

Methods	Data
Conduct of interviews with focal teachers	Audio-recorded interviews (October 2015)
Conduct of an interview with the UK TEFL programme director	Audio-recorded interview (November 2015)
Collection of teaching-related artefacts	Teaching materials (e.g. PowerPoint slides and handouts) and TEFL programme materials (e.g. pamphlets, student handbook, course syllabi) Ella (September 2014–November 2015) Kate (March 2014–November 2015)
Examination of focal teachers' posts in social media during their first year of teaching	Posts on WeChat Ella (September 2014–November 2015) Kate (March 2014–November 2015)

Data coding

Coding procedures informed by Strauss and Corbin (1998) were used to analyse the data. After reading the transcripts repeatedly, we first created codes for themes that we felt were relevant to the research questions. Doing this allowed us to think beyond any stereotypical assumptions we had towards teachers and their teaching practice, given one of the researchers' (Wendy's) familiarity with teaching English in China and with our two teacher participants. Next, based on the axial and selective coding processes, we first identified two central categories: participants' perception of and experience in teacher training programmes and their teaching practices in local teaching contexts. Then, codes relevant to the two categories were separated and collapsed. Finally, guided by our research questions, codes that depicted how our two participants constructed their identities during the TEFL programme and their teaching practices in China were selected and categorised.

Focal participants: Ella and Kate

Ella (a pseudonym) grew up in a small town in Jiangxi Province (an underdeveloped province located in the middle inland area of China). She received her middle school and high school education at a local public school and enrolled at a teacher preparation university in Jiangxi. In 2012 she went to the UK to pursue her Master's degree in TEFL and graduated the following year. Later she returned to the local public school in her hometown as an English teacher, where she worked from September 2014 to February 2015. During this period she taught English to a class of 60 first-year high school students. She then left the job and passed the national public high school teacher recruitment exam in Shanghai. Currently she is an English teacher in a public middle school in Shanghai and her average class size is 35.

Kate (a pseudonym) graduated from the same TEFL programme in the UK in the same year. After returning to China she went through the national public high school teacher recruitment exam and obtained a position as an English teacher in one of the key high schools in Tianjin, a coastal city and one of the five municipalities in China in March 2014. After teaching for one semester, she was assigned another new class comprising more than 50 students. Originally from Tianjin, Kate completed her pre-university education at a prestigious foreign language school where English was a core course. She later entered a top ten comprehensive university for undergraduate study in China.

The data for this study were collected by Wendy, who is friends with Ella and who was later introduced to Kate by Ella. All three of them completed their Masters programme at the same university in the UK. Ella and Kate graduated one year earlier than Wendy. In that respect, from an ethical perspective and in line with the ethical turn in applied linguistics (De Costa, 2016), Wendy's relationship with the two participants enhanced the rapport and provided 'insider' insights when interacting with the participants. Furthermore, attempts were also made to conceal the participants' identities and those of the schools in which they taught through the use of pseudonyms. Finally, a draft of the analyses of our findings were presented to Ella and Kate for member checking (Denzin & Lincoln, 2011) to ensure that they were comfortable with our analyses and that our interpretations did not misrepresent them.

Findings and Discussion: Becoming an English Teacher

In this section, we focus on Ella and Kate's professional trajectory and examine how they came to identify themselves as English teachers as well as how they were acknowledged by the community members, mainly their students, during their first year of teaching. Drawing on Wenger's (1998) conceptualisation of identity construction as a process of becoming and Britzman's (1986, 2003) notion of cultural myths, we explore Ella and Kate's engagement in the focal communities of practice and trace their English teacher identity development.

Learning about 'English learning and teaching'

According to the admission pamphlets of the UK TEFL programme, upon graduation, students should be able to 'demonstrate ability in using relevant theoretical knowledge to develop and implement plans for guiding practical action'. Mandatory courses consisted of mostly teaching-related courses, such as introduction to language teaching, classroom language assessment and curriculum design, all of which were expected to emphasise practical teaching support and pedagogical discussion of content. Nevertheless, unlike students' expectations of learning 'practical'

English teaching skills, those courses were mainly taught through discussions of theories of teaching methods and second language learning. When reflecting on their one-year teacher education experience, both participants pointed out that the programme was too theoretically oriented and lacked practical elements (see Excerpts 1 and 2 below).

Excerpt 1

I spent much time reading research articles about language teaching and learning, and writing essays for each course. I was hoping more time could be devoted to have students do demo classes and get feedback from teachers. (Interview/Kate)

Excerpt 2

I wish we could learn more practical things, such as specific teaching skills, what to do when certain things happen in the class, how to write lesson plans, etc. (Interview/Ella)

As revealed in the above excerpts, Kate and Ella learned how to teach mainly through discussing, reading and writing about topics in the field of English teaching and learning. Moreover, the assessment aspect of the programme, which consisted mainly of essays and dissertations, placed a higher value on student research than on student teaching. According to Wenger's (1998) community of practice, identity is not only reified in the narratives of self-image and social categories, but is constructed through participation in the practices of the community. Therefore, while both Ella and Kate might have been labelled by the community as prospective English teachers, their daily academic engagements, such as reading, discussing academic papers and writing up academic essays in the community constructed and solidified their identity as student researchers. In the absence of actual teaching practice, they were only able to learn things *about* language learning and teaching as students. This academic reality led us to investigate how their one-year UK TEFL experience impacted their teacher identity development.

Teaching philosophies

Through daily participation in the classes and interaction with professors, Ella and Kate, as new members of a teaching community, developed a similar understanding of how to teach and what a teacher should be like. This understanding is instantiated in Ella's interview comments below:

Excerpt 3

We did many group discussions and presentations during the class. The class atmosphere is free and relaxing. We sat in groups and were allowed to ask questions freely. The professors did not always know the answers to every questions and they encouraged us to find the answer together. They treated us with respect and valued our opinions. (Interview/Ella)

Evidently, Ella experienced a learner-centred classroom, which is the cornerstone of Western education (Wette & Barkhuizen, 2009). The relationship between students and teachers was relatively equal (i.e. symmetrical) and born out of mutual respect. As noted by Liu and Fisher (2006), observing a mentor's or advisor's teaching will affect a teacher's identity formation, and novice teachers might follow the way their teachers teach when they are able to benefit from this teaching. Situated in a similar community of teaching practice, Ella and Kate learned about teacher–student relations and how their teachers delivered lessons through their multiple engagements in the community. These engagements in turn contributed to their understanding of being an English teacher and how to teach English. Both Kate and Ella explained in the interviews what English teachers they imagined themselves to be, and how English should be taught upon their return to China.

Excerpt 4

The role of a teacher should be more like a facilitator who provides scaffolding when necessary. The relationship between students and teachers should be equal. For students, more important is to find their own learning method and learn on their own. (Interview/Ella)

Excerpt 5

English is the only language spoken in the classroom. I will ask students to do many group discussions, presentations, and I will create opportunities for them to use English. (Interview/Kate)

Thus, the two participants shared similar views on English teaching and being an English teacher: (1) communicative methods were preferred; and (2) the teacher should not be the only source of learning or the knowledge transmitter.

However, in the interviews that were conducted in October 2015 (see Table 6.1 for a timeline of the data collection process), Ella and Kate conceded the inapplicability of their teaching philosophies in their own teaching contexts of China due to the constraints within the Chinese classroom, which are characterised by large class sizes, institutional pressures and students' poor speaking ability. This problem was exacerbated by the fact that many graduate students like Ella and Kate came to the programme with the false expectation that they would acquire the 'recipe' for teaching English (Britzman, 2003) and earn their graduate degree. However, the director of the TEFL programme herself observed and conceded during an interview in November 2015 that the programme was not practically-oriented enough.

Excerpt 6

Some people come with the expectation that they just want to learn how to teach. We don't want to give them a recipe for, here, how you teach. They are here for their Master's degree, not just a teacher certificate. We hope when they do become teachers they would have theoretical knowledge to draw on and then they are able to make their own choices about what would be the best thing to do in their contexts. (Interview/ Director of the UK TEFL programme)

Admittedly, it is likely that theoretical knowledge might be less helpful at the beginning of teaching when dealing with issues like class management and student–teacher relations became the priority (Wright, 2012). Keeping this observation in mind, in the following section, we examine Ella and Kate's identity construction in their new communities of practice in China.

Becoming an English teacher through practice

Our participants experienced similar challenges at the beginning of their teaching practice in China, although their local teaching contexts varied (as you may recall, Kate taught in a major big city, whereas Ella taught in a small town). Their previous self-image of an English teacher came under much pressure when they had to face the English teaching realities in China. For one, their students' limited English proficiency in the four skills (speaking being the most problematic) impeded their participation in classroom activities.

Excerpt 7
It turned out most of the students barely talked in the group discussion and they could not digest what I said in class well when I use English only. (Interview/Ella)

Excerpt 8
Students complained to me after the class that in order to understand what I said in English they need to spend much time and effort, and doing activities takes up too much class time. They'd rather I spend time explaining vocabulary and grammar rules. (Interview/Kate)

The two excerpts above also demonstrate Ella and Kate's 'English only' classroom language policy, which itself is problematic because such a policy goes against pedagogical benefits associated with translanguaging (e.g. García & Kleyn, 2016). Importantly, their pedagogical practices were not appreciated by students and neither were the classroom activities organised by them. Furthermore, attempts to develop more equitable teacher–student relations in the classroom did not pay off. On the contrary, the friendly and relaxing atmosphere jeopardised their authority as classroom teachers. As described in the Excerpt 9 below, Kate's students treated her as 'one of them' and disrespected her teaching decisions in the classroom, causing much disorder.

Excerpt 9
I tried to be friends with them, smiled a lot to them and talked about funny things or personal things, experiences in class. They probably

thought I was one of them, like a student. And then the class sometimes would lose control. For example, students talked freely in class, and didn't do homework. (Interview/Kate)

As can be seen, practices that were considered normal and even reified in the TEFL programme were not necessarily appropriate in Chinese classrooms. As observed in the Excerpt 8, students in a Chinese classroom context generally expect their teachers to be dominant in the class and teach them grammar rules and vocabulary. In light of these expectations, Richards (1998) suggests that teachers need to meet the demands of their educational environments. Therefore, in order to be acknowledged by the students as competent and qualified, novice teachers would need to adjust their teaching methods to meet students' expectations. In the following excerpt, however, Kate elaborated on how she gained membership into the teaching community.

Excerpt 10

Then, I realized that I should behave like a teacher. I talked to other experienced teachers and asked for their suggestions. Also, when I took over a new class, I started to wear clothes in dark color, hide my personality with less smiling and enforce strict classroom discipline. I tried to keep my distance from them. (Interview/Kate)

Kate's words 'I should behave like a teacher' marked an awareness of constructing her identity as an English teacher in the community. By interacting with other experienced teachers to see how they behaved in the classroom and how they dealt with student–teacher relations, Kate was trying to 'learn certain ways of engaging in action with other people' (Wenger, 1998: 152) in her new community of teaching practice. Similarly, Kate's change in appearance and clothing was to keep her distance from her students and establish her authority in the classroom, which were seen as part of her new plan to behave like a teacher in the community. Building on these findings, Britzman's (1986, 2003) cultural myths construct is employed in the next section in order to unpack the expectations of novice teachers.

Cultural myth #1: Everything depends on the teacher

According to Britzman (1986, 2003), novice teachers are expected to control the whole class and manage students. This holds true especially in large-sized classrooms in China, where classroom management is a major responsibility of novice teachers (Wright, 2012). As demonstrated in the previous excerpts, Kate started to construct her identity as the authority in the classroom through changing her clothing and appearance, disassociating herself in the classroom and enforcing strict classroom discipline. These endeavours could be seen as conforming to social expectations of a high school teacher and a deliberate attempt to gain ratified membership into the teaching community by ensuring that classroom management policies are implemented. However, the consequence of controlling everything, as discussed in Britzman (1986, 2003), is that learning becomes a process of instilling separated rules of knowledge. Evidence of this could be found from our participants' description of their teaching practice during this period because more Chinese was used (which was not necessarily a bad thing), tasks or activities were dropped, and more grammar instruction was included.

Excerpt 11

I used mainly Chinese and some English in the class. Later, I changed my teaching by explicitly pointing out the grammar rules and then helped them understand the reading. (Interview/Ella)

Excerpt 12

I gradually gave up having various activities in the classroom and used more Chinese too. Now it's half Chinese and half English. (Interview/Kate)

Cultural myth #2: Teacher is an expert

In addition to establishing their authority in the classroom, Ella and Kate were subsequently also positioned by the students as experts in English. According to Britzman (1986, 2003), to be an expert in the classroom is another cultural myth novice teachers often face. The students took for granted that their teachers were experts in English, and should therefore be familiar with all the vocabulary and grammar rules that appeared in the textbooks and tests. Kate described her students' perception accordingly:

Excerpt 13

A teacher should be well prepared, including getting familiar with every grammar point in that unit and every vocabulary item relevant to that unit. Then, students would consider you as qualified enough to be their teacher. Students now are quite smart; they would immediately spot if their teachers were well prepared for the class or not. One student once pointed at a new teacher, 'Look, he must be new here, because he looked at his lesson plan several times during the class.' (Interview/Kate)

Kate used the above example to illustrate the power relations between students and teachers. Although teachers should take charge in the classroom, authoritative moves were also initiated by the students. Our data suggest that for teachers to gain authority in the classroom their identities as English experts need to be established first. As a result, more attention might have been given to impressing the students with their grammar and vocabulary knowledge. Along the way, issues such as whether the vocabulary and grammar instruction was understood by the students might, unfortunately, not have been given adequate consideration. In fact, both Ella and Kate discovered that their students were unable to process what was taught in the class due to the massive learning load.

Excerpt 14

I prepared lots of things, including detailed vocabulary explanation and grammar instruction. During the class, I tried to cover all those points, but students would get lost in too many detailed explanations and fail to master the basics due to the overwhelming learning load. (Interview/Kate)

Excerpt 15

It's difficult to decide how much I should include in one class. At that time, I felt like I went too deep in explaining grammar rules and sometimes students got confused. (Interview/Ella)

Identity reconstruction in different communities

As noted in the aforementioned excerpts, our participants' initial efforts to be controllers and experts did not necessarily facilitate students' learning during the class instruction as Ella and Kate expected, even though their efforts helped them gain some recognition as community members from their students. Thus their identities were subject to further refinement, with increasing engagement in teaching practices in their communities. According to Wenger (1998), full members within a community of practice know how to do things and interact with others in the community, and are thus able to make use of the repertoire of resources developed through mutual engagement with community members. However, different communities of practices vary in terms of the resources, practices and expectations developed by members, which might contribute to participants identifying themselves differently despite the same professional identity labels (i.e. English teachers) that they share. In the context of this study, Kate and Ella's teaching contexts varied greatly with respect to the availability of teaching facilities and learning opportunities, as well as teacher quality and school policies. Even though they were English teachers in China, teaching in different school contexts did in fact affect, as we shall see shortly, how they positioned themselves and how they were positioned by others.

Kate's identity reconstruction in her community of practice

After one semester of teaching, Kate was given an opportunity to teach in a new first year high school. While describing her teaching practice for this class, she noted that she was able to incorporate her previous philosophy of learning English for use in the traditional grammar-centred classroom.

Excerpt 16

If you told them (students) that English is for use, and they should practice using English for communication in the class, they won't listen. I totally understand, they have been taught this way and they have to take the Gaokao (China university entrance examination) in the end. What I would do is to create opportunities for them to do some presentations, make speeches and engage in role play, encourage them to participate in activities that require them to use English in and out of school. For one module, I insisted on using English to do the lead-in and to introduce interesting background information on the topic. (Interview/Kate)

As shown, Kate encouraged students to participate in extracurricular activities organised by the school. She also created opportunities for students to engage in communicative activities and provided them with intelligible input, which in turn afforded her much-needed interaction even in such a large class with over 50 students. One of the factors contributing to Kate's incorporation of her own beliefs of English learning in the classroom was the quantity of resources the school provided for both teachers and students. Studying in one of the five municipalities in China and a major coastal Chinese city affords abundant educational resources (Hu, 2016), such as modern teaching facilities and various extracurricular opportunities. These affordances, in Kate's case, allowed her to develop contemporary teaching materials such as PowerPoint lessons and movie clips to enrich the content of her teaching, as well as to introduce popular culture elements (e.g. photographs of celebrities) in her instruction.

In addition, the school policy mandated that Kate conduct at least five demonstration lessons each semester during her first year of teaching. In the demonstration classes, Kate was encouraged to embrace alternative English teaching methods and then received feedback from her colleagues. These practices and resources allowed her to develop appropriate teaching methods that incorporated both communicative and traditional grammar-centred methods. By doing this, Kate could take into consideration her students' needs of passing the exam as well as developing students' communicative competence, which she believed should be a major goal of teaching and learning English. That the practices Kate engaged in on a daily basis shaped her teacher identity is exemplified in Excerpt 17, where she describes herself as an English teacher who was able to make sound decisions in terms of what to teach in her classroom.

Excerpt 17
It's our job to decide how we can apply what we learned in the UK to our own classroom. We have to adjust our teaching between learning English for use and learning English for the Gaokao. (Interview/Kate)

Ella's identity reconstruction in her community of practice
Unlike Kate, Ella's English teaching philosophy was not enacted in her teaching practice. She described her pedagogy at that time as '50% grammar explanation plus 50% drill practice, just like other English teachers in that school' (Interview/Ella). She attributed her adoption of traditional English teaching methods to her 'students' tight schedule and [the] high pressure of the Gaokao (national examinations)' (Interview/Ella). Given

that students in China are under pressure to take the Gaokao, one could argue that what differentiates Ella's choice of teaching instruction from Kate's is their different teaching contexts.

Ella's school was located in a small town in an inland part of China where traditional English teaching methods still dominated English classes. One factor contributing to the situation was that the majority of English teachers lacked experience of employing communicative methods in their classrooms. According to Hansen and Woronov's (2013) report on rural education in China, which holds true in many small towns in China's hinterland, since most Chinese English teachers experienced traditional learning in an exam-oriented system, teachers in rural parts of the country often lack insight into alternative and innovative teaching methods. Secondly, students' English proficiency, especially their deficiency in oral English, impinged on the effectiveness of implementing communicative methods (see Excerpts 7 and 8). Furthermore, living in a small town in China meant that the traditional grammar-focused Gaokao, which favoured students from the big city (Hansen & Woronov, 2013), posed a greater challenge for them because they lacked familiarity with such a high-stakes examination. In that respect, because of their lack of social capital, the traditional method of language teaching had some merits because of its strong grammar focus. The inadequate educational resources and large student population, which are discussed in Hu (2016), also led to Ella's compromised use of communicative methods, leading her to identify herself as 'just like other English teachers in the school' (Interview/Ella).

By contrast, after moving to a public school in Shanghai, Ella enacted in her classroom the teaching philosophy that she had developed in the UK. She elaborated on how her students learned key vocabulary through participating in a meaningful classroom task.

Excerpt 18
The beginning unit in the English book is about family and relatives. For this unit, I gave them a task and told them to explain clearly the relationship between their family members and what they do in English, and put that information in a family tree they need to draw. (Interview/Ella)

When asked why she implemented task-based teaching (Long, 2014) in the new school, in addition to the smaller classroom size (35 students) and the reduced pressure of the Gaokao (her students were in junior high and would not take the exam for another five years), Ella added that the multimedia equipment in her Shanghai school enabled her to incorporate supplementary materials such as videos, songs and pictures to enrich her instruction. Furthermore, Ella's social media posts of her teaching, which were collected between September 2014 and November 2015 (see Table 6.1), revealed various school-initiated English activities in the Shanghai school, such as having foreign teachers come to her school to give lectures, and organising English oral speech club activities for students. In short, her new teaching context in Shanghai afforded her the opportunity to experiment with and enhance the pedagogy to which she was introduced in the UK.

According to Freeman and Johnson (1998), some teaching practices are appreciated whereas others are devalued in varied contexts. In Ella's previous schools, the English teaching practices of explaining grammar rules and preparing students for the Gaokao were favoured. By contrast, Ella's experience with interactive classrooms in the UK that involved engaging students in a variety of English activities and motivating them to use English for communication purposes was more valued in the Shanghai school. In an interview, Ella did not disclose her reason for leaving the school in her hometown after just one semester of teaching. However, one can surmise that the educational resources and socio-economic environment in Ella's school in Shanghai may have been a key draw because it allowed her to practise English teaching in ways that were consistent with her teaching philosophy, much to the appreciation of her students.

Conclusion

This study looked at two cases of novice English teachers' identity construction during their first year of teaching practice in varied teaching contexts in China. Through the lenses of Wenger's (1998) community of practice and Britzman's (1986, 2003) concept of cultural myths, we examined our focal participants' teacher identity construction during their graduate education in the UK and discussed challenges that emerged when they came back to become English teachers in Chinese high schools. The professional identities that they formed in the UK were then subject to negotiation when trying to gain membership into their new teaching communities. To fulfil the expectations desired by these new communities, our participants, Kate and Ella, played roles as managers and English experts in the classroom. Later, with more engagement in their respective communities' practices, their teacher identities were constructed and mediated as they negotiated their individual teaching beliefs and the communities' expectations. Kate, who taught in a public high school in a big city where a variety of teaching and learning resources were available, was able to combine her teaching philosophy principles – in essence English for actual daily use – with the traditional grammar-focused teaching methods. Consequently, her students' needs of passing the exam and her own teaching philosophy were met. Ella, on the other hand, experienced a major change in her pedagogy when changing her job from a rural high school to a junior high school in Shanghai. Moving forward, and taking into consideration Ella and Kate's rich experience of becoming language teaching professionals, we need to remember that teacher identity is always changing, which in turn opens up opportunities for us to find new ways of optimising the learning outcomes of students.

Similar to what Kanno and Stuart (2011) found in their study, our study also demonstrates the key role L2 teachers' identity construction plays in both their classroom practice and their professional career development. Several implications can be drawn from the study in terms of L2 teacher education and future L2 teacher identity research. First, L2 teacher education needs to look beyond the field of SLA as its knowledge base for L2 teachers. Instead, it should explore the possibilities of teacher learning through engagement in specific communities of practice (Freeman, 2002; Kanno & Stuart, 2011). As revealed in this study, Ella and Kate's knowledge of language acquisition and teaching methods contributed to their teacher identity formation in a limited way. If anything, it was their engagement in local communities (i.e. the UK TEFL programme and the teaching community in China) that shaped their professional identities and later explained their evolving teacher identities. Put simply, in addition to imparting student teachers with sound SLA knowledge, L2 teacher education programmes need to pay more attention to LTI construction. Secondly, as proposed by De Costa and Norton (2017), who applied the Douglas Fir Group's (2016) transdisciplinary framework to investigating L2 language learner identity development, teacher identity needs to be examined from an ecological perspective. In other words, a host of factors that reside at multiple levels (e.g. ideologies at the societal and school level, and teachers' practice within classroom) ought to be explored in order to see how teachers' identities are shaped by these factors. Finally, while our study focused on how school ideologies and different teaching contexts affected teachers' classroom practices, it is worthwhile also looking at examples of L2 teachers exercising their agency within the contextual constraints.

Note

(1) Even though Wette and Barkhuizen (2009) identified these challenges as being associated with China, we would argue that the challenges are not specific to China as they bear a universal dimension in that many other countries around the world encounter similar issues when implementing CLT in their English curricula.

References

Barkhuizen, G. (ed.) (2017) *Reflections on Language Teacher Identity.* New York: Routledge/Taylor & Francis.
Beeman-Cadwallader, N., Buck, G. and Trauth-Nare, A. (2014) Tipping the balance from expert to facilitator: Examining myths about being a teacher educator. *Studying Teacher Education* 10 (1), 70–85.
Block, D. (2015) Becoming a language teacher: Constraints and negotiation in the emergence of new identities. *Bellaterra: Journal of Teaching & Learning Language & Literature* 8 (3), 9–26.
Borg, S. (2012) Current approaches to language teacher cognition research: A methodological analysis. In R. Barnard and A. Burns (eds) *Researching Language Teacher Cognition and Practice: International Case Studies* (pp. 11–29). Bristol: Multilingual Matters.

Britzman, D. (1986) Cultural myths in the making of a teacher: Biography and social structure in teacher education. *Harvard Educational Review* 56 (4), 442–457.

Britzman, D.P. (2003) *Practice Makes Practice: A Critical Study of Learning to Teach* (revised edn). Albany, NY: State University of New York Press.

Burns, A., Freeman, D. and Edwards, E. (2015) Theorizing and studying the language-teaching mind: Mapping research on language teacher cognition. *The Modern Language Journal* 99 (3), 585–601.

Cheung, Y.L., Said, S.B. and Park, E. (eds) (2015) *Advances and Current Trends in Language Teacher Identity Research.* New York: Routledge.

Chowdhury, R. and Le Ha, P. (2008) Reflecting on Western TESOL training and communicative language teaching: Bangladeshi teachers' voices. *Asia Pacific Journal of Education* 28 (3), 305–316.

De Costa, P.I. (ed.) (2016) *Ethics in Applied Linguistics Research: Language Researcher Narratives.* New York: Routledge.

De Costa, P.I. and Norton, B. (2017) Introduction: 'Identity, transdisciplinarity, and the good language teacher'. *The Modern Language Journal* 101 (S1), 3–14.

Denzin, N.K. and Lincoln, Y. (eds) (2011) *The SAGE Handbook of Qualitative Research* (4th edn). Thousand Oaks, CA: Sage.

Douglas Fir Group (2016) A transdisciplinary framework for SLA in a multilingual world. *The Modern Language Journal* 100 (Suppl. 2016), 19–47.

Fenimore-Smith, J.K. (2004) Democratic practices and dialogic frameworks: Efforts toward transcending the cultural myths of teaching. *Journal of Teacher Education* 55 (3), 227–239.

Freeman, D. (2002) The hidden side of the work: Teacher knowledge and learning to teach. *Language Teaching* 35 (1), 1–13.

Freeman, D. and Johnson, K.E. (1998) Reconceptualizing the knowledge-base of language teacher education. *TESOL Quarterly* 32 (3), 397–417.

García O. and Kleyn, T. (eds) (2016) *Translanguaging with Multilingual Students: Learning from Classroom Moments.* New York: Routledge.

Hansen, M.H. and Woronov, T.E. (2013) Demanding and resisting vocational education: A comparative study of schools in rural and urban China. *Comparative Education* 49 (2), 242–259.

Hu, G.W. (2002) Recent important developments in secondary English-language teaching in the People's Republic of China. *Language, Culture and Curriculum* 15 (1), 30–49.

Hu, G.W. (2016) Contextual influences on instructional practices: A Chinese case for an ecological approach to ELT. *TESOL Quarterly* 39 (4), 635–660.

Ilieva, R., Li, A. and Li, W. (2015) Negotiating TESOL discourses and EFL teaching contexts in China: Identities and practices of international graduates of a TESOL program. *Comparative and International Education/Éducation Comparée et Internationale* 44 (2), 3.

Kanno, Y. and Stuart, C. (2011) Learning to become a second language teacher: Identities-in-practice. *The Modern Language Journal* 95 (2), 236–252.

Lave, J. and Wenger, E. (1991) *Situated Learning: Legitimate Peripheral Participation.* Cambridge: Cambridge University Press.

Liu, Y. and Fisher, L. (2006) The development patterns of modern foreign language student teachers' conceptions of self and their explanations about change: Three cases. *Teacher Development* 10 (3), 343–360.

Long, M. (2014) *Second Language Acquisition and Task-based Language Teaching.* Malden, MA: Wiley-Blackwell.

Nunan, D. (1991) Communicative tasks and the language curriculum. *TESOL Quarterly* 25 (2), 279–295.

Ouyang, H. (2003) Resistance to the communicative method of language instruction within a progressive Chinese University. In K.M. Anderson-Levitt (ed.) *Local Meanings,*

Global Schooling: Anthropology and World Culture Theory (pp. 121–140). Basingstoke: Palgrave MacMillan.

Richards, J.C. (1998) *Beyond Training: Perspectives on Language Teacher Education.* Cambridge: Cambridge University Press.

Strauss, A. and Corbin, J. (1998) *Basics of Qualitative Research: Techniques and Procedures for Developing Grounded Theory* (2nd edn). Thousand Oaks, CA: Sage.

Tsui, A.B.M. (2007) Complexities of identity formation: A narrative inquiry of an ELT teacher. *TESOL Quarterly* 41 (4), 657–680.

Varghese, M., Morgan, B., Johnston, B. and Johnson, K.A. (2005) Theorizing language teacher identity: Three perspectives and beyond. *Journal of Language, Identity & Education* 4 (1), 21–44.

Wenger, E. (1998) *Communities of Practice: Learning, Meaning, and Identity.* New York: Cambridge University Press.

Wette, R. and Barkhuizen, G. (2009) Teaching the book and educating the person: Challenges for university English language teachers in China. *Asia Pacific Journal of Education* 29 (2), 195–212.

Wolff, D. and De Costa, P.I. (2017) Expanding the language teacher identity landscape: An investigation of the emotions and strategies of a NNEST. *The Modern Language Journal* 101 (S1), 76–90.

Wright, T. (2012) Managing the classroom. In A. Burns and J.C. Richards (eds) *The Cambridge Guide to Pedagogy and Practice in Second Language Teaching* (pp. 60–67). Cambridge: Cambridge University Press.

Xu, H. (2012) Imagined community falling apart: A case study on the transformation of professional identities of novice ESOL teachers in China. *TESOL Quarterly* 46 (3), 568–578.

7 Language Teacher Cognition: An Emergent Phenomenon in an Emergent Field

Anne Feryok

Introduction

The turn towards complex and dynamic systems has sparked interest in emergence and self-organisation in many fields, including psychology and applied linguistics. It is not surprising that language teacher cognition (LTC), located at the intersection of psychology and applied linguistics, has also taken note. Language teacher cognition is here understood as what teachers think, believe and know (Borg, 2006). One issue in LTC research is the relationship between language teacher cognition and practice, which includes whether and how changing cognition changes practice. Underlying this issue is the nature of cognition, and whether emergence can cast any light on issues in LTC research.

In the domain of applied linguistics, Larsen-Freeman and Cameron (2008) discuss self-organisation and emergence. From an ontological perspective, self-organisation is a qualitatively new state that occurs when a system adapts to change through its own properties, without control or external force. If 'self-organization leads to new phenomena on a different scale or level' (Larsen-Freeman & Cameron, 2008: 59), these new phenomena are described as emergent. This description suggests that Larsen-Freeman and Cameron understand an emergent phenomenon, unlike a self-organised phenomenon, to be ontologically distinct from its parts. This is clear from the description of an emergent phenomenon as 'a whole that is more than the sum of its parts' (Larsen-Freeman & Cameron, 2008: 59).

From an epistemological perspective, emergent phenomena 'cannot be explained reductively through the activity of the component parts' (Larsen-Freeman & Cameron, 2008: 59). In other words, the more fundamental parts of an emergent phenomenon cannot be examined and used to make

105

predictions about it (Stephan, 1999). Therefore, a distinction is often made between two types of emergence. In strong emergence, the new phenomenon cannot be predicted from or reduced to its parts. An example would be claiming that human intention cannot be predicted by examining brain states, no matter how sophisticated instruments become. In weak emergence, the new phenomenon can be predicted from or reduced to its parts. Using the same example, this would be claiming that human intention can be predicted by examining brain states once suitable instruments are developed. The weak sense is compatible with self-organisation and scientific explanations. It is based on three assumptions: that the universe is fundamentally material, that there are systemic or collective macro structure properties that are not possessed by any micro structure part of the system, and that those macro structure properties depend on the properties and arrangement or behaviour of the micro structure parts (Stephan, 1999).

Larsen-Freeman and Cameron (2008) approach emergence and self-organisation within complex adaptive systems (CAS) and dynamic systems theory (DST). They will be referred to together as complex dynamic systems (CDS) because their similarities and differences are not the particular focus of this chapter.

Historically, emergence is related to both philosophy and psychology. It is most often associated with 19th century British philosophy, but it also played an important role in early 20th century German Gestalt psychology and field theory (Vintiadis, 2013). In both of these examples, emergence is associated with a monist perspective. Monism is the idea that there is only one fundamental substance, which may be either mental or material. It contrasts with the dualist perspective, most often associated with the philosopher Descartes, that there are two substances, mental (our minds) and material (our bodies).

Modern theories of emergence, like modern theories of science, are materialist. Vygotsky (1987), for example, situated his psychological theory work in materialism. However, it is difficult to account for the phenomenological or felt quality of our mental experiences through materialism (Chalmers, 2006). Therefore, many people are reluctant to completely accept materialism. Vygotsky saw this difficulty as the fundamental problem of psychology. He found a solution in language, which is both biologically material and socially symbolic (Lantolf, 2006). Although language requires our brain and body, we learn language with others, we develop control over ourselves through others, and in those social processes higher level mental functions have developed in our species and in ourselves. The role of language in the emergence of mental functions is especially relevant to LTC. Not only do language teachers play a critical role in creating the social situations through which learners engage with a second language, but they also play this role using language.

There are also pragmatic reasons for looking beyond CDS theory. One reason is that only a handful of studies have examined LTC within a CDS approach. The other reason is that there is an established research agenda in sociocultural theory (SCT), which examines microgenesis, or the development of mental functions, in language teachers. The genetic research method used in these studies may provide the best evidence available for the emergence of LTC.

This chapter begins by examining the tacit dimension in LTC, which has been recognised as central to professional expertise for many years. The tacit dimension is particularly relevant to LTC because language is used on a daily basis from a very young age. Language teachers, like other people, usually have folk psychological beliefs about its nature, learning and use based on their personal experience with language (Pasquale, 2011). The chapter then examines self-organisation and emergence in greater detail by presenting theoretical points which are then illustrated through the LTC research literature. The concepts of self-organisation and emergence are introduced through Aslan's (2015) study of the professional identity development of a novice language teacher who taught French as a native speaker (NS) and German as a non-native speaker (NNS). This study illustrates how the tacit dimension self-organises to become content for reflection-on-action. The critical role played by consciousness as a cause is presented through a microgenetic analysis of emergence from a CDS perspective in Feryok and Oranje's (2015) study of a German as a foreign language teacher as she was planning for a new activity. This study shows how the emergence of cognition acts as both cause and constraint during reflection-in-action. A Vygotskian approach to the emergence is then examined through a microgenetic analysis of the narrative enquiry of an English as a second language teacher (Johnson & Golombek, 2011). This study shows how self-regulation develops. A penultimate section draws together the strands of this chapter by describing the theoretical implications of emergence and development, with the conclusion describing pedagogical and research implications.

Tacit Knowledge and Reflection-in-action

LTC has its roots in early research on teacher beliefs and practices in general education (Borg, 2006). One debate in the early literature turned on whether teacher knowledge was propositional (e.g. Fenstermacher, 1986) or whether it was also experiential (e.g. Munby, 1989). Those who argued that teacher knowledge was largely experiential drew on Polanyi's work on the personal (1962) and tacit (1966) nature of knowledge and skills in both professional practice and everyday life. Polanyi argued that the personal and tacit knowledge used to make judgements when performing activities depended on the interpretative framework supplied by their role within some greater whole that gives them significance. This view drew on Gestalt psychology – an experimental approach to perception based on the idea that people perceived something other than their actual sense perceptions so that 'order emerges from the flow of experience' (Wagemans, 2015: 16).

Schön (1983) drew on Polanyi to argue that 'the workaday life of the professional depends on knowing-in-action' (Schön, 1983: 49), knowledge based on the practical 'knowing how' rather than the propositional 'knowing that'. His close examination of case studies of professional expertise, including that of teachers, showed that both knowledge and experience contributed to the ability to exercise expert judgement without having to consciously deliberate on how to use our knowledge, that is, reflection-in-action, which he distinguished from reflection-on-action (after the action). One characterisation of reflection-in-action is that it is about exercising expert judgement, not reflecting on it later; responding to expected feedback, not monitoring oneself based on feedback; and reframing unexpected feedback, not deliberating over it (Munby, 1989). In other words, reflection-in-action is an immediate, spontaneous, fluent response to the flux of a situation; at the same time, the expert quality of the judgement relies on expert knowledge.

These different modes of knowledge are associated with different memory systems (Ullman, 2015). Declarative knowledge is associated with facts (e.g. content knowledge); it includes semantic and episodic memories. The procedural memory system is associated with behaviours; it also includes priming and perceptual memory, associative learning and conditioned reflexes. To some extent these systems interact, but the different modes of knowledge are separate and do not convert into each other.

In SCT, Vygotsky (1986) described everyday and scientific concepts, which according to Lantolf and Poehner (2014) aligns with the declarative-procedural model (Ullman, 2015). Vygotsky (1986) metaphorically described concept development as two separate processes in which everyday concepts (procedural or tacit knowledge) grow upward while systematic concepts (declarative knowledge) grow downward (Lantolf & Poehner, 2014). Everyday concepts develop spontaneously through exposure and use but are not readily articulated. They are a basis for understanding systematic concepts that rely on verbalisation for their development and understanding, which are usually introduced through formal study. Verbalisation enables concepts to be delineated, organised and manipulated.

In Vygotsky's (1986) account, systematic knowledge reframes, but does not replace everyday knowledge. For example, NSs can intuitively judge what is accurate and appropriate, even if they cannot explain it. Learning enough grammar and linguistics to provide explanations does not eradicate the ability to make intuitive judgements, but provides a framework that encompasses them, which also inhibits everyday concepts such as unfounded prescriptive rules. Vygotsky believed that this ability to inhibit was central to developing the self-regulatory control which enables the development of voluntary attention, planning and other mental functions.

The idea that concept development involves both upward and downward processes resonates with the ideas of self-organisation and emergence. Everyday concepts self-organise into implicit knowledge that is stored in procedural memory, where it can be automatically accessed. Systematic concepts self-organise into explicit knowledge that is stored in declarative memory, where it can be intentionally recalled, which can be done quickly with practice. In language teaching, when systematic concepts are not only learned but are also used in practical experience, a well-integrated body of knowledge develops, known as praxis (Lantolf & Johnson, 2007). Praxis differs from reflection-in-action precisely because of its origins in both procedural and conceptual knowledge.

In the following sections, self-organisation and emergence will be examined, first through theory and then through empirical research.

Self-organisation and Emergence

The core notion in self-organisation is the increase of internal order in a system (O'Connor & Wong, 2015; Vintiadis, 2013). Multi-agent systems, such as birds flocking, are classic examples, and illustrate how self-organised phenomena are not ontologically distinct from their parts, since a flock of birds cannot exist separately from the birds that make it up. This example also illustrates two other points: that self-organisation occurs at a single scale or level in a system among similar interchangeable elements; and that the increase in structure occurs through the rearrangement and integration of these elements. When self-organisation stabilises into a cohesive pattern that constrains systems responses, the pattern is known as an attractor (Larsen-Freeman & Cameron, 2008).

The term 'emergence' was introduced by G.H. Lewes in 1875 to distinguish between two effects, those that were the result of additive or subtractive processes and those that were not, in particular mental properties that develop from neural processes and have their own ontological status (Vintiadis, 2013). O'Connor and Wong (2005) argue that a 'robustly ontological' (O'Connor & Wong, 2005: 622) emergent macro phenomenon must be different nonstructurally (i.e. have other than merely different spatial arrangements of similar features) in order to be irreducible to its parts. They further argue that the relationship between the micro-level system and the macro-level emergent phenomenon must be dynamic and causal. Causal efficacy, or downward causation, is the capacity of the emergent phenomena to act on the micro-level components from which they emerged. This property is important to consciousness and thus also to LTC.

Aslan's (2015) study of a teacher, Ezgi, who taught French as a NS and German as a NNS, shows not only different patterns of self-organisation, but also the emergent beginnings of teacher identity. Aslan used complexity theory to describe the interactions between the teacher's NS and NNS identity and her cognition and practice in her language classes. Aslan collected data in three 30-minute interviews and weekly observations for a semester (alternating between the two language classes) and analysed the data through retrodictive qualitative modelling.

Aslan (2015) focused on the context sensitivity and nonlinearity of the teacher's cognition and practice in the two languages. He described how as a NS of French, Ezgi felt more comfortable teaching culture than grammar, but as a NNS of German, she felt more comfortable teaching grammar than culture. In German class, 'I know that my grammar is very good, and I know how to speak German' (Aslan, 2015: 257). However, the researcher observed that 'in none of the German classes observed was Ezgi found to be using references or explanations pertaining to German culture' (Aslan, 2015: 258), even though she believed she represented European culture in her classes. In French class, the researcher observed that Ezgi 'presented French culture through French songs, videos, and jokes. In addition, she seemed to be more confident when it came to judging and explaining the pragmatic or cultural acceptability or appropriateness of certain phrases and expressions' (Aslan, 2015: 258). However, she 'had difficulty explaining the grammaticality and appropriateness of some of the utterances students generated' (Aslan, 2015: 259). Ezgi's cognition and practice had self-organised into different patterns in the two classes.

Ezgi's understanding of her language speaker identity was associated with the teaching situation. As a teacher, she believed in the need for both grammar and culture teaching, but acted on them differently because she had an emic perspective on French language and culture, but an etic perspective on German language and culture; both sets of practices met with positive student feedback. Aslan explains that even though her 'NS/NNS identities facilitated co-adaptation in Ezgi's teacher cognition' (Aslan, 2015: 259), her 'NS and NNS identities did not affect how she viewed herself as a foreign language teacher, and she perceived the language teaching profession to be independent of the NS/NNS identities associated with the languages she teaches' (Aslan, 2015: 261). Because Ezgi had beliefs about herself as a language teacher that differed from her language speaker-driven practices, her professional language teacher identity cannot be reduced to the different choices she made in the different contexts of her language speaker identity.

Aslan states that 'Ezgi's professional identity as a foreign language teacher mainly consisted of her goals in the classroom' (Aslan, 2015: 259). Ezgi's own words were, 'I think that we don't really learn how to teach through a book because every student is different, every class is different, every grammar is different; so you learn by doing it' (Aslan, 2015: 260). She described her teacher learning process as based on 'her individual efforts and instincts' (Aslan, 2015: 260) and 'the interaction between multiple agents' (Aslan, 2015: 261), so that 'the best way to learn about or improve teaching skills was to be involved in actual teaching' (Aslan,

2015: 261). Thus, although Ezgi could act immediately, spontaneously, and fluently, her teaching actions were not informed by systematic knowledge as much as by personal experience as language learner, user and teacher. There was action and there was reflection-on-action, but it is not clear that there was much reflection-in-action, much less praxis.

This study can be interpreted as underlining the richness of identity as a context for language teacher development. In her study of learner selves, Mercer (2015) shows the difference between expressing identity on a micro-level timescale, which in a teacher would be part of tacit practices, and reflecting on identity on a macro-level timescale, which in a teacher would involve reflection-on-action. In Aslan's (2015) study, there were two different attractors for the tacit practices that self-organised through co-adaptation to the two different micro-level contexts. These actions expressed her nonprofessional, NS identity and thus differed between classes.

Ezgi's language teacher identity appeared to be in the process of emerging through micro-level classroom actions that became fodder for reflection-on-action. The feedback she received from micro-level actions was beginning to integrate itself so that she was consciously aware of herself as a teacher and could articulate her beliefs about it. However, there was little evidence that Ezgi's language teacher identity acted very strongly or intentionally at the micro level. Her practices did not yet reflect her conscious beliefs, such as the value of both culture and grammar teaching, which were associated with her teacher identity. She was not yet able to inhibit her language speaker identity in order to act through her language teacher identity.

Clearly documenting how an older and more firmly entrenched nonprofessional language speaker identity influences a professional activity identity makes this study an important contribution to the CDS literature on language teachers.

Consciousness and Causation

People who find emergence to be a compelling explanation of consciousness may do so because they are reluctant to accept the idea that the mind is fundamentally matter, yet are equally reluctant to abandon the idea that the universe is fundamentally matter. For some, consciousness is the one and only example of an ontologically emergent phenomenon (Chalmers, 2006).

Juarrero (1999) describes intentionality and causality as emergent phenomena in a dynamic relational system. Being a relational system has consequences for both the emergent macro-level system (mental functions) and its micro-level components (fundamental brain processes). Brain processes are necessary to mental functions, but mental functions are the context in which brain processes integrate into patterns. These patterns converge to form attractors, which constrain future behaviour, and 'therefore represent a dynamical system's organisation, including its external structure or boundary conditions' (Juarrero, 1999: 153).

Juarrero (1999), like O'Connor and Wong (2005), notes that constraints not only prevent possibilities from being actualised, but also open up new possibilities because 'previously independent parts are now components of a larger system and as such have acquired new functional roles' (Juarrero, 1999: 144). She argues that intentions are a constraint through which humans have causal efficacy over their actions.

A similar argument appears in SCT, where higher mental development is conceptualised as self-regulation, which crucially involves the ability to inhibit and constrain actions (Vygotsky, 1997). This process is researched through the genetic method, by introducing a mediational means through which a person can control mental functions such as attention and memory, in order to research whether and how it is used (Lantolf & Thorne, 2006). In language teaching and learning, it is most commonly done at the microgenetic, or inter/intrapersonal, level.

Feryok and Oranje (2015) conducted a microgenetic analysis on spoken data collected while a language teacher, Ada, discussed whether, and if so how, a cultural portfolio project could be introduced into her German as a foreign language class as part of the second author's doctoral research. They were able to capture the real-time emergence of a new attractor in the teacher's cognition. Although this approach was limited in that it did not involve the teacher's practices, the planning data avoided the usual LTC methodological issues of researcher-imposed perspectives and retrospective teacher accounts. A follow-up interview demonstrated differences in the teacher's cognition that the authors attributed to these methodological issues.

In the planning session, the researcher explained the project steps in order to discuss them with the teacher, Ada. During the explanation, Ada only asked two questions, one of which confirmed that the project involved a cultural comparison. This turned out to be significant, as Ada seemed to begin thinking of cultural comparison in terms of a speech that she regularly used as an assessment, suggesting that the researcher's explanation had implicitly primed Ada's cognition. The priming was reinforced when the researcher responded to Ada's question about cultural comparison by giving three examples of how students could compare cultures, one of which was a speech. When the researcher had completed the project steps, the teacher then took and maintained topic control for the rest of the planning session. Her first move was to explicitly link the project and the assessment she used in some of her classes by asking 'No, I'm kinda s-, um, um I have the question in my head if can I make that part of an assessment. Um, because, um, we, they're doing a speech' (Feryok & Oranje, 2015: 555–556). This was the first time that the teacher (or researcher) explicitly associated the research project with assessment. The authors call this emergent phenomenon the 'project-as-assessment' since it was similar to and different from both the researcher's outline of the project and the teacher's usual plan for the assessment. Ada's hesitancy, shown by the false start, filled pause and self-repair (which were uncharacteristic of her very confident speaking style) suggest the project-as-assessment was emergent because it was not a stable or pre-formed belief. This is highlighted by Ada articulating the association between 'that' (the research project) and 'part of an assessment' as a question. In other words, Ada realised she had a question, but she had not consciously formulated it. This may have been because her attention was focused on the research project until the term 'cultural comparison' recalled the assessment speech she used, quite literally dividing her attention between two attractors. It was not until Ada actually articulated her question that both her own and the researcher's attention focused on a single phenomenon, the 'project-as-assessment'. The authors noted, 'This process shows new attractors emerging when two or more are competing to stabilize into a pattern' (Feryok & Oranje, 2015: 558).

Once the attractor of project-as-assessment formed, it became a focal point for both the teacher and researcher. Although each returned to their original concepts, the teacher persistently reframed the discussion within the project-as-assessment in order to compare it to her other beliefs. The microgenetic analysis showed that, as the topics of utterances became less directly associated with the project-as-assessment, the teacher would return to it with utterances that referred to both the assessment and project. For example, when the teacher broached the idea of using the project as an assessment, she immediately raised the issue of the students' different spoken proficiency in the levels of classes she taught. She posed this as an issue for Jo's research needs but then reframed that issue within her project-as-assessment idea by saying, 'Cos if I did that [the project] as an assessment' (Feryok & Oranje, 2015: p. 556, line 121) various conditions would have to be met. For example, the teacher raised student self-regulation over research and writing, but again reframed the project-as-assessment with, 'So you know – cos it [the assessment] needs to be valid and work for your, project' (Feryok & Oranje, 2015: p. 556, line 128). The comments showed how not only actual feedback, but also expected or anticipated feedback from the researcher, stabilised the project-as-assessment attractor. The project-as-assessment therefore acted as a top-down constraint on the teacher's (and researcher's) cognition throughout the discussion, shaping the decisions made about implementing the project.

The authors also describe another causal effect of the project-as-assessment on the teacher's cognition. The first author conducted a traditional semi-structured research interview with the teacher after the planning session. Despite having raised and maintained focus on assessment for two-thirds of the planning session (and in 22 of the teacher's 43 turns) and explicitly considering it in light of the national curriculum and assessment standards, the authors state that the teacher said 'she made assessments fit into her teaching but did not teach toward them' (Feryok & Oranje, 2015: 554). They suggest that having planned how to fit the assessment into her teaching, Ada knew she could do it, and therefore her later report reflected her beliefs based on the planning process rather than her general beliefs.

Few studies have examined complex dynamic mental processes in language teachers because of the inherent difficulties in capturing teacher thought as teaching is done. This study shows reflection-in-action in a planning context, with the teacher spontaneously raising concerns through language learning concepts such as spoken proficiency and self-regulation. This study's contribution is to use microgenetic analysis to capture the dynamic process of emergence as it occurs, and not merely the results of a process described retrospectively, as in the other two studies considered here.

Sociocultural Theory and Emergence

There is considerable evidence that Vygotsky considered higher mental functions to be emergent. Therefore, it is not surprising that many studies in SCT focus on the genesis or emergence of a new function in real time, although there are also studies that rely on retrospective narrative accounts, just as has been true of some CDS accounts.

Vygotsky (1997) stated that 'all higher forms of behaviour can always be divided completely and into the natural, elementary neuromental processes that make it up' (Vygotsky, 1997: 80). However, he then pointed out that this does not exhaust psychology, since it only describes the relationship between lower and higher forms. Rather, he underlined, 'if we should want to limit ourselves exclusively to analysis or reducing the higher form to the lower, we would never be able to develop an adequate representation of all the specific features of the higher form and those patterns to which they are subordinate' (Vygotsky, 1997: 81). From Vygotsky's viewpoint, the study of these higher forms without reduction to their physical elements is the domain of psychology. It suggests an ontological as well as an epistemological commitment.

As previously mentioned, Vygotsky (1997) argued that the crucial difference between higher and lower level cognition is that higher level cognition – the domain of psychology – is semiotically and hence socially mediated. He supported this with empirical evidence in which mediated action was examined as it formed in real time. For example, in one series of experiments, children used various materials left near them as potential mnemonic aids, such coloured objects they could use to remember not to the utter the name of a colour forbidden by the 'game rules' of the experiment. The mnemonic aid mediated the children's responses to the prompts, enabling some of them to control their actions in a way they were unable to do without the aids. Vygotsky also noted that the nature of mediation – whether object, sign or word – changed how participants responded in the experiments. If the participants used objects to mediate their behaviours, then objects also regulated the cognitive function that was developing; if they used words to mediate their behaviours, then words also regulated the developing mental function.

The ability to self-regulate is the crucial difference for Vygotsky (1997) between higher and lower level functions. Vygotsky's colleague Luria (1961) later characterised self-regulated or voluntary action as developing with the ability to use others' speech, and then one's own speech, to inhibit automatic responses. This characterisation is similar to Juarrero's (1999) formulation of downward causation as emergent intentions that can constrain actions.

However, Vygotsky (1997) also argued that mediation directed outwardly (e.g. to control others) differed from mediation directed inwardly (e.g. to control oneself) because they functioned differently: the former socially, the latter psychologically. This led him to suggest, 'Self mastery is not constructed on obedience and intention, but, conversely, obedience and intention develop from self mastery' (Vygotsky, 1997: 86). A similar argument is made for attention, which develops through socially mediated actions that become internalised, establishing a new psychological function. Thus, SCT studies focus on identifying where social interactions presage psychological functions. Once a new psychological function is apparent in an individual, its genesis can be traced back to the social interaction.

One approach to microgenesis in language teacher studies has been through narrative enquiry. Johnson and Golombek (2011) outline three stages in the use of narrative enquiry that foster cognitive change: externalisation, verbalisation and systematic examination. In one example, they describe cooperative development, a technique described by Edge (1992) in which teachers non-judgementally discuss their practices, with one of them acting as an 'Understander' who non-judgementally mirrors the other teacher's ideas in order to prompt reflection. The data involved recorded and transcribed sessions between the focal teacher, Michael, and the Understander, teaching videos, and Michael's reflective narrative enquiry.

Michael was concerned about how he dealt with children who were quiet in class. In the first session, the Understander began by mirroring back Michael's uncertainty by paraphrasing his words. Because some paraphrases seemed inaccurate to Michael, he became aware of his uncertainty and was pushed to clarify what he really meant, which revealed that he dominated his students by interrupting them and summarising their words. Although Michael valued his tacit practice as a means of allowing students to assimilate information, he began to see how it discouraged students from speaking. By analysing his tacit practice, Michael became uncertain of it. The process of recognising his uncertainty, articulating it in order to understand it and realising the contradiction underlying it, emerged through his dialogue with the Understander.

Michael then stepped beyond his tacit practice to plan an activity in which students had control, but it was unsuccessful and he became frustrated. In the next session, the Understander mirrored back the teacher's frustration. Michael explained, 'Hearing this made me realise that the reason the quiet children has not been able to use this space may have been exactly because they had never had it before' (Johnson & Golombek, 2011: 318). As Johnson and Golombek (2011: 3019) explain, 'Michael used this "expert" knowledge to mediate himself to be able to make these experiences visible and then reinterpret them'.

The next time when he watched a video of his teaching, Michael wrote that 'after a while, I realised that I had nothing to fear by relinquishing some control' (Johnson & Golombek, 2011: 319), signalling a new emergent understanding of himself as a teacher. He also noted, 'Furthermore, I realised that I had a role to play in creating this space, by providing the structure for, or giving some shape to, the activity itself' (Johnson & Golombek, 2011: 319). It should be underlined that this role Michael envisioned for himself would take place in language. Johnson and Golombek (2011: 319) note this was evidence of the teacher 'regaining internal control in his behaviours' as a consequence of this emergent understanding, possibly through the confidence he developed by acting purposefully, since control was the very issue. What had been missing was teacher control over planning, which underlines the idea that self-regulation was a part of the emergent process. Because the planning and re-planning of the new activity was both causal and intentional, it seems clear that this example of emergence involves downward causation. This is likely to be due to the purposeful process of teacher development in which Michael was engaged, which offers support to the idea that it is not just awareness, but self-awareness, that contributes to emergence in LTC. In a sense, Michael recognised that he needed to use language more effectively in order to teach language more effectively – and this recognition itself also occurred in the language in which he reflected.

Implications: Emergence and Development

LTC research has shown that the tacit dimension develops through self-organisation of micro-level interactions of adapting to contextual changes (Aslan, 2015), which enables the emergence of new ideas (Feryok & Oranje, 2015), which can become the basis for reshaping teacher cognition and practice (Johnson & Golombek, 2011). The last of these provides the fullest account aimed at one of the more intractable issues in LTC: how to help teachers develop and change for the better. The success of that process seems to be attributable to the role of language, especially in narrative enquiry, in fostering self-awareness, especially of dissonance.

Narrative enquiry and the narrative formation of identity are well-established, well-attested constructs in both general teacher education and development (e.g. Clandinin & Connelly, 2000) and language teacher education and development (e.g. Barkhuizen, 2011). Some SCT research looks at how teachers recognise contradictions in their cognition by externalising it in dialogue with others, as in Michael's story. It can also occur in writing for oneself (Golombek & Johnson, 2004), and between colleagues in 'tiny talks' (Zoshak, 2016: 209). What is interesting is that in many of these cases the teachers were able to perform this process themselves, by creating an 'other' through the use of narrative.

Interestingly, Juarrero (2002) suggests that narrative is the most appropriate way to account for the complex and dynamic nature of human actions and intentionality. She states:

> Narrative, interpretive, and historical explanations of action thus require an expanded appreciation of what counts as 'reason' and 'explanation,' for they explain, not by subsuming an explanation under a generalization and thereby predicting it ... but rather by providing insight into and understanding of what actually happened. They do so by supplying a rich description of the precise, detailed path that the agent took, including the temporal and spatial dynamics (both physical and cultural) in which the agent was embedded and in which the action occurred. (Juarrero, 2002: 28)

The detailed stories in Johnson and Golombek (2002), several of which are reinterpreted through SCT (Golombek & Johnson, 2004; Johnson & Golombek, 2011), show this kind of detail and insight. However, the effects of the narrative process on teacher cognition hinge on using language to develop and articulate self-awareness. Through professional language in particular, awareness can be abstracted into 'lessons' that can be generalised to other experiences. This process has been described as 'classroom practices lead to cognitive dissonance, dissonance focuses attention, attention leads to awareness, awareness fosters cognitive change, and cognitive change prompts new practices' (Feryok, 2010: 277). This description is of an emergent sense of consciousness that has causal efficacy, which clearly fits praxis (Lantolf & Johnson, 2007) and perhaps also language teacher identity when it is both discursive and enacted (Varghese et al., 2005), language teacher expertise (Tsui, 2003), and even reflection-in-action (Schön, 1983) insofar as it actually draws on concepts and not only experience.

Juarrero (2002) points out that emergent intentions and plans (such as a teacher developing new beliefs and deciding to change classroom practices) limit the scope of possibilities, decreasing some while increasing others – in other words, it restructures them into a more strongly organised order. The two examples of emergence discussed here (Feryok & Oranje, 2015; Johnson & Golombek, 2011) presented evidence of teachers using language to become conscious of their cognition and its conceptual bases, although only one of them – Michael in Johnson and Golombek (2011) – enacted it in practice. Michael's cognition caused him to act intentionally, which arguably is at a different level from intentions and plans. However, his action then led to reflection, which in turn led to further action and reflection. These repeated cycles of expressing declarative knowledge about practices are also experiences that build up associations and contribute to tacit knowledge. It is this dual process of thinking and acting that may be at the centre of praxis. In the more modern parlance of the declarative-procedural model (Ullman, 2015), this is known as the redundancy hypothesis.

Conclusion

There is a sense in which novices, such as the teacher Aslan (2015) studied, are in the process of developing tacit knowledge because they are in the process of developing its necessary experiential basis – quite literally having sufficient memories to draw on to enable appropriate responses in a range of situations. This is a particular challenge for language teachers who contend with beliefs, knowledge and attitudes about language and its teaching and use based on their first language(s), as did the teacher Aslan studied, or based on practical language teaching experience, as did the teachers in Feryok and Oranje (2015) and Johnson and Golombek (2011).

Teaching practices involve judgements that can be based on systematic concepts, unarticulated everyday ones, trial and error or random choices. On any basis, associative memories of situations, behaviours and outcomes self-organise into patterns. As individual teacher actions increase and integrate with each other, they self-organise to become tacit knowledge or reflection-in-action: a way of acting and thinking like a teacher. Part of tacit knowledge is making judgements, which may or may not have a conceptual basis that enables them to be articulated (Davies, 2015) or, in SCT terms, semiotically mediated (Lantolf, 2006).

We therefore have two things, not one thing, both of which are included under LTC (Borg, 2006): tacit knowledge or reflection-in-action, and conceptual knowledge. From their integration, a macro-level pattern emerges, praxis. Praxis involves higher level thinking that can be articulated, which may be more or less integrated with practices, not only among different teachers, but within a teacher in different situations. This macro-level pattern is not a static characteristic but a dynamic process. It is the ability to act routinely when conscious control is not needed, to exercise conscious control over actions when it is needed, to do both more or less fluently, and to switch between them more or less fluently. This involves the tacit dimension and reflection-in-action, but also conceptual knowledge that enables articulation. Language teachers need to have conceptual knowledge not only of content and pedagogy, but also in the use of the language that they teach, which poses different problems for NSs and

NNSs, as Aslan's study showed. A NS language teacher may have limited conceptual knowledge of their native language, whereas a NNS language teacher may have limited cultural and sociolinguistic competence in the language they teach.

Teachers who have a more conceptual basis for their teaching and are better able to articulate it are able to act more efficaciously – with the intention to cause effects – because they have greater ability to regulate their thoughts and actions. Teachers who act randomly or even through trial and error may not develop such macro-level patterns. Their actions may self-organise, but they do not emerge to the extent of becoming conscious to teachers and potentially subject to their control. However, consciousness can eventually emerge through a variety of means, including those mentioned here: reflecting on teaching, as Ezgi did; participating in a classroom research project, as Ada did; engaging in professional development, as Michael did. It seems that being engaged in thinking and acting self-organises cognition and behaviour and, with purposeful reflection used in practice, emergence emerges.

These ideas suggest that language teacher education needs to focus on developing conceptual knowledge. This does not mean that practice should be ignored. On the contrary, conceptual knowledge needs to be both intentionally exercised in and purposefully extracted from practices so that teachers understand what and how they practise in order to self-regulate (as illustrated above in Johnson & Golombek, 2011). However, self-regulation cannot develop if there is no conceptual knowledge of language and its pedagogy. It is being able to re-conceptualise experience through professional language that transforms a story about teaching from a mere anecdote into a narrative for professional development. As in other professions, a sound body of conceptual knowledge is needed in language teacher education as the starting point for professional development.

This also indicates that LTC research needs to focus on whether conceptual knowledge underlies teaching practices. Of particular relevance to emergence are occurrences that are novel, as in Feryok and Oranje (2015), or difficult, as in Johnson and Golombek (2011); both studies showed how an emergent phenomenon transformed relationships among existing conceptual knowledge. Novelty and difficulty can also reveal whether compensatory redundant knowledge (Ullman, 2015) is available or needs to be developed in both experts and novices, such as whether systematic knowledge enables disrupted routines to be controlled. Retrodiction, as in Aslan (2015), can reveal the contextual influences that point to self-organisation and nascent emergence, which can be a basis for showing when and where conceptual knowledge starts to inhibit routines.

In order to research emergence, LTC research should be genetic, in that cognition should be researched as it emerges; longitudinal, in that emergence necessarily occurs over time; and contextualised, in that at any point a specific and changing set of conditions influences what and how cognition emerges. These specifications are resources as much as constraints on LTC research, in that they suggest that researcher attention needs to be refocused (rather than redirected) on what reveals LTC within the scope of a study. In order to do this, there must be a clear and consistent focus on the multiple roles that language itself plays in LTC: as the content of teaching, the medium through which teaching occurs, and perhaps most importantly for LTC, the means by which LTC develops.

References

Aslan, E. (2015) When the native is also a non-native: 'Retrodicting' the complexity of language teacher cognition. *Canadian Modern Language Review* 71 (3), 244–269.

Barkhuizen, G. (2011) Narrative knowledging in TESOL. *TESOL Quarterly* 45 (3), 391–414.

Borg, S. (2006) *Teacher Cognition and Language Education: Research and Practice*. London: Continuum.

Chalmers, D.J. (2006) Strong and weak emergence. In P. Clayton and P. Davies (eds) *The Reemergence of Emergence* (pp. 244–256). Oxford: Oxford University Press.

Clandinin, D.J. and Connelly, F.M. (2000) *Narrative Inquiry: Experience and Story in Qualitative Research*. San Francisco, CA: Jossey-Bass.

Davies, M. (2015) Knowledge (Implicit, explicit, and tacit): Philosophical aspects. In J.D. Wright (ed.) *International Encyclopaedia of Social and Behavioural Science* (2nd edn; pp. 74–90). Oxford: Elsevier.

Edge, J. (1992) *Cooperative Development*. Harlow: Longman.

Fenstermacher, G. (1986) Philosophy of research on teaching: Three aspects. In M.C. Wittrock (ed.) *Handbook of Research on Teaching* (3rd edn) (pp. 37–49). New York: Macmillan.

Feryok, A. (2010) Language teacher cognitions: Complex dynamic systems? *System* 38 (2), 272–279.

Feryok, A. and Oranje, J. (2015) Adopting a cultural portfolio project in teaching German as a foreign language: Language teacher cognition as a dynamic system. *The Modern Language Journal* 99 (3), 546–564.

Golombek, P.R. and Johnson, K.E. (2004) Narrative inquiry as a meditational space: Explaining emotional and cognitive dissonance in second language teachers' development. *Teachers and Teaching* 10 (3), 307–327.

Johnson, K.E. and Golombek, P.R. (2002) *Teachers' Narrative Inquiry as Professional Development*. Cambridge: Cambridge University Press.

Johnson, K.E. and Golombek, P.R. (2011) The transformative power of narrative in second language teacher education. *TESOL Quarterly* 45 (3), 486–509.

Juarrero, A. (1999) *Dynamics in Action*. Cambridge, MA: MIT Press.

Juarrero, A. (2002) Complex dynamical systems and the problems of identity. *Emergence* 4 (1–2), 94–104.

Lantolf, J.P. (2006) Language emergence: Implications for applied linguistics – a sociocultural perspective. *Applied Linguistics* 27 (4), 717–728.

Lantolf, J.P. and Johnson, K.E. (2007) Extending Firth and Wagner's (1997) ontological perspective to L2 classroom praxis and teacher education. *The Modern Language Journal* 91 (S1), 877–892.

Lantolf, J.P. and Poehner, M.E. (2014) *Sociocultural Theory and the Pedagogical Imperative in L2 Education: Vygotskian Praxis and the Research/Practice Divide*. New York: Routledge.

Lantolf, J.P. and Thorne, S.L. (2006) *Sociocultural Theory and the Genesis of L2 Development*. Oxford: Oxford University Press.

Larsen-Freeman, D. and Cameron, L. (2008) *Complex Systems and Applied Linguistics.* Oxford: Oxford University Press.

Luria, A.R. (1961) *The Role of Speech in the Regulation of Normal and Abnormal Behavior* (trans. J. Tizard). New York: Liveright.

Mercer, S. (2015) Dynamics of the self: A multilevel nested systems approach. In Z. Dörnyei, P.D. MacIntyre and A. Henry (eds) *Motivational Dynamics in Language Learning* (pp. 139–163). Bristol: Multilingual Matters.

Munby, H. (1989) Reflection-in-action and reflection-on-action. *Education and Culture* 9 (1), article 4. See http://docs.lib.purdue.edu/eandc/vol09/iss1/art4 (accessed 29 August 2016).

O'Connor, T. and Wong, H.Y. (2005) The metaphysics of emergence. *Noûs* 39, 658–678.

O'Connor, T. and Wong, H.Y. (2015) Emergent properties. In E.N. Zalta (ed.) *The Stanford Encyclopedia of Philosophy* (Summer 2015 edn). See http://plato.stanford.edu/archives/sum2015/entries/properties-emergent/ (accessed 29 August 2016).

Pasquale, M. (2011) Folk beliefs about second language learning and teaching. *AILA Review* 24, 88–99.

Polanyi, M. (1962) *Personal Knowledge.* New York: Routledge.

Polanyi, M. (1966) *The Tacit Dimension.* New York: Doubleday.

Schön, D.A. (1983) *The Reflective Practitioner: How Professionals Think in Action.* New York: Basic Books.

Stephan, A. (1999) Varieties of emergence. *Evolution and Cognition* 5 (1), 49–59.

Tsui, A. (2003) *Understanding Expertise in Teaching: Case Studies of Second Language Teachers.* Cambridge: Cambridge University Press.

Ullman, M.T. (2015) The declarative/procedural model. In B. VanPatten and J. Williams (eds) *Theories in Second Language Acquisition: An Introduction* (2nd edn) (pp. 135–158). Mahwah, NJ: Lawrence Erlbaum.

Varghese, M., Morgan, B., Johnston, B. and Johnson, K.A. (2005) Theorizing language teacher identity: Three perspectives and beyond. *Journal of language, Identity, and Education* 4 (1), 21–44.

Vintiadis, E. (2013) Emergence. *Internet Encyclopedia of Philosophy.* See http://www.iep.utm.edu/emergenc/ (accessed 29 August 2016).

Vygostky, L.S. (1986) *Thought and Language* (trans. and ed. A. Kozulin). Cambridge, MA: MIT Press.

Vygotsky, L.S. (1987) The historical meaning of the crisis in psychology: A methodological investigation. *The Collected Works of L.S. Vygotsky, Vol. 1.* New York: Plenum Press. (Original work published 1927.)

Vygotsky, L.S. (1997) Genesis of higher mental functions. In R.W. Rieber (ed.) *The Collected Works of L.S. Vygotsky, Vol. 4.* New York: Plenum Press. (Original work published 1931.)

Wagemans, J. (2015) Historical and conceptual background: Gestalt theory. In J. Wagemans (ed.) *The Oxford Handbook of Perceptual Organization* (pp. 3–20). Oxford: Oxford University Press.

Zoshak, R. (2016) 'Tiny talks' between colleagues: Brief narratives as mediation in teacher development. *Language Teaching Research* 20 (2), 209–222.

8 Language Teachers' Self-efficacy Beliefs: An Introduction

Mark Wyatt

Contextualising Self-efficacy Beliefs

In popular culture there has long been an awareness that self-confidence (a lay term relating to self-efficacy beliefs) has a vital role in influencing successful task completion. Indeed, in introducing self-efficacy beliefs, Frank Pajares includes historical quotes to make this point, citing Samuel Johnson's declaration from the 18th century that 'self-confidence is the first requisite to great undertakings' and Mahatma Gandhi's early 20th century affirmation: 'if I have the belief that I can do it, I shall surely acquire the capacity to do it even if I may not have it at the beginning' (Pajares, n.d.). However, in a sense, like positive psychology, the study of self-efficacy beliefs has 'a short history and a long past' (MacIntyre & Mercer, 2014: 154). Indeed, it was only in the middle of the 20th century, as Pintrich and Schunk (1996) report, that psychologists started turning away from Behaviourism to embrace a cognitive view of motivation, in which the individual was positioned as an active decision maker. Expectancy theories recognising the central role of the individual's cognitions in determining their behaviour were developed, and the study of self-efficacy beliefs, defined as 'people's judgements of their capabilities to organise and execute courses of action required to attain designated types of performances' (Bandura, 1986: 391), emerged. Self-efficacy beliefs are task-, domain- and context-specific, and need to be understood in relation to outcome expectations, in other words, the beliefs about the effects actions will have (Bandura, 1986). Since Bandura's work from the 1970s, self-efficacy beliefs have been studied in various domains, including branches of education, with a significant strand of this research focusing on teachers' self-efficacy (TSE) beliefs. Research into *language* teachers' self-efficacy (LTSE) beliefs has appeared more recently and is the focus of this chapter.

Self-efficacy and Expectancy Beliefs

In Bandura's (1986) social cognitive theory, individuals are conceived as symbolising, planning, learning and reflecting beings, who are able to initiate change if they feel sufficiently efficacious. Self-efficacy beliefs are said to emerge from reflected-upon performance accomplishments on previous tasks, vicarious experiences gained from observing or hearing about others' accomplishments, verbal persuasion provided in the form of feedback, and emotional arousal, i.e. information derived through the senses (Bandura, 1986). Self-efficacy beliefs are particularly important because they influence our choice of activities, how much effort we expend on them and how long we persist in the face of challenges (Bandura, 1977). In contrast to outcome expectations, which are 'means-ends' beliefs, efficacy expectations are 'agent-means' beliefs, i.e. beliefs about performing specific actions (Skinner, 1996). Bandura's (1977) conceptualisation of the relationship between self-efficacy beliefs and outcome expectations is depicted in Figure 8.1.

Depending on how efficacy and outcome expectations are aligned, different scenarios, in terms of possible behaviour and the well-being of individuals, can unfold, as the matrix in Table 8.1 suggests. To illustrate this matrix, let us take a hypothetical example from second language education. A sample teaching task might be concerned with helping students skim (a subskill of reading) texts such as newspaper articles for gist. Let us imagine six teachers.

- Teacher A feels inefficacious with regard to the task of teaching skimming for gist, but does not believe enacting it will lead to successful outcomes in any case. The likely result is task avoidance. This teacher's students are unlikely to get much help with skimming.
- Teacher B believes that skimming for gist is useful but, unsure how to make it interesting, feels inefficacious in supporting the development of this subskill. Also influenced by feeling inefficacious in the teaching of other reading subskills, this teacher generalises from these negative experiences and gives up, believing him/herself to be not very good at teaching reading.
- Teacher C believes teaching skimming for gist can lead to beneficial outcomes, but has low self-efficacy beliefs regarding the task of supporting learners in this. Nevertheless, this teacher channels self-doubt into

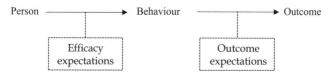

Figure 8.1 Diagrammatic representation of the difference between efficacy expectations and outcome expectations

Source: Reprinted from Bandura (1977: 193). © 1977 APA. Reprinted with permission.

Table 8.1 Matrix suggesting how task-specific efficacy and outcome expectations interact

	Low outcome expectations	High outcome expectations
Low efficacy expectations	Avoidance of the task.	Feelings of inadequacy which, if generalised, can result in giving up easily and withdrawal. However, self-doubt can also prompt reflection and growth.
High efficacy expectations	Relative lack of engagement.	Intense and persistent goal-directed behaviour, unless expectations are unrealistically high and complacency results.

renewed effort, drawing on different sources of efficacy information to support growth, e.g. vicarious experiences gained from seeing others succeed or verbal persuasion in the form of coaching from a mentor, gaining inspiration in the process. This all results in the development of more positive self-efficacy beliefs (and a move from the top right to the bottom right quadrant in Table 8.1).

- Teacher D feels efficacious in helping students skim, but does not really believe this activity will lead to beneficial outcomes and consequently does not engage with it very much. If there is little expectation that tasks will lead to valued outcomes, positive self-efficacy beliefs in enacting them are unlikely to have much beneficial impact on practice.
- Teacher E feels efficacious in helping students skim, believes the activity leads to beneficial outcomes and, in line with Bandura's (1986) theory, exhibits motivated on-task behaviour. This teacher seeks out further opportunities to help students practise skimming by modifying lesson content, expends more effort on the task, persists for longer in the event of difficulties, and also does so with a sense of accomplishment.
- Teacher F recognises the likely benefits of the activity and feels efficacious but, unfortunately, excessively so, with an apparently highly inflated sense of his/her own ability that leads to effort being reduced; complacency sets in.

Language teachers reading the descriptions above might be able to recognise similar configurations of efficacy and outcome expectations in relation to specific classroom tasks in themselves or their colleagues; teachers are likely to perceive the outcomes of tasks differently and feel more efficacious in enacting some of these than others. These beliefs are worth investigating since supporting language learning requires teachers who are highly efficacious in motivating different kinds of students to engage in a whole variety of beneficial language learning activities, while also remaining aware of types of activities in which they need to develop their sense of competence further. Now I will discuss the TSE beliefs literature in general before focusing specifically on the LTSE beliefs research that has more recently emerged from this body of work.

Confusion in the Study of Teachers' Self-efficacy Beliefs

Despite being based on a 'simple idea with significant implications' (Tschannen-Moran & Woolfolk Hoy, 2001: 783), research into TSE beliefs has been mired in conceptual and measurement confusion since its inception in the late 1970s (Klassen *et al.*, 2011; Tschannen-Moran *et al.*, 1998; Wheatley, 2005). As a consequence, there has been considerable debate 'as to what [these beliefs] are, how they are formed and develop, how they can be accessed through research and how the information resulting from such research can be used' (Wyatt, 2014: 166). Since LTSE beliefs research has been shaped by this debate within TSE beliefs research more broadly, key issues of relevance are addressed here to illuminate similar problems in our specific domain.

The first of these issues is a conceptual one. Interest in TSE beliefs can be dated to a 1976 RAND study, in which these beliefs were defined in terms of 'the extent to which the teacher believes he or she has the capacity to produce an effect on the learning of students' (Armor *et al.*, 1976: 23). They were assessed through the following two items:

(1) When it comes right down to it, a teacher really can't do much because most of a student's motivation and performance depends on his or her home environment.
(2) If I try really hard, I can get through to even the most difficult or unmotivated students. (Armor *et al.*, 1976: 23)

However, a conceptual issue that has been noted since then, e.g. by Tschannen-Moran *et al.* (1998), Klassen *et al.* (2011) and Wyatt (2014), is that these survey items actually relate more closely to another theory, not Bandura's (1977), but Rotter's (1966) locus of control; this locus of control can be either internal (if the individual believes they have the strategies to overcome obstacles and succeed) or external (if they believe a negative environment will overwhelm their efforts). Like Bandura (1977), Armor *et al.* (1976) use the term 'efficacy', but their definition, in focusing on the 'effect' the teacher produces, is actually describing an 'agent-ends' belief (Skinner, 1996). As with many definitions of TSE beliefs since (e.g. Tschannen-Moran & Woolfolk Hoy, 2001), there is an insufficient focus on *means* in Armor *et al.*'s (1976) definition: Which specific tasks might the teachers feel (in)efficacious about? Furthermore, regarding Bandura's (1977) concept of outcome expectations, this is quite different from external locus of control: believing that the environment can/cannot defeat your efforts (Armor *et al.*, 1976) is an entirely different concept from believing the strategies you employ can/cannot support learning.

Nevertheless, despite the clear conceptual differences between Rotter's (1966) and Bandura's (1977) theories, researchers influenced by both and seeking to fuse the concepts together dominated TSE beliefs research throughout the 1980s and 1990s. These researchers included Gibson and

Dembo (1984), who developed a subsequently much used and highly influential 16-item survey based on Armor *et al.*'s (1976) original two items. This elicited personal teaching efficacy (PTE) and what has since been labelled general teaching efficacy (GTE) through items including the following:

(1) If a student did not remember information I gave in a previous lesson, I would know how to increase his/her retention in the next lesson.
(2) The hours in my class have little influence on students compared to the influence of the home environment. (Gibson & Dembo, 1984: 581)

While the GTE item on 'the home environment' here clearly owes more to Rotter (1966) than Bandura (1977), Gibson and Dembo's (1984) conceptualisation of TSE beliefs was little challenged until Bandura (1997) intervened decisively, dismissing research into GTE beliefs as irrelevant to his theory, and Tschannen-Moran *et al.* (1998) then largely but not entirely (Wyatt, 2016) reinforced this argument. Nevertheless, Gibson and Dembo's (1984) conceptually flawed instrument remained popular well beyond the late 1990s, as Klassen *et al.*'s (2011) review of the TSE beliefs literature published between 1998 and 2009 reveals, and a minority of LTSE beliefs studies have also been influenced by it.

Conceptually, TSE beliefs research has generally been on a firmer footing since 1997. However, there are still issues with the way these beliefs are typically assessed through quantitative research. Since 2001, the most frequently used survey instrument (by LTSE as well as TSE beliefs researchers more generally) has been one developed by Tschannen-Moran and Woolfolk Hoy (2001). This instrument assesses PTE beliefs across three dimensions of teaching: instructional strategies, classroom management and student engagement. However, some items elicit agent-ends beliefs, e.g. 'How much can you do to control disruptive behaviour in the classroom?', while others elicit agent-means beliefs, e.g. 'To what extent can you use a variety of assessment strategies?' (Tschannen-Moran & Woolfolk Hoy, 2001: 800). These researchers make no attempt to assess outcome expectations, which they justify by following Bandura (1986) in arguing that, 'because they stem from the projected level of competence a person expects to bring to a given situation, outcome expectancies add little to the predictive power of efficacy measures' (Tschannen-Moran & Woolfolk Hoy, 2001: 787). However, while this may certainly be the case, embedded within their argument is an implicit assumption that TSE beliefs are to be elicited only in relation to behaviour that is inherently beneficial (from the perspective of the researcher), e.g. controlling disruptive behaviour (an agent-ends belief). Suppose, though, the above item were to be made more specific through the addition of a few words that incorporated the notion of 'means', e.g. 'How much can you do to control disruptive behaviour in the classroom by (shouting at the students/choosing appropriately motivating tasks/glaring angrily/developing with the students a class charter)?' Teachers may feel efficacious about using a whole range of strategies, not all of which are likely to meet with the approval of child psychologists and teacher educators. TSE beliefs may be more meaningful when elicited alongside data on actual practices.

Further issues relate to task-specificity and how much is lost in the quantification of results. Tschannen-Moran and Woolfolk Hoy (2001: 790) recognise that TSE beliefs are context- and domain-specific, but puzzle over the level of task-specificity to be measured: 'Is efficacy specific to teaching mathematics, or more specific to teaching algebra, or even more specific to teaching quadratic equations?' This is an issue that relates not just to item design but also to the treatment of data and use of results. So, while survey items might probe about classroom management or student engagement, scores are then typically quantified as follows:

> Items address a range of teaching tasks and situations, and scores are averaged across all subscale items. Typically, the reported scores are global measures of [TSE] beliefs – across all aspects of teaching, or all aspects of teaching for specific subjects, or all subscale items. (Wheatley, 2005: 749)

Aggregating scores across survey items in this way allows for the classification of teachers, typically as to whether their TSE beliefs are globally high or low, and this permits, through quantification, generalised relationships to be sought with factors such as student achievement, goal setting, planning and organisation (Tschannen-Moran & Woolfolk Hoy, 2001). As to how these results can then be used, this is rarely discussed. Wheatley (2005) highlights the danger, though, of them unethically influencing the recruitment or retention of teachers. There might also be implications for teacher education. Tschannen-Moran and Woolfolk Hoy (2007) have suggested that the results might be used to help future generations of teachers to become more efficacious, but the notion that in-service teachers might also be supported in developing more positive TSE beliefs, e.g. through engagement in action research (Henson, 2001), has very rarely been explored.

From the perspective of a constructivist teacher educator like Wheatley (2005), much of the literature can seem devoid of practical application, and this may be a product of excessive quantification that has led researchers away from the original TSE beliefs construct. To return to an example above, if we conceive that a teacher can develop more positive TSE beliefs in a task such as supporting learners in developing skimming reading skills (like Teacher C, above), then we can conceive that self-doubt prompting reflection might be part of that growth process (Wheatley, 2002). However, it is unclear whether some researchers in the quantitative tradition have been able to grasp the role of self-doubt, e.g. Tschannen-Moran and Johnson (2011), who describe the notion as a 'puzzle'. This may be because researchers are so used to thinking of TSE beliefs in global terms, with these beliefs furthermore not 'flexible' but 'formed early' and 'fixed' (see, for example, Chacón, 2005).

Consequently, there has been a call to make research into TSE beliefs more useful (Wheatley, 2005), first by recognising that TSE beliefs are task-, context- and domain-specific, in line with the original theory (Bandura, 1977). When conceptualised in this way, TSE beliefs are also conceived of as being 'flexible' not 'fixed', 'dynamic' not 'static' and open to positive change (Pajares, 1992). From this perspective, Wheatley (2002) highlights the importance of self-doubt in supporting growth, while Wyatt (2016) discusses developing task-specific TSE beliefs in relation to a learning cycle. These developments in TSE beliefs research mirror those with regard to research in other self-constructs, e.g. self-concept, which is increasingly understood as complex, dynamic and domain-sensitive (Mercer, 2011).

These developments suggest methodological implications for TSE beliefs researchers. If we accept that TSE beliefs do change dynamically, such as when influenced by teacher education programmes, then qualitative research is needed that is focused on emergent themes of individual importance to teachers and which explores, through methods including observations and interviews, the dynamism in detail. It also requires quantitative studies that go beyond the limitations of much of the correlational work in this field by examining how configurations of beliefs relate to specific practices (e.g. Choi & Lee, 2016), and mixed methods designs that explore the relationships between specific TSE beliefs and behaviour, e.g. Siwatu *et al.* (2016), which employs descriptive analysis of quantitative survey responses to identify TSE doubts to investigate subsequently in interview.

Language Teachers' Self-efficacy Beliefs: An Overview

TSE beliefs research has increasingly spread from general to specific domains, reaching science early (Enoch & Riggs, 1990), but other subject domains only in the 21st century. In their review of the TSE beliefs literature published between 1998 and 2009, Klassen *et al.* (2011) identified 32 studies in science, 17 in technology, nine in maths, seven in sports and physical education but only four in language and literacy (these four perhaps including LTSE beliefs studies, although none is specifically cited). However, in the intervening years there has been an upsurge of research in the language teaching domain. In reviewing the LTSE beliefs literature (Wyatt, 2017), I have located 98 relevant studies (postgraduate theses, book chapters and journal articles) published between 2005 and 2016, and provide a summary below (Table 8.2).

As Table 8.2 demonstrates, LTSE beliefs are being studied in a variety of international contexts, with pre- and in-service teachers mostly of English as a second or foreign language but also of other foreign

Table 8.2 Summary of language teachers' self-efficacy beliefs studies (2005–2016)

Place of origin	Studies of teachers of English as a second or foreign language						Studies of teachers of other languages
	Pre-service teachers (PST)			In-service teachers (IST)			
	Quantitative (Qt)	Mixed methods (M)	Qualitative (Ql)	Quantitative	Mixed methods (M)	Qualitative (Ql)	
Iran				37	3		
Turkey	6	7		3	1	1	1 (Qt, IST, German)
USA	2			1	1		1 (M, IST, French) 3 (Qt, IST, French, German, Spanish)
Oman	1					5	
Vietnam						4	
China	1			1		1	
Korea				2	1		
Taiwan		2			1		
Canada					1		1 (M, IST, French)
Ethiopia				2			
Japan					2		
Singapore						2	
Indonesia				1			
Malaysia							1 (Qt, IST, Arabic)
Thailand				1			
Venezuela					1		

languages, and through a variety of research methods. However, certain patterns are clearly discernible. The bulk of this literature is quantitative, with such methodology being utilised particularly heavily with in-service teachers in Iran. However, the study of LTSE beliefs is also notably common in Turkey, with this research tending to focus much more on pre-service teachers investigated through mixed methods as well as quantitative designs. Qualitative designs are generally in the minority and, indeed, only four different first researchers contributed to the 13 studies identified in five different contexts. Of the 85 studies that collected some quantitative data, 62 of these employed a version of Tschannen-Moran and Woolfolk Hoy's (2001) survey, while only three utilised that of Gibson and Dembo (1984), which represents progress (Klassen *et al.*, 2011), given the conceptual issues with this survey discussed above. However, many of the purely quantitative studies analysed LTSE beliefs in very global terms, searching for correlations between global self-report scores and factors such as emotional intelligence, critical thinking and metacognitive awareness, generally finding the relationships one would expect.

Particular Reasons for Exploring Language Teachers' Self-efficacy Beliefs

Positive LTSE beliefs contribute to psychological well-being crucial to the whole educational process (Mercer *et al.*, 2016), and if teachers feel efficacious across a range of tasks they are more likely to have the characteristics admired in intrinsically motivated, self-determined educators, i.e. 'curious, vital and self-motivated (…) agentic and inspired, striving to learn; extend themselves; master new skills; and apply their talents responsibly' (Ryan & Deci, 2000: 68). However, TSE beliefs can come under threat in various ways (Dörnyei & Ushioda, 2011), and this is perhaps even more so in the case of language teachers than of teachers in some other subject areas. Language teachers do not just need to contend with issues such as stress, limited autonomy and repetitive teaching content (Dörnyei & Ushioda, 2011), as teachers of all subjects tend to, but they may also have to work with highly demotivated language learners (Chambers, 1999), particularly in contexts where the language learning is compulsory but the learners see no obvious need for it (Lamb, 2004).

This affects teachers of different languages in various ways. Due to globalisation, a heavy bias towards English can lead to it being seen as the only foreign language worth learning in some contexts, where consequently the teachers of other foreign languages are suffering (Dörnyei & Ushioda, 2011). Moreover, 'the various critical discourses surrounding the global spread of English and its dominant status in relation to other languages' (Dörnyei & Ushioda, 2011: 184) can also threaten teachers of English, both native speakers (NS) and non-native speakers (NNS). For example, while also suffering from the anxiety that comes from needing to display competence in a language they are learning while teaching (Horwitz, 1996), NNS teachers 'may feel positioned negatively within the profession', experiencing conditions such as 'disempowerment, discrimination, imposter syndrome' (Dörnyei & Ushioda, 2011: 184) which can challenge their LTSE beliefs. Meanwhile, NS teachers 'may also feel vulnerable', particularly if their own variety of British/American English is being dismissed by those promoting World Englishes (Dörnyei & Ushioda, 2011: 184) or if those intent on defending NNS teachers are doing so through tactics including deriding NS teachers as unqualified backpackers. It would seem quite possible that these NS and NNS groups might feel more or less efficacious about different aspects of their work, e.g. grammar teaching or using communicative speaking activities, particularly in fast-changing contexts characterised by radical top-down curriculum change (Wedell, 2008).

What Do We Know to Date about Language Teachers' Self-efficacy Beliefs?

It has been observed by Phan (2015) that studies focused on LTSE beliefs have considered them in relation to the teachers' language proficiency, their attitudes towards the target language and/or their pedagogical practices, e.g. with regard to the use of grammar-translation (GTM) or communicative language teaching (CLT) methodology. Additionally, as Phan (2015) highlights, these beliefs have been explored in relation to teachers' practical knowledge and how this changes. While LTSE beliefs studies that fall into these categories represent a minority of those presented in Table 8.2, they tend to be the most domain-specific and are the focus of attention here.

In deciding how to face the challenge of providing insights into LTSE beliefs research, particularly for readers fairly new to this, I considered two main strategies: either aim for broad coverage through a literature review (my initial idea, but it grew too large and I have developed it separately) or offer descriptive analyses of studies selected to highlight developments in the field, exploring these studies in sufficient depth to shed light on both findings and how the studies were constructed; for reasons of space, I chose the second option here. The studies examined include the first (and most cited) mixed methods study to have explored the relationship between LTSE beliefs, language proficiency and teaching practices. I then review a recent cutting-edge quantitative study exploring similar issues. I also consider a group of mixed methods studies exploring changes in LTSE beliefs in pre-service teachers in the national context in which such change has been most frequently documented (Turkey), and next reflect on a group of qualitative studies of in-service teachers in Oman, whose developing LTSE beliefs were explored in depth through numerous observations and interviews over time, this prolonged longitudinal engagement being extremely rare. Finally, I consider a mixed methods Canadian study of novice teachers of French, which is distinctive in considering the impact of the marginalisation of the foreign language taught on LTSE beliefs. This selection of studies, while subjective, thus addresses the main themes of interest signalled above and is inclusive of research utilising a variety of methodological approaches. This is with a view to helping the reader gain an impression of the field as a whole.

Language teachers' self-efficacy beliefs, language proficiency, and communicative language teaching and grammar-translation methodology approaches in Venezuela

Chacón's (2005) LTSE beliefs study is set in a Venezuelan context in which CLT is actively being promoted by the local Ministry of Education, with the goal of helping school leavers to use English to communicate competently 'with people from English speaking (sic) countries' (Chacón, 2005: 260). However, as Chacón (2005: 260) states, 'the implementation of CLT requires EFL teachers who possess the competency of the language in order to teach it', and she questions the extent to which this is the case in Venezuela. No demonstration of competency is required of new teachers, while teacher education programmes focus not on developing this but on descriptive linguistics. Chacón is interested in the self-reported TSE beliefs for engagement, classroom management and the instructional strategies of EFL teachers in middle schools, their self-reported English proficiency levels in listening, speaking, reading, writing and cultural knowledge, and the pedagogical strategies they report using to teach EFL.

Chacón (2005) adopted a mixed methods design, combining three surveys (one eliciting TSE beliefs, another self-reported English proficiency and the third self-reported pedagogical strategies) completed by 100 in-service teachers, with qualitative semi-structured interviews then conducted with 20 of these teachers, during which vignettes describing teaching situations were presented for comment. The TSE beliefs survey was based on Tschannen-Moran and Woolfolk Hoy (2001), slightly adapted for English (e.g. 'How much can you use a variety of assessment strategies in your English class?'), while the proficiency survey included items such as 'I can understand English films without subtitles'; the third survey contained items describing CLT and GTM practices (e.g. 'Students copy grammar exercises from the blackboard after the teacher's explanation') (Chacón, 2005: 263–264). The vignettes related to using dialogues, songs, group work and problem solving.

With regard to the findings, the most striking is that 'the higher the participants' sense of efficacy, the more likely they were to use either communication-oriented or grammar-oriented strategies' (Chacón, 2005: 265). This suggests that high TSE beliefs might relate to clear methodological choices, but should not necessarily be seen as a goal in themselves – a point made by Wheatley (2005). In this context, for example, given government policies, it might be regarded as undesirable for teachers to be efficacious about using GTM. As argued above and elsewhere (e.g. Wyatt, 2015), it can be very useful to compare TSE beliefs scores with data relating to classroom practices.

Another interesting finding is that quantitative data in Chacón's (2005) study revealed positive correlations between self-reported LTSE beliefs and self-reported proficiency, but in the interviews teachers who had been selected because they had reported high LTSE beliefs overall confessed to limited proficiency, as did teachers selected because they had reported low LTSE beliefs; of course, the more efficacious teachers may have been speaking modestly, but this finding does demonstrate the value of using more than one method to triangulate findings. This is not to suggest, though, that the positive relationship between LTSE beliefs and language proficiency identified in this study was itself surprising. It has been observed elsewhere. A study of NS and NNS teachers of French in the United States, for example, identified higher efficacy levels in the former group, who were presumably more comfortable in the language they were teaching (Mills & Allen, 2007). Finally, in Chacón's (2005) Venezuelan context, most teachers appeared more oriented towards GTM than CLT approaches, which again is perhaps not surprising, given the teachers' educational background, limited language proficiency (which may have made it harder to engage with CLT activities for these, as Chacón argues, can make unpredictable linguistic demands), and the scarcity of in-service teacher education in the context.

Chacón's (2005) study has been partially replicated, e.g. in an Iranian context by Eslami and Fatahi (2008), who used surveys (with 40 novice participants who had up to five years' experience each) but not interviews. Unlike Chacón (2005), Eslami and Fatahi (2008) did find positive correlations between LTSE beliefs and CLT strategies, which may perhaps partly reflect the teacher education available in the Iranian capital (although this is little discussed). Alternatively, the finding could partly be a product of the research design; for example, teachers might readily identify with items such as 'I give students the opportunity to get into groups and discuss answers to problem-solving activities' (Eslami & Fatahi, 2008: 12), as this could be seen as describing 'appropriate' behaviour which might fit with their idealised cognitions (Borg, 2006), even if their actual behaviour is quite different. It is perhaps much easier to say that you encourage problem-solving in groups (and teachers scored themselves highly on this item) than to actually do it or even to go into details about how. Interestingly, none of the ten apparently highly efficacious teachers Chacón (2005) interviewed chose the option of discussing a CLT-oriented vignette about problem-solving through group work in relation to their classes. When evaluating the findings of these studies, we need to look closely at the methodology employed and the implications of this for the findings and further research.

Language teachers' self-efficacy beliefs, target language proficiency and linguistic practices in Korea

Another approach to exploring the impact of LTSE beliefs and self-perceptions of language proficiency on classroom practice is to consider NNS teachers' target language (TL) use in class. This is the focus of Choi and Lee's (2016) quantitative study of 167 secondary school EFL teachers in Korea, a context where English-only policies are mandated but where, previous research suggests, confidence in English language proficiency among NNS teachers may not always be very high. From a theoretical perspective, self-efficacy beliefs affect choice behaviour (Bandura, 1986), and if teachers feel inefficacious with regard to carrying out tasks in English such as instructing and explaining, then they are likely to avoid the TL for these purposes, switching to the mother tongue instead. An unfortunate consequence of such behaviour is that the limited TL exposure can have a negative impact on learners' attempts to acquire the language (Macaro, 2005).

To investigate this issue, Choi and Lee (2016) developed the following quantitative instruments: self-reports on the percentage of class time allocated to English and on the frequency of English used for teaching; self-ratings for English language proficiency and ratings of the minimum proficiency levels required of secondary school English teachers (the difference being a perceived proficiency gap); and an LTSE beliefs survey blending items from Tschannen-Moran and Woolfolk Hoy's (2001) and Dellinger *et al.*'s (2008) tools. Choi and Lee (2016) conducted multiple regression analysis with interaction to help explain the simultaneous influence of self-perceived linguistic and pedagogical competence on practice.

Findings revealed a threshold level below which the NNS teachers appeared to use very little classroom English, but above which language proficiency and LTSE beliefs interacted positively, resulting in expanding TL use. Despite the self-report nature of the data, the study provides strong evidence that teachers need both linguistic and pedagogical preparation (Choi & Lee, 2016).

Choi and Lee's (2016) research design, involving multiple regression analysis with interaction, could usefully be employed to assess the impact of factors besides language proficiency, e.g. attitudes towards World Englishes. With regard to the latter, Lee's (2009) mixed methods study of over 1000 Korean EFL teachers found that NNS teachers who were more bound by NS norms (e.g. valuing American English in the classroom) were also less efficacious, but it is unclear if or how this affected their teaching.

Changes in language teachers' self-efficacy beliefs during pre-service teacher education in Turkey

In the last decade, approximately a dozen studies set in Turkey have explored the impact of the practicum on LTSE beliefs. Given that there had been very little research into efforts to support growth in TSE beliefs prior to Henson (2001), this development is encouraging. Characteristics of this Turkish LTSE beliefs research typically include the use of mixed methods designs, with quantitative surveys, usually based on Tschannen-Moran and Woolfolk Hoy's (2001) instrument which are sometimes translated into Turkish, administered more than once and supplemented by qualitative data from focus group discussions, reflective diaries or open-ended survey questions. This research provides insights into how LTSE beliefs can change, perhaps influenced by different aspects of the practicum experience, and with regard to different dimensions of the tasks faced by the NNS EFL teachers.

To uncover fluctuations in LTSE beliefs and the reasons for these, Turkish researchers have administered surveys at the following time points: at the start of the practicum year (Time 1); after observing classes in schools in the first semester (Time 2); and after practicum teaching in the second semester (Time 3). Teachers have also been followed through to the end of a novice year (Time 4). Yüksel's (2014) study of 40 pre-service teachers, for example, noted an overall fall in LTSE beliefs scores between Times 1 and 2, before an overall rise in Time 3, ascribing these changes, first, to vicarious experiences of observing classes weakening LTSE beliefs, before performance accomplishments in a relatively sheltered environment strengthened them. In Şahin and Atay's (2010) study of 27 pre-service teachers, scores also rose between Times 2 and 3. However, they then fell by the end of the induction year (Time 4); the 'reality shock' that novice teachers often experience (Tschannen-Moran & Woolfolk Hoy, 2007) may have set in. Other studies have examined the impact on LTSE beliefs of teacher education strategies employed on the practicum, such as the beneficial introduction of action research (Cabaroglu, 2014). Examining changes to scores on different items when a survey is being re-administered can provide insights into how training needs are being addressed. In Atay's (2007) study of 78 pre-service teachers, scores fell over time on items related to questioning, suggesting that more support for this may have been needed.

Changes in language teachers' self-efficacy beliefs during in-service teacher education in Oman

A further set of studies I will consider emerged from a qualitative, longitudinal multi-case study of five in-service NNS English teachers in Oman, which made use of observations (five to six per teacher), semi-structured interviews (seven to eight per teacher) and analyses of reflective writing produced throughout a three-year course, during which the researcher, as teacher educator, provided teaching and mentoring (Wyatt, 2008). This intensive and prolonged engagement allowed individual cases within the study to be centred on themes of concern to the teachers.

Emerging through observations and post-lesson discussion interviews, these themes eventually became central to the teachers' undergraduate theses, e.g. on using communicative tasks to develop speaking skills or using group work to support low achievers.

LTSE beliefs were defined as teachers' beliefs in their abilities to support language learning in various task-, domain- and context-specific cognitive, metacognitive, affective and social ways, and there was an emphasis throughout on exploring how developing LTSE beliefs related to developing practical knowledge. This was evident in articles that came out of the original study (e.g. Wyatt, 2010), which explored a teacher's uneven task-specific LTSE beliefs in relation to apparently uneven practical knowledge. A good degree of fit was identified, with the teacher reporting feeling inefficacious, for example, about organising reading races in groups, a curriculum activity which he appeared to struggle with, but efficacious in encouraging learners to scaffold their peers' efforts in other kinds of group work activities, a claim which observational data and further interview data supported. In another case, however, discussed in Wyatt (2015), there did not appear to be such a good degree of fit. A teacher reported feeling efficacious about helping learners overcome difficulties in reading, but the observed strategies, involving reading around the class, did not seem very effective. The teacher appeared to have strong means-ends beliefs (Skinner, 1996) in the value of these strategies and strong agent-means beliefs that he could make use of them, and the role of teacher education in such a situation appeared to revolve around challenging the means-ends beliefs to prompt self-doubt (Wheatley, 2002).

Another article from the same multi-case study focused on a teacher overcoming low LTSE beliefs in teaching young learners, which represented a very different challenge, since she had previously taught much older students (Wyatt, 2013). Suffering from anxiety or negative emotional arousal (Bandura, 1977) manifested in uncertainty in the classroom and sleep loss, she faced classroom management issues she needed to learn how to resolve. However, through reflective learning and supported by a growth mindset (Dweck, 2000), the teacher made considerable progress, becoming much more efficacious in using strategies that appeared to lead to beneficial learning outcomes, as subsequent observational and interview data highlighted (Wyatt, 2013). Prior to this study, Dweck's (2000) work on mindsets, which are increasingly understood as domain-specific and dynamic (Mercer & Ryan, 2009), had rarely been drawn upon in studies of LTSE beliefs.

Novices' LTSE beliefs impacted by the marginalisation of French in Canada

Finally, I consider a Master's dissertation, which is rare in the LTSE beliefs literature in shedding light on how the marginalisation of the foreign language taught is linked to these beliefs. The setting was Cooke's (2013) Canadian context where learners study French as a core subject, for one period per day, in English language elementary schools. As Cooke reports, the marginalisation of French in such schools is an issue that has long been recognised; the teachers do not always have their own classrooms, can feel positioned as outsiders and sometimes need to combat negative attitudes within the school community. Such issues also emerge in the qualitative phase of Cooke's study. Indeed, Cooke quotes a teacher of French as reporting: 'some of the staff [say] "it's just French, it's just French; they are not going to get it anyway". I feel like it's an uphill battle, with the kids and sometimes the staff' (Cooke, 2013: 77). The same teacher also indicates experiencing a sense of isolation as the only French subject teacher in the school, and therefore feeling deprived of positive efficacy-building experiences such as those that can be obtained through mentoring (Wyatt, 2016). Comparing novice teachers in schools where French was a 'core' subject and where a more intensive French immersion programme was followed, Cooke (2013) found that the immersion teachers, working in more supportive environments, were more efficacious. As such, this small-scale study highlights the need to challenge negative attitudes and provide appropriate support systems for novice foreign language teachers as well as consider the status of the language being taught within that specific context.

Conclusions

Inevitably, this brief survey of selected LTSE beliefs studies has left interesting work uncovered, such as the role of culture and gender (Phan, 2015); other pertinent issues are awaiting further research, e.g. the threats to the LTSE beliefs of NS teachers from the global discourse on World Englishes (Dörnyei & Ushioda, 2011).

However, in the research reported on above, it is possible to discern positive trends. First, not only has domain-specific TSE beliefs research relevant to our field developed, but it has also focused on issues that matter: the way these beliefs intersect with language proficiency to shape language practices in class; the recognition that these fluid beliefs grow and change, influenced by a range of experiences, including teacher education (pre- and in-service); the understanding that these beliefs can be evaluated through triangulation in terms of degree of fit with practical knowledge and classroom practice and that an analysis of whether beliefs are agent-means or means-ends can shape strategies employed by teacher educators; the realisation that particular groups of teachers can feel particularly vulnerable and in need of nurturing support, e.g. NNS teachers at the start of their careers, teachers faced with sudden changes to the curriculum or teachers of marginalised foreign languages. This review demonstrates above all that LTSE beliefs studies utilising a range of methodological approaches (quantitative, qualitative and mixed methods) can be useful in identifying ways of helping teachers to become more efficacious, more imbued with positive psychology that will help them in their work.

References

Armor, D., Conroy-Oseguera, P., Cox, M., King, N., McDonnell, L., Pascal, A., Pauly, E. and Zellman, G. (1976) Analysis of the school preferred reading programs in selected Los Angeles minority schools. Report No. R-2007-LAUSD. RAND Corporation, Santa Monica, CA.

Atay, D. (2007) Beginning teacher efficacy and the practicum in an EFL context. *Teacher Development* 11 (2), 203–219.

Bandura, A. (1977) Self-efficacy: Toward a unifying theory of behavioral change. *Psychological Review* 84 (2), 191–215.

Bandura, A. (1986) *Social Foundations of Thought and Action: A Social Cognitive Theory.* New York: Prentice-Hall.

Bandura, A. (1997) *Self-efficacy: The Exercise of Control.* New York: Freeman.

Borg, S. (2006) *Teacher Cognition and Language Education: Research and Practice.* London: Continuum.

Cabaroglu, N. (2014) Professional development through action research: Impact on self-efficacy. *System* 44, 79–88.

Chacón, C.T. (2005) Teachers' perceived efficacy among English as a foreign language teachers in middle schools in Venezuela. *Teaching and Teacher Education* 21 (3), 257–272.

Chambers, G.N. (1999) *Motivating Language Learners.* Clevedon: Multilingual Matters.

Choi, E. and Lee, J. (2016) Investigating the relationship of target language proficiency and self-efficacy among nonnative EFL teachers. *System* 58, 49–63.

Cooke, S. (2013) The self-efficacy beliefs of novice elementary French as a second language teachers. Unpublished Master's dissertation, University of Western Ontario.

Dellinger, A.B., Bobbett, J.J., Olivier, D.F. and Ellett, C.D. (2008) Measuring teachers' self-efficacy beliefs: Development and use of the TEBS-Self. *Teaching and Teacher Education* 24 (3), 751–766.

Dörnyei, Z. and Ushioda, E. (2011) *Teaching and Researching Motivation* (2nd edn). Harlow: Longman.

Dweck, C.S. (2000) *Self-theories: Their Role in Motivation, Personality and Development.* Philadelphia, PA: Taylor & Francis.

Enoch, L.G. and Riggs, I.M. (1990) Further development of an elementary science teaching efficacy belief instrument: A preservice elementary scale. *Social Science and Mathematics* 90 (8), 694–706.

Eslami, Z.R. and Fatahi, A. (2008) Teachers' sense of self-efficacy, English proficiency, and instructional strategies: A study of non-native EFL teachers in Iran. *TESL-EJ* 11 (4), 1–19.

Gibson, S. and Dembo, M. (1984) Teacher efficacy: A construct validation. *Journal of Educational Psychology* 76 (4), 569–582.

Henson, R.K. (2001) The effects of participation in teacher research on teacher efficacy. *Teaching and Teacher Education* 17 (7), 819–836.

Horwitz, E.K. (1996) Even teachers get the blues: Recognizing and alleviating language teachers' feelings of foreign language anxiety. *Foreign Language Annals* 29 (3), 365–372.

Klassen, R.M., Tze, V.M.C., Betts, S.M. and Gordon, K.A. (2011) Teacher efficacy research 1998–2009: Signs of progress or unfulfilled promise? *Educational Psychology Review* 23 (1), 21–43.

Lamb, M. (2004) Integrative motivation in a globalizing world. *System* 32 (1), 3–19.

Lee, J.A. (2009) Teachers' sense of efficacy in teaching English, perceived English language proficiency, and attitudes towards the English language: A case of Korean public elementary school teachers. Unpublished PhD thesis, Ohio State University.

Macaro, E. (2005) Codeswitching in the L2 classroom: A communication and learning strategy. In E. Llurda (ed.) *Non-native Language Teachers: Perceptions, Challenges and Contributions to the Profession* (pp. 63–84). New York: Springer.

MacIntyre, P.D. and Mercer, S. (2014) Introducing positive psychology to SLA. *Studies in Second Language Learning and Teaching* 4 (2), 153–172.

Mercer, S. (2011) The self as a complex dynamic system. *Studies in Second Language Learning and Teaching* 1 (1), 57–82.

Mercer, S. and Ryan, S. (2009) A mindset for EFL: Learners beliefs about the role of natural talent. *ELT Journal* 64 (4), 436–444.

Mercer, S., Oberdorfer, P. and Saleem, M. (2016) Helping language teachers to thrive: Using positive psychology to promote teachers' professional well-being. In D. Gabryś-Barker and D. Gałajda (eds) *Positive Psychology Perspectives on Foreign Language Learning and Teaching* (pp. 213–229). Cham: Springer.

Mills, N.A. and Allen, H. (2007) Teacher self-efficacy of graduate teaching assistants of French. In H.J. Siskin (ed.) *From Thought to Action: Exploring Beliefs and Outcomes in the Foreign Language Program*. Boston, MA: Thomson Heinle.

Pajares, F.M. (n.d.) *Information on Self-efficacy: A Community of Scholars*. See http://www.uky.edu/~eushe2/Pajares/self-efficacy.html (accessed 14 September 2016).

Pajares, F.M. (1992) Teachers' beliefs and educational research: Cleaning up a messy construct. *Review of Educational Research* 62 (3), 307–332.

Phan, N.T.T. (2015) Can I teach these students? A case study of Vietnamese teachers' self-efficacy in relation to teaching English as a foreign language. Unpublished PhD thesis, University of Waikato.

Pintrich, P.R. and Schunk, D.H. (1996) *Motivation in Education: Theory, Research and Applications*. Upper Saddle River, NJ: Prentice Hall.

Rotter, J. (1966) Generalized expectancies for internal versus external control of reinforcement. *Psychological Monographs* 80 (1), 1–28.

Ryan, R.M. and Deci, E.L. (2000) Self-determination theory and the facilitation of intrinsic motivation, social development and well-being. *American Psychologist* 55 (1), 68–78.

Şahin, F.E. and Atay, D. (2010) Sense of efficacy from student teaching to the induction year. *Procedia Social and Behavioral Sciences* 2 (2), 337–341.

Siwatu, K.O., Chesnut, S.R., Alejandro, A.Y. and Young, H.A. (2016) Examining preservice teachers' culturally responsive teaching self-efficacy doubts. *Teacher Educator* 51 (4), 277–296.

Skinner, E.A. (1996) A guide to constructs of control. *Journal of Personality and Social Psychology* 71 (3), 549–570.

Tschannen-Moran, M. and Johnson, D. (2011) Exploring literacy teachers' self-efficacy beliefs: Potential sources at play. *Teaching and Teacher Education* 27 (4), 751–761.

Tschannen-Moran, M. and Woolfolk Hoy, A. (2001) Teacher efficacy: Capturing an elusive construct. *Teaching and Teacher Education* 17 (7), 783–805.

Tschannen-Moran, M. and Woolfolk Hoy, A. (2007) The different antecedents of self-efficacy beliefs of novice and experienced teachers. *Teaching and Teacher Education* 23 (6), 944–956.

Tschannen-Moran, M., Woolfolk Hoy, A. and Hoy, W.K. (1998) Teacher efficacy: Its meaning and measure. *Review of Educational Research* 68 (2), 202–248.

Wedell, M. (2008) Developing a capacity to make 'English for everyone' worthwhile: Reconsidering outcomes and how to start achieving them. *International Journal of Educational Development* 28 (6), 628–639.

Wheatley, K.F. (2002) The potential benefits of teacher efficacy doubts for educational reform. *Teaching and Teacher Education* 18 (1), 5–22.

Wheatley, K.F. (2005) The case for reconceptualizing teacher efficacy research. *Teaching and Teacher Education* 21 (7), 747–766.

Wyatt, M. (2008) Growth in practical knowledge and teachers' self-efficacy during an in-service BA (TESOL) programme. Unpublished PhD thesis, University of Leeds.

Wyatt, M. (2010) An English teacher's developing self-efficacy beliefs in using groupwork. *System* 38 (4), 603–613.

Wyatt, M. (2013) Overcoming low self-efficacy beliefs in teaching English to young learners. *International Journal of Qualitative Studies in Education* 26 (2), 238–255.

Wyatt, M. (2014) Towards a re-conceptualization of teachers' self-efficacy beliefs: Tackling enduring problems with the quantitative research and moving on. *International Journal of Research & Method in Education* 37 (2), 166–189.

Wyatt, M. (2015) Using qualitative research methods to assess the degree of fit between teachers' reported self-efficacy beliefs and their practical knowledge during teacher education. *Australian Journal of Teacher Education* 40 (1), Article 7.

Wyatt, M. (2016) 'Are they becoming more reflective and/or efficacious?' A conceptual model mapping how teachers' self-efficacy beliefs might grow. *Educational Review* 68 (1), 114–137.

Wyatt, M. (2017) Language teachers' self-efficacy beliefs: A review of the literature. (Manuscript submitted for publication.)

Yüksel, H.G. (2014) Becoming a teacher: Tracing changes in pre-service English as a foreign language teacher's sense of efficacy. *South African Journal of Education* 34 (3), 1–8.

9 Teacher Emotions and the Emotional Labour of Second Language Teaching

Jim King and Kwan-Yee Sarah Ng

While it is true that in recent times applied linguistics researchers have begun to show an increased interest in the role that learners' emotions play in the second language acquisition (SLA) process (e.g. Imai, 2010; Mercer, 2006), research on second language (L2) teacher emotions still remains decidedly scant. This is surprising when we consider that both learning *and* teaching are inherently emotional endeavours, with classrooms playing host to a whole gamut of emotional experiences, which can impact upon the effectiveness of learning and the quality of teaching in both positive and negative ways. Taking the stance that emotional experiences are psychological, interactional and social processes (see Denzin, 1984), which emerge from a dynamic interplay between individuals and their immediate environment, this chapter first offers an integrated framework for conceptualising emotions in SLA based on an overview of major studies into teacher emotions. It then goes on to outline a recent study by the lead author (King, 2016), which illustrates how *emotional labour* (Hochschild, 1979, 1983) exemplifies the multidimensional and multilevel forces at play in the SLA teaching and learning process. The study explored how expatriate instructors teaching English within a Japanese university employed emotional labour, that is, managed their in-class emotional displays during interactions with students, in order to achieve educational goals and conform to tacit social norms associated with their professional roles. The forced performance of emotions can be inherently stressful when a dissonance exists between the individual's true feelings and his or her sanctioned emotional display. The chapter therefore considers the link between emotional labour and teacher stress, and concludes by offering some practical suggestions as to how teachers might best enhance their psychological well-being through the use of emotion regulation techniques based on Gross' (2002, 2008) model of the emotion generative process.

Conceptions of Teacher Emotion in Educational Research

Given the social and emotion-laden nature of teaching and learning (Nias, 1996; Schutz & Zembylas, 2009; Sutton & Wheatley, 2003), it was a tremendous surprise to us that research on emotion in education had remained dormant until two decades ago when Nias (1996) initiated a discussion on the emotional nature of teaching in a special edition of the *Cambridge Journal of Education*. With a long history of research in the cognitive and motivational aspects of teaching as the backdrop, educational researchers have only just begun to conceptualise how emotions could influence or enhance one's access to knowledge and skills repertoire. While taking shape fast, this subfield of education research, still in its infancy, has therefore been forced to draw from the literature of various related disciplines, such as social psychology, cultural psychology and organisational management. Based on the major approaches to emotion thus far in these fields, this chapter discusses a possible integration of their ideas in understanding teacher emotion in SLA, with a special focus on the sociocultural and social psychological conceptions of emotion (Schutz & DeCuir, 2002).

Emotion in social psychology

Emotions are a salient feature of the social world and are thus a core topic in social psychology. Geared towards understanding how emotion transacts with cognition, the primary theories of emotion in social psychology are cognitive-orientated and are focused on the intra-organismic dimension, that is, the within-individual processing of emotion in relation to cognition, motivation and behaviour. Among them, the most influential are the appraisal theories of emotions (e.g. Lazarus, 1991), where emotion is viewed as the product of one's evaluation, conscious or subconscious, of the relevance and significance of a situation to one's well-being (for details, see Smith & Lazarus, 1993; for a quick review, see Parrott, 2001; for ongoing debate on the relationship between cognition and emotion, see Storbeck & Clore, 2007). In this view, emotions relate to an appraisal of a personally meaningful goal and to what extent it is achieved. While appraisal theories of emotion are focused on the cognitive relation between the person and environment, they are not so much concerned with the sociocultural or historical forces that are possibly at play in the appraisal or in other parts of emotional processing. Furthermore, the influences of other individuals present within interactions also tend not to be the focus of attention. These forces, referred to as the inter-organismic dimension in our proposed model, are at the heart of teacher education research thus far and of the study presented in this chapter.

Emotion in education and teacher research

The reported study in this chapter is aligned to the key themes of the existing teacher emotion literature. Drawing mainly from social psychology, to date the bulk of teacher emotion studies have focused on two themes: investigating the types of emotions teachers have and the conditions under which they occur (e.g. Chen, 2016; Hagenauer & Volet, 2014; Hargreaves, 2005; van Veen *et al.*, 2005), with many of them conducted as an attempt to understand teachers' conceptual development (e.g. Galman, 2009), teacher burnout (e.g. Zhang & Zhu, 2008) and the impact of education reforms (e.g. Hargreaves, 2005). As will be seen in the proposed framework, teacher emotion in these areas is under pervasive, dynamic, multidirectional sociocultural influences at not only intra- and inter-individual levels, but also across individuals (both teachers and students), institutions and society.

Goals play a key role in directing teachers' emotion. Empirical investigations in teacher emotion research, although scattered, in general validate the applicability of appraisal theories in understanding the sources of teacher emotions, that teacher emotion is closely associated with teachers' perceived level of fulfilment of their goals. Among these goals, the three most frequently recurring appear to be moral, achievement and social goals. While these goals can be gauged easily, it is crucial to look beyond the surface to disentangle the elusive sociocultural forces that teachers and other stakeholders bring to the classroom and educational ecology.

In the SLA field, emotion is both an end and a means to investigating the sociocultural factors in which it is embedded. Although rooted in social psychology, teacher emotion research has developed its own conception of emotion over time, which is very much implicit in the methodological approaches. Unlike social psychologists who are interested in identifying the routes between emotion and cognition, teacher emotion researchers tend to conceptualise emotion as an 'index' (Pierce, 1998) which signifies the presence of cognitive dissonance in response to diverse educational and instructional issues, a precept which probably stems from the evolutionarily significant temporal immediacy of emotion (James, 1969). In other words, emotions serve as a methodologically innovative means to capture teachers' values and beliefs, ranging from their professional self-understanding (e.g. Darby, 2008) and identity development (e.g. Galman, 2009) to conceptual change (e.g. Kubanyiova, 2012) and instructional choices (e.g. Trigwell, 2012). While indexing may be a gateway to tapping into a teacher's cognition, we believe that more work is needed to build an empirically robust and comprehensive theoretical framework that allows for a structured understanding of the dynamic interplay of teacher emotion with other highly interrelated concepts, namely emotion, cognition, motivation and behaviour (intra-organism dimension), as well as the inter-individual and sociocultural factors at play (inter-organismic dimension). Such a framework could be a point of departure where we examine how teacher emotion in other subjects may differ from that in SLA, which is different by nature from content subject learning in that it is highly culturally embedded, identity bound and communication orientated.

Towards an integrated framework to researching teacher emotion

Within teacher emotion literature there are two prominent discourses about the relationship between feeling and thinking: (1) emotion as a product of the transaction between a person and the environment; and (2) emotion as an integral component of a three-part model consisting of emotion, cognition and behaviour, often with bi-directional, dynamic interaction among them. The former is exemplified in Hagenauer and Volet's (2014) investigation, which explored how the participating teachers' cognition of the environment impacted on their emotions. While useful in revealing teachers' cognition, such linear conceptualisation provides only an incomplete picture of the complex sources of emotions. We believe emotions are better captured in the latter three-part dynamic framework, in view of the increasing amount of evidence from cognitive psychology and social psychology that shows that emotion could reciprocally affect cognition in multiple ways (e.g. Storbeck & Clore, 2007). In fact, mood states 'may bias person perception by selectively influencing what people learn about others and by distorting the interpretations and associations they make' (Parrott, 2001: 205). Emotion research that examines the bi-directional flow between emotion and cognition, although slowly emerging (e.g. Golombek & Doran, 2014), could reveal how emotion might impact on teaching instruction and quality. It is also on this premise that we believe teachers' emotional labour deserves more attention than it has received to date.

Among the few proposed frameworks of teacher emotion thus far, we tend to agree with Schutz et al.'s (2006: 344) conception of emotion as 'socially constructed, personally enacted ways of being that emerge from conscious and/or unconscious judgements regarding perceived successes at attaining goals or maintaining standards or beliefs during transactions as part of social-historical contexts'. The most obvious merit of this model is that it underscores the complex interplay between emotions and social-historical contexts which, as we have already noted, are at the heart of people-centred professions such as teaching.

Teacher emotion research, in fact, has mostly been concerned with how affective states are shaped by social, cultural, political and historical forces (e.g. Chen, 2016; Hargreaves, 2005; King, 2014; King & Smith, 2017; Nias, 1996). Mounting evidence shows that those forces shape emotions at two different but inter-related transaction points at least. On the macro, community level, the relationships within an organisation or society could affect teachers' emotional responses to teaching (Schutz *et al.*, 2006). On a micro, individual level, each teacher brings with them, from their own personal and educational backgrounds, their own goals and beliefs shaped over a sustained period by sociocultural, political and historical influences (Rosiek, 2003), which we believe interact with the prevailing macro-level mood. In sum, those global forces shape emotion by exerting influences on cognition (and perhaps emotion and motivation) and transacting at individual, institutional and societal levels. Therefore, in investigating how emotion affects teaching behaviours, it is important to examine not only transient phenomena such as classroom interactions or emotions per se, but also how they might have been moulded by teacher–student relationships (Schutz *et al.*, 2006) or emotional climate (Reyes *et al.*, 2012).

We believe Schutz's *et al.*'s (2006) notion serves well as a starting point for teacher emotion research in SLA, and it can be helpfully supplemented to capture further nuances. First, we need to take into account the reciprocity of teacher emotion, cognition and motivation, as argued above. Secondly, while we agree with Schutz *et al.*'s (2006: 345) idea that emotions are 'ways of being that include physiological, psychological and behavioural aspects', we contend that behaviour should be surfaced as the outcome and likely contributor of the interaction of cognition, emotion and motivation, for it is a distinctive, observable and measurable human characteristic. In short, current teacher emotion literature fits in with our view (Figure 9.1) that teachers' cognition, emotion, motivation and behaviour act on one another. We should note, however, that more studies have yet to be conducted to establish: (1) whether and how goals might be the unifying dimension of cognition, emotion and motivation (Schutz *et al.*, 2006); and (2) how behaviour may influence teacher cognition, emotion and motivation.

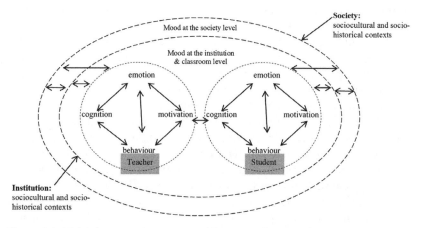

Figure 9.1 Multi-dynamic view proposed for researching teacher emotion

The Interplay between the Intra-organismic and Inter-organismic Dimension of Emotion and its Implication on Teaching

In view of the close connection between the two central goals of teacher emotion research, which are to foster teachers' psychological well-being and to enhance teaching effectiveness (Day & Gu 2009), we argue that it is crucial to have an integrated perspective encompassing interactions within and across intra-organismic and inter-organismic dimensions. The former dimension, as described in the previous section, concerns the origins of emotion, whereas the latter should offer insights into how emotion moves externally between individuals and across individuals and the broader institutional and sociocultural contexts. With regard to the inter-organismic dimension, we hypothesise a processing model in which teacher emotion is conceived as internal emotional processes being channelled into emotional understanding as it is perceived by the recipients (e.g. students). It concerns how emotions may move between human entities, which in this case are teachers, students, the institution and the culture and society at large.

Inter-organismic dimension

The inter-organismic dimension of emotion in SLA deserves more attention than it has received, in part because teacher emotion has 'considerable implications for student learning, school climate and the overall quality of education' (Frenzel *et al.*, 2009: 129). While teachers might not themselves be highly aware of the potential impacts of their emotional expression on student learning (Brackett *et al.*, 2010), there is evidence that the classroom's emotional climate, which comprises teacher-dependent dimensions such as 'positive climate (degree of warmth and connection observed in the classroom)' and 'teacher sensitivity (teacher's awareness and responsiveness to students' academic and social needs)', is linked to better academic outcomes, probably mediated by student engagement (Reyes *et al.*, 2012: 704). Another reason why teacher emotion might influence students' academic success is offered by the attribution theory; for instance, it has been shown that a teacher's anger rather than sympathy could better prompt students to attribute success to effort, which in turn is conducive to their motivation (e.g. Graham, 1990).

The transmission of emotion in the inter-organismic dimension is conducted via behaviours, both verbal and non-verbal, often with the ultimate goal being inter-subjectivity, that is, an alignment of cognition and emotion across the individuals (Denzin, 1984). In teacher–student interaction, non-verbal communication is as essential as verbal communication not only because it aids verbal instructions but also because it exposes teachers' otherwise hidden feelings. While teachers might try to hide their real emotions, students appear to be capable of decrypting what teachers truly feel about them (Babad, 2009). In view of the potentially powerful influence teacher emotion has on student learning, we believe this aspect of teacher psychology needs to be further investigated, particularly in relation to students' own contextualised emotions as they exist within the sociocultural matrix of the classroom.

Believing that emotional support is an integral part of effective teaching (Goldstein, 1999), teachers constantly strive to gauge students' emotional reactions to various instructional tasks and ideas (Rosiek, 2003). To do so, one has to have emotional understanding (Denzin, 1984). Further to detecting and empathising with students' emotions, experienced teachers frequently emotionally scaffold students, often in order to promote learning (Rosiek & Beghetto, 2009). This implicit emotional understanding, which is entangled with the cultural and historical backgrounds of the student, teacher and school, is where teachers may alter instructional details to reduce students' potential negative emotions, such as anger and intimidation (Rosiek, 2003), and possibly enhance their positive ones.

Teacher Emotion in Second Language Acquisition

There is currently scant research on teacher emotion in SLA, and what is available is by no means consistent or systematic in its theory or methodology (for a brief review, see Cowie, 2011). One of the few attempts to provide a theoretical perspective on L2 teacher emotions is Golombek and Doran's (2014) work in which they propose a SCOBA model (*a scheme of a complete orienting basis of the action*) which acknowledges and unifies bi-directional influences among language teacher emotion, cognition and activity. The most prominent feature of this model is that it considers how a teacher's personality, background and experiences transact with their teaching, and thus provides a more complete picture of the dynamic interactions inherent within teaching.

As Reyes *et al.* (2012) argues, research into classroom emotions needs differentiation according to content areas because of the variable nature of learning across subjects. This holds particularly true with language learning. As well as teacher emotion factors that might be universal to all types of teaching, such as emotions associated with workload (Hagenauer & Volet, 2014), the unique role of language in one's identity (Labov, 1972) means that L2 teaching, compared to mainstream subject teaching, might by its pervasive and culture-laden nature engender a higher frequency and a greater range of emotions (intraorganismic dimension). In a similar vein, as L2 teaching requires more emotional understanding on the part of the teacher (interorganismic dimension) in assisting students' psychological adjustment, it necessarily demands even greater levels of emotion regulation. Indeed, an L2 teacher constantly needs to address student anxiety, which is driven not only by worries about competence but also about identity (Stroud & Wee, 2006), a construct that entails 'who you are', 'what you say' and 'how you say it' (Gee, 1996: viii). More than mere language teaching, L2 teachers are likely to need to cater to students' identity, for example by encouraging them to identify with the target language culture to promote intrinsic motivation, and this inevitably involves an emotional dimension. It is therefore crucial that SLA research incorporates investigation into the emotional perspective.

A Case of Teacher Emotion in Second Language Acquisition: The Emotional Labour of Teaching

The construct of emotional labour (also sometimes referred to as emotion labour, emotion work or emotion management) holds rich potential for illustrating how intra-organismic emotions interact with inter-organismic factors which, respectively, can be operationalised as teachers' classroom behaviours and staff–student interactions. The term *emotional labour* originated in the work of the sociologist Arlie Hochschild (1979, 1983), who used it to illustrate how employees, notably within the service sector, are required to manage and display particular emotions when interacting with customers in order to conform to tacit social norms associated with their role. Emotional labour may involve not only attempts to hide the outward display of particular emotions (a strategy known as 'surface acting'), but also the mental work involved in trying to summon up and actually feel emotions deemed 'appropriate' within an organisation or society (the strategy of 'deep acting'). The degree of emotion labour exerted depends on a multitude of factors that rest on the intra-organismic level, such as factors connected to the teacher's sociocultural background, and on the inter-organismic level, including teacher–student interactions and the broader institutional and social context. Emotional dissonance occurs when there is a mismatch between the emotions an employee is obliged to display and what he or she truly feels, and over time this dissonance and the mental effort required to control one's emotions can lead to self-estrangement, depersonalisation, stress and ultimately burnout (Acheson *et al.*, 2016; Hochschild, 1983; Näring *et al.*, 2006, 2011).

That said, Chang and Davis (2009) make the pertinent observation that teacher–student relationships are inherently different from those of service workers and their customers because the former tend to be more long term in orientation (e.g. over the course of an academic year) and are conducted in the very public crucible of the classroom. They therefore argue for a more adaptive view of emotional labour within the teaching profession, suggesting that we should not view the construct in a purely negative light. The management of teachers' emotional displays can, in some circumstances, help to maintain good interpersonal relationships with students, and may also act as a socialising model for younger learners, helping them to effectively regulate and display their own emotions (see Thompson, 1991). Hargreaves (2000) emphasises the potentially positive aspects of emotional labour when he points to its use by teachers seeking to achieve their own agendas, arguing that they can find emotional labour rewarding and pleasurable when working conditions allow.

An Example of Research into the Emotional Labour of Second Language Teaching

As emphasised earlier in the chapter, research investigating teacher emotions within L2 settings is still very much in its infancy. One of the first studies to explore emotional labour within such a context was conducted by the lead author (King, 2016), whose research sought to explore the perceptions and beliefs that a group of mid- to late-career expatriate English as a foreign language instructors working within a private university in Japan held about the emotional dimension of their work.

Data collection and analysis

This small-scale, exploratory study used a series of semi-structured interviews to uncover participants' experiences of actual classroom incidents which had had an emotional element to them and also sought details about how the teachers regulated their own emotions during interactions with students and how they responded to the stress-inducing emotional labour demands of their roles. Exploratory semi-structured interviews were chosen as the primary means of data collection because, when employed skilfully by researchers, this methodology provides participants with opportunities to talk freely and candidly about emotionally loaded topics (Cohen *et al.*, 2011).

A purposive sampling strategy (Patton, 2002) ensured that only experienced expatriate teachers who had been working in Japan for more than five years took part in the study. This approach was taken when selecting participants so that superficial accounts of sociocultural and institutional aspects of the study could be avoided. Five teachers (four males and one female), whose careers spanned between nine and 26 years, gave their consent to be interviewed and they spoke eloquently and at length about the emotional labour involved in teaching English to undergraduates enrolled within a large, private university specialising in foreign language education. Transcription of the interviews took place as soon as possible after each encounter had ended so that concurrent data collection and analysis could be undertaken, with data from one interview session feeding into and informing the next. Grounded theory (Strauss & Corbin, 1998) guided the coding of data within transcripts, with initial low-inference codes being later complemented by higher order, emotional labour-relevant ones. A research journal (Altrichter & Holly, 2011) provided a further source of data and the ideas and post-interview reflections noted down within it contributed to what was an ongoing process of interpretation and analysis within the project.

Findings

The study's findings emphasise the contextually mediated emotional demands that the profession of foreign language teaching entails. They centre around five key themes that emerged from the data: the emotional labour involved in caring for students; the suppression of negative emotions; bearing the motivational burden through emotional labour; the performance of emotions and emotional distancing; and the link between institutional change, working conditions and teachers' emotions. The findings indicate that while sociocultural factors do have influence, whether they have a positive or negative impact on teacher emotion appears to be, to an extent, a cognitive choice. Therefore, changing teachers' perceptions of contextual influences may be of equal importance to their psychological well-being as making changes to the context itself. We will now provide a brief outline of the findings associated with each of these themes in turn which operate at three key levels: the intra-individual level (teacher); the inter-individual level (teacher–students); and the individual–sociocultural level.

Sociocultural influences: Teacher as a cultural mediator in caring for students

The data show that the attributes teachers bring to the classroom shape the emotional climate in the classroom. In particular, a teacher, as an entity embodying certain culture-specific emotions, serves as a cultural and emotional mediator between society and students. A teacher's set of beliefs about caring for students plays a significant role not only in shaping professional identity, but also in guiding the pedagogical approach he or she adopts within the classroom (Isenbarger & Zembylas, 2006; O'Connor, 2008). For some, caring about students forms a natural part of the job, which can be highly rewarding and motivating. For others, dissonance between the care they are expected to display and their true feelings towards students may result in emotional labour as teachers attempt to supress non-caring emotions and summon up caring ones. All of the teachers who took part in the study spoke to some extent about how important it was for them to build and maintain caring relationships with the students they taught, but Jonah, an American with 16 years' teaching experience who had been brought up in Japan, stood out in this regard. He considered himself to be a kind of 'surrogate, third parent' to his students and believed that supporting these young adults through their various non-academic problems was more of a priority in his teaching than actually developing their foreign language skills. Jonah's testimony reflects the notion that teachers' professional identities dynamically evolve in response to the socially situated aspects of their roles which come about through interaction with others (Flores & Day, 2006; O'Connor, 2008). With a great emphasis within Japanese education being placed on interdependency and the transferential nature of teacher–student relationships within that context (Hendry, 1986), Jonah's somewhat 'welfarist' approach to teaching becomes much more understandable. Even so, the asymmetrical nature of care in staff–student relationships, coupled to an inability to engage in some form of emotional distancing, can in the long term leave teachers like Jonah vulnerable and prone to emotional exhaustion.

Cognitive appraisals: Negative emotions being a 'choice'

Data from the study revealed that the cognitive appraisals teacher participants made about the cultural and educational circumstances they were operating in posed a significant influence on their emotions. All of the teachers in the sample spoke about the efforts they made to manage their negative emotions during classes, particularly in relation to feelings of anger, frustration and irritation that occurred when they perceived students not to be cooperating during learning tasks. Data from the study revealed that participants were careful to manage their in-class, public emotional displays by suppressing and masking negative emotions so that their true feelings were not apparent to students. This emotional labour was performed in large part because of a desire to create and maintain a positive learning atmosphere. A recurring theme within the interviews was how some students' silent unresponsiveness during lessons had the potential to trigger negative emotional responses among teachers. For example, Rufus, a highly experienced EFL instructor from the United States who had been teaching in Japan for nine years, recounted in a highly animated fashion the annoyance he felt when individual students just stared at him in 'doe-eyed' silence after he had tried to interact with them while monitoring small-group activities. The silences of language learners within Japanese universities are shaped by any number of complex, interrelated learner-internal and contextual factors (King, 2013a, 2013b, 2014, 2015). Rufus' irritation stemmed from his interpretation of student silence as being a volitional act (rather than purely being down to deficiencies in L2 proficiency), which signified the rejection of him as an interlocutor. Other teachers in the study explained how their improved knowledge of Japanese sociocultural issues and a willingness to extend teacher wait time (see Smith & King, 2017) after posing in-class solicits meant they felt better able to cope both pedagogically and emotionally with their students' silences compared to when they first began teaching at the research site. Silence in itself can be a useful tool for emotion management (Saunders, 1985) and it allows one space to engage in cognitive reappraisal of the events which may have triggered an emotional response in the first place.

Emotional distancing through emotional labour

In our proposed framework it is hypothesised that the emotional interactions between the teacher and students are bi-directional and guided by principles of intersubjectivity. While such interactions can have either a positive or a negative influence on teacher emotion, in this study we identified only negative impacts. Related to this was an awareness of the participants to prevent emotional exhaustion by ensuring a comfortable psychological distance from students. This distance was maintained partly through emotional labour.

Marcus, an American with a background in the theatre who had been teaching English in Japan for 10 years, provided an insightful account of how he prepared for classes in a similar fashion to how he had prepared to go on stage during his former career. It is notable that he framed the 90 minutes of each class as representing a performance and shared how his efforts to appear cheerful, enthusiastic and positive in front of students was somewhat at odds with what he deemed to be his more downbeat, true personality. Marcus' testimony reflects Hochschild's (1983) notion of surface acting which entails manipulating one's outward appearance (through facial expressions, gestures, tone of voice, and so on) to display the surface effects of an emotion but with no attempt made to actually feel the emotion. This behaviour, if engaged in over a prolonged period of time, can eventually lead to mental strain and emotional exhaustion (Näring et al., 2006, 2011; Philipp & Schüpbach, 2010). To protect themselves from such negative psychological consequences of emotional dissonance, a number of the study's teachers revealed that they made efforts to foster a sense of depersonalisation and detachment from their work. For example, Rufus linked his use of this coping strategy to having a situated, transportable identity that he could turn on when he entered the classroom and off when he left. Nora too spoke about maintaining a psychological disconnection from what occurred in her classes. This Australian instructor, who had been teaching at the research site for five years at the time of interview, described her reluctance to engage in truthful self-disclosure during interactions with students. By not allowing them to enter her inner life, Nora was able to create emotional distance from the students and she believed this made her more resilient to the day-to-day stresses of teaching at the university.

The hidden sociocultural rules: Teachers bearing the motivational burden

An interesting theme to emerge in the data was that four of the five participants considered their motivational roles to be different from those of Japanese colleagues at the university, believing their efforts in class to appear bright, cheerful and enthusiastic led some students to view them more as 'entertainers' than as serious language teaching professionals. Although the study did not attempt to discover whether such assertions were true or not, the fact that teachers believed them to be true points towards the existence of tacit, psycho-cultural 'feeling rules' within the university which encouraged non-Japanese teaching staff to engage in sustained regulation of in-class positive emotional displays with the aim of fostering intrinsic motivation within learners.

Participants related how they believed it was primarily the teacher's responsibility to instil intrinsic motivation into learners and that this could be done by manufacturing and exaggerating public displays of positive emotions during interactions with students. Of course the day-to-day reality of teaching is that not all instructors are able to feel an innate, boundless interest in their subject or an infectious enthusiasm for the lesson they are conducting. As a result, when positive emotions are absent, they either have to be summoned up or performed. Interviewees related how they felt obliged to appear bright and cheerful during lessons in order to encourage students and keep them engaged in learning tasks. They also spoke about the emotional energy they expended on efforts to regulate these positive emotional displays in class (cf. Acheson *et al.*, 2016).

The impact of institutional change on teacher emotions

At the time of the interviews, the university which formed the research site was undergoing a period of significant reform brought about by a change in the institution's senior management. These reforms brought with them changes to the teachers' working conditions as curricula, course structures and the administrative duties of teaching staff across the university were altered with little or no prior consultation from the management. Coupled with teachers' concerns about job security and the university's failure to enrol them in the *shakaihoken* (social security) system, an atmosphere of mistrust, malcontent and vulnerability pervaded the institution. Marcus described how at faculty meetings which lacked any debate and were used merely to inform staff of new policies that were to be unquestioningly implemented, he had to hide the shock, anger, disgust and boredom that he felt. He believed the changes being implemented were primarily for financial reasons, that only lip service was paid to educational considerations, and that the views of the university's experienced foreign language teaching staff were completely ignored. Teacher emotions are dynamically shaped by interaction between an individual's sense of professional identity and the situational demands of the institutional/social environment. Reforms to working conditions and teaching practices play a central role in such a process (van Veen & Sleegers, 2009), and this illustrates well the interplay between the intra- and inter-organismic dimensions of teacher emotion.

Conclusion and Suggestions for Emotion Regulation Techniques

The findings in the study outlined above reveal how a sample of mid- to late-career expatriate English language teachers working at a private Japanese university engaged in emotional labour and managed their public displays of emotion in order to accomplish educational goals and conform to their institution's socially derived, tacit rules of 'appropriate' teacher emotions. Although space constraints do not allow us to discuss the various coping measures available to those who teach for effectively dealing with the negative psychological consequences of emotional labour in the form of work-related stress (see Kyriacou, 2000), we would like to conclude by drawing attention to three preventative strategy areas that teachers can draw from in order to successfully downregulate negative in-class emotions. From changing jobs to keeping a stiff upper lip, Gross (2008) makes the point that there is an overwhelming number of processes that can be used to regulate emotion. However, we suggest his process model of emotion regulation (Gross, 2002, 2008) is a good starting point from which educators can begin to consider what strategies may be most suitable for both themselves and their own teaching situation. Rather than response-focused strategies, which suppress emotions after they have occurred, we recommend teachers employ antecedent-focused regulation strategies in the form of (1) *modifying situations*, (2) *deploying attention* and (3) *cognitive change*.

Regarding *modifying situations*, learning tasks may be tailored to preclude student behaviours which are likely to trigger a negative emotional response in the teacher. The key here is to anticipate such behaviours before they occur and modify one's lesson plan accordingly. *Deploying attention* could simply just involve ignoring students' trigger behaviours (if they are minor enough) and focusing on positive behaviours instead. And finally, *cognitive change* might involve the reappraisal of a situation through the use of self-talk so that its emotional significance is altered, for example, thinking about a learner's silence in terms of the inhibiting social anxiety he or she may be feeling rather than seeing the failure to respond as a personal slight. Although the emotion regulation strategy examples described here are necessarily brief and far from a full taxonomy, the three types of antecedent-focused approaches outlined do represent a good starting point from which we can begin to develop practical, research-based ideas about how to tackle the negative psychological consequences of emotional labour in language teaching and thus promote the emotional well-being of second language teachers everywhere.

References

Acheson, K., Taylor, J. and Luna, K. (2016) The burnout spiral: The emotion labor of five rural U.S. foreign language teachers. *The Modern Language Journal* 100 (2), 522–537.
Altrichter, H. and Holly, M.L. (2011) Research diaries. In B. Somekh and C. Lewin (eds) *Research Methods in the Social Sciences* (2nd edn) (pp. 43–52). London: Sage.
Babad, E. (2009) *The Social Psychology of the Classroom*. New York: Routledge.
Brackett, M.A., Palomera, R., Mojsa-Kaja, J., Reyes, M.R. and Salovey, P. (2010) Emotion regulation ability, burnout, and job satisfaction among British secondary school teachers. *Psychology in the Schools* 47 (4), 406–417.
Chang, M.-L. and Davis, H.A. (2009) Understanding the role of teacher appraisals in shaping the dynamics of their relationships with students: Deconstructing teachers' judgments of disruptive behaviour/students. In P.A. Schutz and M. Zembylas (eds)

Advances in Teacher Emotion Research: The Impact on Teachers' Lives (pp. 95–127). Dordrecht: Springer.

Chen, J. (2016) Understanding teacher emotions: The development of a teacher emotion inventory. *Teaching and Teacher Education* 55, 68–77.

Cohen, L., Manion, L. and Morrison, K. (2011) *Research Methods in Education* (7th edn). Abingdon: Routledge.

Cowie, N. (2011) Emotions that experienced English as a foreign language (EFL) teachers feel about their students, their colleagues and their work. *Teaching and Teacher Education* 27 (1), 235–242.

Darby, A. (2008) Teachers' emotions in the reconstruction of professional self-understanding. *Teaching and Teacher Education* 24 (5), 1160–1172.

Day, C. and Gu, Q. (2009) Teacher emotions: Well being and effectiveness. In P.A. Schutz and M. Zembylas (eds) *Advances in Teacher Emotion Research: The Impact on Teachers' Lives* (pp. 15–31). Dordrecht: Springer.

Denzin, N. (1984) *On Understanding Emotion*. San Francisco, CA: Jossey-Bass.

Flores, M.A. and Day, C. (2006) Contexts which shape and reshape new teachers' identities: A multi-perspective study. *Teaching and Teacher Education* 22 (2), 219–232.

Frenzel, A.C., Goetz, T., Stephens, E.J. and Jacob, B. (2009) Antecedents and effects of teachers' emotional experiences: An integrated perspective and empirical test. In P.A. Schutz and M. Zembylas (eds) *Advances in Teacher Emotion Research: The Impact on Teachers' Lives* (pp. 129–151). Dordrecht: Springer.

Galman, S. (2009) Doth the lady protest too much? Pre-service teachers and the experience of dissonance as a catalyst for development. *Teaching and Teacher Education* 25 (3), 468–481.

Gee, J.P. (1996) *Social Linguistics and Literacies: Ideologies in Discourses* (2nd edn). London: Taylor and Francis.

Goldstein, L.S. (1999) The relational zone: The role of caring relationships in the co-construction of mind. *American Educational Research Journal* 36 (3), 647–673.

Golombek, P. and Doran, M. (2014) Unifying cognition, emotion, and activity in language teacher professional development. *Teaching and Teacher Education* 39, 102–111.

Graham, S. (1990) Communicating low ability in the classroom: Bad things good teachers sometimes do. In S. Graham and V.S. Folker (eds) *Attribution Theory: Applications to Achievement, Mental Health, and Interpersonal Conflict* (pp. 17–52). Hillsdale, NJ: Lawrence Erlbaum.

Gross, J.J. (2002) Emotion regulation: Affective, cognitive, and social consequences. *Psychophysiology* 39 (3), 281–291

Gross, J.J. (2008) Emotion regulation. In M. Lewis, J.M. Haviland-Jones and L. Feldman Barrett (eds) *Handbook of Emotions* (3rd edn) (pp. 497–512). New York: Guilford Press.

Hagenauer, G. and Volet, S. (2014) 'I don't think I could, you know, just teach without any emotion': Exploring the nature and origin of university teachers' emotions. *Research Papers in Education* 29 (2), 240–262.

Hargreaves, A. (2000) Mixed emotions: Teachers' perceptions of their interactions with students. *Teaching and Teacher Education* 16 (8), 811–826.

Hargreaves, A. (2005) Educational change takes ages: Life, career and generational factors in teachers' emotional responses to educational change. *Teaching and Teacher Education* 21 (8), 967–983.

Hendry, J. (1986) *Becoming Japanese: The World of the Pre-school Child*. Manchester: Manchester University Press.

Hochschild, A.R. (1979) Emotion work, feeling rules, and social structures. *Journal of Sociology* 85, 551–575.

Hochschild, A.R. (1983) *The Managed Heart: The Commercialization of Human Feeling*. Berkeley, CA: University of California Press.

Imai, Y. (2010) Emotions in SLA: New insights from collaborative learning for an EFL classroom. *The Modern Language Journal* 94 (2), 278–292.

Isenbarger, L. and Zembylas, M. (2006) The emotional labour of caring in teaching. *Teaching and Teacher Education* 22 (1), 120–134.

James, W. (1969) What is an emotion? In W. James (ed.) *Collected Essays and Reviews* (pp. 244–280). New York: Russell and Russell. (Original work published 1884.)

King, J. (2013a) *Silence in the Second Language Classroom*. Basingstoke: Palgrave Macmillan.

King, J. (2013b) Silence in the second language classrooms of Japanese universities. *Applied Linguistics* 34 (3), 325–343.

King, J. (2014) Fear of the true self: Social anxiety and the silent behaviour of Japanese learners of English. In K. Csizér and M. Magid (eds) *The Impact of Self-Concept on Language Learning* (pp. 232–249). Bristol: Multilingual Matters.

King, J. (ed.) (2015) *The Dynamic Interplay between Context and the Language Learner*. Basingstoke: Palgrave Macmillan.

King, J. (2016) 'It's time, put on the smile, it's time!': The emotional labour of second language teaching within a Japanese university. In C. Gkonou, D. Tatzl and S. Mercer (eds) *New Directions in Language Learning Psychology* (pp. 97–112). Dordrecht: Springer.

King, J. and Smith, L. (2017) Social anxiety and silence in Japan's tertiary foreign language classrooms. In C. Gkonou, M. Daubney and J.-M. Dewaele (eds) *New Insights into Language Anxiety: Theory, Research and Educational Implications* (pp. 92–110). Bristol: Multilingual Matters.

Kubanyiova, M. (2012) *Teacher Development in Action: Understanding Language Teachers' Conceptual Change*. New York: Palgrave Macmillan.

Kyriacou, C. (2000) *Stress-busting for Teachers*. Cheltenham: Stanley Thornes.

Labov, W. (1972) *Sociolinguistic Patterns*. Philadelphia, PA: University of Pennsylvania Press.

Lazarus, R.S. (1991) Cognition and motivation in emotion. *American Psychologist* 46 (4), 352–367.

Mercer, S. (2006) Using journals to investigate the learners' emotional experience of the language classroom. *Estudios de Linguistica Inglesa Aplicada (ELIA)* 6, 63–91.

Näring, G., Briët, M. and Brouwers, A. (2006) Beyond demand-control: Emotional labour and symptoms of burnout in teachers. *Work and Stress* 20 (4), 303–315.

Näring, G., Vlerick, P. and Van de Ven, B. (2011) Emotion work and emotional exhaustion in teachers: The job and individual perspective. *Educational Studies* 38 (1), 63–72.

Nias, J. (1996) Thinking about feeling: The emotions of teaching. *Cambridge Journal of Education* 26 (3), 293–306.

O'Connor, K.E. (2008) 'You choose to care': Teachers, emotions and professional identity. *Teaching and Teacher Education* 24 (1), 117–126.

Parrott, W.G. (2001) *Emotions in Social Psychology: Essential Readings*. Philadelphia, PA: Psychology Press.

Patton, M.Q. (2002) *Qualitative Evaluation and Research Methods* (3rd edn). Thousand Oaks, CA: Sage.

Philipp, A. and Schüpbach, H. (2010) Longitudinal effects of emotional labour on emotional exhaustion and dedication of teachers. *Journal of Occupational Health Psychology* 15, 494–504.

Pierce, C.S. (1998) What is a sign? In Peirce Edition Project (ed.) *The Essential Peirce, Vol. 2* (pp. 4–10). Bloomington, IN: Indiana University Press. (Original work published 1894.)

Reyes, M.A., Brackett, S.E., Rivers, M.W. and Salovey, P. (2012) Classroom emotional climate, student engagement, and academic achievement. *Journal of Educational Psychology* 104 (3), 700–712.

Rosiek, J. (2003) Emotional scaffolding: An exploration of teacher knowledge at the intersection of student emotion and subject matter content. *Journal of Teacher Education* 54 (5), 399–412.

Rosiek, J. and Beghetto, R.A. (2009) Emotional scaffolding: The emotional and imaginative dimensions of teaching and learning. In P.A. Schutz and M. Zembylas (eds) *Advances in Teacher Emotion Research: The Impact on Teachers' Lives* (pp. 175–194). Dordrecht: Springer.

Saunders, G.R. (1985) Silence and noise as emotion management styles: An Italian case. In D. Tannen and M. Saville-Troike (eds) *Perspectives on Silence* (pp. 165–183). Norwood: Ablex.

Schutz, P.A. and DeCuir, J.T. (2002) Inquiry on emotions in education. *Educational Psychologist* 37 (2), 125–134.

Schutz, P.A. and Zembylas, M. (eds) (2009) *Advances in Teacher Emotion Research: The Impact on Teachers' Lives*. Dordrecht: Springer.

Schutz, P.A., Hong, J.Y., Cross, D.I. and Osbon, J.N. (2006) Reflections on investigating emotion in educational activity settings. *Educational Psychology Review* 18 (4), 343–360.

Smith, C.A. and Lazarus, R.S. (1993) Appraisal components, core relational themes, and the emotions. *Cognition and Emotion* 7 (3–4), 295–323.

Smith, L. and King, J. (2017) A dynamic systems approach to wait time in the second language classroom. *System* 68, 1–14.

Storbeck, J. and Clore, G. (2007) On the interdependence of cognition and emotion. *Cognition and Emotion* 21 (6), 1212–1237.

Strauss, A.L. and Corbin, J. (1998) *Basics of Qualitative Research: Techniques and Procedures for Developing Grounded Theory*. Thousand Oaks, CA: Sage.

Stroud, C. and Wee, L. (2006) Anxiety and identity in the language classroom. *RELC Journal: A Journal of Language Teaching and Research* 37 (3), 299–307.

Sutton, R.E. and Wheatley, K.F. (2003) Teachers' emotions and teaching: A review of the literature and directions for future research. *Educational Psychology Review* 15 (4), 327–358.

Thompson, R.A. (1991) Emotional regulation and emotional development. *Educational Psychology Review* 3 (4), 269–307.

Trigwell, K. (2012) Relations between teachers' emotions in teaching and their approaches to teaching in higher education. *Instructional Science* 40 (3), 607–621.

van Veen, K. and Sleegers, P. (2009) Teachers' emotions in a context of reforms: To a deeper understanding of teachers and reforms. In P.A. Schutz and M. Zembylas (eds) *Advances in Teacher Emotion Research: The Impact on Teachers' Lives* (pp. 233–251). Dordrecht: Springer.

van Veen, K., Sleegers, P. and van de Ven, P. (2005) One teacher's identity, emotions, and commitment to change: A case study into the cognitive-affective processes of a secondary school teacher in the context of reforms. *Teaching and Teacher Education* 21 (8), 917–934.

Zhang, Q. and Zhu, W. (2008) Exploring emotion in teaching: Emotional labor, burnout, and satisfaction in Chinese higher education. *Communication Education* 57 (1), 105–122.

10 The Relational Beliefs and Practices of Highly Socio-emotionally Competent Language Teachers[1]

Christina Gkonou and Sarah Mercer

In this chapter we discuss the nature of socio-emotional competences, which we argue are essential for effective language teaching. We begin by outlining what socio-emotional competences are and why we believe these are especially important in the language classroom. We then report on one aspect of a large-scale British Council funded study examining the beliefs and practices of highly socio-emotionally competent teachers (Gkonou & Mercer, 2017). We discuss data collected through observations and stimulated recall interviews with six teachers who scored very highly on a socio-emotional competence questionnaire. In this chapter we focus in particular on how the teachers see the role of interpersonal relationships within and beyond the classroom in their professional practice. We explore their beliefs in respect to different types of relationships as well as their practices in these areas. We conclude the chapter by reflecting on the implications of the findings for understanding the relational dimension of language education, teachers' socio-emotional competences and how these can be fostered in teacher education programmes.

Socio-emotional Competences

Socio-emotional competences encompass a range of key life skills which help individuals to recognise and regulate their emotions, care for others, take responsible decisions and actions, build healthy, positive interpersonal relationships and deal effectively with the challenges and difficulties of daily life. Within psychology-based research, these skills are broadly categorised under the constructs of emotional intelligence (EI) and social intelligence (SI). In what follows, we discuss each of these in turn.

EI refers to the ability of individuals to be aware of their own emotions and those of others, manage their own emotions efficiently, empathise with people in their immediate social environment by taking their perspective, participate in social interactions and manage interpersonal relationships effectively, and have a positive outlook on life by remaining motivated to work on daily tasks (Goleman, 1995, 1998). EI has often been confused with other variables such as personality traits, motivation or optimism. However, as Mayer *et al.* (2008: 514) explain,

> groups of widely studied personality traits, including motives such as the need for achievement, self-related concepts such as self-control, emotional traits such as happiness, and social styles such as assertiveness should be called what they are, rather than being mixed together in haphazard-seeming assortments and named emotional intelligence.

The second competence we are focusing on here is SI, which refers to individuals' ability to manage their interpersonal relationships intelligently and efficiently in order to create genuine, caring and healthy relationships (Goleman, 2006). Although EI and SI might often be seen as overlapping, as Goleman (2006) clarifies, they reflect two distinct skills: the former centres on an *intra*personal dimension (i.e. what goes on within an individual), whereas the latter concentrates on an *inter*personal dimension (i.e. what goes on within interactions among individuals).

A key debate within psychology and most importantly general education concerns the extent to which EI and SI are stable personality traits or can be explicitly and formally taught to people and thus be enhanced. Discussing learners and school programmes, Humphrey (2013: 18–19) suggests that learning, in order to be emotionally and socially intelligent, is a 'process', which takes place through 'an explicit course of action, a method or practice (...) the emphasis is on the *taught* first and foremost, with the *caught* a secondary consideration' (italics in the original). Emmerling and Goleman (2003) distinguish between nature and nurture and conclude that training can further boost an individual's EI and SI skills. In addition, numerous intervention-based studies have shown that EI and SI are malleable and that individuals who receive training on EI and SI are more self-aware and better able to empathise with others and regulate their emotions within social contexts (Brackett & Katulak, 2006; Matthews *et al.*, 2002; Nelis *et al.*, 2009; Zins *et al.*, 2004). We believe that the nature of EI and SI is not a question of either/or but rather that they reflect a combination of both trait and state characteristics; thus, socio-emotional competences can be learnt and socio-emotionally competent individuals can further develop these skills through experience, attention and sustained effort.

Socio-emotional Competences in Language Education

Within general education, a field known as social and emotional learning (SEL) emerged in the 1990s with a focus of research conducted at the

Collaborative for Academic, Social, and Emotional Learning (CASEL). As the name suggests, SEL comprises two aspects: the social aspect represents the crucial role that interpersonal development plays in successful learning, and the emotional aspect mirrors the importance of intrapersonal development in the sense that learners need to be able to recognise their emotions and the cognition and behaviour associated with these emotions (Humphrey, 2013; Kusché & Greenberg, 2006; Merrell & Gueldner, 2010).

Within second language acquisition (SLA), research into these socio-emotional competences and their influence on language learning and teaching remains scarce. Although the relevance of a range of constructs from general and social psychology has been examined by key scholars in the field (see, for example, Mercer *et al.*, 2012), EI and SI appear in only a few publications. Specifically, strong EI skills have been found to predict lower levels of language anxiety (Dewaele *et al.*, 2008; Shao *et al.*, 2013), positive attitudes towards foreign language learning (Oz *et al.*, 2015), and higher teacher self-efficacy (Moafian & Ghanizadeh, 2009). Additionally, enhanced SI skills were shown to help language learners to experience positive emotions in social interactions and support their peers towards academic achievement and success (Imai, 2010).

Our own interest in socio-emotional competences and their potential applicability to SLA stemmed from our shared conviction that developed EI and SI skills are crucial for language teachers to survive and thrive in their jobs (Castle & Buckler, 2009). It has been shown that developed EI and SI skills contribute towards teachers' psychological and professional well-being (Brackett *et al.*, 2010; Holmes, 2005; Mercer *et al.*, 2016; Zembylas, 2005). In addition, we recognised that teachers' high EI and SI are likely to influence the quality of teacher–student relationships as well as group dynamics and also classroom management (Patti, 2006; Reissman, 2006). Further, language teaching in multicultural settings but also language communicative competence per se necessitate an ability to create positive relationships with others and here dimensions of EI and SI, such as empathy, can play a central role (Mercer, 2016). Therefore, we felt it was surprising to note the relative paucity of research into EI and SI among language teachers, given the key role we felt it could play for both teachers and learners.

Relationships in Language Education

Quality relationships in education have been found to be connected to a range of positive outcomes beneficial to both learners and teachers (Cornelius-White, 2007; Davis, 2003; Fredricks *et al.*, 2004; Furrer & Skinner, 2003; Jennings & Greenberg, 2009; Skinner & Belmont, 1993). Wentzel (2015: 167) explains, 'teacher–student relationships that are emotionally close, safe, trusting, that provide access to instrumental help, and that foster a more general ethos of community and caring in classrooms appear to be highly effective in promoting positive student outcomes'. In Hattie's (2009) meta-analysis of 138 influential factors on learning, teacher–pupil relationships emerge in position 11, which is incredibly high compared to other constructs considered as centrally important such as motivation, which only comes in at position 51. The evidence is clear. The relationship between teachers and pupils is vitally important for effective teaching and learning. We can have the best materials and resources available, but if as teachers we do not build the right connections with our learners, then we will not be able to reap the benefits of the affordances at our disposal. As Rita Pierson so succinctly said in her famous TED talk, 'Kids don't learn from people they don't like'. She argues powerfully in her talk for the importance of understanding human connection and the power of relationships for effective learning. In language teaching, Breen (2001: 309) stresses the same thing, saying, 'social relationships in the classroom orchestrate what is made available for learning, how learning is done and what we achieve'. Indeed, there are increasing numbers of voices suggesting that the focus of classroom life should not be on managing individuals but rather managing relationships between them (Bingham & Sidorkin, 2010; Fredricks et al., 2004; Gieve & Miller, 2006; Hart & Hodson, 2004; see also CASEL). However, quality relationships in class are not only beneficial for pupils but for teachers too. From a self-determination perspective, teachers also need to feel connected to their pupils and colleagues and in doing so they can draw strength and positive professional well-being from positive relationships (Davis et al., 2012).

It is understandable that teachers who score highly in EI and SI are in the best position to build quality interpersonal relationships in their classrooms with and among learners (Gehlbach, 2010; Hattie, 2009; Jennings & Greenberg, 2009; Kress et al., 2004; Lopes et al., 2003; Moafian & Ghanizadeh, 2009; Powell & Kusuma-Powell, 2010; Saarni, 1999). Therefore, if we want to take a relational perspective on classroom life, we felt it would be a good place to start by exploring the beliefs and practices of English language teachers who scored highly on EI and SI scales. One of our primary aims was to see what quality relationships meant to these teachers and how they enacted such relationships and relational beliefs in their actual teaching practice.

Outline of the Study

Participants and context

To explore the relational beliefs and practices of highly socially and emotionally competent teachers, we first gathered data from an online survey which recorded EI/SI scores for ELT teachers across the globe. All the data came from part of a larger mixed methods study funded by the

British Council (Gkonou & Mercer, 2017). From the survey data, we selected six volunteer highly socio-emotionally competent English language teachers working in Austria and the UK at secondary school level (i.e. three EFL teachers in Austria, three ESL teachers in the UK). The demographic information for the participants is summarised in Table 10.1.

Data collection

To investigate the relational beliefs and practices of the participating teachers, we employed non-participant classroom observations and stimulated-recall interviews. For the classroom observations, we designed a semi-structured observation protocol to ensure that both researchers would focus on comparable aspects of the lessons in the two different countries and attend to similar aspects of classroom life of particular relevance to EI/SI. The observation protocols contained the following aspects for each lesson stage and activity type: teacher classroom management techniques, teacher body language (position and movement), teacher facial expressions, teacher communicating emotions non-verbally, teacher use of voice, and teacher visual behaviour (e.g. eye contact and duration). These observation protocols were intended to complement the lesson videos and thereby centred on aspects of teacher behaviour and classroom management that would potentially be difficult to notice by re-watching the films after the lessons. In both research settings, only one camera was used, which was placed at the back of the class and focused on the teacher only and not on the students.

The follow-up, semi-structured, stimulated-recall interviews with the teachers were conducted within a maximum of two weeks of the actual observations. The interview guide was divided into three main sections: (a) background and understanding the context where the focus was on teachers' experiences, emotions at the workplace, sharing practices with colleagues and general beliefs about what makes a good language lesson and teacher; (b) discussion about the concepts of EI and SI which elicited responses on teachers' awareness generally of the two constructs, their reported practices with relation to them, any training opportunities they have had on EI and SI and advice they would give to novice teachers; and (c) looking at the videos which included questions on segments of the lessons chosen by the teachers and/or the researchers and how teachers viewed them in respect to EI and SI. At the same time, the design was left open to allow for interesting points raised by the participants during the interview to be followed up with additional questions by the researchers. The interviews lasted between 80 and 134 minutes. It is worth noting that some of the interviewed teachers were already known to the researchers. This was felt to facilitate rapport during the interviews and enhance nuanced understandings on the part of the interviewers with regard to contextual and personal issues.

Table 10.1 Demographic information for teacher participants

Code	Age	Gender	Years of teaching experience	Experience of living abroad (in years)	Relevant qualifications	Total EI/SI score	Context	L1 English
T1UK	49	Female	23	6	BA modern languages PGCE TESOL Diploma	241	ESL	Yes
T2UK	36	Female	3	0	BA education TESOL Certificate	201	ESL	No
T3UK	39	Male	16	8	TESOL Certificate Bell Delta	235	ESL	Yes
T1A	42	Male	4	2	MA teaching English and history	214	EFL	No
T2A	53	Female	28	4	MA teaching English and sport	253	EFL	No
T3A	62	Female	29	37	MA modern languages MA English	247	EFL	Yes

Notes: EI, emotional intelligence; SI, social intelligence.

Data analysis

Each researcher read their classroom observation notes and watched the films of the lessons they had observed. A list of common themes that emerged across all lessons in each setting was compiled. This list was then exchanged between the two researchers and was also inserted into the data management software Atlas.ti for coding. All interviews were transcribed digitally for coding, again using Atlas.ti. This generated 107,352 words. Both researchers first read the interview transcripts and took notes making ongoing memos. Multiple waves of coding were done alternately by the researchers, constantly comparing, refining and checking for agreement. Based on the discussion, the codes from the classroom observations and interviews were assimilated and a first draft of the analysis was written by one of the authors. This was then reviewed and checked by the other author and it was exchanged until a joint final analysis was prepared. In this chapter we report on the key relational beliefs and practices of these teachers as observed in their classes and discussed in their stimulated recall interviews. For more detail on the larger study from which this is taken, please see Gkonou and Mercer (2017).

Findings

Unsurprisingly, also given the focus of the study, all of the teachers talked explicitly about working to promote positive relationships in their classes. They did this on two levels primarily: first, in terms of their own relationships with learners and, secondly, in terms of the relationships among the learners and the centrality of group dynamics. We will deal with each set of relationships in turn, with the primary focus being on the teacher–pupil relationship as was the focus of the study.

Teacher relationships with learners

There were four core features that the teachers shared in terms of what they believed supported or characterised a quality relationship with their learners. The most notable element concerned *empathy*. All of the teachers spoke either explicitly of seeking to get in the minds of their learners or, as T3A put it, trying to get on the kids' wavelength (T3A: 5287). Alternatively, they displayed the qualities of empathy in how they spoke about their pupils, often seeking to understand or explain their behaviour or responses, rather than judging them. Their empathy was especially notable in terms of their sensitivity to the pupils' need to protect face at this age. This meant that teachers reported being careful and thoughtful about how they gave and worded feedback, the arrangement of speaking activities, especially in plenary format, and also how to discipline appropriately ensuring neither teacher nor pupils lost face, typically by discussing problem issues outside of class. As T3UK (1048) explained,

> I'm always careful. I'm very, very careful about what I say even just if they've got an answer. Because for some of them to actually put a hand out and to answer your question or even answer a question, when you've asked an open question and because it's very hard just to get an answer. So when they actually do answer, they're really going out their way and putting themselves potentially in quite vulnerable situations to answer that question. So then to turn around and just say no bluntly, you see them. When they realized they've got it wrong and you see how upset and sort of how hurt they are. So I think you wouldn't want to reinforce that because and then they are not going to answer again. So yeah I think I'm very careful with that. So just soften it a little bit.

Four teachers also explicitly drew attention to the importance of being able to read pupils' emotions and using non-verbals to get a sense of the classroom atmosphere and individual emotional states. Some examples from the data illustrate this:

> I think I'm fairly sensitive when I see people blushing or reacting or you know. (T3A: 5343)

> I think I can read the students' emotions and feelings quite well in class. So I can feel if they're a bit flustered. I can tell when that student was a bit annoyed because he couldn't find the words out and I can tell when it's time not to go down, not to persevere and not to push one area or focus on one student too much because sometimes you're monitoring. (T3UK: 0908)

From the observational data, we also noted that the teachers used a lot of smiling and eye contact with pupils across all of the groups. Indeed, all of the teachers tended to move around the room making use of the classroom space and moving physically closer in and among the learners. T3UK described this most eloquently:

> I'd always feel that you've got this desk and this is the barrier. So when you're behind that desk you are the teacher and the students are there. But I try and get away from that all the time now. I won't make a big deal and I'll just say can you move your bag and I'll sit then and so I try to make it collective and move around a bit and put chairs differently. So it is very much us together rather than the teachers there behind the desk with this barrier and they're there teaching the students. (T3UK: 0924)

Another quality mentioned explicitly by half of the teachers was the idea of bi-directional respect. In this way, teachers spoke of trying to show their respect for their pupils and their opinions, listening actively to them, but they also expected the respect to be returned by the pupils.

> But you can always learn to respect the student and I think that is abso-lutely key and sometimes you will respect them and empathise with

them. Sometimes you naturally empathise with them and just love them but obviously your behaviour is the same for everybody. And sometimes you find it difficult to understand them but you can still respect them. (T1UK: 0063)

I think it's respect I try to respect them they respect me (T1A: 1447)

T2A talks of an incident when the pupils were being disrespectful. She explains that she only needs to explicitly remind them or ask them whether she has ever shown them such disrespect and they recognise she has not and, as such, the problem is then typically resolved.

T: And not showing respect. I don't have to do anything I just ask them sorry have you ever have I ever talked to you like that?
R: mhm mhm mhm
T: Do you think I don't respect you? And they cannot say I think so because it's just not true
R: True mhm
T: And they never ever they say okay you respect me and could you please do the same to me? And usually it's okay. (T2A: 3379–3383)

Teachers also talked about trust and making learners feel safe. It is possible that this dimension of relationships is especially important in language classrooms given the need for learners to present themselves in a foreign language and risk losing face. T1A explains the need to ensure that this sense of trust is exercised in respect of the other learners' behaviour in class as well:

That if you have created if you have the feeling that there is a person you can trust and if you have the feeling that ah this person is going to make sure that the others are not going to make fun of you then ah or establish ah an atmosphere that allows you to to to to speak up you're going to do it. (T1A: 2118)

T1UK reports on a group that she worked with where the trust among the learners had been broken and how difficult it was to get them talking and engaged. This draws attention to the role of the teacher in managing and creating a sense of trust not only with themselves but also among the learners.

But this particular class, they were just all really miserable and I think that looking back, it was because the group dynamic which I was talking about before had not been worked on, they didn't trust each other, they didn't want to work together. (T1UK: 0044)

Finally, the most notable characteristic that all of these teachers talked about or displayed was a responsiveness to the group as a whole as well as individuals. They all recognised the diversity and how groups can differ from each other. They all took trouble to not only know their pupils' names but also to know personal stories or information about them as individuals. They reported trying to use this to connect with the students and to help make the pupils feel involved and cared for.

> I try and remember little things about them that again I will use in my humor ... If you can remember things about the students I think that makes a big difference as well. (T3UK: 0864)

> T: Or X for example the Afro-
> R: Yeah
> T: Austrian girl in that row she she was blown away by Ireland when they went there last year and now she would love to go to X you know
> R: Oh nice!
> T: And I try to you know I try to mention these little things to them when I'm marking their homework for example. (T3A: 5203–5207)

T3A explained that she wanted her pupils in this way to feel liked and valued as people (T3A: 6640).

Another issue that emerged from the data was the issue of fairness, with teachers wanting to treat everyone fairly and equally.

> ... but you've got to treat them the same as everybody else and you've got to smile at them too ... and try to treat them equally. (T3A: 6614–6616)

Yet, this did not mean treating all the learners in the same way. As T3A went on to explain,

> T: And I think you've got to you've got to ah vary it according to the individual
> R: Yes
> T: Now take X for example brilliant student brilliant mind very clever lazy as anything
> R: mhm
> T: So ah if you know if he'll hand me in an essay the last minute that he's quickly written by hand and it's actually it's pretty good eh but you know there are things and I'll say X I'm not accepting anything without title
> R: Yeah
> T: I'm not I'm not taking it now another kid who has terrible problems
> R: Yeah
> T: even finding the thoughts to put in an essay who forgets the title I'm not gonna make a fuss about the title yeah?
> R: Yeah yeah
> T: I'm going to take what he has you know what I mean?
> R: Yeah yeah it's the everybody should be doing to their limits what they can do. (T3A: 6998–7009)

This differentiation between learners was linked to the sensitivity on the part of the teachers to learners' individual needs and how this was reflected in working structures. All the teachers talked about the benefits of knowing learners as individuals and trying to accommodate and acknowledge this diversity in interactions.

The teachers also talked about adjusting their teaching to suit the learners and their ongoing needs or mood.

> I realized if something is not working don't keep flogging that dead horse. (T3UK: 0920)

> T: If I love a short story and I think ah this is gonna be great and I'll do it with the kids and I see that it's it's above their heads it's too difficult it's too ...
> R: Yeah
> T: boring for them I have absolutely no problem abandoning it
> R: Yeah
> T: and doing something else. (T3A: 6538–6542)

This flexibility was characteristic of all the teachers but especially notable among all the ESL teachers who all worked with culturally diverse classes, which they attempted to accommodate and work with in a culturally sensitive manner.

> Then maybe choose one of them to read out all the things that you learn later, about ways to encourage people to speak if they're not confident. But, yes it was that again it, it was the lack of, perhaps cultural understanding, but also the contrast between these very lively expressive Europeans and the vast majority of the class who were basically just waiting for me to tell them stuff, and so they could learn so that was quite hard. (T1UK: 0042)

> You learn that certain cultures will respond to this and other cultures will respond to that. (T1UK: 0061)

An especially interesting dimension to the relationship between teacher and pupils was the fact that the effects were bi-directional. Previous research (see, for example, Wentzel, 2015) has tended to emphasise the effects of quality teacher–pupil relationships for learners, but the effects on teachers are less often discussed. However, these teachers showed awareness not only of reaping the benefits when the relationship was good but also feeling it negatively when there are problems. For example,

> ... sometimes if you're not feeling up to teaching but then anyway you get into the mood anyway just by being in the class and interacting. (T3UK: 0752)

Generally, the teachers consciously took steps to enact their socio-emotional competences with regard to building and maintaining healthy relationships with learners as a group and with the individuals in the class. While they differed in some of their concrete actions, their general concerns were very similar. All of the teachers also attended to the relationships among the learners and this is discussed in the next section.

Teachers' view of relationships among learners

The most salient topic raised among the teachers was that of group dynamics. Indeed, T1UK expressed this best, saying, 'Teaching is a group thing, it's got to be, and the group dynamics is so key' (0036). All of the teachers talked about the importance of group dynamics for classroom life to function effectively, especially in a language classroom which typically depends on people feeling comfortable enough to speak up and be happy to work with others. The teachers each took specific actions to try to ensure positive relationships among learners, such as using self-depreciating humour to lower anxiety and create a positive rapport as well as ensuring that learners knew one another's names.

> ... but by making fool out of myself ah I allow them to make fools out of themselves ... And the here we are again with this ah safe environment. (T1A: 2315–2317)

However, it was interesting to note that teachers differed in the degree of control they felt they had over the group dynamics that emerged, especially at the early stages of group formation:

> Yes, because of classroom dynamics. Because of the good interactions between students and students. Sometimes it is not down to me, it is down to them. (T2UK: 0519)

> T: I'm not talking about now who is in charge but what the climate is going to be that is decided by the kids by the the
> R: And how much influence do you think the teachers have on the climate?
> T: If once has been established it's very difficult to change a class climate I think if you have a class from the beginning you can do a lot. (T3A: 6578–6580)

This is an important dimension of teacher competences, namely, having a sense that a skill or ability is within your locus of control and something that you can work on and affect.

Teacher relationships with significant others (professional and personal)

The teachers in the study not only talked about the relationships in class – although these were clearly the focus of the data collection – but they also spoke about how important other relationships are for their well-being. Notably, several teachers talked about how the relationship with the head teacher can positively or negatively affect the morale among staff and their own relationship to the head and school as a whole. The two data extracts below show clearly the contrasting experiences that are possible in a school:

> She is lovely. She always has time to listen to us. She has always ... we know that she has got plenty on her plate already. We know that all the

inspections, and all the paper work but she is so good at managing her time. Whenever you come to her, whenever whether she is busy or not, she stops and ok come in … She is very welcoming. I think this is very important for people. We feel like … some people can show this that they are stressed with work and then they just take out on other people. This is what happens to X so he is not so good boss. (T2UK: 0379)

Because there's really no support from our head teacher … Because I know that he is satisfied our work and to the outside world … my teachers are great but he never ever tells us … It's just when we make a mistake it's terrible and but eh I don't think that anyone of us has ever heard you did a great job here or there. (T2A: 3561–3565)

A generally more supportive experience was reported by the teachers in their relationships with colleagues. Several of the teachers talked positively about being able to share materials and ideas with colleagues or simply just enjoy a 'debrief' about school life with their colleagues.

So you often get teachers send in materials and emails and ideas and discussing what you do and just helping each other out. There's a nice veil of camaraderie there I think. I think there is a nice support there. You just kind of brainstorm and pick each other's brains and get ideas. Even just talking about how students respond to materials and how you deal with particular students. I think that's the massive part of teaching being able to bounce these ideas around and reflect on it with other teachers. (T3UK: 0888)

And we support each other just by you know having fun during the breaks meeting for drink after work and you know writing stupid things on whatsapp. (T2A: 3553)

However, for some teachers, their relationships with their partners at home were an especially important source of well-being giving them strength to cope with life in school.

T: I keep talking to my husband I tell him that maybe he doesn't really listen this doesn't really matter and while I tell him I realise things
R: mhm
T: and I don't really we don't really want any answers because for most of us talking is just you know analysing and then putting the things into the right shelves
R: Yeah
T: onto the right shelves and then you can see at least
R: Yeah
T: For me I can see that. (T2A: 3515–3519)

As these non-school related relationships were not the focus of the study, we did not collect data in depth about them; however, they represent a potentially important source of well-being for the teachers despite or perhaps because of not being from the same domain and sphere of work.

Teacher beliefs

All of the teachers in our study believed strongly in the value of a communicative language teaching (CLT) approach. This meant that they prioritised meaningful personal communication above language accuracy. Indeed, for one teacher (T1A), this was so much more important for rapport building as well that he supported a boy in one class in telling a story in his L1 because he wanted to help him get his story across as a matter of priority. For him, the communication per se was more important than an insistence on use of the L2, which could have frustrated the learner given his lack of L2 proficiency at this stage. As he explains,

> T: Ahm and I told them before we started I wasn't thinking of him but there was another girl at the class where I knew she had second language informally and I said 'Ok you can' the task was to write down for you know 2–3 minutes without stopping for everything they knew or they associated with ah a new topic we were going to talk about this task to just warm them up. I said 'Use use the language that comes to you naturally' and he wrote in X because he had a X background and (laughter) after the class he came to me and he was like almost as tall as I'm in the fifth form and he came and he had tears in his eyes and he said you know this was the first time that in Austria I could do something with my language in the school system and that makes you think doesn't it? We have these huge resources and we don't have any structure or anything to develop these structures we know about the X talk and all these things and we know how important it is to have a good developed first language in order not only for your language classes but also for mathematics and physics and whatever
>
> R: Everything
>
> T: And we just don't make any use of the knowledge and that's a shame. (T1A: 1725–1727)

Generally, all the teachers adhered to a CLT perspective and had distinct beliefs about what classed as successful language teaching. An interesting dimension of this was the amount of self-disclosure deemed to be appropriate from teachers. Research has shown that a degree of self-disclosure can create more positive relationships between teacher and pupils (Lannutti & Strauman, 2006), but it is a fine balance and too much disclosure would be inappropriate. In the language classroom there is naturally more opportunity for self-disclosure on the part of both learners and teachers. As learners were expected to share so much about themselves through the materials typical in CLT settings, T3UK felt it only fair to share some aspects of his own life as well. However, as he cautioned, 'I don't go overboard' (0812). Two teachers explain that such self-disclosure is valuable in helping learners to see another more human side of you as a teacher and therefore as a way to build trust:

> That's not fair if I'm asking them to do that then I should be sharing too and sometimes they ask sometimes they ask 'what do you think?' which

is actually great isn't it because they're seeing you as a person and not just as a teacher and that's very important. (T1UK: 0079)

But at the same time again I think if that's kind of who you are and you get to know the students in class I think they can see that you're a human as well and they're not just a teacher. (T3UK: 0812)

A specific set of beliefs that raised some questions of concern for us were teacher mindset beliefs about the socio-emotional competences at the focus of this study. During the interviews, neither of us thought to follow up on the comments on these beliefs in any detail and that must remain for another study to explore in more depth. However, four of the teachers explicitly raised questions about whether these skills are 'learnable' or not. As T2UK explains, 'sometimes I do something and I realise OMG I have done it wrong. I should have not said this. I should have empathised more with this. Sometimes I feel like that, I feel like I need to learn how to master this. But I do not know if it is learnable?' (T2UK: 0391). T3UK (1056) also commented on this:

I think some people perhaps are more sensitive anyway because they are more sensitive themselves. So I think they might be a bit more tuned in to the students' feelings or might be more aware of how they're feeling, by nature, by their own by their own character. Sometimes I'll put myself in that situation so I think in that sense, despite how you deal with people, there is an element by your own character by being responsive. So I know some teachers who are brilliant of responding to student's emotions and I'm very, very aware of how to deal with students and how to respect student's needs and emotions in the class and perhaps others who might not be as good at it. But having said that, I think there are, you can also say develop the skills, yes, I think you can also become intuitive to how students are likely to react to things you say in the classroom ... I think first of all I think part of your character just naturally you kind of respond, but because of who you are and the way you deal with different people and emotionally in that sense, but also, I think you can also develop these skills and I think things like workshops would be a good thing.

This idea of these competences being immutable would match another study by Irie *et al.* (under review), which suggests that pre-service teachers may also feel that these less technical and more 'soft skills' or 'personality traits' are not competences that can be developed, thereby holding a more fixed mindset about them. This is naturally of concern for pre-service and in-service training that can only be effective if the teachers taking part start from the premise that they can improve their abilities as a teacher in these areas.

Implications for Practice and Questions for Further Research

In this chapter we have reported on the kinds of beliefs and practices ESL/EFL teachers who score highly on EI/SI have in regard to relationships in their professional roles. We have seen that although the teachers differed in some respects, there were also commonalities in terms of some of the key qualities of relationships that they recognised. We reflect that socio-emotional competences are likely to foster teachers who are sensitive to the interpersonal dimensions of language learning and teaching but their practices will be mediated by their beliefs which in turn will potentially generate individual behaviours. This means any training programmes will need to be sensitive in not prescribing specific behaviours but instead seeking to promote principles, which teachers can enact in ways that reflect their own personalities, belief systems and sense of authenticity as a teacher. There is not just one way to be socio-emotionally competent as a language teacher, and how a teacher chooses to express their 'caring' for learners may vary.

We also noted that the teachers commented on the degree to which certain aspects of socio-emotional competences can be developed and are within a teacher's locus of control. This raises important questions for us in respect to teacher development. As outlined earlier, evidence from intervention studies suggests that EI/SI competences are malleable, at least to some degree, and can be promoted through training (see, for example, Brackett & Katulak, 2006; Nelis *et al.*, 2009; Zins *et al.*, 2004). We suggest that training needs to begin by getting teachers to have a 'growth mindset' in these areas in order to create facilitative attitudes, which will help teachers to be open to working on improving their skills in these areas.

At present, we note that there tend to be very few pre-service or, indeed, in-service training programmes that attend to these skill areas. However, given their centrality for successful and effective teaching as well as for teacher professional well-being, we argue that space should be made within respective curricula and development programmes as a matter of urgency. However, there is often little time or space made for these supposed 'soft skills', with priority being given to technical skills. Yet we concur with Day and Gu (2010: 36) who conclude that creating a dichotomy between these two sets of skills is ultimately a mistake.

We are only at the beginning of understanding the nature of language teacher EI/SI and how this interconnects with teacher beliefs and practices and there remain many exciting questions for further research to investigate. We are especially keen to explore the nature of teacher–pupil relationships with the focus on the relationship per se as an emergent quality of the interaction of the individuals involved. We are also keen to understand how teacher mindsets about their socio-emotional competences may affect their willingness to engage in training programmes in this area. We also recognise the need to develop empirically based intervention programmes that allow for teacher individuality and cultural appropriacy. As other work in this area suggests that emotions are likely to be understood and worked on differently in different cultures (e.g. Weare, 2004), future models of language teacher socio-emotional competences will need to be developed in light of this contextual variation.

Conclusion

In this chapter we have focused on the teachers' use of their EI/SI to understand the role and nature of relationships in their professional lives, focusing on classroom life. We have ourselves been positively inspired by the experience and have learned a lot from watching teachers who care about their learners and convey this in terms of their interest in them as individuals and their interest in the quality of their learning (see also Davis *et al.*, 2012). From our study, it is apparent that all the teachers were caring in respect to their learners but their caring was expressed in different ways which reflected the different characters and experiences of the teachers. Teachers will need to enact their EI/SI in ways which enable them to express their authentic teaching selves and there cannot be any prescriptive lessons drawn from this study. Instead, we saw that caring did not imply 'coddling' (Cavanagh, n.d.), but it did mean a level of relational quality between teachers and pupils that embodied the mutual respect, trust and warmth which are characteristic of positive and healthy interpersonal relationships. Relationships are the key to successful classrooms and the teachers' own psychology will be defining in the nature and quality of the relationships they are able and willing to construct. As we begin to better understand teacher psychology, we will start to appreciate what competences teachers believe they can develop, such as their socio-emotional competences, and how we can work with these understandings for better teacher development programmes that not only foster the technical skills of teaching but also the socio-emotional skills that we believe are so central to successful educational encounters from both the learner and teacher perspective.

Note

(1) This document is an output from the ELT Research Award scheme funded by the British Council to promote innovation in English language teaching research. The views expressed are not necessarily those of the British Council.

References

Bingham, C. and Sidorkin, A.M. (eds) (2010) *No Education Without Relation*. New York: Peter Lang.

Brackett, M.A. and Katulak, N. (2006) The emotionally intelligent classroom: Skill-based training for teachers and students. In J. Ciarrochi and J.D. Mayer (eds) *Improving Emotional Intelligence: A Practitioner's Guide* (pp. 1–27). New York: Psychology Press/Taylor & Francis.

Brackett, M.A., Palomera, R., Mojsa-Kaja, J., Reyes, M.R. and Salovey, P. (2010) Emotion-regulation ability, burnout, and job satisfaction among British secondary-school teachers. *Psychology in the Schools* 47 (4), 406–417.

Breen, M.P. (2001) Navigating the discourse: On what is learned in the language classroom. In C.N. Candlin and N. Mercer (eds) *English Language Teaching in its Social Context: A Reader*. Abingdon: Routledge.

CASEL (Collaborative for Academic, Social, and Emotional Learning) (n.d.) Website. See www.casel.org (accessed 20 September 2016).

Castle, P. and Buckler, S. (2009) *How to Be a Successful Teacher: Strategies for Personal and Professional Development*. Thousand Oaks, CA: Sage.

Cavanagh, S.R. (n.d.) *Caring Isn't Coddling*. See https://chroniclevitae.com/news/1621-caring-isn-t-coddling (accessed 12 December 2016).

Cornelius-White, J. (2007) Learner-centered teacher–student relationships are effective: A meta-analysis. *Review of Educational Research* 77 (1), 113–143.

Davis, H.A. (2003) Conceptualizing the role and influence of student–teacher relationships on children's social and cognitive development. *Educational Psychologist* 38 (4), 207–234.

Davis, H.A., Summers, J.J. and Miller, L.M. (2012) *An Interpersonal Approach to Classroom Management*. Thousand Oaks, CA: Corwin Press.

Day, C. and Gu, Q. (2010) *The New Lives of Teachers*. Abingdon: Routledge.

Dewaele, J.-M., Petrides, K.V. and Furnham, A. (2008) The effects of trait emotional intelligence and sociobiographical variables on communicative anxiety and foreign language anxiety among adult multilinguals: A review and empirical investigation. *Language Learning* 58 (4), 911–960.

Emmerling, R.J. and Goleman, D. (2003) *Emotional Intelligence: Issues and Common Misunderstandings*. The Consortium for Research on Emotional Intelligence in Organizations. See http://www.eiconsortium.org/pdf/EI_Issues_And_Common_Misunderstandings.pdf (accessed 25 September 2016).

Fredricks, J.A., Blumenfeld, P.C. and Paris, A. (2004) School engagement: Potential of the concept, state of the evidence. *Review of Educational Research* 74 (1), 59–109.

Furrer, C. and Skinner, E. (2003) Sense of relatedness as a factor in children's academic engagement and performance. *Journal of Educational Psychology* 95 (1), 148–162.

Gehlbach, H. (2010) The social side of school: Why teachers need social psychology. *Educational Psychology Review* 22 (3), 349–362.

Gieve, S. and Miller, I.K. (2006) *Understanding the Language Classroom*. Basingstoke: Palgrave.

Gkonou, C. and Mercer, S. (2017) *Understanding Emotional and Social Intelligence among English Language Teachers*. London: British Council.

Goleman, D. (1995) *Emotional Intelligence: Why It Can Matter More Than IQ*. New York: Bantam Books.

Goleman, D. (1998) *Working with Emotional Intelligence*. New York: Bantam Books.

Goleman, D. (2006) *Social Intelligence: The New Science of Human Relationships*. London: Arrow Books.

Hart, S. and Hodson, V.K. (2004) *The Compassionate Classroom: Relationship Based Teaching and Learning*. Encinitas, CA: PuddleDancer Press.

Hattie, J. (2009) *Visible Learning: A Synthesis of Over 800 Meta-Analyses Relating to Achievement*. Abingdon: Routledge.

Holmes, E. (2005) *Teacher Wellbeing: Looking After Yourself and Your Career in the Classroom*. London: Taylor & Francis.

Humphrey, N. (2013) *Social and Emotional Learning: A Critical Appraisal*. London: Sage.

Imai, Y. (2010) Emotions in SLA: New insights from collaborative learning for an EFL classroom. *The Modern Language Journal* 94 (2), 278–292.

Irie, K., Ryan, S. and Mercer, S. (under review) Using Q methodology to investigate pre-service EFL teachers' mindsets about teaching competences.

Jennings, P.A. and Greenberg, M.T. (2009) The prosocial classroom: Teacher social and emotional competence in relation to student and classroom outcomes. *Review of Educational Research* 79 (1), 491–525.

Kress, J.S., Norris, J.A., Schoenholz, Z.A., Elias, M.J. and Seigle, P. (2004) Bringing together educational standards and social and emotional learning: Making the case for educators. *American Journal of Education* 111 (1), 68–89.

Kusché, C.A. and Greenberg, M.T. (2006) Teaching emotional literacy in elementary school classrooms: The PATHS Curriculum. In M.J. Elias and H. Arnold (eds) *The Educator's Guide to Emotional Intelligence and Academic Achievement: Social-Emotional Learning in the Classroom* (pp. 150–160). Thousand Oaks, CA: Corwin Press.

Lannutti, P.J. and Strauman, E.C. (2006) Classroom communication: The influence of instructor self-disclosure on student evaluations. *Communication Quarterly* 54 (1), 89–99.

Lopes, P.N., Salovey, P. and Straus, R. (2003) Emotional intelligence, personality, and the perceived quality of social relationships. *Personality and Individual Differences* 35 (3), 641–658.

Matthews, G., Zeidner, M. and Roberts, R.D. (2002) *Emotional Intelligence: Science and Myth*. Boston, MA: MIT Press.

Mayer, J.D., Salovey, P. and Caruso, D.R. (2008) Emotional intelligence: New ability or eclectic mix of traits? *American Psychologist* 63 (6), 503–517.

Mercer, S. (2016) Seeing the world through your eyes: Empathy in language learning and teaching. In P.D. MacIntyre, T. Gregersen and S. Mercer (eds) *Positive Psychology in Second Language Acquisition* (pp. 91–111). Bristol: Multilingual Matters.

Mercer, S., Ryan, S. and Williams, M. (eds) (2012) *Psychology for Language Learning: Insights from Research, Theory and Practice*. Basingstoke: Palgrave Macmillan.

Mercer, S., Oberdorfer, P. and Saleem, M. (2016) Helping language teachers to thrive: Using positive psychology to promote teachers' professional well-being. In D. Gabryś-Barker and D. Gałajda (eds) *Positive Psychology Perspectives on Foreign Language Learning and Teaching* (pp. 213–229). Cham: Springer.

Merrell, K.W. and Gueldner, B.A. (2010) *Social and Emotional Learning in the Classroom: Promoting Mental Health and Academic Success*. New York: Guildford Press.

Moafian, F. and Ghanizadeh, A. (2009) The relationship between Iranian EFL teachers' emotional intelligence and their self-efficacy in language institutes. *System* 37 (4), 708–718.

Nelis, D., Quoidbach, J., Mikolajczak, M. and Hansenne, M. (2009) Increasing emotional intelligence: (How) is it possible? *Personality and Individual Differences* 47 (1), 36–41.

Oz, H., Demirezen, M. and Pourfeiz, J. (2015) Emotional intelligence and attitudes towards foreign language learning: Pursuit of relevance and implications. *Procedia – Social and Behavioral Sciences* 186, 416–423.

Patti, J. (2006) Addressing social-emotional education in teacher education. In M.J. Elias and H. Arnold (eds) *The Educator's Guide to Emotional Intelligence and Academic Achievement: Social-Emotional Learning in the Classroom* (pp. 67–75). Thousand Oaks, CA: Corwin Press.

Powell, W. and Kusuma-Powell, O. (2010) *Becoming an Emotionally Intelligent Teacher*. Thousand Oaks, CA: Corwin Press.

Reissman, R. (2006) Raising your new teacher's emotional intelligence: How using social-emotional competences can make your first year of teaching less stressful and more successful. In M.J. Elias and H. Arnold (eds) *The Educator's Guide to Emotional Intelligence and Academic Achievement: Social-Emotional Learning in the Classroom* (pp. 76–82). Thousand Oaks, CA: Corwin Press.

Saarni, C. (1999) *The Development of Emotional Competence*. New York: Guildford Press.

Shao, K., Yu, W. and Ji, Z. (2013) An exploration of Chinese EFL students' emotional intelligence and foreign language anxiety. *The Modern Language Journal* 97 (4), 917–929.

Skinner, E. and Belmont, M.J. (1993) Motivation in the classroom: Reciprocal effect of teacher behavior and student engagement across the school year. *Journal of Educational Psychology* 85 (4), 571–581.

Weare, K. (2004) *Developing the Emotionally Literate School*. London: Paul Chapman.

Wentzel, K.R. (2015) *Teacher–Student Relationships, Motivation, and Competence at School*. New York: Routledge.

Zembylas, M. (2005) *Teaching with Emotion: A Postmodern Enactment*. Greenwich, CT: Information Age.

Zins, J.E., Weissberg, R.P., Wang, M.C. and Walberg, H.J. (eds) (2004) *Building Academic Success on Social and Emotional Learning: What Does the Research Say?* New York: Teachers College Press.

11 Variation in ESL/EFL Teachers' Attitudes towards their Students

Jean-Marc Dewaele and Sarah Mercer

Mercer *et al.* (2016) have called for more teacher-centredness in the field of language learning psychology, arguing that teacher psychology plays a central role not just for the teachers themselves but also for their students and their psychology. As Day and Gu (2009) argue, teacher well-being is crucial in a rewarding but very demanding profession, not only for teachers' own job satisfaction and motivation but also for the effectiveness of their teaching and ultimately for their learners' well-being as well. Indeed, the effects of a healthy teacher psychology imply a better teacher in terms of pedagogy and didactics too. As Bajorek *et al.* (2014: 6) explain, a 'teacher with high job satisfaction, positive morale and who is healthy should be more likely to teach lessons which are creative, challenging and effective'.

To date, research in the field of teacher psychology in second language acquisition (SLA) has concentrated on a relatively narrow number of variables, especially when compared with the breadth of variables considered in learner psychology in SLA (Mercer, 2016). This has resulted in a relatively patchy understanding of the complexity of teacher psychology. This volume seeks to redress the balance and, in this chapter, we hope to contribute to the emerging field by considering a number of independent variables in teachers which we hypothesise might be linked to the attitudes they have towards their students. More specifically, we focus on the role of ESL/EFL teachers' emotional intelligence, English proficiency, teaching experience, gender, and their attitudes towards various types of learners and how these may be interrelated. The idea to include two dependent variables, where one represents a subcategory of the other (teacher attitudes towards lively students versus towards students in general) stems from the realisation that teachers may have different attitudes towards students who are more lively and more challenging than average. In the service industry there are parallels examining the skills of providers regarding how they deal with challenging rather than average customers (Harris, 2002).

One key factor known to contribute positively to learner achievement is their rapport and relationship with their teacher (Hattie, 2009; see also Gkonou & Mercer, this volume). In this study we seek to understand, first, teachers' attitudes towards their students, which is a key dimension of this rapport and relationship. One can expect that positive teacher attitudes are likely to be reflected in positive attitudes in the learners too through processes such as contagion and the role of mirror neurons (Frenzel & Stephens, 2013; Iacoboni *et al.*, 2005). A second reason for focusing on teacher attitudes is because several studies have found that there is a link between teacher and pupil emotions and motivation (see, for example, Frenzel & Stephens, 2013). It can thus be supposed that teachers' negative attitudes towards their students would negatively affect the atmosphere during classes and dampen students' enjoyment, potentially leading to demotivation and the weakening of their desire to learn the target language (Dewaele *et al.*, 2017). The second characteristic we wish to examine in relation to teacher attitudes to their learners is their emotional intelligence (EI). EI is known to be a key characteristic that contributes to positive relationships; teachers scoring high in EI have been shown to have better relationships with learners and to be able to create a better, more positive classroom atmosphere (Albrecht, 2006; Corcoran & Tormey, 2012).

Thus, the questions we wish to investigate in this study are to what extent teacher attitudes are linked to relatively stable characteristics of the teacher. Might EI make a difference, as suggested by studies that document its impact on positive relations and classroom experience (Albrecht, 2006; Corcoran & Tormey, 2012)? Or – given the findings by Gkonou and Mercer (2017) and Dewaele *et al.* (in preparation) that teachers with more experience scored more highly in EI – might teaching experience play a role too? Given the language specificity of the domain, could teachers' level of proficiency in English have any effect on their attitudes towards their students? Finally, given research which suggests gender differences in EI (Corcoran & Tormey, 2012; Gkonou & Mercer, 2017; Petrides *et al.*, 2004), we also wondered whether male and female EFL/ESL teachers have comparable attitudes towards their students. The present study aims to address these questions and, by doing so, start to fill this particular gap in our understanding of teacher psychology, reflecting also specifically on its potential contribution to classroom dynamics and the nature of the teacher–student relationship.

Literature Review

Empirical work on teacher attitudes had traced connections between these and a number of constructs, including learner characteristics, and teacher-related factors such as teacher experience, gender, cultural affinity and EI levels. Most research on teachers' attitudes towards their students has centred on special needs students in mainstream schools (Avramidis & Norwich, 2002). The motivation for the research was to find out whether inclusive policies were supported by educators in practice. Reviewing the existing research, the authors concluded that a host of factors might impact upon teacher acceptance of the inclusion principle. Teachers' attitudes were more dependent on the nature and severity of the disabling condition of the student than on teacher-related variables. Pursuing this line of enquiry, Avramidis and Kalyva (2007) considered the attitudes of 155 Greek general education primary teachers towards inclusion. The authors found that teachers with longer experience in teaching special needs students held more positive attitudes towards them.

In the field of language education, Walker *et al.* (2004) collected data from 422 mainstream K-12 teachers in 28 US schools, and supplementary interview data from six teachers, on their ideological beliefs and attitudes towards English language learners (ELLs). Their aim was to use a mixed methods approach to identify negative, ethnocentric or racist attitudes among teachers in order to confront and transform these attitudes. At the time of the data collection, the United States was still reeling from the ban on bilingual education and the downsizing of ELL education. Independent variables included '(1) whether or not the teacher had received training in working with language-minority students, (2) whether the teacher had previously taught ELLs, (3) the ethnic backgrounds of ELLs taught, (4) teacher's total years of teaching (…) (5) teacher's gender, and (6) teacher's educational background' (Walker *et al.*, 2004: 138). The analysis revealed that 70% of teachers were 'not actively interested in having ELL students in their classroom' (Walker *et al.*, 2004: 140) and that close to 90% had never received any training on how to work with ELL students. Despite this, close to two-thirds of teachers felt that their school was welcoming towards ELL students and their native cultures and three-quarters felt that these language-minority students 'bring needed diversity to schools' (Walker *et al.*, 2004: 140). Numerous teachers declared that ELL students should be the sole responsibility of specialised ELL teachers rather than them, the mainstream teachers. The negative attitudes were found to result from negative experiences with ELL students and from an ethnocentric bias (Walker *et al.*, 2004: 154). More experienced teachers, having had more positive experiences with ELL students, developed more positive attitudes (Walker *et al.*, 2004: 153).

Another study of teacher attitudes towards ELLs in mainstream classes was conducted by Reeves (2006). From her study of 279 high school teachers, she explored a range of teacher attitudes and found a neutral to slightly positive attitude towards ELL inclusion. Clearly, teacher attitudes towards minority groups in their classrooms is an important dimension to explore further and, in terms of expectations, could be defining for the teacher–pupil relationship and teacher actions in class.

Teacher–student relationships can also be affected by gender issues. Split *et al.* (2012) collected data from 649 primary school teachers teaching a total of 1493 students and found that 'female teachers reported better (i.e. more close, less conflictual, and less dependent) relationships with students than male teachers' (Split *et al.*, 2012: 363). They also reported that female teachers had equally good relationships with male students as male teachers. Other studies have suggested that perceived similarity (which can be through gender among other factors such as ethnicity) can affect the quality of a relationship. For example, Ensher and Murphy (1997) found that the quality of relationship between mentor and protégé was higher with perceived similarity in terms of both race and gender, although others such as Turban *et al.* (2002) have found that similarity effects can dissipate with time depending on the duration of the actual relationships. Clearly, these are important dimensions to the potential quality of teacher–student relationships that need to be better understood as possible mediating variables.

Teacher attitudes towards their students are also reflected in the emotions that teachers experience and express both consciously and unconsciously in their behaviours in class. Frenzel and Stephens (2013) use the concept of emotional contagion to explain what happens when students recognise their teacher's emotions and subsequently experience similar emotions. Teachers who enjoyed teaching maths classes used lively gestures and humour, and they also made frequent eye contact with students. Unsurprisingly, these teachers were rated as more enthusiastic by their students, who felt more motivated as a consequence (Frenzel & Stephens, 2013: 49). Becker *et al.* (2015) focused on the antecedents of 39 teachers' emotions in 9th or 10th grade mathematics classes with a total of 758 students. The researchers looked specifically at the relationships between students' motivation and discipline and the level of enjoyment and anger experienced by their teachers. The students' motivation and discipline was found to explain a quarter of the variance in their teachers' emotions. The inclusion of the teachers' subjective appraisals as a mediating mechanism increased the amount of variance explained to almost two-thirds. The authors concluded that 'since teachers' emotions depend to a large extent on subjective evaluations of a situation, teachers should be able to directly modify their emotional experiences during a lesson through cognitive reappraisals' (Becker *et al.*, 2015: 1).

Our additional hypothesised construct that we feel may mediate the attitudes teachers hold about their pupils and the possible relationship they form with pupils is their levels of EI. The theory of trait emotional intelligence (TEI) emerged from the distinction between two EI constructs (ability EI and trait EI; Petrides & Furnham, 2000, 2001). TEI is formally defined as a constellation of emotional perceptions located at the lower levels of personality hierarchies typically assessed through questionnaires and rating scales (Petrides *et al.*, 2007). Although TEI is linked to higher order personality traits (the so-called Big Five), it explains unique variance. TEI essentially concerns people's self-perceptions of their emotional abilities and their inner world. The authors distinguish between four trait EI factors: well-being, self-control, emotionality and sociability. In the field of EFL/ESL, Moafian and Ghanizadeh (2009) looked at the relationship between EI, measured with a Persian version (Dehshiri, 2003) of the Bar-On EI test (Bar-On, 1997), and teacher self-efficacy, measured with the Ohio State Teacher Efficacy Scale (Tschannen-Moran & Woolfolk Hoy, 2001) of 89 Iranian EFL teachers. They found a significant correlation between EFL teachers' EI and their scores in self-efficacy ($r = 0.5$, $p < 0.05$). Three components of EI were most strongly correlated with teacher efficacy: emotional self-awareness, interpersonal relationship and problem solving. The authors argue that training could enhance teachers' EI which could then increase their sense of efficacy. The intended result would be more effective teaching through enhanced group dynamics, less anxiety and more empathetic communication.

Enhancing teachers' EI was also the aim of Vesely *et al.* (2014), whose starting point was the observation that, 'teaching is a profession of high occupational stress and "emotional labour"' (Vesely *et al.*, 2014: 81). Teachers who can no longer deal with the stress may abandon the profession. The researchers thus tried to boost 49 pre-service teachers' EI over a five-week period to help them manage their stress levels and remain in the profession in the future. They found a marginally significant increase between the start and the end of the treatment on Petrides' (2009) Trait Emotional Intelligence Questionnaire (Short Form) and a significant increase on Wong, Law and Wong's Emotional Intelligence Questionnaire (WEIS) (Wong *et al.*, 2004).

Gkonou and Mercer (2017; see also this volume) also examined levels of EI and social intelligence (SI) with EFL teachers across the globe. They found generally high scores for all teachers but with some gender, length of experience and possible cultural differences. In their stimulated recall interviews following in-class observations of teachers, they found that teachers scoring highly on EI/SI shared many interpersonal goals and values but some of their actual specific classroom behaviours differed according to intrapersonal and contextual characteristics.

As can be seen in the preceding paragraphs, research on teacher attitudes has shed light on how they relate to multiple factors, including relatively stable variables (e.g. gender) and more dynamic ones, such as EI and SI. To date, however, research into the attitudes of language teachers seems relatively scarce, and our study aims to begin to address this gap by tracing the connections between the factors identified in the literature and the reported attitudes of English language teachers.

Research Questions

The present study aims to address the following four research questions:

(1) What is the effect of TEI on teachers' attitudes towards their students and their enjoyment of lively students in particular?
(2) What is the effect of years of teaching experience on teachers' attitudes towards their students and their enjoyment of lively students in particular?
(3) What is the effect of English proficiency on teachers' attitudes towards their students and their enjoyment of lively students in particular?
(4) What is the effect of gender on teachers' attitudes towards their students and their enjoyment of lively students in particular?

Method

Instruments

An open-access anonymous online questionnaire was created for the purposes of this study. This remained online for six months in 2016. Snowball sampling, which is a form of non-probability sampling (Ness Evans & Rooney, 2013), was used to generate responses. Calls for participation with a link to the questionnaire were forwarded through emails to teachers and students, and informal contacts asking them to forward the link to other teachers. In total, 520 mono- and multilingual ESL/EFL teachers across the world filled out the questionnaire, of which 513 did so completely.

Online questionnaires are ideal for collecting large amounts of data from participants from different parts of the world belonging to various age groups and language profiles (Wilson & Dewaele, 2010). The geographical diversity boosts the ecological validity of the results, as the effects of local educational practices are averaged out. It has been found that the psychometric properties of online versions of traditional questionnaires are very similar to the pen-and-paper versions (Denissen *et al.*, 2010).

The research design and questionnaires received ethical clearance from the lead research institution. Participants started by filling out a number of demographic questions about gender, age, nationality, country of residence, language history and numbers of years in the profession. Participants also filled out the short version of the TEIQue-SF (Petrides, 2009), which contains 30 items and yields a global trait EI score. Items include: 'On the whole, I'm able to deal with stress', 'Expressing my emotions with words is not a problem for me' and 'Generally, I'm able to adapt to new environments'. We ran a Cronbach alpha analysis on the 30 items to investigate the internal consistency of the questionnaire. The Cronbach alpha score was 0.88. The mean score was 4.55 ($SD = 0.6$), with scores ranging from 2.7 to 5.9 (absolute minimum = 1, absolute maximum = 7). Three groups were created: those within one standard deviation (SD) around the mean (the middle group: $n = 339$), those with scores more than one SD above the mean (the high group: $n = 74$), and those with scores with more than one SD below the mean (the low group: $n = 85$).

The next part of the survey consisted of the English version of the LEXTALE, a 60-item lexical test developed by Lemhöfer and Broersma (2012). The authors describe LEXTALE as a quick and practically feasible test of vocabulary knowledge for medium to highly proficient speakers of English as a second language. It consists of a simple un-speeded visual lexical decision task which takes less than four minutes to complete (Lemhöfer & Broersma, 2012). The test gives a good indication of overall English proficiency. LEXTALE scores have been found to correlate highly with TOEIC test results, an established test of English proficiency (www. lextale.com/validity.html). Thus, even though LEXTALE was not designed to capture general English proficiency fully, it is nevertheless a useful indicator of it (Lemhöfer & Broersma, 2012). The mean score was 86.5 ($SD = 12.7$). Scores ranged from a minimum of 15 to the maximum possible score of 100. Three groups were created following the procedure for TEI, the 'low' linguistic proficiency group with scores more than 1 SD below the mean ($n = 94$), the 'medium' linguistic proficiency group ($n = 306$), and the 'high' linguistic proficiency group ($n = 53$).

Participants

A total of 513 participants (377 females, 131 males, five not stated) filled out the questionnaire in full. A majority of female participants is the norm in web-based language questionnaires (Wilson & Dewaele, 2010). The mean age was 40 years ($SD = 10$).

The largest group were British ($n = 71$), Americans ($n = 40$), followed by Ukrainians ($n = 37$), Greek ($n = 30$), Azerbaijani ($n = 30$), Argentinian ($n = 30$), Chinese ($n = 30$), Indian ($n = 30$), Spanish ($n = 30$), Turkish ($n = 30$), Macedonian ($n = 30$), Canadian ($n = 30$), and smaller groups of participants with the following nationalities: Austrian, Croatian, Pakistani, Belgian, Bulgarian, Egyptian, French, Polish, Portuguese, Swiss, Hungarian, Iranian, Japanese, Saudi, Slovenian, Australian, German, Brazilian, Finnish, Italian, Jordanian, Romanian, Serbian, Singaporean, South African, South Korean, Uruguayan, Irish, Israeli, Mexican, Russian, Swedish, Algerian, Angolan, Dutch, Indonesian, Libyan, Moroccan, Nigerian, Taiwanese, Thai, Armenian, Belarusian, Bosnian, Chilean, Cuban, Czech, Ethiopian, Filipino, Iraqi, Jamaican, Kenyan, Malaysian, Montenegrin, Mozambican, Nepalese, New Zealander, Panamanian, Peruvian, Syrian, Tunisian, Turkish Cypriot and Venezuelan.

The sample of participants consisted of 15 monolinguals, 113 bilinguals, 174 trilinguals, 104 quadrilinguals, 81 pentalinguals, 22 sextalinguals and 4 septalinguals.

English was the most frequent L1 ($n = 136$) and the remaining 376 participants had English as an additional language.

A majority of participants were teaching English at university ($n = 290$), with smaller numbers teaching in secondary schools ($n = 154$), primary schools ($n = 63$) and nursery schools ($n = 6$).

The largest group of participants were working in Ukraine ($n = 37$), Greece ($n = 32$), Spain ($n = 30$), Azerbaijan ($n = 25$), Japan ($n = 25$), the UK ($n = 17$) and the United States ($n = 17$). The remaining participants worked in 103 different countries.

Some participants had only just started teaching, while one had been a teacher for 52 years (mean = 15 years, $SD = 10$). We created three groups: those who had been teaching for less than five years, i.e. more than one SD below the mean ($n = 78$), those who had been teaching more than five and less than 26 years, i.e. within one SD on either side of the mean ($n = 348$), and finally those with 26 years or longer experience, i.e. more than one SD above the mean ($n = 87$).

Dependent variables

Data about attitudes were elicited through the following two closed questions:

(1) What is your attitude towards your students? Possible answers included: (1) Very unfavourable, (2) Unfavourable, (3) Neutral, (4) Favourable, (5) Very favourable.
(2) Do you enjoy having lively students? Possible answers included: (1) Absolutely not, (2) Not particularly, (3) To some extent, (4) Yes, (5) Absolutely yes.

A one-sample Kolmogorov–Smirnov test revealed that the scores on the first 5-point Likert question were not normally distributed (KS = 0.31, $p < 0.0001$), and a similar result emerged for the second question (KS = 0.30, $p < 0.0001$). A look at Figure 11.1 shows that over half of the participants gave a maximal score of 5 on the first question and close to half gave a maximal score in response to the second question. The median score for attitudes towards students was 5 (mean = 4.4, $SD = 0.8$), the median score for attitudes towards lively students was 4 (mean = 4.3, $SD = 0.7$). Despite the fact that the scores are skewed towards the high end of the scale, there is sufficient variation to investigate individual differences using non-parametric statistics. We used the non-parametric equivalent of ANOVAs, namely, Kruskal–Wallis tests, and we used the Mann–Whitney test instead of the independent t-test as it does not require the assumption of normal distribution.

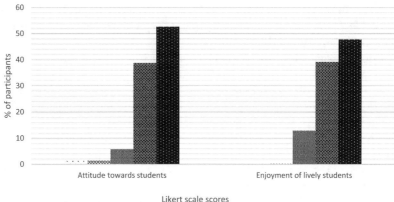

Figure 11.1 Proportion of participants choosing a specific Likert scale score for the two questions

Results

Kruskal–Wallis tests revealed that TEI had a significant effect on teachers' attitudes towards students and towards enjoyment of lively students (see Table 11.1). The results are visualised in Figure 11.2 (based on mean scores). The analyses show that increased levels of TEI are linked to more positive attitudes towards students and higher enjoyment of lively students. The differences in scores are broadly constant across the three TEI groups.

The Kruskal–Wallis tests also revealed that the length of teachers' experience had a significant effect on attitudes towards students but not on their enjoyment of lively students. More experienced teachers reported more positive attitudes towards their students (see Table 11.2 and Figure 11.3).

Table 11.1 Effect of *trait emotional intelligence* (TEI) on attitudes towards students and enjoyment of lively students (mean ranks)

Level TEI	Attitudes towards students	Enjoyment of lively students
Low	206	230
Medium	244	244
High	323	296
χ^2	34.8	11.6
df	2	2
p	0.0001	0.003

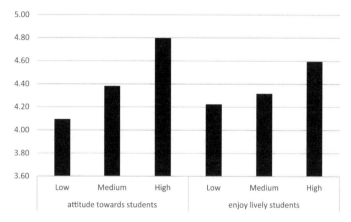

Figure 11.2 Effect of *trait emotional intelligence* (TEI) on attitudes towards students and enjoyment of lively students (mean scores)

Table 11.2 Effect of *years of teaching experience* on attitudes towards students and enjoyment of lively students (mean ranks)

Years of teaching experience	Attitudes towards students	Enjoyment of lively students
Low	228	233
Medium	256	256
High	287	287
χ^2	8.2	2.9
df	2	2
p	0.017	NS

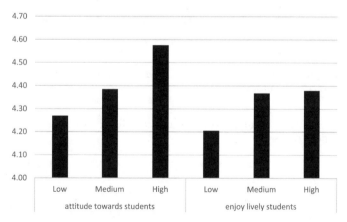

Figure 11.3 Effect of *teacher experience* on attitudes towards students and enjoyment of lively students (mean scores)

Teachers' English proficiency was positively – and significantly – linked to attitudes towards students and enjoyment of lively students (see Table 11.3 and Figure 11.4)

A Mann–Whitney test revealed that a significant gender difference exists for attitudes towards students but none appeared in the enjoyment of lively students (see Table 11.4 and Figure 11.5).

Table 11.3 Effect of *proficiency level* on attitudes towards students and enjoyment of lively students (mean ranks)

Proficiency level	Attitudes towards students	Enjoyment of lively students
Low	212	222
Medium	267	263
High	267	281
χ^2	13.1	8.5
df	2	2
p	0.001	0.014

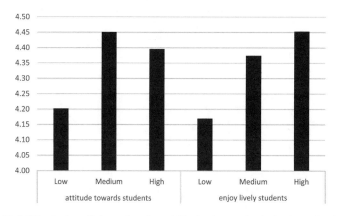

Figure 11.4 Effect of *proficiency level* on attitudes towards students and enjoyment of lively students (mean scores)

Table 11.4 Effect of *gender* on attitudes towards students and enjoyment of lively students (mean ranks)

Gender	Attitudes towards students	Enjoyment of lively students
Female	261	255
Male	234	253
Mann–Whitney U	23,392	24,538
Z	–2.12	–0.12
p	0.034	NS

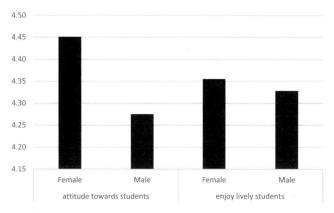

Figure 11.5 Effect of *gender* on attitudes towards students and enjoyment of lively students (mean scores)

Discussion

The first research question looked into the effect of TEI on teachers' attitudes towards their students and their enjoyment of working with lively students. This personality trait turned out to be positively linked to both attitudes towards the students and the enjoyment of lively students. We had anticipated this because individuals with higher levels of TEI are typically better able to understand and control their own emotions (including negative emotions), which means they are less likely to become angry with students. They are also likely to be better able to read the emotional atmosphere in the class, their own emotional state and that of individual students and can thus make adjustments when needed. Dewaele (2015) argued that good language teachers are able to harness the combined emotions of their students in order to channel them towards the learning objectives. This is not an easy thing to do, and having a high level of TEI could be an asset. Teachers with high TEI also tend to be more sociable (as sociability is one of the four TEI factors), which presumably helps them to develop good relations with their students, which can be reflected in more positive attitudes. They are also likely to be better able to channel the energy of lively students because they know how to work with them effectively. Their skills in managing their own as well as others' emotions will probably translate into an effective teaching style, especially in interpersonal terms but also possibly in other pedagogical dimensions. Vesely *et al.* (2013) pointed out that EI skills largely overlap with the positive factors comprising teacher efficacy, which explains the positive relationship between EI and teacher efficacy (Moafian & Ghanizadeh, 2009). In a separate study on the same database that this chapter is based on, Dewaele *et al.* (in preparation) found that TEI was significantly and positively linked to self-reported creativity, classroom management and pedagogical skills, and negatively linked with predictability. In other words, participants with high scores on TEI reported being more creative in their classes, less predictable, with better class management and better pedagogical skills compared to participants with lower TEI scores. In a study by Gkonou and Mercer (2017; see also Gkonou & Mercer, this volume), teachers who scored highly on EI/SI were found to differ in many of their specific classroom practices but generally they all shared a similar emphasis on the importance of empathy, recognising learner individuality and diversity and the need to be accordingly responsive in teaching. This too would help us to explain their positive attitudes to learners of all types.

The second research question focused on the effect of years of teaching experience. Interestingly, a longer experience had a positive effect on teachers' attitudes towards their students but had no effect on their enjoyment of lively students. This could suggest that teachers perhaps gradually learn to appreciate their students more (cf. Avramidis & Kalyva, 2007; Walker *et al.*, 2004) or simply that those who did not have positive attitudes towards their students have eventually left the profession. Powell and Kusuma-Powell (2010: 166) cite Kegan (1982), who presented the theory that 'people become progressively more socially mature as they move through their lives'. This could mean that the teachers become more tolerant of learners as individuals and possibly develop more realistic expectations about students' abilities and progress. More experienced teachers perhaps simply become wiser and more emotionally intelligent over time as suggested in other studies (see also Gkonou & Mercer, 2017). Indeed, a Pearson correlation analysis confirmed that older teachers scored significantly higher on TEI ($r = 0.12$, $p < 0.005$). This is not an unusual phenomenon, as personality psychologists agree that scores on personality traits are determined by both nature and nurture and shift with time (Furnham & Heaven, 1999). A lifetime of teaching is likely to shape some aspects of a person's personality, especially those drawn on frequently in the profession.

Surprisingly, our more experienced teachers did not enjoy working with lively students more than less experienced teachers. One possible explanation is that our more experienced teachers were also significantly older (confirmed by a Pearson correlation analysis: $r = 0.87$, $p < 0.0001$), and that having to manage lively students could perhaps feel less tiring for younger teachers.

The third research question considered the effect of English proficiency on teachers' attitudes towards their students and their enjoyment of working with lively students. It turned out that teachers with lower levels of linguistic proficiency have less positive attitudes towards their students and were also less likely to enjoy lively students. This could be linked to a certain sense of linguistic insecurity (cf. Lim, 2011; Santiago Sanchez, 2014). It is known that teacher self-efficacy is linked to EI and teacher professional well-being (Vesely *et al.*, 2013). Teachers with higher levels of English proficiency in our study could have realised that they had the necessary linguistic capital to do their job to a high standard, which probably gave them the requisite confidence in front on their class, their colleagues and their institution. As Wyatt (this volume) explains, 'if teachers feel efficacious across a range of tasks, they are more likely to have the characteristics admired in intrinsically-motivated, self-determined educators'. An alternative explanation could be that the finding indicates the differentiated effect of social desirability bias. In other words, teachers who are keen to make a good impression would be more likely to report that they have both good language skills and positive attitudes towards their learners.

The final research question looked at the effect of gender on teachers' attitudes towards their students and their enjoyment of lively students. The female teachers reported having more positive attitudes towards their students but they did not enjoy the lively students any more than their male peers. We considered whether the higher score of the female teachers might be linked to a gender difference in TEI scores (see Dewaele *et al.*, 2008). However, an independent *t*-test showed that female participants did not score significantly higher on TEI (Mann–Whitney $U = 24,038$, $Z = -0.45$, $p = NS$). Female teachers' closer, less conflictual and less dependent relationships with students have been highlighted in other research (Spilt *et al.*, 2012) and could be one reason for the findings.

The present research design is not without its limitations. Adopting a purely quantitative cross-sectional design allowed us to identify significant patterns in the data at one moment in time. We are aware that attitudes can shift over short (minutes, hours) and longer periods of time (years). A teacher can be disappointed or delighted by students' behaviour or performance during a specific segment of a class and this would be likely to affect the teacher's attitude towards the students. The sum of the highs and lows will be reflected in the answer to the single question about 'your attitudes towards your students': it might not shift as wildly from month to month or year to year but it is likely to be dynamic. Also the variation might be unrelated to students but linked to factors that were not considered in the present study, such as the teaching approach in the institution, the relationship with colleagues and superiors, or the mental and physical health of the teacher. A qualitative approach could reveal other factors linked to attitudes of individual teachers as well as further illuminate the nature of the relationship between teachers and learners. Yet, here, the strength of the quantitative approach is the ability to identify patterns of relationships between variables that could potentially be generalisable to other contexts and populations (Dörnyei, 2007).

This brings us to the second limitation: participant self-selection and the consequence of this on the representativeness of the sample. Looking at the distribution of responses (Figure 11.1), it is clear that very few teachers with negative attitudes participated in the survey. We were not expecting this variable to be normally distributed: indeed, why would anyone wish to remain in the teaching profession with negative attitudes towards students? However, teachers with less positive attitudes were less likely to want to spend time filling out a questionnaire related to their profession, which could lead to an under-representation of this type of teacher. This does not directly affect the relations between dependent and independent variables, but it has to be kept in mind in reflecting on their broader implications. A particular strength of the present study is the geographical and linguistic diversity of our sample: no single country or nationality dominated, which means that the findings are not strongly influenced by local factors and thus makes them more representative of EFL/ESL teachers across the world. In other words, the sample's diversity strengthens the present study's ecological validity.

However, in turn, we are also aware that there is the potential for cultural diversity in how respondents understand the nature of relationships, emotions and, thus, items in this survey (Molinsky, 2015; Saarni, 1999; Triandis *et al.*, 1988). Molinsky (2015) warns that emotions are expressed very differently across cultures and that their meaning can vary considerably, which makes this area a potential communication minefield. Weare (2003: 19) explains that, 'deciding what goes on a list of emotional and social competences cannot be value-free, culture-free or an apolitical exercise'. Subsequently, we feel that a degree of caution needs to be kept in mind when reflecting on the findings and potential implications across cultures.

Conclusion

The present study was initiated after our surprise at finding very little research about variation in teachers' attitudes towards their students, especially in an EFL/ESL setting. Our hypothesis that teachers with high levels of EI would have more positive attitudes and enjoy lively students more was confirmed. A potential implication of this finding is that pre-service teachers with low levels of EI need to be aware of the challenges posed by the teaching profession and reflect on their ability and willingness to engage with the relational dimensions of the language classroom. Teacher trainers should also reflect on ways to boost trainee teachers' levels of EI (cf. Veseley *et al.*, 2014). Our study hinted at the possibility that, over time, teachers may develop more positive attitudes towards their students, although they do not necessarily enjoy lively students more. A particularly striking finding was that teachers' English proficiency had affective consequences as more proficient teachers reported more positive attitudes towards their students and enjoyed lively students more. We interpreted this in terms of self-efficacy and linguistic in/security and the consequence this could have on the relationship between teacher and students. Finally, we found that female teachers had more positive attitudes towards their students. No gender difference emerged in the enjoyment of lively students.

In sum, it seems likely that, in this study, the teachers' attitudes towards their learners are determined by their TEI, their length of professional experience, their level of English proficiency and their gender. We conclude that teachers need to reflect on their own EI competences as well as their sense of self-efficacy, especially in linguistic terms, not only for their own professional well-being but also for the nature of the relationships they are likely to create with learners in their classrooms. This study represents a first step in seeking to better understand the complexity of EFL/ESL teachers' personality, such as in the case of TEI. It also begins to cast some light on the nature of relationships between teachers and pupils and the teacher-related factors that may affect this. There remains much work still to be done in fleshing out the details of these relationships across settings and populations; however, given the centrality of teachers' personality and their relationships with pupils, it promises to be an important strand of research in the emergent field of teacher psychology.

References

Albrecht, K. (2006) *Social Intelligence: The New Science of Success*. San Francisco, CA: Jossey-Bass.

Avramidis, E. and Kalyva, E. (2007) The influence of teaching experience and professional development on Greek teachers' attitudes towards inclusion. *European Journal of Special Needs Education* 22 (4), 367–389.

Avramidis, E. and Norwich, B. (2002) Teachers' attitudes towards integration/inclusion: A review of the literature. *European Journal of Special Needs Education* 17 (2), 129–147.

Bajorek, Z., Gulliford, J. and Taskila, T. (2014) *Healthy Teachers, Higher Marks? Establishing a Link between Teacher Health and Wellbeing, and Student Outcomes*. London: The Work Foundation. See https://www.educationsupportpartnership.org.uk/sites/default/files/resources/healthy_teachers_higher_marks_report_0.pdf

Bar-On, R. (1997) *The Emotional Quotient Inventory (EQ-I): Technical Manual*. Toronto: Multi-Health Systems.

Becker, E.S., Keller, M.M., Goetz, T., Frenzel, A.C. and Taxer, J.L. (2015) Antecedents of teachers' emotions in the classroom: An intraindividual approach. *Frontiers in Psychology* 6, 635.

Corcoran, R.P. and Tormey, R. (2012) How emotionally intelligent are pre-service teachers? *Teaching and Teacher Education* 28 (5), 750–759.

Day, C. and Gu, Q. (2009) Teacher emotions: Well being and effectiveness. In M. Zembylas and P. Schutz (eds) *Teachers' Emotions in the Age of School Reform and the Demands for Performativity* (pp. 15–31). Basel: Springer.

Dehshiri, R. (2003) The reliability and validity of EQ-I in Iran's context. Unpublished MA dissertation, Allame Tabatabaee University.

Denissen, J.J.A., Neumann, L. and van Zalk, M. (2010) How the internet is changing the implementation of traditional research methods, people's daily lives, and the way in which developmental scientists conduct research. *International Journal of Behavioral Development* 34 (6), 564–575.

Dewaele, J.-M. (2015) On emotions in foreign language learning and use. *Language Teacher* 39 (3), 13–15.

Dewaele, J.-M., Petrides, K.V. and Furnham, A. (2008) Effects of trait emotional intelligence and sociobiographical variables on communicative anxiety and foreign language anxiety among adult multilinguals: A review and empirical investigation. *Language Learning* 58 (4), 911–960.

Dewaele, J.-M., Witney, J., Saito, K. and Dewaele, L. (2017) Foreign language enjoyment and anxiety in the FL classroom: The effect of teacher and learner variables. *Language Teaching Research*; doi:10.1177/1362168817692161.

Dewaele, J.-M., Gkonou, C. and Mercer, S. (in preparation) Do ESL/EFL teachers' emotional intelligence, teaching experience, proficiency and gender affect their classroom practice?

Dörnyei, Z. (2007) *Research Methods in Applied Linguistics: Quantitative, Qualitative and Mixed Methodologies*. Oxford: Oxford University Press.

Ensher, E.A. and Murphy, S.E. (1997) Effects of race, gender, perceived similarity, and contact on mentor relationships. *Journal of Vocational Behavior* 50 (3), 460–481.

Frenzel, A.C. and Stephens, E.J. (2013) Emotions. In N.C. Hall and T. Goetz (eds) *Emotion, Motivation and Self-regulation: A Handbook for Teachers* (pp. 1–56). Bingley: Emerald Group.

Furnham, A. and Heaven, P.C.L. (1999) *Personality and Social Behaviour*. New York: Oxford University Press.

Gkonou, C. and Mercer, S. (2017) *Understanding Emotional and Social Intelligence among English Language Teachers*. London: British Council.

Harris, E.K. (2002) *Customer Service: A Practical Approach*. Upper Saddle River, NJ: Prentice-Hall.

Hattie, J. (2009) *Visible Learning*. London: Routledge.

Iacoboni, M., Molnar-Szakacs, I., Gallese, V., *et al.* (2005) Grasping the intentions of others with one's own mirror neuron system. *PLoS Biology* 3 (3), e79; doi:10.1371/journal.pbio.0030079.

Kegan, R. (1982) *The Evolving Self*. Cambridge, MA: Harvard University Press.

Lemhöfer, K. and Broersma, M. (2012) Introducing LexTALE: A quick and valid lexical test for advanced learners of English. *Behavior Research Methods* 44 (2), 325–343.

Lim, H.W. (2011) Concept maps of Korean EFL student teachers' autobiographical reflections on their professional identity formation. *Teaching and Teacher Education* 27 (6), 969–981.

Mercer, S. (2016) Psychology for language learning: Spare a thought for the teacher. Plenary address at *PLL2*, Jyväskylä, Finland.

Mercer, S., Oberdorfer, P. and Saleem, M. (2016) Helping language teachers to thrive: Using positive psychology to promote teachers' professional well-being. In D. Gabryś-Barker and D. Gałajda (eds) *Positive Psychology Perspectives on Foreign Language Learning and Teaching, Second Language Learning and Teaching* (pp. 213–229). Cham: Springer.

Moafian, F. and Ghanizadeh, A. (2009) The relationship between Iranian EFL teachers' emotional intelligence and their self-efficacy in language institutes. *System* 37 (4), 708–718.

Molinsky, A. (2015) Emotional intelligence doesn't translate across borders. *Harvard Business Review*, 20 April. See https://hbr.org/2015/04/emotional-intelligence-doesnt-translate-across-borders

Ness Evans, A. and Rooney, B.J. (2013) *Methods in Psychological Research* (3rd edn). New York: Sage.

Petrides, K.V. (2009) Psychometric properties of the Trait Emotional Intelligence Questionnaire. In C. Stough, D.H. Saklofske and J.D. Parker (eds) *Advances in the Assessment of Emotional Intelligence* (pp. 85–101). New York: Springer.

Petrides, K.V. and Furnham, A. (2000) On the dimensional structure of emotional intelligence. *Personality and Individual Differences*, 29 (2), 313–320.

Petrides, K.V. and Furnham, A. (2001) Trait emotional intelligence: Psychometric investigation with reference to established trait taxonomies. *European Journal of Personality* 15 (6), 425–448.

Petrides, K.V., Furnham, A. and Martin, G.N. (2004) Estimates of emotional and psychometric intelligence: Evidence for gender-based stereotypes. *Journal of Social Psychology* 144 (2), 149–162.

Petrides, K.V., Pita, R. and Kokkinaki, F. (2007) The location of trait emotional intelligence in personality factor space. *British Journal of Psychology* 98 (2), 273–289.

Powell, W. and Kusuma-Powell, O. (2010) *Becoming an Emotionally Intelligent Teacher.* Thousand Oaks, CA: Corwin.

Reeves, J. (2006) Secondary teacher attitudes toward including English-language learners in mainstream classrooms. Faculty Publication, Department of Teaching, Learning and Teacher Education, University of Nebraska-Lincoln. See http://digitalcommons.unl.edu/teachlearnfacpub/116

Saarni, C. (1999) *The Development of Emotional Competence.* New York: Guilford Press.

Santiago Sanchez, H. (2014) The impact of self-perceived subject matter knowledge on pedagogical decisions in EFL grammar teaching practices. *Language Awareness* 23 (3), 220–233.

Split, J.L., Koomen, H.Y.Y. and Jak, S. (2012) Are boys better off with male and girls with female teachers? A multilevel investigation of measurement invariance and gender match in teacher–student relationship quality. *Journal of School Psychology* 50 (3), 363–378.

Triandis, H.C., Bontempo, R., Villareal, M.J., Asai, M. and Lucca, N. (1988) Individualism and collectivism: Cross-cultural perspectives on self-ingroup relationships. *Journal of Personality and Social Psychology* 54 (2), 323–338.

Tschannen-Moran, M. and Woolfolk Hoy, A. (2001) Teacher efficacy: Capturing and elusive construct. *Teaching and Teacher Education* 17 (7), 783–805.

Turban, D.B., Dougherty, T.W. and Lee, F.K. (2002) Gender, race and perceived similarity effects in developmental relationships: The moderating role of relationship duration. *Journal of Vocational Behaviour* 61, 240–262.

Vesely, A.K., Saklofske, D.H. and Leschied, A.D.W. (2013) Teachers – the vital resource: The contribution of emotional intelligence to teacher efficacy and well-being. *Canadian Journal of School Psychology* 28 (1), 71–89.

Vesely, A.K., Saklofske, D.H. and Nordstokk, D.W. (2014) EI training and pre-service teacher wellbeing. *Personality and Individual Differences* 65, 81–85.

Walker, A., Shafer, J. and Iiams, M. (2004) 'Not in my classroom': Teachers' attitudes towards English language learners in the mainstream classroom. *NABE Journal of Research and Practice* 2 (1), 130–160.

Weare, K. (2003) *Developing the Emotionally Literate School.* London: Sage.

Wilson, R. and Dewaele, J.-M. (2010) The use of web questionnaires in second language acquisition and bilingualism research. *Second Language Research* 26 (1), 103–123.

Wong, C.S., Law, K.S. and Wong, P.M. (2004) Development and validation of a forced choice emotional intelligence for Chinese respondents in Hong Kong. *Asia Pacific Journal of Management* 21 (4), 535–559.

12 Language Teacher Agency

Cynthia J. White

The idea of language teachers as active agents both inside and outside the classroom has long been a guiding concept in applied linguistics and education. At its core, teacher agency aims to describe teachers' efforts to make choices within a host of contexts: in establishing and maintaining relationships with learners and colleagues, in engaging with new curricular requirements and assessment practices, in innovative learning, in participating in ongoing professional development opportunities and teacher workplace learning initiatives, in adapting themselves to the diverse requirements of their working contexts, and so on. Lack of agency in relation to such areas as pedagogical tasks, workplace relationships, innovation and student learning has long been recognised as a problem for teachers. Yet, until recently, the concept of *teacher* agency has received relatively little attention in applied linguistics research, with teachers being seen more in relation to learners than as 'agents in their own right' (Kalaja *et al.*, 2015: 14).

Recent and current approaches to teacher agency have also included a focus on emotion and identity together with such notions as identity-agency (Ruohotie-Lyhty & Moate, 2016) and life-course agency (Ruohotie-Lyhty & Moate, 2015). New lines of enquiry have emerged in Ng and Boucher-Yip's (2016) edited collection on teacher agency and policy responses in English language teaching, and in recent articles on teacher agency in relation to norms and varieties of English (Hamid *et al.*, 2014), to the interactional dynamics of bilingual classrooms (Palmer & Martínez, 2013), and to language planning and policy in Vietnam (Van Huy *et al.*, 2016). Studies such as these reveal the wide currency of the construct of teacher agency together with the studies reviewed later in this chapter, which are concerned with the influence of experiences outside the classroom (Feryok, 2012), identity negotiations and teacher agency (Kayi-Aydar, 2015), the emergence of agency through CALL practice (Kitade, 2015), and teacher agency in narrative accounts of classroom conflict (White, 2016). Taken together, they advance our understandings of language teacher agency and are both framed by and contribute to broader agendas within applied linguistics and society.

This chapter aims to provide a critical overview of language teacher agency beginning with a review of the emergence of the concept and associated theoretical approaches. The chapter then examines empirical studies into language teacher agency – studies which have used activity theory, sociocultural theory or dialogical frameworks – to show how the concept of language teacher agency extends our understanding of the lived experiences and trajectories of language teachers.

The Emergence of the Concept of Language Teacher Agency

In approaching the notion of language teacher agency, it is important to acknowledge the wider, more long-standing debates about agency itself that have taken place in applied linguistics and related fields. An early and still widely used definition of agency comes from Ahearn (2001), as the socioculturally mediated capacity to act in relation to one's environment, emphasising that all action is mediated 'both in its production and in its interpretation' (Ahearn, 2001: 112). Lantolf and Pavlenko (2001) depict agency as arising out of the engagement of individuals in the social world, arguing that it involves both what is done and how it is understood as meaningful. They elaborate on agency as being a 'relationship' (Lantolf & Pavlenko, 2001: 145) that an individual has with those around them; individuals are seen as 'defining the terms and conditions of such relationships' (Lantolf & Pavlenko, 2001: 145), and as assigning meanings to objects and events. The importance of the reflexive capacities of humans in relation to agentive processes are identified in Candlin and Sarangi's (2004: xiii) definition of agency as 'the self-conscious reflexive actions of human beings'. In a slightly later contribution, Lantolf and Thorne (2006: 238) emphasise that agency is socioculturally mediated in that 'within a given time and space, there are constraints and affordances that make certain actions probable, others possible, and yet others impossible'. They highlight the limitations of viewing agency as simply voluntary control over actions and behaviour, emphasising that it also 'entails the ability to assign relevance and significance to things and events' (Lantolf & Thorne, 2006: 142–143). Van Lier has also emerged as an important contributor to our understandings of agency: he defines agency as 'action potential mediated by social, interactional, cultural, institutional and other contextual factors' (van Lier, 2008: 171).

This preliminary background will be extended further – and linked specifically to language teacher agency – in the following section on theoretical approaches. However, it does reveal something of the divergence in how agency can be conceptualised: a significant divide exists in terms of how agency is understood as relating to structures on the one hand and subjectivities on the other. For example, there is a view of agency as encoded in and shaped by linguistic structure: Bamberg (1997: 317), in his early work exploring the narrative construction of agency in terms of 'who is doing what to whom', argues that anger narratives often operate with an agentive other with self as an object, while helplessness may involve such grammatical features as modal auxiliaries, 'try' predicates and negation. In terms of the salience of subjectivities, Mercer's research into language learner agency is helpful in revealing that agency is 'not only concerned with what is observable but it also involves nonvisible behaviours, beliefs, thoughts and feelings' (Mercer, 2012: 42). Approaches to agency also vary considerably, as identified by Feryok (2012), in terms of their focus – from a concern with power and control in one paradigm to seeing relationship as central to agency in others. Examples in terms of the former include McNay's (2000: 16) definition of agency as 'the capacity to manage actively the often discontinuous, overlapping or conflicting relations of power' and Duranti's approach emphasising agency as:

> the property of those entities (i) that have some degree of control over their own behaviour, (ii) whose actions in the world affect other entities' (and sometimes their own), and (iii) whose actions are the object of evaluation (e.g. in terms of their responsibility for a given outcome). (Duranti, 2004: 453)

By contrast, approaches which emphasise relationships as central to agency argue that it is located in particular contexts (in both time and space), and is always tied to the affordances and constraints of those contexts. Agency has also been theorised at different scales: from being a part of large-scale social, political and historical processes, down to as emerging from discourse at the micro level of interaction.

The emergence of the concept of teacher agency also needs to be seen in relation to other key concepts such as autonomy (Huang & Benson, 2013), identity (Li & De Kosta, this volume; Ruohotie-Lyhty & Moate, 2016; Varghese, this volume) and emotion (King & Ng, this volume; White, 2016). Several decades of research into autonomy provided a significant foundation for the advent of the concept of agency in applied linguistics: Esch and Zähner (2000), for example, refer to individuals as being 'active agents' within a wider discussion of actions and autonomy in a range of technology-mediated environments. The article marks an important shift that was taking place from a focus on autonomy as an individual attribute to agency focusing on how individuals act within and in relation to specific contexts. As Kalaja *et al.* (2015) note, referring to the early stages of the emergence of agency as a construct distinct from autonomy, 'agency began now to be seen as a phenomenon that was necessarily dependent on both the individual and his or her social environment' (Kalaja *et al.*, 2015: 14). In terms of autonomy, Benson (2007: 30) observes that 'agency can perhaps be viewed as a point of origin for the development of autonomy, while identity might be viewed as one of its more important outcomes'. Also referring to autonomy, van Lier (2007) argues that his earlier (1996) work ultimately identifies motivation and autonomy as two sides of the same coin of agency. And, more recently, Duff (2012) in writing about identity and agency argues that agency 'refers to people's ability to make choices, take control, self-regulate, and thereby pursue their goals as individuals leading, potentially, to personal or social transformation' (Duff, 2012: 413); equally important is that agency is seen as the ability to 'actively resist certain behaviours, practices, or positionings' (Duff, 2012: 417). Referring to emotion, Kalaja *et al.* (2015: 212) in the conclusion to their work on beliefs argue that emotions pervade agency since 'they permeate (…) how we choose to act (or not) in the world'. Teacher agency can also be related to a number of other constructs such as decisional capital, defined by Hargreaves and Fullan (2012: 93–94) as 'the capital that professionals acquire and accumulate through structured and unstructured experience, practice, and reflection – capital that enables them to make wise judgements in circumstances where there is no fixed rule or piece of incontrovertible evidence to guide them'. Having traced the emergence of the concept of (teacher) agency, we now turn to a consideration of theoretical underpinnings and approaches.

Theoretical Approaches to Language Teacher Agency

While a number of theoretical approaches to language teacher agency have been developed, the most influential are based within sociocultural and dialogical frameworks. Accordingly, they are a significant part of this overview together with detail on socioculturally based ecological studies and activity theory. This is followed by a review of dialogical approaches to understanding teacher agency. This section ends with a consideration of complexity perspectives, which offer considerable promise for studies of language teacher agency in line with understandings of learner agency as a complex dynamic system (Mercer, 2011).

Arguably, sociocultural theory has provided the most influential underpinnings for research into language teacher agency. The prominence of sociocultural perspectives can be seen as part of the social turn (Block, 2003) in applied linguistics and as a reaction against purely cognitivist or highly individualistic views of human actions. In terms of agency, the work of Vygotsky (1978, 1986) has provided a strong foundation for subsequent theorising, as the focus turned to individuals acting in particular sociocultural settings. Van Lier (2004), for example, relates actions to their social context through the concept of affordances, 'what is available to the person to do something with' (van Lier, 2004: 91), either directly in the environment, or in a mediated form, through people. Again from his classroom-based article, van Lier (2008) depicts agency as interdependent with the social contexts of L2 teaching and learning. From this perspective, teachers respond to the affordances and constraints of each particular context, and the modified conditions that emerge then serve as the context for ensuing actions. The core of this approach is articulated by van Lier where he makes the case that agency must be understood as a 'contextually enacted way of being in the world' (van Lier, 2008: 163) which is always 'mediated by social, interactional, cultural, institutional and other contextual factors' (van Lier, 2008: 171). Later, Block (2013) expands the social context of agency to include spatial, temporal, cultural and semiotic parameters. Importantly, for van Lier a core feature of agency is 'awareness of the responsibility for one's actions vis-a-vis the environment, including affected others' (van Lier, 2008: 172). He thus emphasises that agency is always a social event in that it is socially motivated and socially interpreted.

Agency from an ecological perspective can be understood in terms of the focus on the relationship between the individual and their environment (van Lier, 2004), with an emphasis on concrete settings, and in relation to transactions in particular ecological conditions and circumstances. The notion of affordance is central to agency, defined by van Lier to refer to the possibilities for action that the environment offers to the individual (van Lier, 2004: 79). Ecological views of agency emphasise that agency is not an attribute of an individual but an emergent phenomenon within the ecological conditions through which it is exercised and enacted. Thus individuals act *by means of* their environment, not simply *in* their environment: it is the result of the ongoing interplay between individual efforts, available resources and contextual and structural factors, moment by moment. Thus it is possible to see individuals as both enabled and constrained by their material environments and also as able to be reflexive and creative in taking actions which are counter to particular constraints. Importantly, this approach emphasises that even if individuals have particular capacities, whether they can enact agency depends on the interaction of those capacities and the particular ecological conditions. Thus agency is viewed as a relational effect. A recent study on foreign language teachers' agency and beliefs using an ecological framework comes from Ruohotie-Lyhty (2015), analysing the emerging beliefs of 11 new language teachers in Finland during their first three to four years of teaching. Drawing on van Lier (2004), she emphasises that a teacher's *perception* of the environment is a crucial factor in determining what affordances are available to the individual, and that the individual's perception of the environment is not necessarily how it actually is, 'but as it is to them, in other words, how it enables or restrains their actions' (Ruohotie-Lyhty, 2015: 151). Further, individuals are not seen as being controlled by their environment but as having possibilities of acting – or not – in relation to the affordances as seen by them of that context. Specifically, her study explores the relationship of the teachers with their professional environment and the agency that emerges in those ongoing interactions and relationships. The study uses interpretative repertoires (Potter & Wetherell, 1987) as an analytical tool to identify the kinds of environments (including affordances) that teachers construct in their narratives. Further to this, she analyses the subject positions of the individuals within that environment and identifies two contrasting subject positions: one pointing towards independence and agency, and the other suggesting dependence on a constraining environment. Agency is thus shown to be mediated by the environment (the physical, social and emotional aspects of their work) and by the way individuals construct those aspects of context in relation to their identity and beliefs.

The study of teacher agency from an activity theory perspective analyses individual teacher actions within the context of activity networks, namely 'the social and historical context of the activity system in which they occur' (Feryok, 2012: 97). As Kalaja *et al.* (2015) note, activity theory includes more of an outsider's perspective on activity, whereby both the individual and society are viewed as co-evolving processes. In generating new activities, individuals can transform their social reality, hence the link between individual agency, emerging forms of activity, and change. The significance of activity-based approaches to teacher agency will be discussed in more detail later in the chapter through the work of Feryok (2012) and Kitade (2015). However, both draw on Valsiner's (1998) notion of 'active appropriation', which underlines the role of the individual in actively constructing new choices and thereby not being restricted to local environments. Within activity theory, individual agency is seen as displayed through actions at the individual level within an activity system at the social level. Agency is thus conceptualised as being on a continuum with society, with both viewed as co-evolving processes that are mutually influential.

Sullivan and McCarthy (2004) identify a number of limitations of sociocultural approaches to agency: they argue that in focusing largely on individuals acting in particular contexts they have tended to overlook individual sensibility in terms of how individuals feel, live and express agency. They also argue that sociocultural analyses of agency have tended 'to miss the centrifugal messiness of lived and felt relations between people' (Sullivan & McCarthy, 2004: 291–292). Dialogical theories of agency address these gaps, drawing on the work of Bakhtin (1984, 2010), which has been introduced into applied linguistics through the work of Hall *et al.* (2005), Vitanova (2005, 2010), Dufva and Aro (2014), Aro (2015), and others. They are distinctive in their focus on personal viewpoints, individual sensibilities, and the emotions, values and feelings that human beings bring to their relationships with others. While sociocultural theorists have given emphasis to sociocultural contexts and systems, dialogical approaches focus on the lived experience of agency as individuals relate to others. Dialogically informed stances on agency focus on individual sensibility, but are not confined to the individual and are instead viewed as part of dialogical relationships that govern the human condition. Thus, Dufva and Aro (2014) argue that agency is dialogical and relational and needs to be analysed as both subjectively experienced and collectively emergent. Bakhtin introduced the notion of authoring as a further aspect of agency, whereby 'selves author themselves in the midst of complex relationships with others' (Vitanova, 2010: 132). Agency is part of the process by which individuals make sense of events and their lived experiences and, as Aro (2015: 50) notes, 'constantly author their life story, and their role in it'. For Bakhtin, dialogism is the antithesis of individualism and Cartesian views of self: agency is essentially determined by the subjectivity of another and answerability. For Bakhtin (1984: 147), individuals are located on a 'threshold' where, in everyday acts, they face the question 'how ought I to act?' which includes a sense of answerability. The value of dialogical approaches to understanding teacher agency will be discussed later in this chapter in a study I carried out (White, 2016), where sudden, protracted conflict arose in a class for refugees and the teacher had to decide how she would act while also addressing her own feelings and those of other members of the class.

Complexity theory has emerged as a valuable framework for understanding that human activity in language learning and teaching is part of a complex dynamic system involving the interplay of multiple, interconnected elements. Larsen-Freeman and Cameron (2008) identify a number of attributes of complex systems such as emergentism, ecology, dynamism, change, unpredictability, interconnectedness and nonlinearity, all of which have challenged notions of the conceptual stability of systems and activities. For example, interaction in a complex system results in emergent structures, the influence of which is nonlinear: large changes can have small effects and small changes can have large effects. In terms of agency from a complexity perspective, contexts, environments and individuals constitute systems that are constantly interacting and dynamic. Part of this constant state of flux is the dynamic reciprocity between an agent and the environment, whereby an individual makes use of the affordances in the environment and at the same time shapes the environment. Drawing on Mercer (2011, 2012), agency can be seen as being made up of two interrelated dimensions – the individual's sense of agency and their observable actions, meaning that conceptualisations of agency from a complexity perspective also consider 'the teachers' experience of agency as an inherent part of the system of agency' (Kalaja et al., 2015: 17). Viewing teacher agency in terms of complex systems is a promising, as yet underexplored, avenue of enquiry in applied linguistics.

Empirical Work on Language Teacher Agency

Another useful way of accessing the construct of teacher agency is through an analysis of recent empirical work. In the remainder of the chapter I review a number of studies which have investigated how teachers choose to act at particular moments of tension or struggle, how they develop their sense of agency, how agency emerges in relation to various kinds of sociocultural and historical change, how teachers give accounts of their agency when confronted with intense conflict in the classroom, and how agency and emotion are interrelated from a dialogical perspective. The five studies (Feryok, 2012; Kayi-Aydar, 2015; Kitade, 2015; Ruohotie-Lyhty & Moate, 2016; White, 2016) were chosen to represent the range of enquiry and scholarship in relation to this construct, and the diverse theoretical perspectives (activity theory, sociocultural theory, dialogical frameworks) used to investigate language teacher agency.

The influence of experiences outside the classroom on teacher agency

In an article entitled 'Activity theory and language teacher agency', Feryok (2012) analyses how actions and life experiences outside the classroom exert an influence on the agency a teacher develops. Specifically, she examines the narrative data (email and oral interviews) and classroom observations of one Armenian teacher of English, Nune. In taking a broadly sociocultural approach, Feryok acknowledges the role of both social forces and individual experience. She draws on Galperin's notion of orienting activity, defined as the visualisation or verbalisation of the performance of an action that contributes to its internalisation (Galperin, 1989); the significance of the orienting activity is that it presents a horizon of possible actions wherein procedural options can be considered, rather than haphazardly chosen through trial and error (Galperin, 1989). In this case, Nune's early experiences at school with her English teacher acted an image which mediated her emerging sense of agency by guiding the ways in which she engaged in actions as a language teaching student, an English teacher and also as a teacher trainer. The analysis shows how Nune's actions in relation to different social constraints within the continuum of the activity system reshaped the conditions that prevailed – and in so doing created affordances for her next action. The study demonstrates very clearly that 'individuals can transform social reality in the production of new activities in everyday social practices and in that sense they "lead" emerging forms of activity through individual agency' (Feryok, 2012: 97). Feryok's study emphasises that L2 teachers' subjectivity, which is impacted by their previous experiences, also plays a crucial role for the emergence of agency. Importantly too, the scope of the study draws attention to the need to focus on wider time frames than the immediate, taking into account teachers' prior experiences, and lived experiences across a lifetime.

Identity negotiations and a teacher candidate's sense of agency

Kayi-Aydar (2015) draws on post-structural theories and uses narrative inquiry to enquire into how the identity negotiations of one foreign language teacher candidate, Janelle, interact with her sense of agency. She draws on Rogers and Wetzel's work to define agency as 'the capacity of people to act purposefully and reflectively on their world' (Rogers

& Wetzel, 2013: 63), but also stresses that individual agency is connected to the conditions and settings within which it is enacted. As background to the study, she cites Ruohotie-Lyhty's (2013: 122) view that it is important to investigate 'how teachers use their agency in interpreting their experiences', which is closely linked to identity formation. The data collection was based on interviews and journal entries. The three semi-structured interviews each lasting two to 2.5 hours focused on Janelle's past, present and future narratives; Janelle's journal entries were written when she was a teacher candidate and a student in Kayi-Aydar's classes. The analysis of these narratives reveals the dynamic nature of Janelle's agency, as it fluctuated and was shaped not only in different settings but by interactions with others in those settings. The study is significant in revealing how matters of 'race, ethnicity and nonnativism are all intertwined in complex ways, interacting with one's agency' (Kayi-Aydar, 2015: 154). Specifically, the study sheds light on how Janelle's status as a nonnative speaker of Spanish and her ethnic and racial identity as a white American impacted on her agency; she ultimately decided to withdraw from her profession as a Spanish language teacher and to become instead an ESOL teacher. A further contribution of the study is in focusing on the time period when language learners intend to become language teachers and the questions of proficiency that then arise. Kayi-Aydar notes that while Janelle 'felt confident in her other abilities, her fear of speaking Spanish immensely hurt her agency' (Kayi-Aydar, 2015: 155). A conclusion of this study is that it is important to focus on language teachers' experiences as both language learners and teachers, and to examine 'sites of tension' (Kayi-Aydar, 2015: 157) in their life stories in order to gain deeper views of their identities and agency.

The long-term emergence of teacher agency through computer assisted language learning (CALL) practice

Kitade (2015) takes a longitudinal perspective in examining the emergence of language teachers' agency; she draws on reflections given by two Japanese as a foreign language teachers covering a period of 16 years as they developed their work as computer assisted language learning (CALL) practitioners. Using an activity theory framework, Kitade traces the very different life trajectories of the two teachers described as 'pioneers' in CALL; she analyses how the challenges they faced, and the ways they responded, relate to the development of their agency as CALL practitioners. To do this, Kitade draws on narrative inquiry data gathered through semi-structured interviews carried out by a combination of asynchronous and synchronous media (both text and audio) through email and Skype, which provided opportunities for deep reflection and also opportunities to elicit further information. The interviews made use of the 'life-line interview method' (Schroots & Ten Kate, 1989) where participants were invited to sketch a line to represent fluctuations in their involvement in CALL, and to narrate what took place at different points.

The results provide insights into the trajectories of the teachers as CALL practitioners, into critical points within that trajectory, and into each teacher's development of agency at those points. Specifically, the study traces how the teachers became aware of the social dimensions of technology as they encountered students' responses to ICT, and at times the 'mismatched values' (Kitade, 2015: 396) between themselves and their students. Importantly, Kitade concludes that the change in perceptions that resulted from these encounters not only influenced the teachers' pedagogical use of technology but it was those changes that in turn underpinned the development of their agency. The study also illustrates how ICT as a newly emergent cultural artefact affected the development of teacher agency largely through their ongoing recognition of their new role in relation to technology as that role emerged. Results reveal that in both cases the teachers met with divergent attitudes towards ICT and its value in language learning and teaching processes; such dissonances occurred between themselves and their students and within wider communities. Importantly, both teachers saw themselves as having a 'mediating mission' (Kitade, 2015: 413) in addressing these tensions (both within the classroom and across communities) and that these processes became a site for the emergence and development of their agency. Kitade draws on Engeström's (2009) view that the emergence of agency can be analysed through Leont'ev's (1978) concepts of 'need, object and motive', and of contradictions that arise between them. In this study it was the teachers' awareness of tensions in their teaching practice that became central to the emergence and enacting of their agency. Kitade concludes that the teachers were both in well-resourced contexts and stable positions and that had they been in 'more marginalized positions (…) their support or recognition by the community as innovative teachers would likely be restricted and the development of their agency might have been more complicated' (Kitade, 2015: 415). Kitade sees the emergence of agency as relating to teachers' ongoing transformations in response to 'various types of social, cultural and historical change' (Kitade, 2015: 418), arguing that analysing such transformations in relation to agency enhances our understanding of the development of L2 teachers.

The development of identity-agency among pre-service teachers

The agentic nature of pre-service teachers' identity development in Finland is the focus of a study by Ruohotie-Lyhty and Moate (2016). Specifically, it focuses on eight teachers over a period of two years, and aims to identify the different kinds of agency involved in identity development, drawing on the theoretical notion of identity-agency, defined as 'the agency individuals invest in the development of their professional identity'

(Eteläpelto *et al.*, 2015: 318). The study explores identity-agency as 'the capacity to use experiences and participation in the development of professional identity' (Eteläpelto *et al.*, 2015: 319); this approach reflects the assumption that participation per se in a community does not establish identity but rather that it is in being 'active in using agentic experiences' (Eteläpelto *et al.*, 2015: 319) that professional identities are forged. The focus is first on identifying different forms of identity-agency and then on the experiences pre-service teachers relate to when exercising those different forms of identity-agency. As in Kayi-Aydar's (2015) work, experiences are defined in a broad sense including past, present and potential experiences that act as a resource preservice teachers can draw on as they form their identity-agency. Like Kitade, the study analyses teachers' activity within their own development, but from a dialogical perspective, using an autobiographical narrative approach, based on the assignments the participants submitted as students, including reflective accounts from teaching practice. Expansive, reductive and attentive forms of identity-agency were found to underpin the narrative accounts. Ruohotie-Lyhty and Moate note that attentive identity-agency aligns with dialogic theories (Bakhtin, 1993; Holquist, 1990) which highlight the relationship between self and other, and the ongoing monitoring of that relationship as integral to the development of self. The research presents a complex and nuanced perspective on the different categories of identity-agency: for example, Ruohotie-Lyhty and Moate observe that unremitting expansion of identity-agency has drawbacks in that it 'precludes opportunities for reconciliation or learning who I am now' (Ruohotie-Lyhty & Moate, 2016: 326). Correspondingly, the reductive tendencies can be functional in that they may support metacognitive development in the understanding of self; equally, instances of withdrawal may be the basis of further development. To conclude, the study brings to light relational perspectives on identity development, in showing how identity-agency is highly contextualised, either promoted or constrained by the nature of the relationship between self and other, and as such dependent on experience.

Teacher agency in narrative accounts of classroom conflict

Classes for asylum seekers and refugees have been identified as complex communicative spaces marked by diverse, often urgent issues and crises which students face in their everyday lives; referring to these contexts, Baynham (2006) advocates the need for a more complex and more nuanced perspectives on agency and the contingent responsiveness of teachers within classes for refugee learners of English. In a recent New Zealand-based study, White (2016) examines the interrelationships between emotion and agency in teacher accounts of an incident of sudden, intense conflict in an English language class for immigrants and refugees. Narrative accounts of the conflict are given by the teacher, Anna, in three different settings: in an initial written account, then revisited in an individual oral interview, and finally when Anna chose to talk about the conflict in an informal teacher group discussion. The study has two aims: to examine and elucidate how agency and emotion are related from a dialogical perspective, and to show *how* and *why* emotions and agency get talked about in teachers' lives. The analytical framework for the study draws on the notion of narrative accounts (Talmy, 2010), where the data are viewed as 'accounts' of events, interior mental states and so on: they are also seen as co-constructed between Anna and her imagined audiences in the written narrative, then between Anna and myself as interviewer, and finally between Anna and the other teachers in the teacher group discussion. A further meaning of the term 'accounts', identified by Prior (2011: 62), incorporates how narrators bring together and comment on their social worlds and in so doing are 'accounting for (events) and accountable (to others)'. This latter perspective is markedly congruent with dialogically based enquiry into how individuals draw on emotion and agency in accounting for conflict and in being accountable to others at different moments.

In the first narrative, Anna relates the problematic event, in terms of a prolonged attack on herself (and New Zealand society) by one of the students, connected to the topic of care of the elderly. In Bakhtinian terms, Anna authors herself as on a threshold: she must decide how she will act, the words she will choose and what her relationship to others will be, including to the implicit audience of the narrative. In this part of the study the salience of agency and emotion across different timescales is underlined: in accounting for herself and events Anna draws on and provides glimpses of her family history, she reconstructs the non-judgemental interactive norms established over time in the class, and she shows awareness of participants' values and expectations. The analysis of the individual interview reveals affective dimensions of the notion of active answerability (Vitanova, 2010) as Anna contemplates how she (and others) would feel if the conflict escalated further, or if she were to be seen as someone who critiqued the cultural practices of others. In the teacher group discussion, emotion was represented as at once constraining and enabling agency with control over the projected affective stance constructed as both an affordance and as a key dimension of the teachers' answerability. The study also reveals that teachers use emotions as a resource in talking about their agency to construct wider, shared discourses about their ideals, constraints and answerability as teachers, and in so doing co-author themselves as a fundamental part of their agency.

Conclusion

In this chapter I have marked out current theorising and research into language teacher agency, emphasising the multiple aspects of agency, the range of research and real-world problems to which it can be applied, and the effects of multiple contexts, actors and moments on teacher agency. Here the focus has largely been on individual agency, with collective agency largely unexplored (although implicit in the evident importance of relationships which runs through many of the studies). A potentially rich approach to studying teacher agency identified by Ahearn (2001) is to analyse meta-agentive discourse, that is, how people talk about agency, providing insight into people's own theories of agency which is a promising avenue of enquiry into teacher agency. While policy demands and shifts in teaching contexts have emerged as salient for teachers in terms of their agency, there is also room for more fine-grained enquiry into the demands that teachers identify and respond to in what can be termed the dialectic of person and practice. To conclude, perhaps the richest site for exploring agency is within what Kubaniyova and Feryok (2015: 439) term the 'ecologies of teachers' inner lives', which incorporates 'individual intentional mental processes' and 'purposeful actions at the individual level' situated within teachers' lives, classrooms and wider systems.

References

Ahearn, L.M. (2001) Language and agency. *Annual Review of Anthropology* 30, 109–137.

Aro, M. (2015) In action and inaction: English learners authoring their agency. In P. Kalaja, A.M.F. Barcelos, M. Aro and M. Ruohotie-Lyhty (eds) *Beliefs, Agency and Identity in Foreign Language Learning and Teaching* (pp. 48–65). Basingstoke: Palgrave Macmillan.

Bakhtin, M.M. (1984) *Problems of Dostoevsky's Poetics* (ed. and trans. C. Emerson). Minneapolis, MN: University of Minnesota Press.

Bakhtin, M.M. (1993) *Toward a Philosophy of the Act*. Austin, TX: University of Texas Press.

Bakhtin, M.M. (2010) *The Dialogic Imagination: Four Essays* (ed. and trans. M. Holquist, trans. C. Emerson). Austin, TX: University of Texas Press.

Bamberg, M. (1997) Language, concepts and emotions: The role of language in the construction of emotions. *Language Sciences* 19 (4), 309–340.

Baynham, M. (2006) Agency and contingency in the language learning of refugees and asylum seekers. *Linguistics and Education* 17 (1), 24–39.

Benson, P. (2007) Autonomy in language teaching and learning. *Language Teaching* 40 (1), 21–40.

Block, D. (2003) *The Social Turn in Second Language Acquisition*. Edinburgh: Edinburgh University Press.

Block, D. (2013) The structure and agency dilemma in identity and intercultural communication research. *Language and Intercultural Communication* 13 (2), 126–147.

Candlin, C.N. and Sarangi, S. (2004) Making applied linguistics matter. *Journal of Applied Linguistics* 1 (1), 1–8.

Duff, P. (2012) Identity, agency, and second language acquisition. In C.J. Doughty and M.H. Long (eds) *Handbook of Second Language Acquisition* (pp. 410–426). Oxford: Blackwell.

Dufva, H. and Aro, M. (2014) Dialogical view on language learners' agency: Connecting intrapersonal with interpersonal. In P. Deters, X. Gao, E. Miller and G. Vitanova (eds) *Theorizing and Analyzing Agency in Second Language Learning: Interdisciplinary Approaches* (pp. 37–53). Bristol: Multilingual Matters.

Duranti, A. (2004) Agency in language. In A. Duranti (ed.) *A Companion to Linguistic Anthropology* (pp. 451–473). Oxford: Blackwell.

Engeström, Y. (2009) The future of activity theory: A rough draft. In A. Sannino, H. Daniels and K.D. Gutiérrez (eds) *Learning and Expanding with Activity Theory* (pp. 303–328). Cambridge: Cambridge University Press.

Esch, E. and Zähner, C. (2000) The contribution of information and communication technology (ICT) to language learning environments or the mystery of the secret agent. *ReCALL* 12 (1), 5–18.

Eteläpelto, A., Vähäsantanen, K. and Hökkä, P. (2015) How do novice teachers in Finland perceive their professional agency? *Teachers and Teaching: Theory and Practice* 21 (6), 660–680.

Feryok, A. (2012) Activity theory and language teacher agency. *The Modern Language Journal* 96 (1), 95–107.

Galperin, P. Ya. (1989) The problem of attention. *Soviet Psychology* 27, 83–92.

Hall, J.K., Vitanova, G. and Marchenkova, L. (eds) (2005) *Dialogue with Bakhtin on Second and Foreign Language Learning: New Perspectives.* Mahwah, NJ: Lawrence Erlbaum.

Hamid, M.O., Zhu, L. and Baldauf, R.B. (2014) Norms and varieties of English and TESOL teacher agency. *Australian Journal of Teacher Education* 39 (10), 77–95.

Hargreaves, A. and Fullan, M. (2012) *Professional Capital: Transforming Teaching in Every School.* New York: Teachers College Press.

Holquist, M. (1990) *Dialogism: Mikhail Bakhtin and his World.* London: Routledge.

Huang, J.P. and Benson, P. (2013) Autonomy, agency and identity in foreign and second language education. *Chinese Journal of Applied Linguistics* 36 (1), 7–28.

Kalaja, P., Barcelos, A.M.F., Aro, M. and Ruohotie-Lyhty, M. (eds) (2015) *Beliefs, Agency and Identity in Foreign Language Learning and Teaching.* Basingstoke: Palgrave Macmillan.

Kayi-Aydar, H. (2015) Multiple identities, negotiations, and agency across time and space: A narrative inquiry of a foreign language teacher candidate. *Critical Inquiry in Language Studies* 12 (2), 137–160.

Kitade, K. (2015) Second language teacher development through CALL practice: The emergence of teachers' agency. *CALICO Journal* 32 (3), 396–425.

Lantolf, J.P. and Pavlenko, A. (2001) Second (L)anguage (A)ctivity theory: Understanding second language learners as people. In M.P. Breen (ed.) *Learner Contributions to Language Learning: New Directions in Research* (pp. 141–158). Harlow: Pearson.

Lantolf, J.P. and Thorne, S.L. (2006) *Sociocultural Theory and the Genesis of L2 Development.* Oxford: Oxford University Press.

Larsen-Freeman, D. and Cameron, L. (2008) *Complex Systems and Applied Linguistics.* Oxford: Oxford University Press.

Leont'ev, A.N. (1978) *Activity, Consciousness, and Personality* (trans. M.J. Hall). Englewood Cliffs, NJ: Prentice Hall.

McNay, L. (2000) *Gender and Agency: Reconfiguring the Subject in Feminist and Social Theory.* Cambridge: Polity Press.

Mercer, S. (2011) Understanding learner agency as a complex dynamic system. *System* 39 (4), 427–436.

Mercer, S. (2012) The complexity of learner agency. *Apples – Journal of Applied Language Studies* 62, 41–59.

Ng, P.C. and Boucher-Yip, E.F. (eds) (2016) *Teacher Agency and Policy Response in English Language Teaching.* London: Routledge.

Palmer, D. and Martínez, R.A. (2013) Teacher agency in bilingual spaces: A fresh look at preparing teachers to educate Latina/o bilingual children. *Review of Research in Education* 37 (1), 269–297.

Potter, J. and Wetherell, M. (1987) *Discourse and Social Psychology: Beyond Attitudes and Behaviour.* Thousand Oaks, CA: Sage.

Prior, M.T. (2011) Self-presentation in L2 interview talk: Narrative versions, account-ability, and emotionality. *Applied Linguistics* 32 (1), 60–76.

Rogers, R. and Wetzel, M.M. (2013) Studying agency in literacy teacher education: A layered approach to positive discourse analysis. *Critical Inquiry in Language Studies* 10 (1), 62–92.

Ruohotie-Lyhty, M. (2013) Struggling for a professional identity: Two newly qualified language teachers' identity narratives during the first years at work. *Teaching and Teacher Education* 30, 120–129.

Ruohotie-Lyhty, M. (2015) Dependent or independent: The construction of the beliefs of newly qualified foreign language teachers. In P. Kalaja, A.M.F. Barcelos, M. Aro and M. Ruohotie-Lyhty (eds) *Beliefs, Agency and Identity in Foreign Language Learning and Teaching* (pp. 149–171). Basingstoke: Palgrave Macmillan UK.

Ruohotie-Lyhty, M. and Moate, J. (2015) Proactive and reactive dimensions of life-course agency: Mapping student teachers' language learning experiences. *Language and Education* 29 (1), 46–61.

Ruohotie-Lyhty, M. and Moate, J. (2016) Who and how? Preservice teachers as active agents developing professional identities. *Teaching and Teacher Education* 55, 318–327.

Schroots, J.J.F. and Ten Kate, C.A. (1989) Metaphors, aging and the life-line interview method. In D. Unruh and G. Livings (eds) *Current Perspectives on Aging and the Life Cycle: Personal History Through the Life Course* (pp. 281–298). London: JAI Press.

Sullivan, P. and McCarthy, J. (2004) Toward a dialogical perspective on agency. *Journal for the Theory of Social Behaviour* 34 (3), 291–309.

Talmy, S. (2010) Qualitative interviews in applied linguistics: From research instrument to social practice. *Annual Review of Applied Linguistics* 30, 128–148.

Valsiner, J. (1998) *The Guided Mind: A Sociogenetic Approach to Personality*: Cambridge, MA: Harvard University Press.

Van Huy, N., Hamid, M.O. and Renshaw, P. (2016) Language education policy enactment and individual agency: The cauldron of conflicts in policy positions in implementing the Common European Framework of Reference for languages in Vietnam. *Language Problems and Language Planning* 40 (1), 69–84.

van Lier, L. (1996) *Interaction in the Language Classroom: Awareness, Autonomy and Authenticity*. London: Longman.

van Lier, L. (2004) The semiotics and ecology of language learning: Perception, voice, identity, and democracy. *Utbildning and Demokrati* 13 (3), 79–103.

van Lier, L. (2007) Action-based teaching, autonomy and identity. *International Journal of Innovation in Language Learning and Teaching* 1 (1), 46–65.

van Lier, L. (2008) Agency in the classroom. In J.P. Lantolf and M.E. Poehner (eds) *Sociocultural Theory and the Teaching of Second Languages* (pp. 163–186). London: Equinox.

Vitanova, G. (2005) Authoring the self in a non-native language: A dialogic approach to agency and subjectivity. In J. Kelly Hall, G. Vitanova and L. Marchenkova (eds) *Dialogue with Bakhtin on Second and Foreign Language Learning: New Perspectives* (pp. 149–169). Mahwah, NJ: Lawrence Erlbaum.

Vitanova, G. (2010) *Authoring the Dialogic Self: Gender, Agency and Language Practices*. Amsterdam: John Benjamins.

Vygotsky, L.S. (1978) *Mind in Society: The Development of Higher Mental Process*. Cambridge, MA: Harvard University Press.

Vygotsky, L.S. (1986) *Thought and Language* (revised edn, ed. A. Kozulin). Cambridge, MA: Harvard University Press.

White, C.J. (2016) Agency and emotion in narrative accounts of emergent conflict in an L2 classroom. *Applied Linguistics*; doi:10.1093/applin/amw026.

13 Teachers Crafting Job Crafting

Joseph Falout and Tim Murphey

Finding possible ways to make work more meaningful can contribute to the psychological well-being in the jobs and lives of language teachers and their students. This study took an approach from positive psychology – which enquires into how people find, maintain or regain well-being – of presenting descriptive, rather than prescriptive, research (Seligman, 2011). Job crafting happens when people make alterations in the conventional tasks, relationships and roles involved with their work so it becomes subjectively more meaningful to them (Wrzesniewski, 2016). Thus, different ways teachers say they are achieving job crafting became the first focus of our study. The second focus was the hypothesis that sharing descriptions of job crafting among teachers could inspire them to find more meaning in their work.

These focuses were investigated, respectively, by two phases. In Phase 1, 41 language teachers from around the world described what they do in their job that goes beyond the basic job description and gives their job meaningfulness. Their responses were sorted into 12 descriptive job roles within four categories. For Phase 2, we sent this information to the original respondents who had said they were interested in the results. They then responded to our further questions about to what extent they believed they were job crafting in each of the categories. They also provided us with their reflections on the research results from Phase 1. Phase 2 findings suggest that sharing descriptions of job crafting among teachers did make a difference to their own meaning-making about their work. Thus this study itself presents an example of how teachers can inspire each other to do greater job crafting. As our title suggests, they became a group of teachers who were crafting their job crafting.

Meaning and Job Crafting

People feel their lives are meaningful when they are investing their energies in something they value and perceive as bigger than themselves (e.g. Compton & Hoffman, 2015; Lopez *et al.*, 2015). Generally, meaning in life has been found to contribute to a wide range of positive emotions (e.g. Fredrickson, 2009). It also appears to be strongly connected to a sense of purpose in one's career (Steger & Dik, 2009). The meaning teachers make in their lives, particularly in their jobs, is important as it contributes to their overall well-being (Chan, 2009, 2013). Furthermore, a sense of purpose can also be positively reflected in teachers' approaches to their work, particularly in the care and attention they give to their daily tasks (Albuquerque *et al.*, 2014).

Meaning is one of the primary elements of well-being in one of the most prominent conceptions of positive psychology, Seligman's (2011) acronym, **PERMA**. This stands for Positive emotion, Engagement, positive Relationships, Meaning and Accomplishment (or Achievement). Meaning also appears in Oxford's (2016) recently proposed framework of well-being for language learners, called **EMPATHICS**, which relates the cognitive, emotional and behavioural interrelationships of: Emotion and Empathy; Meaning and Motivation; Perseverance, including resilience, hope and optimism; Agency and Autonomy; Time; Hardiness and Habits of mind; Intelligences; Character strengths; and Self factors, including Self-efficacy, Self-concept, Self-esteem and Self-verification. Meaning-making in language education can signify making sense of, giving explanations about or attaching values to experiences. Teachers and learners make sense of their experiences co-constructively. For example, learners make sense of their learning from the small experiences to the trajectories of their language development – including the challenges, suffering and ecstasy – and listeners of such learner narratives, notably teachers, also make meaning from the learners' experiences (Oxford, 2016).

The concept of meaning in language education is increasingly becoming recognised as crucial because meaning is made 'inside and between the people in the classroom' (Stevick, 1980: 4). These interactions in their classroom life, their individual psychologies and their capacities to value and participate in making a positive difference in the world around them relate to a whole range of goals, needs, processes and desires, as explored in the recent volume, *Meaningful Action: Earl Stevick's Influence on Language Learning and Teaching* (Arnold & Murphey, 2013). Meaning in the language classroom is therefore derived from and invested into creating social harmony, as attested by the turn of interest in applied linguistics towards classroom atmosphere, group dynamics, community, learner voices, embodied and extended learning, agency and trust (Arnold & Murphey, 2013). Through such social dynamics, meaning influences the psychological well-being of language learners and teachers at school and in their out-of-school lives.

Regardless of occupation, education, salary and occupational demands, the reasons people give for working correlates with the meaningfulness they find in their jobs and overall lives. Their main motivations can be oriented towards a *job* (working for the pay cheque), *career* (working for advancement up the career ladder) or *calling* (following a mission to benefit others and to make the world a better place). Working for a calling, compared with working for a job and career, relates significantly to greater job performance, job and life satisfaction and physical health (Wrzesniewski *et al.*, 1997).

Even if they think they do not have a calling, people can modify their approaches to their jobs to create greater meaningfulness and psychological well-being (Wrzesniewski, 2016; Wrzesniewski & Dutton, 2001). This is job crafting. It happens when employees do their job differently from how it is supposed to be done, by large or small measures, particularly as expected by the employer and stated in job descriptions, manuals and guidelines. In job crafting, employees customise the work by reconfiguring: (1) the boundaries of their actions; (2) the nature of their interactions among the people there; and (3) the nature of their job identity or definition of the role. These three forms of job crafting are known, respectively, as *task crafting, relational crafting* and *cognitive crafting*. Job crafting includes reformulating usual job procedures, choosing newer procedures and opting out of others. It also involves reframing one's identity on the job and reasons for doing it. The degrees to which people enjoy augmenting their work (i.e. affect), feel the power and desire to do it (i.e. agency and motivation), and imagine beyond the norms of who they are on the job (i.e. identity) can determine whether they even try job crafting (Wrzesniewski & Dutton, 2001).

When employees who normally view their work as a job or career customise the moments they have and the efforts they make with one of the three forms of job crafting, they begin understanding that there may be ways for them to cultivate purposefulness. They believe their jobs are improvable, that they are capable of performing better at work and attaining greater job and life satisfaction. This occurs in connection with the belief that other people's lives are improvable or that the surrounding world can become better. Employees can become hopeful, feeling they are striving towards something greater than themselves. Thus, meaningfulness in work can happen incrementally through what is known as a growth mindset (Dweck, 2006). Furthermore, the reasons language teachers work can be multiple, flexible and complex (see Hiver *et al.*, this volume). Their identities can likewise be multiple, influenced by roles and relationships both inside and outside school, and inform meaning-making in teaching and determination to stay in the profession (Werbińska, 2016). Therefore, motivational orientations of work for teachers concern a complex flow of dynamic meaning-making (Figure 13.1), and incremental job crafting through a variety of small ways over time can help teachers sustain the psychological benefits of having a calling throughout the ups and downs within trajectories of their teaching and the course of their lives.

Specific descriptions of job crafting come from a range of professions (e.g. Wrzesniewski & Dutton, 2001). However, we found little in the literature about how teachers do job crafting. Wellman and Spreitzer (2010)

Figure 13.1 Complex flow dynamics of meaning-making

use their own casual observations to illustrate a few examples from the academic field of organisational behaviour. For task crafting, one of their colleagues took on a new challenge of creating a computer-based teaching simulation to research reciprocation in networks, in which his students eventually participated for adding experimental data, but afterwards were found to behave more altruistically towards each other in the classroom. Another teacher from a business school took on an additional position as an administrator and reinvented herself as a leader of the school. For relational crafting, one scholar researching burnout with at-risk individuals spent additional time with the participants to teach them coping strategies. For cognitive crafting, one teacher challenged his students with a course project of raising money for a charity. For each case, Wellman and Spreitzer (2010) asserted that job crafting brought increased personal meaningfulness to everyone involved, be it teachers or students, because they were helping to improve the lives of others.

A study (Leana *et al.*, 2009) involving 232 teachers and teacher helpers at 62 childcare centres used scaled questionnaires, open-ended interviews, mixed focus groups and independent observational raters to assess the job performance and psychological benefits of those engaging in job crafting. The study presented robust evidence that individual job crafting (i.e. by oneself) and collaborative job crafting (i.e. by mutual decision making among colleagues within the workplace) are two distinct constructs. Moreover, it found that those engaging in collaborative job crafting, as opposed to individual job crafting, engaged in significantly higher quality care in children's personal and academic needs and experienced significantly higher levels of job satisfaction, job performance, job attachment and commitment to organisational aims. In short, teachers and their helpers, in collaborating to alter what is expected of them by the organisation, even to the extent of bending the rules at times, wound up providing more for the students on a daily basis in ways that aligned with the overarching goals of their employers. What they specifically did for job crafting, however, was not reported.

The primary motivations for the present study were to find out for ourselves how teachers are job crafting in language education, and then to share these examples with other language teachers, with the aim of inspiring us all with ways we might create more meaningfulness in our professional work and overall lives.

Methods

This study was conducted in two phases. In the first phase we gathered descriptions of the different ways the participants reported doing job crafting. In the second phase we sent a summary of these descriptions back to all the teachers who had said they were interested in the Phase 1 results. The specific methods for each of the two phases are presented in their respective procedures sections.

Procedures: Phase 1

Participants

A total of 44 teachers participated in Phase 1. Table 13.1 shows the details of their circumstances at the time of responding.

Instrument

We aimed for a positive psychology approach to find what works in making meaning in language teaching and to inspire teachers to make more meaning in their jobs. Therefore, we wanted to attract teachers who found meaning in their work, but we did not want to exclude teachers who could not find meaning. Also, we recognise there is potentially a great range of

Table 13.1 Participant circumstances

Educational institution	n	%
Primary school	4	9.1
Junior high school	10	22.7
High school	7	15.9
College or university	26	59.1
Graduate school	3	6.8
Conversation school	2	4.5
Cram school or test preparation	1	2.3
Other (including pre-school, kindergarten, corporate and adult education, language school, private tutoring and teacher training)	10	22.7
One category of the above (teaching in)	31	70.5
Two categories of the above (teaching in)	9	20.5
Three categories of the above (teaching in)	4	9.1
Country		
Japan	19	43.2
Indonesia, United States	5 each	11.4 each
Brazil	3	6.8
Qatar, South Korea, United Kingdom	2 each	4.5 each
Afghanistan, Colombia, Finland, Germany, Greece, Hong Kong, Iraq, Oman, Uruguay	1 each	2.3 each
Two countries of the above (teaching in)	3	6.8
Language being taught		
English	43	97.9
Japanese	4	9.1
Indonesian	3	6.8
Portuguese, Spanish	1 each	2.3 each
Two languages above (English and Indonesian)	2	4.5
Three languages above (English, Portuguese and Spanish)	1	2.3

reasons to teach and ways to find meaning in teaching. In considering all this, we intended to appeal to those who both had found and had not found meaning in teaching. The questionnaire thus began with the heading: *A call for 'teachers with a calling' stories and those who wish to have a calling.* Although we did not wish to elicit negative emotional responses – and in fact just the opposite; that of hope – we can now see problematic effects from the wording of this heading, including an unintended idealisation of having a calling. The goal is not necessarily having a calling, but managing the psychological resources one has in order to create meaning, and to incrementally maintain one's resilience (cf. Hiver, this volume; Kostoulas & Lämmerer, this volume) in meaning-making in teaching.

This heading was followed by ten questions (Table 13.2) to assess the extent to which participants were experiencing meaningfulness in their teaching. The first question, in the present perfect, 'I have experienced great meaningfulness as a teacher', was intended to elicit a eudaemonic appraisal, meaning a summary of things up through now that would relate to the degree of job satisfaction. The questions that followed, in the present tense, were to help determine in which situations teachers

Table 13.2 Areas of meaningfulness for teacher job crafters

Question	Non-crafters (n = 3)	Job crafters (n = 41)			
	Mean	Mean	SD	Skewness	Kurtosis
(1) I have experienced great meaningfulness as a teacher.	1.67	3.20	0.80	−0.38	−1.38
(2) Meaningfulness happens when I interact with students in classes.	1.33	3.20	0.77	−0.69	0.05
(3) Meaningfulness happens when I read my students work.	1.00	2.68	0.90	0.06	−0.88
(4) Meaningfulness happens when I see my students perform.	1.33	3.32	0.71	−0.57	−0.86
(5) Meaningfulness happens when students confide in me personally.	1.67	3.17	0.88	−0.57	−0.94
(6) Meaningfulness happens when I see my students developing in some way.	2.00	3.46	0.67	−0.89	−0.31
(7) Meaningfulness happens when I interact with other teachers.	1.33	2.46	0.89	0.22	−0.63
(8) Meaningfulness happens when I interact with administrators.	1.00	1.70	0.81	1.20	1.27
(9) Meaningfulness happens when I produce research and publish articles.	2.00	2.59	1.08	−0.17	−1.25
(10) Meaningfulness happens when I share teaching ideas with others (informally, at conferences or in publications).	2.33	3.07	0.81	−0.71	0.29

Note: Four-point Likert scale of 1 = rarely or never, 2 = sometimes, 3 = regularly, 4 = very frequently.

currently find meaning, such as when interacting with students, teachers or administrators, or when presenting teaching ideas or publishing research. These questions were also intended to help prime the participants' thinking about what brings them meaningfulness in teaching. Then questions were given to gain the demographics of the survey population.

In the next part of the questionnaire, we summarised the benefits of teachers seeing their job as a calling (Leana *et al.*, 2009). We explained to respondents that we intended to use their stories of how they make their work purposeful in order to benefit other teachers. Then came two short, exemplary descriptions of job crafting in altered tasks (i.e. changing the work of simply making language tests into a chance of including reading material for teaching healthy habits of living) and roles (i.e. changing self-perception from a teacher of language to a teacher of making worldwide friendships). Finally, the core part was an open-ended question, designed from interview questions in a job crafting study conducted by Berg *et al.* (2010), which prompted:

> What things do you do in your job that goes beyond the job description and that you think gives your job meaningfulness? (please describe as many things as you can in your tasks and roles)

The questionnaire concluded: 'This research is anonymous. If you would like to receive a summary of this research and tips on how teachers make their work more meaningful, please leave your name and email address.' The last question asked whether or not participants were willing to answer follow-up questions. Thirty-seven (84.1%) indicated they were indeed willing, and 35 (79.5%) included contact information; these latter participants became the base population for Phase 2 of this study.

Procedure

Within teacher circles, the questionnaire was sent by email and passed around on social network sites by contacts of the authors. The data were collected over a period of five weeks, then read multiple times. Few responses explicitly involved cognitive crafting, in which teachers mentioned their job crafting roles: one wished to be a 'better teacher'; another expressed the differences in meaning between duties as 'homeroom teacher' and 'language teacher'; one was an International Relations Committee member; one said 'lifelong learner' and 'friendly but not a friend'; two mentioned other areas of teaching experience (maths and history); one mentioned a former profession in business; and one talked about the student role in becoming 'a better citizen in our community'.

Meanwhile, job crafting descriptions involving actions, activities and relationships were given in so much detail – and sometimes elaborated with abstract reasoning, pedagogies or ideologies – that we found it difficult to accurately and meaningfully capture it all in categorical summarisations short enough for reporting back to the participants. Certain descriptions of actions, activities and relationships, we realised, could often be reformulated into roles. For example, 'counselling' and 'guiding' students could be intuited as teacher as counsellor and guide, and 'modelling and discussing the learning process' became teacher as role model. In this manner, we could infer roles these language teachers had taken on, and thus we determined that the rich and varied descriptions of activities could be more easily captured and presented as roles. After emic readings of the data, 12 distinct roles emerged from our coding efforts. These were then grouped by similar type and given meta-role labels.

Results: Phase 1

This study was designed to investigate what works well for teachers, specifically in terms of the things they do in their jobs that go beyond the job description and that they think give their job meaningfulness (i.e. job crafting). However, three participants (6.2%) did not provide answers about job crafting. Also, they responded having low-to-no levels of meaning in their work (Table 13.2), indicating they found little purpose in teaching. One participant's self-description was that of a 'mercenary' (the only non-job-crafting role mentioned in the survey), as teaching English was only a means to make a living, and this teacher planned to leave the profession soon. Another participant answered the open-ended job crafting question in one word: 'nothing', while the last avoided answering by instead asking: 'By what metrics do [job crafting] teachers teach better and become more productive', to which we can refer inquisitive readers to Leana *et al.* (2009). Our study was not tailored to investigating why teachers feel a lack of meaningfulness in their work, or wish to avoid describing what gives their job meaning, although such research in the future would certainly benefit the field of teacher psychology.

Forty-one participants (93.2%) responded that they found meaning in some if not many areas of their work, notably by interacting with students and seeing their progress, with a skewness towards experiencing meaningfulness very frequently. Their solid ideas and, in many instances, detailed descriptions, provided raw data from which we derived the roles that these teachers take on (Table 13.3). The only area surveyed in which meaning was not found to happen often was when interacting with administrators, and it was the only question missing a response (Q8, $n = 40$).

These roles are not discrete; there are many overlapping qualities among the roles, not only within but also across the four categories. Moreover, taking on multiple roles at once is possible if not usual for many teachers. Given here are descriptions of language teacher job crafting. Note: orthographic infelicities, grammatical choices and other deviations from editorial style (often attributable to busy days and imperfect typing software) were kept.

Advisors

Advisors volunteer to explicitly teach language learning and use, sometimes advising for specific purposes or situations, such as hunting for jobs or conducting research.

Respondent #1: I want students to have a hands-on experience of what they are learning about. For example, in my nutrition classes, after doing a unit on the slow food movement, which I created from authentic materials, I have students come to my house and we all cook lunch together … I host an English club in my office and get students to volunteer for activities that I think will benefit them, such as ELT conferences on campus, or multicultural activities.

Respondent #9: I open study groups or individualized tutoring sessions. Through out those chances I can understand my students better and help them in a way that I can't do in a large class setting.

Guides

Guides show what is possible through examples of what other people are capable of doing and of what awaits students in the wider world beyond the classroom. They point out pathways beyond for the future self-possibility of arriving at physical locales or metaphorical states of being.

Respondent #14: We frequently have classes outside the classroom in open air spaces, squares, the beach, the park even on the street where we practice giving directions or treasure hunts.

Respondent #40: I'm doing video interviews with graduates who are either studying/using English in Japan or overseas. Giving them a chance to share their story (in both English and Japanese) is inspiring to me (to see how far they've come) and a chance for current students to see how far they can go.

Role models

They consciously set examples in their characteristics and appearances. They remember that their personal example can change the way students learn language and live life.

Respondent #26: I care for my students on a personal level and make sure that my teaching is not limited within the classroom walls. I try to set myself as an example of a lifelong learner to motivate them to study more …

Respondent #34: On occasion I let my hair down. In Latin America, males have short hair, but now some of them are trying to compete with me (good luck, I' from Hawai'i), and they all have learned the 'Shaka' hand sign which means to 'Hang Loose'. They're starting to understand that 'Aloha' is a greeting for coming & going.

Creators

Creators appeal to the creativity and holistic aspects of their students as well as bring their own various talents into teaching. Time-honoured practices and new technologies both come into play.

> **Respondent #14**: I always teach with an open mind so even though I plan my classes, if the students' interest lead us to other topics, grammar points or activities I'm flexible to change. I try to engage students with different kinds of activities where they can practice all skills and also to perform creatively by singing, playing, acting, listening to music, watching videos, painting and discussing ideas freely.

> **Respondent #39**: When I create an activity and learn that it needed to be adjusted to fit the students' needs and I see how that adjustment positively affected my students' learning and participation in the activity.

Intermediaries

Intermediaries act as social network builders among classmates and even beyond the classroom walls. They act as a conduit for students' interests and mediate social spaces for students' growth.

> **Respondent #3**: Facilitating new friendships for students from around the globe and knowing that these connections may last a lifetime for my students brings a high degree of satisfaction. I have had the pleasure of teaching students from every continent and most major people groups. This globalization being realized within the confines of my classroom has been a Much loved hallmark of my teaching career.

> **Respondent #7**: When there was no teacher yet having idea of sending students to do a voluntary service activities, I myself had that kind of challenging idea of taking students abroad. In fact, I managed to help parents trust their children to go. I also used to challenge my students to have a kind of teleconference through skype on certain projects done together with our partners abroad.

Teachers of more than language

They act as cultural informants and they raise awareness of local and global problems. They also consider themselves to be teachers of practical life skills, critical thinking, community and global citizenship, and more, promoting student autonomy, voice and empowerment.

> **Respondent #27**: I realized that teaching civics in a disadvantaged community was so empowering to them. These are students who are taught to fear or hate the justice system. But, they are also students who will likely interact with the government more often than most. Having students ask about slavery and immigration and the many injustices in American History gave them (and me) new perspective. Much to the dismay of their other teachers, I'm sure, I wanted them to challenge what they had always been told was true in the US. I want them to ask the tough questions. But, more importantly, I wanted them to find their own answers.

Respondent #35: Teaching the students how to search for good quality information, how to effectively weigh up differing points of view on a topic and how to critically assess the information that was provided to them on the internet and by the media was an incredibly powerful thing. The students seemed to mature before my eyes as their projects progressed and, dare I say it, turned from being rather passive, accepting adolescents into informed, passionate and questioning young adults. And their English improved too!

Companions

Companions share their own personal information when considered appropriate and provide compassion when needed. They spend their free time with students in many different spaces, opening up their offices and even homes for social activities that often relate to the learning in class.

Respondent #16: Interact with students outside of class: have tea together as a group or individual students, assist with English (from class or not) when not in class, discuss each other's culture, and show an interest in their lives, language, and culture.

Respondent #43: ... I sometimes talk with my students during a break and after school. For instance, things they couldn't understand in the class, something they are interested in, how to study English, and so on. I think that is important to enhance their motivation for learning language.

Devotees

Devotees show appreciation and dedication to their students. Devotees believe in their students and make a point in letting them know about it.

Respondent #4: I give achievable challenges to students who may have not felt much success with English before, and I praise them (good! nice! interesting!), and gradually, they gain in how much pride, confidence and fun they have while meeting new challenges.

Respondent #32: I was discouraged by the education system during my first year of teaching. I felt like the system both placed an undue amount of pressure on students and judged them arbitrarily. I found meaning in the job once I was able to see past the curriculum and realize that the classes were more about the people in the room than the material we were supposed to cover. The most meaningful thing for me was realizing that the students felt the same way and that by making a connection, I could support them in working to make a better system.

Psychologists

Psychologists are concerned with the internal world of learners and their potential growth as learners and as human beings. They help students adjust to learning or living in new situations and to emerging learner identities and values.

Respondent #8: The institution at which I work is a small school so interaction with the students can be quite close at times so we are able to keep relatively close tabs on student performance. This allows us to recognize changes in behavior over time. We also meet with a portion of the students each semester to monitor their adjustment and performance. This gives us a chance to take steps to work with students who are having difficulties. In more than one case, as a result of these meetings, I've been fortunate enough to have students trust me enough to confide in me about difficulties they are having.

Respondent #30: By addressing the metacognitive processes we go through, we can demonstrate that even experts experience failure and that healthy learning comes from reflecting on the processes and considering strategies or behaviors that we can use to achieve better outcomes from our efforts … I find meaning in setting up the classroom conditions for students to experience cognitive dissonance so that they can practice learning in a thoughtful way and so that they can explore new ways to think through learning. In many ways, I think of myself not as a teacher of content or of language, but of the learning process. The students are the ones doing all the work. Not me. And when I see them improving their self understanding, it sends tingles up my spine. That's what makes this profession a way of life rather than a job.

Witnesses

Witnesses feel rewarded from observing learner development in a myriad of areas. Although they may not always see the progress they want to see, they have future hopes for their students.

Respondent #10: As a language teacher, I feel the sense of meaningfulness when …
- I see the students do not stop talking English unless I put a stopper.
- I see the students keep talking about the things they learned even after the bell.
- I ask for questions and get immidiate responces.
- I see the students' great outcomes, for example, in writing essays, making speeches/presentations, or even in English proficiency test such as STEP test.
- I give a questionairre to students and see positive answers about their self-esteem.
- I hear that the students I taught keep using English in their life or career.

Respondent #29: Many times there is joy in their learning … Together we 'fall in love' with learning. It is an honor for me to teach all students.

Practitioners in progress

They view their teaching skills and accomplishments as a work in progress. They are strivers and survivors in the face of difficulties throughout various career challenges, highlights and stages.

Respondent #28: I always apply new ideas and experiment with new notions I've picked up mostly through interacting with other teachers online or reading books/articles in ELT.

Respondent #40: It's taken 9 years of tweaking my program to get this far but there is still more to change.

Teacher trainers

They voluntarily work with other teachers for improving teaching. They conduct their training from informal to formal settings.

Respondent #2: I took times twice a week to train the teachers assistant in my school to speak better English and to learn about Montessori. It isn't school program, just my own.

Respondent #11: Sharing good teaching resources to as many teachers (that I can reach) as possible, doing research and many other professional development activities to become a better teacher to my students and help other teachers (who have or wish to have the calling) to do the same.

Procedures: Phase 2

To recap Phase 1, we collected descriptions about how the participants make their work meaningful. From emic readings of their descriptions, we determined 12 roles that could capture how they formulate or approach their tasks (i.e. task crafting), interact with others (i.e. relationship crafting) and perceive their identities (i.e. cognitive crafting). We looped these 12 descriptive roles back to the participants in Phase 2, with the hypothesis that reading about their own job crafting and that of others would help them to appreciate what works in meaning-making, if not to inspire greater job crafting.

Participants

Of the 35 participants from Phase 1 who indicated agreeableness to answer follow-up questions, 13 (37.1%) actually responded in Phase 2.

Instrument

The Phase 2 questionnaire, following the procedures of critical participatory looping (Murphey & Falout, 2010), first looped back the Phase 1 results in Table 13.3, which gave an overview of the 12 roles of language teacher job crafting. The first four questions were for assessing to what extent the participants felt they were job crafting in each of the four categories of roles. Then two open-ended questions were for providing feedback from the participants about this study.

Table 13.3 Meaningful roles of language teachers

Navigators

Advisors	Volunteer their time to tutor or advise outside of class.
Guides	Show learners where they can possibly go, physically or metaphorically.
Role models	Strive to embody ideal characteristics, such as being a lifelong learner.

Transformers

Creators	Bring variety to learning with original materials that stimulate various senses.
Intermediaries	Act as social network builders in the classroom and beyond.
Teachers of more than language	Teach practical life skills, culture, critical thinking, etc.

Nurturers

Companions	Build personal relationships with their students.
Devotees	Show dedication to students and give personalised feedback and praise.
Psychologists	Address the internal world of students, helping them adjust and grow.

Wonderers

Witnesses	Find fulfilment from observing learner developments and achievements.
Practitioners in progress	Work on professional development throughout their careers.
Teacher trainers	Voluntarily train teachers to better teach students.

Results: Phase 2

The participants, on average, felt they perform job crafting in most role categories somewhat regularly in their daily work (Table 13.4). Not all participants in Phase 2 responded to the open-ended questions, but here we provide everything that we did receive, without any expurgation or other manipulation, and so answers are presented with integrity, including orthographic infelicities, grammatical choices and other deviations from editorial style (Tables 13.5 and 13.6).

Crafting job crafting

How people view the meaning of their work may be more influential on their satisfaction with work and life than their salary or job prestige (Wrzesniewski *et al.*, 1997). Even if the nature of the job is not meaningful to an employee, aspects of the work can become more meaningful when the employee reformulates and transforms given tasks, relationships and roles. This is a process known as job crafting, which also corresponds to

Table 13.4 Frequency of job crafting in four categorical roles (n = 13)

Question	Mean	SD	Skewness	Kurtosis
(1) How much do you feel you act as a Navigator in your daily work?	2.92	0.73	0.14	−1.05
(2) How much do you feel you act as a Transformer in your daily work?	2.92	0.83	0.16	−1.68
(3) How much do you feel you act as a Nurturer in your daily work?	2.46	0.84	0.58	−0.12
(4) How much do you feel you act as a Wonderer in your daily work?	2.69	1.07	−0.14	−1.28

Note: Four-point Likert scale of 1 = rarely or never, 2 = sometimes, 3 = regularly, 4 = very frequently.

psychological well-being (Wrzesniewski, 2016). The present study provides descriptions of job crafting about actual ways language teachers are making alterations related to their work that makes them feel more purposeful in what they are doing and more useful to others than if they had simply done their teaching duties as given. These teachers suggested that they have increased for themselves the complexities of their work and positive affect towards it (cf. Gkonou & Mercer, this volume; Gregersen & MacIntyre, this volume), the agency and motivation to make these changes (cf. Hiver *et al.*, this volume; Sahakyan *et al.*, this volume; White, this volume), their resilience (cf. Hiver, this volume; Kostoulas & Lämmerer, this volume) and the diversity of their own teacher identities (cf. Li & De Kosta, this volume; Varghese, this volume).

The primary focus in these adaptations to their jobs appears to be in the relationships with their students, as can be seen in the results (Tables 13.2 and 13.3). Few descriptions involved other colleagues, and none of

Table 13.5 Q5: What roles might be missing and in which category might they belong?

(1) How about Entertainers? They could be close to Creators, but I value more on teacher's positive attitude towards enjoying learning with students. They find joy in entertaining students and by doing so they enjoy themselves finding students smile, laugh, or any positive emotional reaction from students as well as growth or positive changes in them.

(2) Transformer → reinventor (someone who is able to take a fresh approach to an existing situation with success).

(3) I cannot think of any.

(4) Some teachers are like fixtures, they have little to no impact, rather they are like cogs in a machine, working towards their summer off and retirement.

(5) Care-taker

(6) Encouragers in category Navigator or even Nurturer.

(7) Similar to 'Role Model' perhaps, but 'Cultural Representative' might be useful in one of these categories. I think an important aspect of my job is to be a positive example of an 'American' and to address stereotypes that learners might have.

Table 13.6 Q6: What do you think about this research?

(1) This quick glimpse of your research has already given me a chance to reconcider where I am now and wherefore I am heading. Just by answering these questions, teachers can reflectively think about their career or confirm their identities. Also, it was useful to know what teachers with calling are actually viewing themselves. More detailed numbers and examples would be of great help for teachers development. Thank you Tim-sensei and professor Falout for this.
(2) I am very interested to see how your research develops in the direction of professional development. In particular, teaching methods that focus more on the learner and where content is more based on what learners need and want, rather than on units of a textbook. Please keep me posted on your progress.
(3) I think it works well as a taxonomy to show developing teachers where their strengths lie and which aspects are less developed and thus may be worthy of attention in either formal or informal CPD.
(4) I enjoyed the reflectivity it brings.
(5) I feel that this can answer some of my pondering about who I am as a teacher.
(6) It seems like an excellent research topic that would help everyone in education or going into education, as well as leaders, parents, etc. learn and realize that there is more to being a teacher than teaching subjects and the importance of having teachers with these qualities or goals in their teaching because teachers are training and preparing students for life and building students' character.
(7) interesting
(8) If by 'this research' you mean this form in particular, I think it would have been better to let each subcategory stand alone. For example, concerning the larger 'Nurturer' category, I strive to be a 'Devotee' but not a 'Companion' or a 'Psychologist', so it was hard for me to respond to the whole category.
(9) Valuable perhaps in showing teachers where they are, and where they might want to go next.

them involved administrators or other personnel encountered at educational institutions (e.g. janitorial, vending or security staff). Additionally, none of the participants mentioned mentors, and only one participant wrote about students' parents (Respondent #7 in the Intermediaries example). However, depersonalisation from students *and colleagues* may be regarded as a major psychological risk to teachers, especially those who have chosen to teach and live abroad (Falout, 2010). Moreover, both demotivation and unintentional remotivation most often came from relationships with students *and colleagues*, as reported in one study of 75 English teachers from ten countries around the world (Falout *et al.*, 2012). Teachers seeking belonging may want to consider three further approaches, as suggested by Falout (2013): (a) engaging with colleagues and others inside and outside school, by asking for help, sharing resources, teaching in teams and greeting everyone daily; (b) imagining what is possible for one's self, with mentors, professional organisations, peer study groups, continuing education classes, online communities and books; and (c) aligning with explicit and implicit local values, rules, customs and courtesies.

The job crafting data from this study are not intended to be comprehensive or prescriptive; rather, these examples of creating more meaning in language teaching are for descriptive purposes. That is, we present these ideas for other teachers to compare and confirm what works for them, and perhaps to choose for themselves what they might wish to try. It is important to note that different teachers have different ways of finding meaning. What works for some teachers might not work for other teachers. Tasks, relationships and roles considered inventive in one context might be standard in other contexts. Furthermore, teachers cannot be expected to do everything or be all. Teachers from this study reported that they could do job crafting often, but not daily. These teachers may also have had more latitude than other teachers to do things beyond the job description that make teaching feel more purposeful. However, job crafting involves evaluating what is possible for each individual to change the balance of responsibilities, focus of goals and means of accomplishments, as well as understanding the implications of shaping work experiences towards what the individual hopes to enjoy (Wrzesniewski, 2016).

Limitations and Invitations

More work could be done in future studies by improving the questionnaire, dispersing it to wider groups, and collecting different types of data such as observational data on teacher performance or longitudinal data on dynamic trajectories of job crafting. Perhaps also a study on student job crafting would reveal further possibilities in the work of learners. To teachers reflecting upon the present research and looking for greater meaning in their work, we suggest they can promote more effective action taking, meaningfulness and dialogue by forming their own groups to share and study the kinds of job crafting that work for them in their circumstances.

Conclusions

Positive psychology studies the well-being and the well-becoming (Murphey, 2016) of people to find strategies, beliefs and activities that might help others increase and spread positive psychodynamics. In this chapter we presented the positive perspectives of language teachers who often work beyond their job descriptions in ways that bring them meaningfulness. We assume they also have had bad days, like most of us, and may have at times likely lost their sense of calling and struggled to regain it. We teachers are all on dynamic trajectories of job crafting and learning and may at times be lost with seemingly little or no meaning. Thus, having a calling does not mean we are not challenged and do not face adversity, and not having a calling does not mean that we are without purpose, but from job crafting we can create resilience, hope and optimism. So we muster our strength to weather hard times, knowing deep inside there will be better days ahead, and continue to seek to fill our work and lives with meaningfulness.

Acknowledgements

Our appreciation goes to the teachers who inspired us by sharing their stories and comments for this research, and to the editors who helped us craft this chapter. We also extend gratitude to Tetsuya Fukada for technical support in gathering the data and looping it back to the teachers.

References

Albuquerque, I., de Lima, M.P., Matos, M. and Figueiredo, C. (2014) Work matters: Work personal projects and the idiosyncratic linkages between traits, eudaimonic and hedonic well-being. *Social Indicators Research* 115, 885–906.

Arnold, J. and Murphey, T. (2013) *Meaningful Action: Earl Stevick's Influence on Language Learning and Teaching.* Cambridge: Cambridge University Press.

Berg, J.M., Wrzesniewski, A. and Dutton, J.E. (2010) Perceiving and responding to challenges in job crafting at different ranks: When proactivity requires adaptivity. *Journal of Organizational Behavior* 31, 158–186.

Chan, D.W. (2009) Orientations to happiness and subjective well being among Chinese prospective and in service teachers in Hong Kong. *Educational Psychology* 29 (2), 139–151.

Chan, D.W. (2013) Subjective well-being of Hong Kong Chinese teachers: The contribution of gratitude, forgiveness, and the orientations to happiness. *Teaching and Teacher Education* 32, 22–30.

Compton, W.C. and Hoffman, E. (2015) *Positive Psychology: The Science of Happiness and Flourishing* (2nd edn). Belmont, CA: Wadsworth.

Dweck, C.S. (2006) *Mindset: The New Psychology of Success.* New York: Ballantine.

Falout, J. (2010) Strategies for teacher motivation. *Language Teacher* 34 (6), 27–32.

Falout, J. (2013) Forming pathways of belonging: Social inclusion for teachers abroad. In S.A. Houghton and D.J. Rivers (eds) *Native-speakerism in Japan: Intergroup Dynamics in Foreign Language Education* (pp. 105–115). Bristol: Multilingual Matters.

Falout, J., Murphey, T. and Stillwell, C. (2012) Avoiding burnout by lighting fires: Three contexts of change. In C. Coombe, L. England and J. Schmidt (eds) *Reigniting, Retooling, and Retiring in English Language Teaching* (pp. 9–22). Ann Arbor, MI: University of Michigan Press.

Fredrickson, B.L. (2009) *Positivity: Top-Notch Research Reveals the Upward Spiral that Will Change Your Life.* New York: Three Rivers Press.

Leana, C., Appelbaum, E. and Shevchuk, I. (2009) Work process and quality of care in early childhood education: The role of job crafting. *Academy of Management Review* 52 (6), 1169–1192.

Lopez, S.J., Pedrotti, J.T. and Snyder, C.R. (2015) *Positive Psychology: The Scientific and Practical Explorations of Human Strengths* (3rd edn). Thousand Oaks, CA: Sage.

Murphey, T. (2016) Teaching to learn and well-become: Many mini-renaissances. In P.D. MacIntyre, T. Gregersen and S. Mercer (eds) *Positive Psychology in SLA* (pp. 324–343). Bristol: Multilingual Matters.

Murphey, T. and Falout, J. (2010) Critical participatory looping: Dialogic member checking with whole classes. *TESOL Quarterly* 44 (4), 811–821.

Oxford, O. (2016) Toward a psychology of well-being for language learners: The 'EMPATHICS' vision. In P.D. MacIntyre, T. Gregersen and S. Mercer (eds) *Positive Psychology in SLA* (pp. 10–87). Bristol: Multilingual Matters.

Seligman, M.E.P. (2011) *Flourish: A New Understanding of Happiness and Well-being – and How to Achieve Them.* London: Nicholas Brealey.

Steger, M.F. and Dik, B.J. (2009) If one is looking for meaning in life, does it help to find meaning in work? *Applied Psychology: Health and Well-Being* 1 (3) 303–320.

Stevick, E.W. (1980) *Teaching Languages: A Way and Ways.* Rowley, MA: Newbury House.

Wellman, N. and Spreitzer, G. (2010) Crafting scholarly life: Strategies for creating meaning in academic careers. *Journal of Organizational Behavior* 32, 927–931.

Werbińska, D. (2016) Language-teacher professional identity: Focus on *discontinuities* from the perspective of teacher affiliation, attachment and autonomy. In C. Gkonou, D. Tatzl and S. Mercer (eds) *New Directions in Language Learning Psychology* (pp. 135–157). Cham: Springer.

Wrzesniewski, A. (2016) How to build a better job. A. Wrzesniewski interviewed by S. Vedantam. *Hidden Brain: Conversation about Life's Unseen Patterns.* Podcast, 29 March 2016. See http://www.npr.org/2016/03/28/471859161/how-to-build-a-better-job (accessed August 2016).

Wrzesniewski, A. and Dutton, J.E. (2001) Crafting a job: Revisioning employees as active crafters of their work. *Academy of Management Review* 26 (2), 179–201.

Wrzesniewski, A., McCauley, C. and Rozin, P. (1997) Jobs, careers, and callings: People's relations to their work. *Journal of Research in Personality* 31, 21–33.

14 Teachstrong: The Power of Teacher Resilience for Second Language Practitioners

Phil Hiver

In this century of transnational mobility, growing multilingualism and cross-cultural interactions, language teaching remains a crucial profession. The majority of instructed language learning worldwide occurs in increasingly diverse classroom settings, characterised by complex and challenging conditions. Languages are often compulsory subjects taught in large, mixed-ability groups. However, the climate in many institutions is one of increasingly stringent accountability measures and unpredictable reform mandates, accompanied by a lack of support and teacher autonomy; these can undermine teachers' professional self-worth and psychological well-being. These structural conditions of the language teaching profession may prevent teachers from developing feelings of effectiveness and building confidence and self-reliance. Enter *teacher resilience*: the positive capacity of teachers to maintain effective functioning in their practice despite threatening circumstances and to develop increased productivity through consistent achievement in the classroom (Day *et al.*, 2007; Gu & Day, 2013). The aim of this chapter is to explore the applicability of this commonplace personal strength in the work and lives of second and foreign language (L2) practitioners. The first part of the chapter will provide an in-depth, conceptual overview of the construct. Then I will examine its utility for the language teaching profession, with particular implications for L2 pedagogy. Finally, I propose an agenda for research specific to the field of applied linguistics that endeavours to accommodate the dynamic, multifaceted and relational nature of teacher resilience.

A Little Bit of Background

The beginnings of resilience research can be traced back to developmental psychologists in the 1970s and 1980s studying the origins of mental illness and behavioural problems (e.g. Garmezy *et al.*, 1984; Rutter *et al.*, 1976; Werner, 1982). These researchers were surprised to find that many children and adolescents who appeared to be at severe risk for psychopathology due to genetic or experiential hazards were in fact developing well. Studies of youngsters raised in extreme poverty, foster homes and other institutional settings and children of criminal or abusive parents grown to adulthood consistently showed that, even in the face of extreme deprivation or threats to their development, these children possessed protective factors that provided a form of invulnerability (Werner, 1993). This resilience was defined by Ann Masten, one of the influential originators of the construct, as the capacity to recover from experiences of psychological adversity and to function effectively and grow adaptively while navigating these traumatic circumstances (Masten, 2001).

Conceptualising Resilience

The very first operational definitions interpreted resilience as a latent intrapersonal quality (e.g. Masten *et al.*, 1990). From this perspective, resilience is a trait-like resource that exists within an individual and functions to protect that individual from adversity. A related conceptualisation, an outcome-oriented approach, regards resilience as a behavioural outcome, distinct from lay definitions of invulnerability. Resilient individuals, in this sense, are individuals who, when encountering a demonstrable risk or threat, effectively adapt or achieve a positive outcome through it (Hu *et al.*, 2015). This view of resilience signifies the achievement of positive adaptation or adjustment which defies expectations in the face of significant adversity (Wilkes, 2002). Two complementary aspects of this early definition are *sustainability* – i.e. the capacity for individuals to maintain a positive outcome despite the occurrence of traumatic experiences, and *recovery* – i.e. the ability of individuals to bounce back from these challenges (Zautra *et al.*, 2008). The agenda of the first two decades of resilience research was to systematically uncover the characteristics which foster resilience by differentiating individuals who thrive in the face of substantial risk and adversity from those who succumb to destructive forces (Richardson, 2002). These factors concern: (a) attributes of the resilient individuals themselves; (b) aspects of their relationships with significant others; and (c) characteristics of their wider social-cultural environments (see, for example, Wu *et al.*, 2013).

The second wave of resilience research (i.e. since 2000) saw researchers begin to view resilience in terms of a dynamic developmental process involving the interaction of psychological and social factors in a given environment that enable individuals to successfully resolve or adapt to risks and threats (Chiccetti, 2010). Researchers recognised that identifying the factors which help individuals turn adversity into advantage – as in the earliest studies – was crucial, but also that approaching resilience as an underlying protective process would allow them to investigate exactly how and why resilient individuals achieve this outcome of effective functioning despite traumatic events (Ungar, 2012). The consensus in most current theorising is that the development of this self-righting and steeling capacity is the result of fundamental systems for human development and adaptation operating normally, and that it can be found in every human to varying degrees at various times in one's lifespan (Reich *et al.*, 2010). This perspective is more inclusive as it proposes multiple pathways to resilience, and sees the individual as an active participant in this developmental process in context and across time, with prior experiences and interactions shaping the organisation of this protective functioning (Bonanno, 2004). Clear implications for prevention and intervention emerged from this developmental perspective. Through this focus on the mechanisms underlying resilient functioning, researchers began to study how to engineer the conditions for resilience to develop, for instance, by increasing the relative balance of protective factors over risk factors (Luthar *et al.*, 2000).

Another prominent issue to come out of this expanding research agenda concerns the surprisingly widespread occurrence of resilience (Murray & Zautra, 2012). The design of initial studies on the development of resilience was only sensitive to the most extreme forms of the context, and as such implied that successful adaptation in the face of debilitating circumstances was an extraordinary capacity, which was not questioned until more recently (Masten, 2001). Masten (2009) has termed this 'ordinary magic', to emphasise that resilience is a naturally occurring phenomenon which arises from the interaction of the adaptive systems that foster and protect human development and psychological recovery. Lately, some scholars have highlighted the need to refine previous conceptualisations of resilience (Rutter, 2006; Windle, 2011). One reason for this is the recognition that positive adaptation may not occur across all spheres of life, and thus the dynamics of resilience across varied domains need to be probed more fully. Another reason relates to the nature of risk and the extent of adversity: resilience has typically been associated with acute and chronic adversities, but may apply equally well to individuals who are faced with more routine hassles, setbacks, challenges and pressures that are part of the ordinary course of life – what some have called an 'everyday life' approach to resilience (Ong *et al.*, 2009).

While there is no shortage in psychology of models and theories related to constructive explanatory styles and mindsets, positive emotionality, beliefs about self and personhood, and faith, hopes and goals for the future (for one review, see Seligman *et al.*, 2005), resilience provides what is perhaps the most comprehensive picture of the relational processes and emergent qualities that enable an individual to adapt effectively and function positively despite challenging circumstances (Lipsitt & Demick, 2012). Resilience research has become multidisciplinary and is moving rapidly into fields across all the social and human sciences; there is also growing evidence for the importance of building resilience in educational settings (Martin, 2013). The potential impact of resilience on health, well-being and quality of life has received increasing interest from those involved with policy and practice over the last decade, and this has brought insights and agendas from this positively oriented psychology literature to educational research. I will now turn to focusing on the growing body of research that examines the phenomenon of resilience in connection to teachers and the work of teaching (e.g. Day & Gu, 2014).

Situating Teacher Resilience

Teacher resilience is most meaningful if it is located within the discourse of the 21st century educational environments that provide context. With regard to education policy more broadly, the emphasis on standards, outcomes and teacher accountability has intensified in many educational settings, as the progress and achievement of students faces greater scrutiny than ever (Darling-Hammond & Lieberman, 2012). Socially and culturally in many countries, the makeup of the local communities which schools serve has become more diversified, pushing schools and teachers to manage a broader role in supporting their community (Wentzel & Ramani, 2016). The field-specific concerns and contributions of the language teacher have also begun to receive increasing attention from applied linguists considering particular political, societal and cultural challenges and questions of the 21st century, such as policies of language ideology and power, growing linguistic commodification and social marginalisation, and the rising norm of multilingualism and transnational mobility (Crookes, 2013; Hall, 2016). In their proposed reconceptualisation of the language teacher's roles for the 21st century, Kubanyiova and Crookes (2016) argue that language teachers' stance towards their own roles, the pedagogical choices made regarding instructional practices and the language practices promoted institutionally and beyond (e.g. use of language assessment as a policy tool) suggest critical value-oriented, moral and ethical dimensions of language teaching – and indeed of language teacher education.

In the context of these increased challenges and pressurised conditions in contemporary teaching settings, a fairly in-depth understanding of the reasons for teacher burnout and attrition exists in mainstream teacher research (see, for example, Borman & Dowling, 2008) that has only begun to be explored with language teachers (Hiver, 2016a; Swanson, 2012). Research into teacher resilience is part of the shift towards models of success and perseverance that promote retention and teacher effectiveness; it is concerned with how teachers manage and sustain their motivation and commitment, recover in the face of adversity, and develop increased self-efficacy through consistent achievement in the classroom (Hong, 2012).

Teacher resilience has been defined as a teacher using all the resources available to maintain personal well-being alongside professional productivity in the face of adversity and detrimental conditions, what Gu and Day (2013: 26) have termed 'the capacity to maintain equilibrium and a sense of commitment, agency and moral purpose in the everyday worlds in which teachers teach'. However, this concept has experienced limited cross-over to the applied linguistics literature or to language teacher research. Indeed, adopting a psychological perspective of *what* language teachers do, *why* they do what they do, and *how* they adapt and develop is still relatively new for the domain of applied linguistics concerned with the knowledge base of language teachers and the purposes and practices of language teacher education and professional development (cf. Burns *et al.*, 2015). Mercer *et al.* (2016) have proposed that 'in respect to psychology in language learning specifically, (...) teachers have been somewhat neglected' (Mercer *et al.*, 2016: 213–214), but that this lack of attention may be wrong in light of the central role language teachers play in the dynamics of the classroom ecology and in learners' engagement within that instructional setting.

Relationships, clearly, are at the centre of teachers' work (Day & Gu, 2010), and teachers' professional worlds are organised around critical role relationships – teachers with learners, and teachers with other colleagues or superiors in the workplace; this is equally the case in the language teaching profession (Benesch, 2012). Teacher resilience, perhaps more so than resilience for other professionals, must be viewed as relational, developmental and dynamic rather than an innate individual trait (Luthar, 2006). This is echoed in the work of Noddings (2012) and Zembylas (2014) who propose that, fundamentally, teaching should be seen as the creation of caring connections and encounters between individuals. In language teaching, the fact that these relationships cannot be taken for granted but must be cultivated as a matter of effort acknowledges the role of individual agency in language teachers' work to reach and engage their students regardless of the challenges this might bring them (Feryok, 2012). Teacher resilience, then, is constructed as a dynamic process within a given context. It encompasses the teachers' sense of purpose, entails meaningful action and participation, and is shaped in the interaction of personal and social dimensions.

Lessons from Teacher Resilience Research

There are extensive programmes of research on teacher resilience in Australia (e.g. Johnson *et al.*, 2014; Le Cornu, 2013) and the UK (e.g. Day & Gu, 2014; Day *et al.*, 2007), with equally important – although less prominent – work also being done across North America (e.g. Castro *et al.*, 2010), Africa (e.g. Ebersöhn, 2014) and Asia (e.g. Gu & Li, 2013). The current educational climate of many of these contexts places teacher quality at the forefront of educational reforms and initiatives to boost student outcomes and ongoing professional learning. Because of this, the picture emerging from these studies of thousands of teachers at various career phases is that a form of psychological invulnerability may be a key factor in teachers' instructional effectiveness, their capacity to adapt and survive, and their long-term commitment to the profession (Gibbs & Miller, 2014). While there is very little existing research on language teacher resilience, these characteristics parallel recent research on the complex, emergent and contextually mediated role of language teacher motivation (Hiver, 2015; Kubanyiova, 2012), language teacher agency (Feryok, 2012), language teacher identity (Johnson & Golombek, 2011; Kanno & Stuart, 2011) and language teacher cognition (Burns *et al.*, 2015; Kubanyiova & Feryok, 2015) in the work and lives of language teachers. This suggests that evaluating and integrating established insights from teacher resilience into the growing body of language teacher research would be relatively straightforward.

As it is multidimensional and socially constructed in nature, teacher resilience should not be seen as an idealised state – it is developed and sustained by drawing on multiple capacities (Gu & Day, 2007). The socio-emotional resources resilient teachers draw on are perhaps the most note-worthy part of existing research. Resilient teachers approach their practice with higher self-efficacy and draw more on active coping strategies. They possess the meta-cognition and self-regulation skills needed to be autono-mous, exhibit greater altruism and sense of purpose in life, and have posi-tive self-perceptions and a generally optimistic disposition. At the collegial level of their work, they build positive relationships with competent and nurturing colleagues and superiors, seek out friends and partners who are supportive, and use the support and attachment of social networks in their professional lives. A variety of personal and social or professional factors can enhance or inhibit the extent to which teachers acquire these resilient qualities (Mansfield *et al.*, 2016), and as teacher resilience manifests itself in response to situational demands it can develop and change continu-ously with emerging conditions or contexts (Gu, 2014). Thus, rather than an essentialised view of teacher resilience as innate, it should be seen instead as a dynamic, relational and developmental quality; I provide fur-ther examples of this immediately below.

Several researchers have focused specifically on the potential for resil-ience in pre-service or novice teachers (e.g. Howard & Johnson, 2004). For instance, Tait's (2008) analysis of the teacher recruiting, training and induction process in Canada indicated that resilient teachers developed characteristics, such as mirroring more highly efficacious and emotionally intelligent teachers, which appeared to provide the foundation for success and long-term commitment to the profession. Johnson *et al.* (2014) identi-fied similar components of teacher resilience in teachers-in-training, citing productive relationships, career competence and skills, personal ownership and a sense of accomplishment as the necessary resources for teachers to develop resilience early on in their careers. Given the varying levels of preparation and competence of beginning teachers, these studies all argue that resilience is a crucial contributor to career preparation, teaching effectiveness and persistence in the profession past the first year or two (Gibbs & Miller, 2014). There are parallels here with the small body of work on novice language teachers (see, for example, Farrell, 2008, 2012, 2016). Although this scholarship has not been framed from a resilience perspective, the psychological resources available to novice language teachers in their early years have been recognised as influential for how successfully these practitioners navigate their first years in the classroom (Freeman & Johnson, 1998) and develop over their careers (Tarone & Allwright, 2005). Developing a strong sense of agency and self-efficacy gives beginning language teachers the ability to remain in control of events occurring to them and around them, strong professional networks contribute a culture of collaboration and support, and gaining a sense of purpose and competence provides the necessary stimulus for identity growth – all of which contribute to their survival (Farrell, 2008, 2012, 2016).

The agenda of other recent research has been to investigate whether teachers can practise resilience and thus develop it through intervention (Beltman *et al.*, 2016; Mansfield *et al.*, 2016). The research to date provides evidence not only that teacher resilience can be built, but also that developing it is necessary to sustain teachers' commitment to the profession and help them achieve optimal teaching effectiveness. For instance, teachers employing specific resilience strategies when experiencing anxiety provoking or disruptive encounters at school are able to overcome the pressures and adversity inherent in these situations (Castro *et al.*, 2010). Le Cornu's (2009, 2013) studies have examined the potential role of learning communities in fostering and building resilience during the professional experiences of teachers. She reported that providing opportunities for peer support, explicitly teaching protective skills or attitudes, and adopting clear supportive roles in the workplace contributed to mutual empowerment and resilience building in teachers who previously did not exhibit this capacity. Collecting data from teachers working in inner city high schools in California, Brunetti (2006) also reported that in spite of the challenges these teachers faced, they were able to sustain their resilience while under fire, persist in the profession and even achieve a measure of success with their students. These findings suggest that resilience can be enhanced, strengthened or honed if the conditions and support that teachers need to perform at their best are available.

Resilience research offers a way to investigate the attitudes and behaviours of teachers within the context of their work and professional lives, and sheds light on how these individuals maintain their commitment, motivation and engagement (Mansfield *et al.*, 2012). However, the broader implication from this research is that teacher resilience plays an additional role: that of maximising students' well-being, progress and achievement. Research into academic resilience has shown that the capacity for resilience in students is linked to prosocial behaviour and peer acceptance, school attendance, class participation and perseverance, self-efficacy, motivation and aspirations and, ultimately, long-term academic success (Martin & Marsh, 2006, 2008). Some have stated explicitly that students cannot be expected to develop resilience if their teachers do not exhibit this ability themselves, and that educators who want their students to develop the capacity to successfully adjust to challenging circumstances and overcome setbacks and failures must first develop resilience themselves (Day, 2004; Parker & Martin, 2009). This is echoed in recent scholarship on the impact of language teachers' vision on students' learning and processes of sense-making (Dörnyei & Kubanyiova, 2014). Learner vision cannot flourish without teacher vision, but if the teacher is disengaged and lacks vision, this is just as readily transmitted to students through the socially mediated encounters of the language classroom (Dörnyei & Ryan, 2015). For this reason, teachers who hope to foster positive capacities in their learners must first develop those capacities, and the picture emerging from the above review is that teachers can intentionally cultivate these character strengths in their own practice.

Beyond Resilience to Immunity

When conceptualised as dynamic, relational and contextual, resilience is both immediately relevant and valuable to understanding language teaching. In addition, building from the literature examining the psychological aspects of teaching and ways to maximise teacher psychological well-being, a very recent line of research with L2 teachers has extended this by integrating notions of professional identity and teacher cognition and exploring how these might interface with the contextual realities that influence classroom practice. This work has identified a novel construct – language teacher immunity (e.g. Hiver, 2015, 2016b; Hiver & Dörnyei, 2017). In this section I briefly introduce this construct which grew out of the application of resilience for L2 teaching and learning, as it remains one of the few applications of the core invulnerability metaphor from resilience in the L2 teaching and learning field. Language teacher immunity has been conceptualised (see, for example, Hiver & Dörnyei, 2017) in close parallel to the biological definition of acquired (also known as *adaptive*) immunity, and it describes a robust armouring system that emerges in response to high-intensity threats and which allows teachers to maintain professional equilibrium and instructional effectiveness. Existing evidence suggests that L2 teachers who are emotionally well-adjusted, open to change and resilient to burnout, and motivated and productive in their practice possess this superordinate psychological quality which other teachers have not developed.

When contrasted with resilience, the uniqueness of the metaphor of teacher immunity revolves around three aspects (Hiver & Dörnyei, 2017). First, like an acquired immune response to viral pathogens, language teacher immunity emerges only through a self-organised (i.e. spontaneously coordinated) adaptive reaction to repeated instances of domain-specific crisis. Thus, rather than an innate, trait-like disposition, teacher immunity is a situated and teaching-specific construct which emerges in relation to conflicts that are particular to classroom practice. Given its primary function of ensuring the system's survival, developing a robust teacher immunity appears to be indispensable to surviving in the profession (see also Day & Gu, 2014). However, unlike teacher resilience, this outcome is not the commonplace result of ordinary systems for development and adaptation. Secondly, language teacher immunity develops a protective configuration that is dual natured – at times serving a necessary safeguarding purpose, but at other times threatening the individual's functioning and becoming a professional liability by mounting resistance to change. Resilience, by definition, cannot promote either resistance to change or maladaptive functioning because it has only positive valence (Richardson, 2002; Wilkes, 2002). Language teacher immunity, however, similarly to its biological parallel, may develop into a counterproductive form that unexpectedly threatens the survival of the individual through cynicism, apathy or fossilisation. Finally, language teacher immunity is integrated into the fabric of teachers' professional identity through the formation of analytical narratives that consciously legitimise classroom experiences (e.g. Johnson & Golombek, 2011; McAdams & McLean, 2013). Resilience, on the other hand, has not been implicated explicitly in the more global scheme of professional identity formation or as part of the self-concept. Thus, the metaphor of language teacher immunity provides a more nuanced and balanced appraisal which sheds light not only on practitioners' psychological well-being, but also on issues such as teachers' adaptivity and openness to change, their commitment to the profession and investment in the quality of students' learning.

Work framed from a complexity theory perspective, in which teacher immunity is seen as an emergent outcome, has suggested that teacher immunity manifests itself in four global categories within which precise archetypes develop: L2 teachers may be (a) productively immunised (i.e. possessing a robust, beneficial form of teacher immunity); (b) maladaptively immunised (i.e. possessing a rigid, counterproductive form of teacher immunity); (c) immunocompromised (i.e. having not developed any coherent form of teacher immunity); or (d) partially immunised (i.e. having developed half-way features of teacher immunity). Additionally, the developmental process has been shown to follow a self-organised sequence of four stages – triggering, linking, realignment and stabilisation – with unique signature trajectories or pathways of development for particular outcomes. In each case, the teacher immunity outcomes are assembled into teachers' professional identity through analytical narratives designed to make sense of the events that are part of their experience and help them gain resolution and purpose from this adversity (Johnson & Golombek, 2011). These outcomes are ultimately displayed in language teachers' emotions and beliefs, instructional practice, and commitment and persistence within challenging instructional settings. Thus, this multifaceted and dynamic construct provides a potential tool for integrating teacher resilience into larger questions surrounding the profession and revolutionising the way in-service teachers are mentored and new language teachers are prepared.

Researching Language Teacher Resilience

This section provides a brief look at several existing traditions of resilience research, both in developmental and educational psychology, in order to propose a principled agenda for resilience research that connects to the life, work and experience of language teachers. These approaches can be exploited to explore the field-specific contribution of teacher resilience beyond established constructs and existing frameworks, and to make explicit links to the work of language teachers – i.e. creating rich, meaningful L2 learning environments for their learners – and the accompanying objectives and outcomes of their classroom practice.

First and foremost, research will need to establish the relevance of teacher resilience to our field empirically and conceptually – its applicability cannot be assumed a priori. Resilience research emerged from phenomenological studies looking for explanatory clues in the characteristics of survivors living in high-risk situations, rather than from theoretically grounded models (Richardson, 2002). The typical design of these person-based studies of teacher resilience identified educators with a resilient profile, often comparing these with individuals from the same high-risk context who had a maladaptive functioning in order to determine what attributes accounted for the differences in outcome (Day & Hong, 2016). While a range of protective factors has been identified consistently in the teacher resilience literature, there are notable instances where protective factors were shown to be in operation and yet resilient outcomes did not result. This issue reflects the complexity of resilience formation; implicit in this approach to resilience research is the fact that personal and contextual factors may exert an influence on each other at different levels and thus impact important outcomes (Gu, 2014).

With regard to determining precisely what relevance teacher resilience has to our field, this attention to situational and within-individual factors lends itself well to investigating whether language teachers routinely encounter the type of significant challenges and adversity necessary for resilience to blossom – and, if this initial criterion can be established, to explore what sets apart language teachers who achieve positive adaptation and adjustment despite these high-risk environments. While language teacher resilience research designed in this way is likely to be exploratory and build incremental insights, it does not follow that a person-focused programme of language teacher resilience research must result in disconnected idiographic findings unique to certain individuals and settings. Because it can pay close attention to commonalities and still remain sensitive to variations in time and context, this approach is well-suited to searching for patterns and characteristic differences among the qualities, components and subtle influences that make some teachers more resilient and others less so (Beltman *et al.*, 2016).

As the early resilience research gradually became more applied, variable-focused approaches began to identify links between the degree of adversity, outcome and individual or contextual qualities that exert a protective function from the consequences of the adversity, usually relying on multivariate statistical procedures to do so (Masten, 2001). In contrast to the sense of the whole in many person-based studies, this variable-focused design is better suited to searching for links between individual predictors, such as risks and assets, and resilience outcomes across larger samples of teachers (see, for example, Rutter, 2012). One objective of researching these main effects is to offer models of intervention that might offset the risks by counterbalancing or mediating them with positive assets (Mansfield *et al.*, 2016). This type of teacher resilience research often measures the independent contribution that a combination of risks or assets makes to the outcome of resilience and the implications this has for the roles and practices teachers adopt professionally.

The strength of this tradition of teacher resilience research is that it encourages explicit links to be made with constructs already established within research specific to the field of language teachers – such as their agency, beliefs and emotions – in order to investigate areas of convergence as well as the unique insights that language teacher resilience might bring to applied research in the sense of its contribution to reflective and innovative L2 classroom practice. This programme of language teacher resilience research is likely to take a more integrated and transactional view of all the individual and contextual variables that contribute to the development of this outcome, as doing so would enable researchers to incorporate these findings within contemporary frameworks for the study of the work and life of language teachers, such as language teacher cognition, language teacher identity and language teacher development (Mercer *et al.*, 2016).

Finally, while research from both of the above approaches has argued for the multidimensional situated nature of teacher resilience, very few designs are concerned with its dynamic, adaptive nature, nor have they fully addressed the question of how teacher resilience is developed. Teacher resilience is not absolute, and even resilient individuals show considerable fluctuation over time. However, little attention has been paid to fluctuations and adjustments of teacher resilience *in situ* (Robertson *et al.*,

2015). This issue is perhaps not surprising given that few teacher resilience studies are designed to collect longitudinal data or record the fluctuations of adaptation that some suggest is the norm in most resilient individuals. Thus, an agenda for language teacher resilience should be to investigate the dynamic interaction between the various people, practices and policies at play in the social ecology of the language classroom (cf. Mercer, 2016) and how these may lead to productive or maladaptive developmental pathways and outcomes over the course of teachers' professional lives – as in the strand of work on language teacher immunity.

Conclusion

This chapter has explored how the capacity of resilience might advance the field's understanding of L2 practitioners' psychological well-being, and their commitment and effectiveness in the increasingly complex, challenging L2 classroom settings worldwide. It is apparent from this overview that, rather than a fixed, latent capacity, teacher resilience should be seen as dynamically shaped by the social and professional contexts in which ordinary teachers work and live. My position throughout has been that, because teacher resilience provides unique explanatory power for practitioners' psychological, emotional, behavioural and even cognitive functioning in professional settings, it may be an indispensable quality for understanding how language teachers manage and sustain their passion, enthusiasm and commitment to making a difference in the L2 classroom. Situating the study of language teachers in the larger discourse of educators more broadly will allow a more robust psychological perspective of *what* language teachers do, *why* they do what they do and *how* they adapt and develop. However, while there is particular promise for future research avenues specific to language teachers, this programme of research must establish the precise contribution of teacher resilience to L2 teachers and teaching and embed this research within existing frameworks for studying the work and life of language practitioners.

References

Beltman, S., Mansfield, C. and Harris, A. (2016) Quietly sharing the load? The role of school psychologists in enabling teacher resilience. *School Psychology International* 37 (2), 172–188.

Benesch, S. (2012) *Considering Emotions in Critical English Language Teaching: Theories and Praxis.* New York: Routledge.

Bonanno, G. (2004) Loss, trauma, and human resilience: Have we underestimated the human capacity to thrive after extremely averse events? *American Psychologist* 59 (1), 20–28.

Borman, G. and Dowling, N. (2008) Teacher attrition and retention: A meta-analytic and narrative review of the research. *Review of Educational Research* 78 (3), 367–409.

Brunetti, G. (2006) Resilience under fire: Perspectives on the work of experienced, inner city high school teachers in the United States. *Teaching and Teacher Education* 22 (7), 812–825.

Burns, A., Freeman, D. and Edwards, E. (2015) Theorizing and studying the language-teaching mind: Mapping research on language teacher cognition. *The Modern Language Journal* 99 (3), 585–601.

Castro, A., Kelly, J. and Shih, M. (2010) Resilience strategies for new teachers in high-needs areas. *Teaching and Teacher Education* 26 (3), 622–629.

Chiccetti, D. (2010) Resilience under conditions of extreme stress: A multilevel perspective. *World Psychiatry* 9 (3), 145–154.

Crookes, G. (2013) *Critical ELT in Action: Foundations, Promises, Praxis.* New York: Routledge.

Darling-Hammond, L. and Leiberman, A. (eds) (2012) *Teacher Education around the World: Changing Policies and Practices.* New York: Routledge.

Day, C. (2004) *A Passion for Teaching.* New York: Routledge.

Day, C. and Gu, Q. (2010) *The New Lives of Teachers.* New York: Routledge.

Day, C. and Gu, Q. (2014) *Resilient Teachers, Resilient Schools: Building and Sustaining Quality in Testing Times.* New York: Routledge.

Day, C. and Hong, J. (2016) Influences on the capacities for emotional resilience of teachers in schools serving disadvantaged urban communities: Challenges of living on the edge. *Teaching and Teacher Education* 59, 115–125.

Day, C., Sammons, P., Stobart, G., Kington, A. and Gu, Q. (2007) *Teachers Matter: Connecting Lives, Work and Effectiveness.* New York: McGraw-Hill.

Dörnyei, Z. and Kubanyiova, M. (2014) *Motivating Learners, Motivating Teachers: Building Vision in the Language Classroom.* Cambridge: Cambridge University Press.

Dörnyei, Z. and Ryan, S. (2015) *The Psychology of the Language Learner Revisited.* New York: Routledge.

Ebersöhn, L. (2014) Teacher resilience: Theorizing resilience and poverty. *Teachers and Teaching: Theory and Practice* 20 (5), 568–594.

Farrell, T.S.C. (ed.) (2008) *Novice Language Teachers: Insights and Perspectives for the First Year.* London: Continuum.

Farrell, T.S.C. (2012) Novice-service language teacher development: Bridging the gap between pre-service and in-service education and development. *TESOL Quarterly* 46, 435–449.

Farrell, T.S.C. (2016) Surviving the transition shock in the first year of teaching through reflective practice. *System* 61, 12–19.

Feryok, A. (2012) Activity theory and language teacher agency. *The Modern Language Journal* 96 (1), 95–107.

Freeman, D. and Johnson, K. (1998) Reconceptualizing the knowledge-base of language teacher education. *TESOL Quarterly* 32, 397–417.

Garmezy, N., Masten, A. and Tellegen, A. (1984) The study of stress and competence in children: A building block for developmental psychopathology. *Child Development* 55, 97–111.

Gibbs, S. and Miller, A. (2014) Teachers' resilience and well-being: A role for educational psychology. *Teachers and Teaching: Theory and Practice* 20 (5), 609–621,

Gu, Q. (2014) The role of relational resilience in teachers' career-long commitment and effectiveness. *Teachers and Teaching: Theory and Practice* 20 (5), 502–529.

Gu, Q. and Day, C. (2007) Teachers resilience: A necessary condition for effectiveness. *Teaching and Teacher Education* 23 (8), 1302–1316.

Gu, Q. and Day, C. (2013) Challenges to teacher resilience: Conditions count. *British Educational Research Journal* 39 (1), 22–44.

Gu, Q. and Li, Q. (2013) Sustaining resilience in times of change: Stories from Chinese teachers. *Asia-Pacific Journal of Teacher Education* 41 (3), 288–303.

Hall, G. (ed.) (2016) *The Routledge Handbook of English Language Teaching.* New York: Routledge.

Hiver, P. (2015) Once burned, twice shy: The dynamic development of system immunity in language teachers. In Z. Dörnyei, P.D. MacIntyre and A. Henry (eds) *Motivational Dynamics in Language Learning* (pp. 214–237). Bristol: Multilingual Matters.

Hiver, P. (2016a) The triumph over experience: Hope and hardiness in novice L2 teachers. In P.D. MacIntyre, T. Gregersen and S. Mercer (eds) *Positive Psychology in SLA* (pp. 168–192). Bristol: Multilingual Matters.

Hiver, P. (2016b) Tracing the signature dynamics of language teacher immunity. Unpublished PhD thesis, University of Nottingham.

Hiver, P. and Dörnyei, Z. (2017) Language teacher immunity: A double-edged sword. *Applied Linguistics* 38 (3), 405–423.

Hong, J. (2012) Why do some beginning teachers leave the school, and others stay? Understanding teacher resilience through psychological lenses. *Teachers and Teaching: Theory and Practice* 18 (4), 417–440.

Howard, S. and Johnson, B. (2004) Resilient teachers: Resisting stress and burnout. *Social Psychology of Education* 7 (4), 399–420.

Hu, T., Zhang, D. and Wang, J. (2015) A meta-analysis of the trait resilience and mental health. *Personality and Individual Differences* 76, 18–27.

Johnson, B., Down, B., Le Cornu, R., Peters, J., Sullivan, A., Pearce, J. and Hunter, J. (2014) Promoting early career teacher resilience: a framework for understanding and acting. *Teachers and Teaching* 20 (5), 530–546.

Johnson, K. and Golombek, P. (2011) The transformative power of narrative in second language teacher education. *TESOL Quarterly* 45, 486–509.

Kanno, Y. and Stuart, C. (2011) Learning to become a second language teacher: Identities-in-practice. *The Modern Language Journal* 95 (2), 236–252.

Kubanyiova, M. (2012) *Teacher Development in Action: Understanding Language Teachers' Conceptual Change*. Basingstoke: Palgrave Macmillan.

Kubanyiova, M. and Crookes, G. (2016) Re-envisioning the roles, tasks, and contributions of language teachers in the multilingual era of language education research and practice. *The Modern Language Journal* 100 (S1), 117–132.

Kubanyiova, M. and Feryok, A. (2015) Language teacher cognition in applied linguistics research: Revisiting the territory, redrawing the boundaries, reclaiming the relevance. *The Modern Language Journal* 99 (3), 435–449.

Le Cornu, R. (2009) Building resilience in pre-service teachers. *Teaching and Teacher Education* 25 (5), 717–723.

Le Cornu, R. (2013) Building early career teacher resilience: The role of relationships. *Australian Journal of Teacher Education* 38 (4), 1–16.

Lipsitt, L. and Demick, J. (2012) Theory and measurement of resilience: Views from development. In M. Ungar (ed.) *The Social Ecology of Resilience: A Handbook of Theory and Practice* (pp. 43–52). New York: Springer.

Luthar, S. (2006) Resilience in development: A synthesis of research across five decades. In D. Chiccetti and D. Cohen (eds) *Developmental Psychopathology, Vol. 3* (2nd edn) (pp. 739–795). Hoboken, NJ: John Wiley.

Luthar, S., Chiccetti, D. and Becker, B. (2000) The construct of resilience: A critical evaluation and guidelines for future work. *Child Development* 71 (3), 543–562.

Mansfield, C., Beltman, S., Price, A. and McConney, A. (2012) 'Don't sweat the small stuff': Understanding teacher resilience at the chalkface. *Teaching and Teacher Education* 28 (3), 357–367.

Mansfield, C., Beltman, S., Broadley, T. and Wetherby-Fell, N. (2016) Building resilience in teacher education: An evidenced informed framework. *Teaching and Teacher Education* 54, 77–87.

Martin, A. (2013) Academic buoyancy and academic resilience: Exploring 'everyday' and 'classic' resilience in the face of academic adversity. *School Psychology International* 34 (5), 488–500.

Martin, A. and Marsh, H. (2006) Academic resilience and its psychological and educational correlates: A construct validity approach. *Psychology in the Schools* 43 (3), 267–281.

Martin, A. and Marsh, H. (2008) Academic buoyancy: Towards an understanding of students' everyday academic resilience. *Journal of School Psychology* 46 (1), 53–83.

Masten, A. (2001) Ordinary magic: Resilience processes in development. *American Psychologist* 56 (3), 227–238.

Masten, A. (2009) Ordinary magic: Lessons from research on resilience in human development. *Education Canada* 49 (3), 28–33.

Masten, A., Best, K. and Garmezy, N. (1990) Resilience and development: Contributions from the study of children who overcome adversity. *Development and Psychopathology* 2 (4), 425–444.

McAdams, D. and McLean, K. (2013) Narrative identity. *Current Directions in Psychological Science* 22 (3), 233–238.

Mercer, S. (2016) Complexity and language teaching. In G. Hall (ed.) *The Routledge Handbook of English Language Teaching* (pp. 473–485). New York: Routledge.

Mercer, S., Oberdorfer, P. and Saleem, M. (2016) Helping language teachers to thrive: Using positive psychology to promote teachers' professional well-being. In D. Gabryś-Barker and D. Gałajda (eds) *Positive Psychology Perspectives on Foreign Language Learning and Teaching* (pp. 213–232). Cham: Springer.

Murray, K. and Zautra, A. (2012) Community resilience: Fostering recovery, sustainability, and growth. In M. Ungar (ed.) *The Social Ecology of Resilience: A Handbook of Theory and Practice* (pp. 337–345). New York: Springer.

Noddings, N. (2012) The caring relation in teaching. *Oxford Review of Education* 38, 771–781.

Ong, A., Bergeman, C. and Boker, S. (2009) Resilience comes of age: Defining features in later adulthood. *Journal of Personality* 77 (6), 1777–1804.

Parker, P. and Martin, A. (2009) Coping and buoyancy in the workplace: Understanding their effects on teachers' work-related well-being and engagement. *Teaching and Teacher Education* 25 (1), 68–75.

Reich, J., Zautra, A. and Hall, J. (eds) (2010) *Handbook of Adult Resilience*. New York: Guilford Press.

Richardson, G. (2002) The metatheory of resilience and resiliency. *Journal of Clinical Psychology* 58 (3), 307–321.

Robertson, I., Cooper, C., Sarkar, M. and Curran, T. (2015) Resilience training in the workplace from 2003 to 2014: A systematic review. *Journal of Occupational and Organizational Psychology* 88 (3), 533–562.

Rutter, M. (2006) Implications of resilience concepts for scientific understanding. *Annals of the New York Academy of Sciences* 1094, 1–12.

Rutter, M. (2012) Resilience: Causal pathways and social ecology. In M. Ungar (ed.) *The Social Ecology of Resilience: A Handbook of Theory and Practice* (pp. 33–42). New York: Springer.

Rutter, M., Tizard, J., Yule, W, Graham, P. and Whitmore, K. (1976) Research report: Isle of Wight studies, 1964–1974. *Psychological Medicine* 6 (2), 313–332.

Seligman, M.E.P., Steen, T., Park, N. and Peterson, C. (2005) Positive psychology progress: Empirical validation of interventions. *American Psychologist* 60 (5), 410–421.

Swanson, P. (2012) Second/foreign language teacher efficacy and its relationship to professional attrition. *Canadian Modern Language Review* 68 (1), 78–101.

Tait, M. (2008) Resilience as a contributor to novice teacher success, commitment, and retention. *Teacher Education Quarterly* 35, 57–75.

Tarone, E. and Allwright, D. (2005) Language teacher-learning and student language learning: Shaping the knowledge-base. In D.J. Tedick (ed.) *Language Teacher Education: International Perspectives on Research and Practice* (pp. 5–23). Mahwah, NJ: Lawrence Erlbaum.

Ungar, M. (2012) Social ecologies and their contribution to resilience. In M. Ungar (ed.) *The Social Ecology of Resilience: A Handbook of Theory and Practice* (pp. 13–31). New York: Springer.

Wentzel, K. and Ramani, G. (eds) (2016) *Handbook of Social Influences in School Contexts: Social-emotional, Motivational, and Cognitive Outcomes.* New York: Routledge.

Werner, E. (1982) *Vulnerable but Invincible: A Longitudinal Study of Resilient Children and Youth.* New York: McGraw-Hill.

Werner, E. (1993) Risk, resilience, and recovery: Perspectives from the Kauai longitudinal study. *Development and Psychopathology* 5 (4), 503–515.

Wilkes, G. (2002) Introduction: A second generation of resilience research. *Journal of Clinical Psychology* 58 (3), 229–232.

Windle, G. (2011) What is resilience? A review and concept analysis. *Reviews in Clinical Gerontology* 21 (2), 152–169.

Wu, G., Feder, A., Cohen, H., Kim, J., Calderon, S., Charney, D. and Mathé, A. (2013) Understanding resilience. *Frontiers in Behavioral Neuroscience* 7 (10), 1–15.

Zautra, A., Hall, J. and Murray, K. (2008) Resilience: A new integrative approach to health and mental health research. *Health Psychology Review* 2, 41–64.

Zembylas, M. (2014) Making sense of the complex entanglement between emotion and pedagogy: Contributions of the affective turn. *Cultural Studies in Science Education* 9, 1–12.

15 Making the Transition into Teacher Education: Resilience as a Process of Growth

Achilleas Kostoulas and Anita Lämmerer

Whereas most contributions to this volume discuss aspects of the psychology of language teachers, in this chapter we focus on a related demographic, language teacher educators. This shift in focus is motivated by the observation that the psychology of teacher educators has received very little empirical attention to date, despite their key role as 'lynchpins to the educational enterprise' (Hadar & Brody, 2016: 102). Helping teachers develop can be a very rewarding experience for those of us involved in teacher education, but it comes with a unique set of challenges, among which one might include the expectation to model best practice by continually adjusting to theoretical developments and empirical findings, or the intricate balancing of academic and professional identities.

This chapter aims to develop our understanding of how teacher educators might deal with such challenges in their professional circumstances. The transition from school to teacher education at a university level has been the subject of some recent research, which has highlighted the psychological challenges associated with adjusting to new roles and contexts (e.g. Dinkelman, 2011; Trent, 2013; Williams *et al.*, 2012). However, our own focus is on the construct of resilience, which we define as an emergent, dynamic process of psychological growth that enables one to cope with adversity. Resilience has been slowly gaining currency in educational research, often in response to concerns about burnout and attrition rates, especially among teachers at the start of their careers (Farrell, 2016; Howard & Johnson, 2004; Le Cornu, 2009, 2013). In our chapter we extend this strand of enquiry by reporting on a case study that looked into the resilience of a language teacher educator, Claire (pseudonym), who – at the time of our study – had just completed her first semester as a university lecturer. In doing so, we advance a theoretical understanding of resilience, which we argue is of particular relevance to the particularities of language teacher psychology.

Developing an understanding of the resilience of language teacher educators addresses many arguments analogous to the ones that have been raised in the literature (e.g. Kostoulas & Mercer, 2016; Mercer et al., 2016) about empirically attending to the psychology of language teachers, as the two groups are subject to a comparable range of experiences. These include increased workloads, challenges associated with time management, and the perceived pressure of modelling appropriate learning outcomes for their learners (e.g. Boyd & Harris, 2010). However, the process of becoming a teacher of teachers is also associated with a number of distinctive challenges, especially for those teacher educators who transition into this role mid-career after years of classroom teaching. For example, Hamilton et al. (2009: 210) note that this particular transition from school to the tertiary context involves a shift to 'more expansive academic expectations (...) for the development, communication and critique of knowledge in scholarly ways'. The dual transition from the school context to that of higher education, and from the role of a teacher to that of an academic, has been described as a 'complex, challenging process' (Griffiths et al., 2010: 252), which can put pressure on the ways in which beginner teacher educators perceive themselves, and on their sense of self-worth (Harrison & McKeon, 2008; McKeon & Harrison, 2010; Murray & Male, 2005). The typical stressors of academic life, made more intensive by the lack of experience, direction and clarity often associated with transition periods, suggest that novice teacher educators might find their coping resources overstretched at the start of this career stage. This period therefore lends itself well to observing how resilience is experienced.

Our study aimed at developing an understanding of the role resilience can play during such periods of transition in the career trajectory of language educators. Specifically, we wanted to gain insights into: (a) how individuals like Claire could draw on resilience to cope with the more challenging aspects of the transition; and (b) how such transitions might trigger changes in one's resilience. In our attempt to make sense of how Claire coped with her transition into her new professional role, we were wary of imposing onto our data conceptualisations of resilience that had been developed within the contexts of clinical or counselling psychology. Our concern was that such theoretical accounts, which tend to foreground adversity and adjustment to it (Alvord & Grados, 2005), are best suited for understanding responses to 'negative circumstances with negative consequences' (Fletcher & Sarkar, 2013: 14). Therefore, they might not always be suitable for examining phenomena such as a starting a desired new job, which are not readily described as adversities. Our perspective, which we view as complementary to existing accounts of resilience, focuses instead on understanding resilience as an adjustment to of the challenges of everyday professional practice.

We begin the chapter with an overview of how resilience has been described in the literature, arguing how existing conceptualisations might be further developed in order to become more suited to the specific needs of language teacher psychology. Drawing on this literature as a broad frame of reference, we then describe a tentative model of resilience, which consists of a 'resilience system' and a definition of resilience as an emergent phenomenon (see Feryok, this volume). We then move on to describe our study, which aimed at empirically validating the model.

Rethinking Resilience

In the literature, resilience is broadly defined as an individual's capacity to withstand adversity or recover from it. Within this general conceptualisation, there are a number of different theoretical strands (for comprehensive reviews, see Hiver, this volume; Hu et al., 2015; Richardson, 2002), which for our present purposes can be summarised in a 'trait'–'process' dichotomy. One set of definitions, which is typical of earlier resilience research, has tended to focus on the protective factors ('traits'), which enable individuals to successfully respond to adverse circumstances (e.g. Connor & Davidson, 2003; Rutter, 1987). Rutter's (1987: 316) definition of resilience as a constellation of 'protective factors which modify, ameliorate or alter a person's response to some environmental hazard that predisposes to a maladaptive outcome' is a typical example of such conceptualisations. Research associated with this line of thinking has often taken a phenomenological approach and has resulted in identifying a medley of 'protective factors', or traits associated with resilience, such as optimism (Werner, 1984), intelligence (Alvord & Grados, 2005), internal motivation (Masten, 2001), internal locus of control (Kuterovac-Jagodic, 2003) and a sense of belonging (Gonzales & Padilla, 1997), to name just a few examples. These findings are potentially problematic in that they privilege static understandings of resilience, and may therefore not be fully compatible with the context-sensitive and dynamic nature that the construct is now understood to have by some researchers (Masten & Coatsworth, 1998; Winfield, 1991).

A different approach to understanding resilience involves viewing it as the process through which individuals attain positive psychological outcomes in the face of unfavourable conditions (Leipold & Greve, 2009; Zolkoski & Bullock, 2012). This approach involves looking into psychological 'phenomena characterised by good outcomes in spite of serious threats to adaptation or development' (Masten, 2001: 228). As stated by Luthar et al. (2000):

> Rather than simply studying which child, family, and environmental factors are involved in resilience, researchers are increasingly striving to understand *how* such factors may contribute to positive outcomes. (Luthar et al., 2000: 544, original emphasis)

Empirical work informed by this perspective has often taken an ecological view of behavioural tendencies, by focusing on the transactions between the individual and the environment (e.g. Cicchetti & Lynch, 1993; Galli & Vealey, 2008; Garmezy, 1991).

The multiplicity of perspectives on resilience has been helpful in shedding light on different facets of the phenomenon, but our concern is that it can hinder a holistic understanding of resilience. The decontextualised studies of protective factors are particularly problematic in this regard, due to the fragmented findings that they produce, their lack of sensitivity to the culturally specific ways in which personality traits and practices are perceived, and their tendency to reinforce the 'conceptually grievous' (Fletcher & Sarkar, 2013: 15) notion that resilience is a property that an individual either possesses or does not. In a similar vein, outcome-oriented theories of resilience are definitionally dependent on the existence of discernible risk (Zolkoski & Bullock, 2012) and therefore do not lend themselves well to explaining how the psychological resources connected to resilience are enacted when such adversity is not perceived. These concerns suggest a need for a holistic theory of resilience, which highlights the interconnections among different psychological resources and environmental influences that are available to individuals, regardless of the perceived levels of risk.

Another aspect of resilience that warrants problematisation is its relation to adversity. As hinted in the previous paragraph, resilience theories have been closely linked to notions of risk, or threat to well-being. Initially, this was the result of research design: the first empirical studies of resilience aimed at identifying the traits that enabled exceptional individuals to cope with extreme adversity, such as deprived childhood (e.g. Rutter, 1976, 1979) or cohabitation with family members who suffered from mental illness (e.g. Bleuler, 1972/1978). In later conceptualisations, adversity was incorporated into the definition of resilience, because a positive outcome, the cornerstone of most definitions, is only meaningful in the context of threat (Zolkoski & Bullock, 2012). However, in recent years, there has been an increasing readiness to understand adversity, and by extension resilience, not only in connection to potentially catastrophic risk, but also as in connection to persistent, if less intensive, stressors. In the context of education in particular, Day and Gu (2014) have put forward the concept of 'everyday resilience' that teachers need to develop in order to cope with the challenges of their professional lives, such as accountability pressures, increasing workloads and micro-aggression in their workspace.

Building on the above, we suggest that a theory of resilience for language teaching psychology should address three requirements. First, it should be compatible with the dynamic and situated nature of human psychology. Secondly, it should account for the ways in which resilience emerges from the psychological resources available to the individual, and how it recursively shapes them. Furthermore, it needs to be sensitive to the particular kinds of low-intensity stressors that language educators face in their day-to-day professional lives.

Resilience as growth

To address these theoretical requirements, we put forward a tentative definition of teacher resilience as an emergent process of psychological growth, which is produced by the complex interplay of intrapersonal and contextual factors. Using complex systems theory (e.g. Byrne & Callaghan, 2013; Cilliers, 1998) as an epistemological lens, we view resilience as a phenomenon that emerges from a broad set of psychological constructs but is ontologically distinct from them, and transcends their individual properties (Feryok, this volume; Juarrero, 1999).

Resilience, thus defined, can be conceptualised as emerging within a 'resilience system'. We conceptualise this as a system of relations that develop among different aspects of an individual's psychology. These relations are rarely straightforward or predictable, because of the dense web of interconnections between the constructs that the system encompasses (Davis & Sumara, 2006). An example of such unpredictability, although not explicitly framed from a complexity perspective, is provided by Ungar *et al.* (2013), who point out that the pursuit of hobbies could be a predictor of resilience among children in privileged social strata contexts, whereas for children growing up in economic disadvantage, resilience might be fostered through child labour that contributes to the family income.

By synthesising empirical work that has been conducted on resilience in mainstream psychology (see previous section), it is possible to produce a broad-strokes description of the system, which encompasses three clusters of interrelating constructs (Figure 15.1). The first cluster, *inner strengths*, is understood as a subsystem of personal qualities or traits connected to resilience. Indicatively, these might include self-efficacy (Gillespie *et al.*, 2007; Gu & Day, 2007), background and identities (Mancini & Bonnano, 2009), and future-oriented beliefs, such as a sense of purpose,

Figure 15.1 Hypothetical model of a resilience system

hope and optimism (Gillespie *et al.*, 2007; Werner, 1984). Another cluster, *external support structures*, includes elements such as family and social support networks, workplace 'small cultures' (Holliday, 1999), mentorship and leadership, and institutional expectations. The importance of these factors is a common finding in several studies of resilience, which have highlighted the role of connectedness to the social environment (Denz-Penhey & Murdoch, 2008), the supportive role of family and peers (Gonzales & Padilla, 1997), and connections and attachment (Alvord & Grados, 2005). The final cluster, *learned strategies*, refers to the 'complex repertoire of behavioural tendencies' which some researchers have used to define resilience (Agaibi & Wilson, 2005: 197). This cluster includes both cognitive patterns (e.g. rationalising setbacks in the workspace) and behavioural ones (e.g. avoiding or seeking new challenges), whether they are consciously deployed or produced by the subconscious mind.

This system depicted in Figure 15.1 is intended as a frame for bringing together those aspects of an individual's psychology which might be relevant to resilience, as well as the relations developing among them. Although it would have been possible to further specify the system, by populating each cluster with the protective factors that have been identified in the literature, we deliberately avoided this for two reasons. One was that, in our view, such an over-specification would detract from the theoretical utility of the model, which is to foreground the phenomenon of resilience as an overarching construct that connects the interrelations between the nodes of the system. The second reason was that we conceptualise the system as being idiosyncratic, context-dependent and dynamic. That is to say, different individuals will likely have different constellations of resilience-connected characteristics, and the relations among them can be expected to vary in different contexts and times. In the next sections, we show how this system can facilitate our understanding of the role of resilience during a period of transition in a teacher educator's career trajectory.

The Study

The conceptual model that was presented above was used to examine the resilience of a teacher educator, Claire, who retrospectively reported on her transition into her new professional role. Claire is a teacher and teacher educator in her forties, who at the time of the study had just taken up a new part-time post as a lecturer in teacher education. Claire already had extensive and varied teaching experience. Early in her career she had been employed in an English-speaking country, and upon her return to Austria she worked in a number of language teaching contexts. She was eventually hired as an English language teacher in secondary education, where she continued to be employed part-time when the study took place.

Data for the study were generated by means of two semi-structured interviews that were conducted immediately after Claire had completed her first semester as a teacher educator. In the first interview, we explored her teaching history, her beliefs about teaching and the ways in which she perceived herself as a teacher, and we also retrospectively discussed her first experiences as a lecturer. We began the second interview with follow-up questions and clarifications, following which Claire was presented with 24 statements taken from the CD-RISC resilience scale (Connor & Davidson, 2003), and she was invited to discuss the extent to which these statements were consistent with her experiences during the past six months. An example of such a question (slightly paraphrased due to the confidentiality agreement with the scale's copyright owners) is presented below:

Interviewer:	'When I face difficulties, I try to see the humorous aspects of the situation'. Has this applied to you?
Claire:	Yes. <u>Here</u>, yes.
Interviewer:	Can you give me an example?
Claire:	For example in [name of course]. I mean I told you that I was really worried and scared about this course. So I started off ...

This interview design allowed us to capitalise on the strengths of a well-established research instrument, while deriving more situated and contextualised insights than would have been produced by a scale-type instrument. Both interviews lasted about an hour and were audio-recorded and transcribed. In addition, memos were made by the research team immediately after the interview to capture initial insights.

The transcribed data were read and pre-coded manually using a system of marginal remarks (Miles & Huberman, 1994), which were then further developed into a proto-coding scheme, by connecting themes from the data to the literature on resilience and our tentative model. This scheme was subsequently used by both researchers to independently code the data using ATLAS.ti. The coded data and the memos that were created during coding were then compared, leading to the development of the final coding framework. The coding framework was then applied to the data through a third wave of coding. In addition, conceptual network diagrams were used to trace connections between themes, and we followed up on negative and contradictory evidence to refine our interpretations through theory elaboration. Our emerging understanding was recorded in analytical memos of increasing detail, and we also tried to account for researcher effects by reflexively interrogating our interpretations. The end product of this process was a model of Claire's resilience (Figure 15.2), aspects of which will be presented next.

Claire's First Semester

Space considerations preclude the full descriptions of Claire's resilience system, so in the paragraphs that follow we present examples of each

Figure 15.2 Claire's resilience system

category (inner strengths, external support and learned strategies) and trace connections between system constituents. To illustrate inner strengths by means of an example, we describe how Claire's self-efficacy beliefs grew during her first teaching semester. Following that, we outline how her support network fostered a feeling of trust, which enabled Claire to cope with challenges in her professional context. Finally, we move on to show some cognitive and behavioural patterns that Claire deployed in response to specific challenges.

Growing stronger, again

One of the things that was striking about the way in which Claire described herself was her strong self-efficacy beliefs as a teacher (e.g. 'Teaching? I am <u>very</u> safe with the teaching as such'). Whether discussing her university courses or her lessons in secondary school, Claire confidently talked about her didactic competence (e.g. 'I wasn't worried about my teaching. You know I can do this.'). These self-efficacy beliefs were associated with broader views Claire held about herself. For example, she repeatedly described herself as a creative person, and connected this belief to her ability to teach in non-routine ways ('I am very creative and I have lots of ideas'). Such was the strength of her self-efficacy beliefs that they enabled Claire to take a positive perspective on aspects of her personality that might be construed as negative in non-teaching contexts. This was, for example, the case when Claire talked about her lack of organisational skills ('I will have to accept that whatever kind of course I will teach, will always be a bit chaotic'). Although she describes being disorganised as a 'terrible weakness', which reflects clearly 'ought' beliefs about teachers, she pointed out teaching situations where she was able to capitalise on this aspect of her personality by modelling improvisation skills or by demonstrating a growth mindset:

> And then there was this situation where I had- I don't know how many sheets in front of me. And then I just looked at them [the students] and said: 'Well, you know, one of the most important things when you are a teacher is that you are really well organised. So, you can see I am not there yet.'

Claire's confidence in her didactic competence was a recurring theme in the interviews, and it was evident that she drew on these positive self-beliefs in order to cope with challenges and setbacks during her first semester as a lecturer.

A large part of Claire's teacher self-efficacy beliefs appeared to derive from her teaching background. In the interviews, Claire often reiterated that she was an experienced teacher ('I worked in [...] education of a long time', 'I had a lot of experience', 'I have been basically teaching for thirty years'). She was able to draw on this experience, she explained, to answer practical questions posed by her students (e.g. 'It helps me because [...] they ask us a lot of things, like "How do we do this?" and so on. Then I can really tell them and I can show them, this is what we do'). She also noted that it was helpful in dealing with classroom management issues:

> Or you know, they [i.e. the students] come late: the first person, then the second, then the third. And I know these things, I know it from school, ... Well, what I do then, is what I always do ... I just tell that 'I don't want this' and they should do ((directive finger pointing)) >this and this and this<. And it works out well.

While these examples show how Claire appeared to derive confidence from her professional background, the latter was not just a source of practical knowledge. Another theme recurring throughout the interviews connected to the expertise and the professional ethos Claire developed in the various posts she held, other than secondary education:

> When I was self-employed, (...) I went to a lot of conferences. And my field of expertise then was telling them or teaching people how to use (...) videos and scenes from films and stuff like that. (...) And I had a lot of success with that. So people loved it. And I started working for [a private language education provider] and all that added up.

When narrating her past in such terms, Claire projected the image of a confident professional. However, and interestingly, it appears that she was only able to narratively construct this identity from the vantage point of her new professional role. As she goes on to remark, 'to be really honest that was gone (...) [after] I started school. And when I started working at university that came back.'

Claire's self-efficacy beliefs also seemed to connect to the professional validation that she received from her students and from her section head. Claire explicitly acknowledges that 'it is very important for me to get feedback from students', and she was proactive in eliciting regular feedback on the content of her courses and her teaching style ('I'd ask them "Do I go on teacher, you know, schoolteacher mode?"'). While it seems that the possibility of being negatively evaluated was always a persistent background concern, Claire's open communication with the students helped her to challenge such fears, as seen in the following incident:

> One student, who I thought was a very, very critical student, came to me after the lesson. And I thought 'He is gonna say now "what are you doing!" or whatever' ((laughs)) And then he said 'I just wanted to tell you that I really, really enjoy what we are doing here' and then 'I learn a lot'.

This incident, which Claire singled out as one of her most pleasant memories of the semester, and several other similar exchanges that she narrated, seemed to have a very strong impact on Claire ('one of them last week made me cry [...] and I was so happy because I really, really, really put so much effort into this'), and appeared to reinforce her positive self-image as a teacher.

What seems interesting about Claire's self-efficacy beliefs is that these appeared to be dynamic, and to fluctuate in response to contextual conditions. Earlier in this section, we hinted that the evolution of Claire's self-efficacy was not linear, in the sense that it increased over time, as she accumulated more experience; rather, based on her self-reports, these beliefs appeared to have weakened at some point in Claire's past, when she found herself in an environment that she perceived as non-supportive, and they only manifested themselves again after being triggered by her new professional role. Similarly, her ability to obtain validation from the students appeared to be conditional on establishing relations of trust with them, and it seems reasonable to assume that this source of support also changed as she built stronger relations with her students over time. The dynamic nature of her self-efficacy beliefs was neatly summarised when Claire was asked to what extent she thought she could achieve her goals in the face of possible obstacles; she responded that she believed this to be 'definitely' the case, but also pointed out that 'if you had talked to me a year ago, I would have told you: "Don't know how"'. She elaborated on this by stating that it was teaching at university that 'gave [her] back this belief'.

The discussion in the paragraphs above already hints at the difficulty of maintaining a sharp distinction between Claire's inner strengths and her interpersonal relationships. With this caveat in mind, we now turn our attention to her support network.

Feeling trusted and appreciated

Despite being a newcomer to her academic department, Claire was able to count on the support of an extensive support network, which consisted of her family, her colleagues at the university, some of whom were also personal friends, and other people at the university with whom she interacted professionally. The nature and frequency of her interactions with different members of this network varied, but its overall psychological function was to generate a feeling of security. Claire defined this as 'being able to trust people', and she signalled it as one of the most important features that helped her to adjust to her new professional role.

Claire claimed that her family were always a steady source of emotional support for her, and that she felt confident discussing her professional decisions with them. These included her decision to start additional work at university, despite the impact it would have on their family life ('My partner has been very, very supportive, because he was just so happy [...] And he just said "We will handle it. We will cope with it. Just go there."') Although Claire did not experience any major challenges during her first semester at university, she claimed that being able to rely on support from her family made a difference to her ability to cope.

Alongside her family, Claire drew considerable support from a close friend, Lily, who also taught at the same university. She notes that: 'I've known Lily for a very, very long time and the great thing with Lily (...) is: Lily and I became friends after working together (...) the friendship developed out of working together.' Lily, with whom Claire had a strong pre-existing professional and personal relationship, proved to be constant source of practical and emotional support. For example, she was the first person Claire called right after receiving a job offer, in order to get reassurance:

> I called Lily and the first thing that I said was 'Lily, I need help here ((laughs)) because I am not sure I can do this.' And Lily said 'of course you can do this.'

Claire was also able to turn to Lily for advice about her day-to-day teaching ('We usually speak on the phone quite late at night'), and she jokingly described her as her backup plan if things went wrong.

Notably, however, this strong supportive relationship appeared to depend on Claire's pre-existing familiarity and trust, as her relationships with other colleagues developed differently. For example, when discussing her relationship with Rose, another lecturer who was teaching the same course, Claire seemed more reserved:

> I think if I had called Rose more often, I would have had the same kind of guidance. Not the same, because I don't know Rose so well. But she would have helped me too. But, there was no time.

Such differences in interpersonal dynamics are, of course, commonplace, but a comparison of Claire's relationship with her two colleagues hints both at the importance of trust as a component of her resilience, and at the context-specific nature of her resilience.

In addition, Claire also reportedly drew a lot of support from the administrative staff and Violet, the head of the section. She named several administrators, whom she considered 'really supportive' and 'really nice and helpful', and claimed that the rapport she developed made her feel 'more self-confident'. Similarly, she described Violet as being 'very encouraging and very helpful' and pointed out that Violet's trust was influencing on her self-efficacy beliefs ('Whenever I thought "Maybe I can't do this", I thought "Then she wouldn't have hired me"'). Summarising her supportive relationships, Claire explicitly stated that at university she feels 'in general appreciated', and this fostered feelings of security that helped her to cope with the transition into her new role.

Dealing with difficulties

In order to cope with the various challenges she encountered during her first semester in her new professional role, Claire employed a wide repertoire of strategies, often in a deliberate, purposeful way. One set of such strategies involved the active use of her cognition to challenge unhelpful perceptions or feelings. When faced with stressful situations, Claire reported that she consciously attempted to regulate her emotions by trying to 'calm down sometimes a bit, and to just see things a bit cooler'. She also mentioned using self-talk extensively to control her stress, relax and motivate herself. For example, this is how she described her immediate reaction to a classroom situation in which she unexpectedly had to improvise: 'I said "come on, I can do this, this is ridiculous. I mean, I can come up with something"'.

Another cognitive strategy that Claire used involved extensive reflection-on-action following challenging classroom situations ('I go home and I think "oh, I've made this mistake"'). When reflecting on the choices and decisions she made, she made an effort to retrospectively reformulate her choices and decisions in positive terms (e.g. 'at least I was authentic'). She also used rational processing to evaluate her experiences: when thinking of a lesson that had not gone as she had planned, she claimed that she would not view it as a failure, since 'there are so many things that work, and things that don't work'. Elsewhere in the data, when reflecting on the likelihood that some of her students might not have been satisfied by the courses she taught, she rationally pointed out that 'sometimes you cannot meet everybody's needs'. In addition to helping her set realistic goals for the future, this process of rational reflection often involved re-assessing the significance of any unsuccessful experiences. For example, when asked to describe any possible setbacks in her first semester at university, she emphasised that 'they were just tiny, tiny little things', which did not have a negative impact on the way she perceived her teaching competence.

Using such strategies, Claire managed to maintain a realistic perception of her professional self, which was not distorted by perfectionistic expectations or unhelpful comparisons with her more experienced peers.

Apart from cognitive strategies, Claire also reported using several behavioural strategies to cope with challenges. The most important of these involved actively seeking support and guidance from people who might help her ('I start asking'). As seen in the previous section, Claire frequently built on the supportive relations she enjoyed with her peers and her students, but she was also proactive in seeking institutional and expert support where necessary. For instance, she reported being very comfortable with seeking guidance and feedback from her section head ('Here I have the impression that if I do something that is really not OK, [she] would tell me'). She also mentioned several instances where she sought expert support to prepare her lessons, and to deal with challenging classroom management issues. On the whole, Claire reported that she benefited greatly from 'working with people who I can learn something from' and was keen to point out that 'when you work together, it is so much better'.

While Claire was happy to provide multiple examples of receiving such support at the university, she also noted that such proactivity was less appropriate in what she perceived as a competitive atmosphere at her school:

> It's just the system. (…) I get from one trouble into the next. (…) For me, the way I am, is I would ask somebody what they do. (…) They don't. Everybody plans their own thing. (…) And at the beginning, when I started, I would just go up to people and would say 'Are we going to meet there?' (…) But some people really felt I was being intrusive.

What this extract seems to suggest is that while Claire seemed skilled at eliciting the support she needed, the effects of this strategy appeared to be context-specific.

When faced with potentially threatening situations, Claire used a variety of strategies, including humour, withdrawal and confrontational responses. In the interviews she cited several instances where she used humour to defuse awkward situations in her courses. She also made multiple self-depreciating jokes during the interviews at instances when she appeared relatively nervous. However, she mentioned that she was only comfortable using humour in situations where she felt safe, such as interacting with her students ('In class with my students, yes. In the teachers' room, no'). When faced with more threatening situations, such as interacting with colleagues whom she perceived as unfriendly, she reported that 'I withdraw myself totally'. This often meant physically distancing herself from the threatening situation by either returning home ('I teach my lessons, and I go home. And if I have a first and a third lesson, I go home') or taking a walk outside the school ('I love going outside, and I walk a lot'). That said, she also stated that she was prone to vigorously standing her ground in situations that she perceived as particularly threatening ('Sometimes I freaked out, because I am very emotional. So when I get angry, I get really angry'). The diversity of behavioural responses Claire used in response to threats of different intensity hints at the nonlinearity of outcomes, which is often regarded as a hallmark of complex systems.

Conclusions

By looking into aspects of Claire's resilience system, we hope to have achieved two goals. The first one was to develop insights into the ways in which educators might experience the transition from experienced teacher to novice teacher educators. Claire's experiences were broadly consistent with what has been reported in the literature (e.g. Ben-Peretz *et al.*, 2010; McGregor *et al.*, 2010; Ritter, 2014). Some common themes include the importance of background experience as a psychological resource (cf. Boyd & Harris, 2010), the role of self-efficacy beliefs (cf. Gu & Day, 2007) and the supportive role of colleagues (cf. Minott, 2010). Perhaps unsurprisingly, the differences between the norms at school and university (cf. Griffiths *et al.*, 2010) also came up in the data, as does the differentiated effect they had on her resilience. In the literature, it has been suggested that many teacher educators who move into higher education from classroom teaching go through a transition period that might last for up to three years (Murray & Male, 2005). The considerably more rapid adjustment that Claire reported is difficult to trace back to any single contributing factor, which is why we believe that a holistic view, such as the one advocated in this chapter, can be useful in understanding the role of her resilience. Our second goal was to develop an understanding of resilience for language teaching psychology. While the insights from this single case study are proportional to its restricted scope, we believe that they form a useful starting point for further empirical and theoretical work that will flesh out and validate our emerging theorisation.

Our initial expectation was that Claire's description of her first semester as a teacher educator would involve formidable challenges and her struggle to adjust to them. Instead, we were presented with an account of growth and empowerment, triggered by Claire's transition into her new professional role. In the context of discourse about education which often highlights the challenges facing the profession, this unexpected finding was, in our view, a source of inspiration.

References

Agaibi, C.E. and Wilson, J.P. (2005) Trauma, PTSD, and resilience: A review of the literature. *Trauma, Violence, and Abuse* 6 (3), 195–216.

Alvord, M.K. and Grados, J.J. (2005) Enhancing resilience in children: A proactive approach. *Professional Psychology: Research and Practice* 36 (3), 238–245.

Ben-Peretz, M., Kleeman, S., Reichenberg, R. and Shimoni, S. (2010) Educators of educators: Their goals, perceptions and practices. *Professional Development in Education* 36 (1–2), 111–129.

Bleuler, M. (1972/1978) *The Schizophrenic Disorders: Long-Term Patient and Family Studies*. New Haven, CT: Yale University Press.

Boyd, P. and Harris, K. (2010) Becoming a university lecturer in teacher education: Expert school teachers reconstructing their pedagogy and identity. *Professional Development in Education* 36 (1–2), 9–24.

Byrne, D. and Callaghan, G. (2013) *Complexity Theory and the Social Sciences: The State of the Art*. London: Routledge.

Cicchetti, D. and Lynch, M. (1993) An ecological-transactional analysis of children and contexts: The longitudinal interplay among child maltreatment, community violence, and children's symptomatology. *Development and Psychopathology* 10, 235–257.

Cilliers, P. (1998) *Complexity and Postmodernism: Understanding Complex Systems*. London: Routledge.

Connor, K.M. and Davidson, J.R.T. (2003) Development of a new resilience scale: The Connor–Davidson resilience scale (CD-RISC). *Depression and Anxiety* 18 (2), 76–82.

Davis, B. and Sumara, D. (2006) *Complexity and Education: Inquiries into Learning, Teaching, and Research*. London: Routledge.

Day, C. and Gu, Q. (2014) *Resilient Teachers, Resilient Schools: Building and Sustaining Quality in Testing Times*. London: Routledge.

Denz-Penhey, H. and Murdoch, C. (2008) Personal resiliency: Serious diagnosis and prognosis with unexpected quality outcomes. *Qualitative Health Research* 18 (3), 391–404.

Dinkelman, T. (2011) Forming a teacher educator identity: Uncertain standards, practice and relationships. *Journal of Education for Teaching* 37 (3), 309–323.

Farrell, T.S.C. (2016) Surviving the transition shock in the first year of teaching through reflective practice. *System* 61, 12–19.

Fletcher, D. and Sarkar, M. (2013) A review of psychological resilience. *European Psychologist* 18 (1), 12–23.

Galli, N. and Vealey, R.S. (2008) 'Bouncing back' from adversity: Athletes' experiences of resilience. *Sport Psychologist* 22, 316–335.

Garmezy, N. (1991) Resiliency and vulnerability to adverse developmental outcomes associated with poverty. *American Behavioral Scientist* 34 (4), 416–430.

Gillespie, B.M., Chaboyer, W., Wallis, M. and Grimbeek, P. (2007) Resilience in the operating room: Developing and testing of a resilience model. *Journal of Advanced Nursing* 59 (4), 427–438.

Gonzalez, R. and Padilla, A.M. (1997) The academic resilience of Mexican American high school students. *Hispanic Journal of Behavioral Science* 19, 309–317.

Griffiths, V., Thompson, S. and Hryniewicz, L. (2010) Developing a research profile: Mentoring and support for teacher educators. *Professional Development in Education* 36 (1–2), 245–262.

Gu, Q. and Day, C. (2007) Teachers' resilience: A necessary condition for effectiveness. *Teaching and Teacher Education* 23 (8), 1302–1316.

Hadar, L.L. and Brody, D.L. (2016) Talk about student learning: Promoting professional growth among teacher educators. *Teaching and Teacher Education* 59, 101–114.

Hamilton, M., Loughran, J. and Marcondes, M. (2009) Teacher educators and the self-study of teaching practices. In A. Swennen and M. Van der Klink (eds) *Becoming a Teacher Educator: Theory and Practice for Teacher Educators* (pp. 205–217). Dordrecht: Springer.

Harrison, J. and McKeon, F. (2008) The formal and situated learning of beginning teacher educators in England: Identifying characteristics for successful induction in the transition from workplace in schools to workplace in higher education. *European Journal of Teacher Education* 31 (2), 151–168.

Holliday, A. (1999) Small cultures. *Applied Linguistics* 20 (2), 237–264.

Howard, S. and Johnson, B. (2004) Resilient teachers: Resisting stress and burnout. *Social Psychology of Education* 7 (4), 399–420.

Hu, T., Zhang, D. and Wang, J. (2015) A meta-analysis of the trait resilience and mental health. *Personality and Individual Differences* 76, 18–27.

Juarrero, A. (1999) *Dynamics in Action.* Cambridge, MA: MIT Press.

Kostoulas, A. and Mercer, S. (2016) Fifteen years of research on self and identity in System. *System* 60, 128–134.

Kuterovac-Jagodic, G. (2003) Posttraumatic stress symptoms in Croatian children exposed to war: A prospective study. *Journal of Clinical Psychology* 59 (1), 9–25.

Le Cornu, R. (2009) Building resilience in pre-service teachers. *Teaching and Teacher Education* 25 (5), 717–723.

Le Cornu, R. (2013) Building early career teacher resilience: The role of relationships. *Australian Journal of Teacher Education* 38 (4), 1–16.

Leipold, B. and Greve, W. (2009) Resilience: A conceptual bridge between coping and development. *European Psychologist* 14, 40–50.

Luthar, S.S., Cicchetti, D. and Becker, B. (2000) The construct of resilience: A critical evaluation and guidelines for future work. *Child Development* 71 (3), 543–562.

Mancini, A.D. and Bonanno, G.A. (2009) Predictors and parameters of resilience to loss: Toward an individual differences model. *Journal of Personality* 77 (6), 1805–1832.

Masten, A.S. (2001) Ordinary magic: Resilience processes in development. *American Psychologist* 56 (3), 227–238.

Masten, A.S. and Coatsworth, J.D. (1998) The development of competence in favorable and unfavorable environments: Lessons from research on successful children. *American Psychologist* 53 (2), 205–220.

McGregor, D., Hooker, B., Wise, D. and Devlin, L. (2010) Supporting professional learning through teacher educator enquiries: An ethnographic insight into developing understandings and changing identities. *Professional Development in Education* 36 (1–2), 169–195.

McKeon, F. and Harrison, J. (2010) Developing pedagogical practice and professional identities of beginning teacher educators. *Professional Development in Education* 36 (1–2), 25–44.

Mercer, S., Oberdorfer, P. and Saleem, M. (2016) Helping language teachers to thrive: Using positive psychology to promote teachers' professional well-being. In D. Gabryś-Barker and D. Gałajda (eds) *Positive Psychology Perspectives on Foreign Language Learning and Teaching, Second Language Learning and Teaching* (pp. 213–229). Cham: Springer.

Miles, M.B. and Huberman, A.M. (1994) *Qualitative Data Analysis: An Expanded Sourcebook* (2nd edn). Thousand Oaks, CA: Sage.

Minott, M.A. (2010) Reflective teaching as self-directed professional development: Building practical or work-related knowledge. *Professional Development in Education* 36 (1–2), 325–338.

Murray, J. and Male, T. (2005) Becoming a teacher educator: Evidence from the field. *Teaching and Teacher Education* 21 (2), 125–142.

Richardson, G.E. (2002) The metatheory of resilience and resiliency. *Journal of Clinical Psychology* 58 (3), 307–321.

Ritter, J.K. (2014) 'You would think I could pull it off differently': A teacher educator returns to classroom teaching. *Issues in Teacher Education* 23 (2), 29–46.

Rutter, M. (1976) Research report: Isle of Wight studies. *Psychological Medicine* 6, 313–332.

Rutter, M. (1979) Protective factors in children's responses to stress and disadvantage. *Annals of the Academy of Medicine, Singapore* 8 (3), 324–338.

Rutter, M. (1987) Psychosocial resilience and protective mechanisms. *American Journal of Orthopsychiatry* 57, 316–331.

Trent, J. (2013) Becoming a teacher educator: The multiple boundary-crossing experiences of beginning teacher educators. *Journal of Teacher Education* 64 (3), 262–275.

Ungar, M., Ghazinour, M. and Richter, J. (2013) Annual research review: What is resilience within the social ecology of human development? *Journal of Child Psychology and Psychiatry* 54 (4), 348–366.

Werner, E.E. (1984) Resilient children. *Young Children* 40, 68–72.

Williams, J., Ritter, J. and Bullock, S.M. (2012) Understanding the complexity of becoming a teacher educator: Experience, belonging, and practice within a professional learning community. *Studying Teacher Education* 8 (3), 245–260.

Winfield, L.F. (1991) Resilience, schooling, and development in African-American youth: A conceptual framework. *Education and Urban Society* 24 (1), 5–14.

Zolkoski, S.M. and Bullock, L.M. (2012) Resilience in children and youth: A review. *Children and Youth Services Review* 34 (12), 2295–2303.

16 Signature Strengths as a Gateway to Mentoring: Facilitating Emergent Teachers' Transition into Language Teaching

Tammy Gregersen and Peter D. MacIntyre

> One looks back with appreciation to the brilliant teachers,
> but with gratitude to those who touched our human feelings.
> Carl Jung

Emergent teachers,[1] and in particular language teachers, undergo an evolution of their personal and professional identities over time, one that taps into key processes in teacher psychology (cf. Li & De Costa, this volume; Sahakyan *et al.*, this volume). Developing new roles, different perspectives, engaging in new behaviours, and shifts in attitudes within the classrooms where they may once have thrived as students highlight a few of the changes encountered by emergent teachers (Kanno & Stuart, 2011). As a result of the shaping of their nascent professional identities, emergent teachers may experience considerable tension and self-doubt, especially if the personal and professional dimensions of becoming a teacher are not well balanced (Beijaard *et al.*, 2004). Among the tensions experienced by teachers are wanting to care for students but being expected to be tough, balancing work and private life, feeling incompetent but feeling compelled to be an expert, maintaining emotional distance, harmonising teaching with other work-related tasks, depending on a mentor yet wanting to go it alone, respecting students' integrity, shifting from being a student to being a teacher, dealing with contradictory institutional attitudes, and wanting to take on more responsibility. Personality theorist Karen Horney described the 'tyranny of the shoulds', which reflects a neurotic need to be perfect, to meet impossibly conflicting standards (e.g. enjoy life but to be above personal pleasure), to be fully in control, and to '... know, understand and foresee everything' (Horney, 1950: 65). Being aware of their apparent shortcomings, emergent teachers can feel that they are not being taken seriously, can feel fed up and as if they are being pushed (Pillen *et al.*, 2013). Numerous studies have reported that as many as half of new teachers abandon their careers in their first five years (Jonson, 2002; Smith & Ingersoll, 2004). Multiple reasons have been proposed for this mass exodus, including a dearth of supportive mentoring. Emergent teachers who remain in the profession have most likely had some help in facing the many challenges inherent in the process of gaining their initial experience (Asención Delaney, 2012).

As emergent teachers are initiated into the educational community, they participate in a dynamic and continuous process of adaptation. As they take on new roles and responsibilities, they experience novel interactions with students, administrative staff and other teachers, among others. Various tensions are inherent in the teaching process itself, which can be stressful for beginning teachers (Flores, 2004; Kelchtermans & Ballet, 2002). Nias (1996) contends that teachers' emotional reactions to their work are closely linked to their views of self and others. For the emergent teacher, coping with the novelty of the situation and the various, sometimes conflicting relationship demands within it can be emotionally difficult at times; emotions will play an important role in the ways in which developing tensions are experienced (Hargreaves, 2005; Kelchtermans, 2005; Olsen, 2010; Volkmann & Anderson, 1998).

Developing a professional identity as a teacher is a complex and emotional process. Language teacher educators and experienced teacher mentors can help to guide emergent teachers through their initial experiences in their classrooms. In contemplating ways in which to approach structuring the mentor–mentee discussions, our thinking has been informed by the notion of 'signature strengths'.

Signature Strengths

Underlying this project is our belief that capitalising on one's areas of strength is likely to lead to greater success than investing comparable time and effort in remediating areas of weakness (Clifton & Harter, 2003; Gregersen & MacIntyre, 2014). The strengths-based approach implemented in the present study draws upon research in positive psychology, with our attention directed towards teachers thriving – not merely surviving – and being more attuned to their uniquely personal configuration of strengths rather than to their deficiencies (Schreiner *et al.*, 2009).

A focus on strengths development is an investment in personal resources, as captured in the notion of positive psychological capital, which is defined as:

> (a)n individual's positive psychological state of development that is characterized by (1) having confidence (self-efficacy) to take on and put in the necessary effort to succeed at challenging tasks; (2) making positive

attribution (optimism) about succeeding now and in the future; (3) perse-
vering toward goals, and when necessary, redirecting paths to goals
(hope) in order to succeed; and (4) when beset by problems and adversity,
sustaining and bouncing back and even beyond (resiliency) to attain success. (Luthans *et al.*, 2007: 3)

Much like financial capital, positive psychological capital can be accumulated over time and invested to accomplish future goals, including those
of teachers and language learners (Gregersen *et al.*, 2016). Hargraves and
Fullan (2012) recast the familiar notion of developing teachers' capacity,
proposing instead a refined term 'professional capital', with components
that include decisional capital, social capital and human capital (i.e. the
qualities of the individual teacher). They argue that whereas the word
'capacity' suggests a need for deficiencies and remediation, moving teachers towards meeting externally imposed standards, the term 'professional
capital' points to school and system-wide investments that are necessary
for success among emergent teachers, as well as the other stakeholders in
the system. We must emphasise that teachers do not arrive at their (first)
classroom *de novo*; there is a person inside the role and a role inside the
person; that person has a particular configuration of strengths. Prior work
has emphasised the *role* of a teacher in considering appropriate mentorship (Buchmann, 1993). In the present research we emphasise that the
character strengths that emergent teachers bring into the profession must
be considered a vital component of their positive psychological capital,
ready to be invested in their ongoing personal and professional development, and is one of the bases for professional accountability (Fullan *et al.*,
2015). We argue that, whereas is it appropriate to consider the role a
teacher plays in designing mentorship opportunities, it is more appropriate to consider the assets of the person-in-the-role (or role-within-person
if the emphasis is on the individual teacher); specifically we advocate capitalising on the shared strengths of mentor and mentee.

Park *et al.* (2004) describe character strengths as moral traits that exist
in degrees and which are measurable as individual differences and which
are reflected in thought, feeling and behaviour. Partly in response to the
widely used mental illness classification system, the Diagnostic and
Statistical Manual of Mental Disorders (DSM), Peterson and Seligman
(2004) published what they saw as its positive psychology counterpart, the
Values In Action (VIA) Classification of Strengths. To turn a phrase, it is
an attempt at 'classification of the sanities' (Seligman, 2002: 131). The
VIA taxonomy of strengths describes six ubiquitous, valued and respected
virtues, which are common to all major religions and cultural traditions:
wisdom, courage, love, justice, temperance and spirituality. Theoretically
categorised under the six broad virtues are 24 distinct strengths including
appreciating beauty, bravery, creativity, curiosity, fairness, gratitude,
humour, kindness, learning, love, perspective, spirituality, teamwork and
zest (Peterson & Seligman, 2004). Park and Peterson (2009) developed the

VIA Inventory of Strengths (VIA-IS) as an online assessment tool to be used in identifying one's signature strengths (for a complete list of inclusion criteria, see Park *et al.*, 2004). The VIA-IS consists of 240 items that measure one's character strengths, and has been taken by over four million people to date (VIA Institute, 2016). A subsample of over 117,000 respondents from 54 different countries showed that the strengths most frequently endorsed included kindness, fairness, honesty, gratitude and judgement, while the least common strengths were prudence, modesty and self-regulation (Park *et al.*, 2006). More recent analysis of the VIA Inventory suggests that three broad factors capture the major components of the VIA strengths: caring, inquisitiveness and self-control which, respectively, reflect the ability to care for others, love of learning, and willingness to work hard – '... a triumvirate of heart, head and guts' (McGrath, 2015: 422). The literature on character strengths is developing rapidly, with scholarly publications, various assessment inventories and strength interventions (Biswas-Diener *et al.*, 2011).

In his book, *Authentic Happiness*, Seligman (2002) describes signature strengths as those one owns, celebrates and displays frequently; these are defining characteristics of a person. A strength should meet the following criteria in order to be considered signature:

- a sense of ownership and authenticity surrounding the strength;
- a feeling of excitement (particularly at first) while displaying it;
- a rapid learning curve;
- intrinsic motivation to use the strength;
- a sense of yearning to act in accordance with it;
- the creation and pursuit of fundamental projects that revolve around the strength;
- continuous learning of new ways to use the strength;
- invigoration rather than exhaustion when using the strength;
- the discovery of the strength as owned in an epiphany;
- a feeling of inevitability in using the strength (i.e. 'try and stop me').

An exercise to develop strengths, supported by empirical research, is called *Using Signature Strengths in a New Way* (Peterson, 2006). In this exercise, participants are asked first to complete the VIA online inventory. After signature strengths are identified, participants are asked to take one of the top five identified strengths and use it in a new way every day for one week. In a six-group, randomised, placebo-controlled trial, this exercise was found to have lasting impacts on well-being for up to six months (Seligman *et al.*, 2005) and led to improvements in patients with mild-to-moderate depression, as well as higher remission rates in patients with severe depression for up to one year post-intervention (Seligman *et al.*, 2006). Follow-up studies, using variations in methods and analyses, have found more modest but significant effects of the signature strengths exercise, particularly with increasing positive affect (Mongrain

& Anselmo-Matthews, 2012; Woodworth *et al.*, 2016). Applications of interventions such as this one have contributed to the developing literature on positive psychology interventions (Rashid, 2015), including in the SLA field (Gregersen *et al.*, 2015; MacIntyre & Mercer, 2014).

The literature on strengths development suggests that there can be advantages to focusing on using one's strengths in new ways, in contrast to a focus on compensating for deficiencies (Peterson, 2006). This chapter examines how the strengths that emergent teachers bring to the profession might be optimised through individualised guidance provided by more experienced teacher mentors. Specifically, mentors will suggest novel ways for new teachers to use their personal signature strengths. To study the reactions to this exercise, we will employ a small-scale, individualised, qualitative research design. We chose this approach because strengths profiles may differ substantially across participants and the effectiveness of positive psychology interventions has been shown to increase when individuals are able to self-select interventions (Sin & Lyubomirsky, 2009; Woodworth *et al.*, 2016). Furthermore, the general applicability of group-level statistical comparisons to individual cases is questionable and in many cases should be avoided (Molenaar & Campbell, 2009). Finally, there remains some question about the processes by which the signature strengths exercise works and the types of effects it might have are not yet well understood (Mongrain & Anselmo-Matthews, 2012; Woodworth *et al.*, 2016). These factors argue for an individual-level, qualitative approach to the present research.

Because signature strengths are the ones people (in our case, emergent teachers) already possess, it may be easier and more enjoyable to work with them to build positive psychological capital. To the extent that emergent teachers experience more fulfilment, greater character strengths and healthy collective social support, they likely will endure fewer psychological or physical difficulties when challenges arise in their profession (Peterson *et al.*, 2006). The building and enhancing of character strengths not only tends to reduce the possibility of negative outcomes (Botvin *et al.*, 1995) but strengths themselves contribute to healthy positive life-long growth and flourishing (Colby & Damon, 1992; Park, 2004; Weissberg & Greenberg, 1997). The question becomes – how does an emerging teacher develop specific, protective character strengths, and what role can a mentor play in promoting these?

Benefits of Mentoring

A language teacher's perception of self can be modified with every linguistic concept taught, every new expectation from the school administration and every new package of teaching materials. However, perhaps most profoundly, one's identity as a teacher shifts in relationships with other people – teaching peers and learners alike. There is perhaps no relationship with more potential for transforming teachers than that between a mentor teacher and an emergent teacher.

For our specific purpose in defining mentoring for emerging teachers, we draw upon He's (2009: 297) definition: '… enhancing pre-service teachers' resilience in teaching by introducing ways to identify one's strengths and assets; co-constructing goals and establishing motivation and strategies to achieve goals; and self-monitoring one's growth, optimism and resilience as a teacher.' It is a personal and professional relationship in which participants – mentors and mentees together – co-construct their identities. This interpretation originates in a sociocultural view of learning in which collaboration between the already emerged and the emergent is necessary to build new professional knowledge (Freeman & Johnson, 1998; Malderez & Wedell, 2007; Richards, 2008; Smith, 2001; Wright, 2010). Forming reflective teachers who engage in collaborative learning and evaluate their personal and professional development therein is the primary objective of the constructivist view of L2 teacher education in the 21st century (Wright, 2010). Consequently, these reflective practitioners glean fresh understanding about their practice by engaging in a critical study of it, which in turn then leads to improvement and intervention. In this view, mentors are indispensable in the promotion of reflective practices through their supportive partnership wherein mentors and mentees together and alone contemplate their practice, re-examine the 'what', 'how' and 'why' of their teaching, and make efforts towards improving their professional practice (Schön, 1983, 1987).

Effective mentors extend themselves beyond merely modelling skilled practice. They support the emergent teacher's emotional and cognitive development in the process of forming a professional identity (Malderez & Bódoczky, 1999). Consequently, emergent teachers can benefit from reduced feelings of isolation, increased confidence and self-esteem, professional growth, improved self-reflection and problem-solving capacities (Flores, 2004; Pillen et al., 2013; Wright, 2010). The emotional and psychological support emergent teachers receive can enable them to put difficulties into perspective and boost their morale and job satisfaction (Bullough, 2005; Johnson et al., 2005; Lindgren, 2005; Marable & Raimondi, 2007).

Effective mentoring is individualised, delivering equally valuable *but not identical* treatment to different mentees. Differentiation and individualisation of recommendations are critical to the successful mentoring of emergent teachers (van Fleet, 1973). According to Leaver and Oxford (2001), less effective mentors sometimes fail to consider that mentees are unique in many ways, particularly when considering variables such as personality, ways of processing information and learning preferences. Recently, Mitchell et al. (2015) suggested that mentor–mentee relationships would be facilitated by sharing personal information about each other early in their relationship, such as by completing a personality test or '... worksheets in which they jointly reflect on how their past experiences have informed their career progression' (Mitchell *et al.*, 2015: 8). In this study, we propose that signature strengths be used as a focused way of documenting similarities between mentor and mentee.

Mentoring is more likely to be successful in situations where decisions about mentor–mentee pairings consider the strengths and limitations of those involved, and where the mentor and mentee connect both personally and professionally (Abell *et al.*, 1995). Similarity between mentor and mentee has also been shown to predict the success of the relationship (Eby *et al.*, 2013; Ensher & Murphy, 1997). Additionally, mentoring effectiveness is increased when mentors teach the same subject specialisation as their mentees (Hobson *et al.*, 2009; Smith & Ingersoll, 2004). For these reasons, the current research project carefully paired mentors with mentees based on character strengths included in the VIA inventory in order to provide personalised feedback and to encourage reflection over practice, helping to refine participants' developing professional identity.

The Present Study

This study focuses on the reactions of emergent teachers (mentees) to being guided by experienced teachers (mentors), who share the majority of their signature strengths. The process began with each participant emergent teacher identifying and then reflecting on their signature strengths and thinking about ways to use them in new ways in their daily (not necessarily classroom) life. Participant experienced teachers also identified their signature strengths and were then paired with emergent teachers who shared at least three of the top five strengths. Subsequently, the experienced mentors provided advice to the emergent mentees on how to use their top five signature strengths *in the classroom*. The procedure concluded with emergent teachers implementing the advice and responding to questions about the efficacy of the guidance. With evidence from the strengths profile of participants, the detailed mentors' advice and mentees' reactions, we sought to answer the following questions:

RQ1: What signature strengths do emergent teachers bring to their classrooms and are they different from the strengths found in prior, large-scale research using the VIA inventory?

RQ2: What is the nature of the advice that carefully paired experienced teachers offer to their less experienced counterparts who share similar signature strengths?

RQ3: Do emergent teachers respond positively to the acted upon advice provided by their mentors? If so, in what ways?

Methodology

Participants

Two groups of participants were necessary to carry out this series of five case studies: (1) the 'mentees' (i.e. emergent teachers) and (2) the 'mentors' (i.e. experienced teachers). The original sample of participants in the mentee group consisted of 25 undergraduate emergent teachers who were enrolled in a teaching English to speakers of other languages (TESOL) course at a mid-sized university in the Midwestern United States. From this group of 25, we chose five mentees based upon similarity between their top strengths as shown by the VIA online survey and those of the mentors who took the same survey. All five mentees were females between the ages of 19 and 24 and had lived most of their lives in the Midwestern United States. The mentors group originally had five participants but the size was later reduced to three to match as well as possible the strengths of mentors and mentees. All of the mentors had graduated as TESOL educators from the same university from which the mentees were drawn. All mentors were females between the ages of 28 and 35 and they had between six and 12 years of teaching experience. All three mentors had been raised in the same geographical area as the mentees.

Instruments

(1) Values In Action survey

Published by Peterson and Seligman (2004), the VIA survey of character strengths is an online 240-item self-report questionnaire. Using a 5-point Likert-type scale (1 = very much unlike me to 5 = very much like me), the VIA determines the extent to which participants agree or disagree with items reflecting the 24 character strengths. Although there are no time restrictions, the survey typically takes approximately 25 minutes to complete. Upon completion of the survey, respondents are immediately sent their results by email, with their strengths rank ordered from one to 24. The four to seven strengths at the top of the list can be deemed 'signature strengths'. For consistency across persons, we are focusing on the top five strengths. Permission was granted by administrators of the VIA survey to use the results in this research project.

(2) Strengths-based advice from mentors

Mentors were sent the strengths profile of mentees with whom they shared at least three of their top five strengths. The overlapping strengths between mentors and mentees were highlighted. Mentors then were asked to consider how they use each of the shared strengths and to provide advice to an emergent teacher on using the strength in new ways that the mentee might not have yet considered. The guideline given to mentors is reported in the procedure section and the content of the advice is reported in the results section. Mentees implemented the advice during their semester-long practice teaching assignments.

(3) The Post-application of Signature Strength Survey (PASSS)

The PASSS is a 7-item Likert-type questionnaire, written for the present study, with possible responses ranging from 1 (strongly disagree) to 5 (strongly agree). Space is provided after each item to add further commentary, if desired. Each item was written based on empirical findings about the potential positive outcomes of using signature strengths in novel ways. Items include a strengthened sense of well-being, greater relational satisfaction with others, heightened resilience, enhanced competence, more refined coping skills and greater persistence in goal attainment. The PASSS was developed to encourage mentees to reflect on the efficacy of the suggestions they received for using strengths in a new way in their language classrooms.

Procedure

As part of a class assignment in an undergraduate course for preparing educators in teaching English as a second language at a mid-sized university in the Midwestern United States, 25 students took the VIA online survey in order to discover their signature strengths. They were instructed to come up with novel ways to use their strengths and then to write a four- to five-page narrative about what they had learned about themselves and their individual strengths in the process of using them in new ways. At the same time, five experienced teachers were recruited via social media to also take the VIA online survey. Emergent teachers were paired with the experienced teachers based on the compatibility of their responses. To be matched, mentors and mentees had to share at least three of their top five signature strengths. An excerpt from the mentors' instructions read as follows:

> Provide real-life ways of applying [your] partner's strengths in new ways [because] research demonstrates that new applications of signature strengths have long-term positive effects on happiness [and that] the important idea is that the strength is used in NEW ways.

Teachers gave their advice once, and throughout the next semester emergent teachers used the advice provided by their assigned mentors in one of their pre-service teacher fieldwork placements in a local school, while working with culturally and linguistically diverse students.

After completion of the signature strength exercise, emergent teachers were asked to respond to the second Likert-type survey, the PASSS, which instructed them to reflect on the advice they received from their mentors and provide an evaluation of their experience in the classroom after using their signature strengths in novel ways. The PASSS also provided space for emergent teachers to add comments and explanations to describe their microteaching, producing additional qualitative data.

Results and Interpretations

RQ1: What signature strengths do emergent teachers bring to their classrooms and are they different from the strengths found in groups of differing demographics?

Table 16.1 contains the 24 signature strengths found in the VIA Classification, ranked in the order of most commonly endorsed ('most like me') strengths in the general US population to the least commonly endorsed ('least like me') strengths. Researchers have reported remarkable similarity in the relative endorsement of the 24 character strengths by adults around the world. The most commonly endorsed strengths in 54 countries are kindness, fairness, authenticity, gratitude and open-mindedness; the least prominent strengths were prudence, humility and self-regulation (Park *et al.*, 2006). Because the sample for the present study was drawn from the Midwestern United States, it is important to know that the same ranking of greater versus lesser strengths also characterised all 50 states in the USA – except for spirituality which tends to be somewhat more evident in the South – and held steady even when controlled for gender, age, education and political affiliation.

Table 16.1 shows the rankings of strengths of the emergent teachers, from most frequently to least frequently endorsed. At the top of the list for both the population of VIA test takers and for the present sample are kindness (16 hits), fairness (16 hits) and honesty (nine hits). However, seemingly out of order in the emergent teacher population, are the virtues of love (eight hits) and humour (eight hits), which superseded the more commonly endorsed values of gratitude and judgement found in the general population. The strength of perspective (eight hits) also was unusually well endorsed by the mentees, although we hasten to add that this is a small sample.

More detail on the strengths profile of the participants is provided in Table 16.2, which also identifies which of the three top signature strengths coincided between the mentors and the mentees. For example, in the first pairing, mentee Shelley and mentor Jackie (pseudonyms) were paired because they shared the strengths of creativity, fairness and humour. The second pairing showed mentee Brianna and mentor Ginger sharing humour, love and kindness. The third mentor, Morgan, was matched up with three mentees. Morgan was matched with mentees Helen, Maria and Harriet, all of whom identified spirituality and kindness as top strengths.

RQ2: What is the nature of the advice that experienced teachers offer to less experienced counterparts with similar signature strengths?

The mentors provided a variety of types of advice to the emerging teachers (a detailed list of mentors' advice, organised by its associated VIA

Table 16.1 Frequency with which each of the 24 signature strengths from the Values In Action Classification were cited as being in the top five responses of emergent teachers

VIA signature strengths	Rank in population	No. of emergent teachers endorsing	Rank among emergent teachers
Kindness	1	16	*T-1
Fairness	2	16	T-1
Honesty	3	9	3
Gratitude	4	4	T-12
Judgement	5	5	T-9
Love	6	8	T-4
Humour	7	8	T-4
Curiosity	8	5	T-9
Appreciation of beauty	9	5	T-9
Creativity	10	4	T-12
Perspective	11	8	T-4
Social intelligence	12	2	T-19
Leadership	13	3	T-16
Teamwork	14	1	22
Bravery	15	4	T-12
Love of learning	16	3	T-16
Forgiveness	17	6	T-7
Hope	18	2	T-19
Persistence	19	0	T-23
Spirituality	20	6	T-7
Zest	21	2	T-19
Prudence	22	3	T-16
Humility	23	4	T-12
Self-regulation	24	0	T-23

Note: *T indicates a tied ranking in the present study.

strength, is available from the authors). Table 16.3 shows the categories into which the advice offered by mentors was coded. Categories were generated by reading the text of the advice as one document and extracting six major themes: *specific classroom activities; relationship formation and maintenance; creating a positive classroom (or course) atmosphere; advice for self-care; learn about yourself as a teacher* and *awareness of issues (e.g. cultural differences).* Two independent coders applied the categories to the text of the advice. The initial coding produced just over 77% agreement (47/61) between coders. Seven of the discrepancies between coders pertained to interpretation of 'classroom activity' versus

Table 16.2 Strengths pairings of experienced teacher mentors and emerging teacher mentees

Emergent teachers	Experienced teachers
Shelley	*Jackie*
1. Bravery	**1. Creativity**
2. Creativity	2. Love
3. Fairness	3. Kindness
4. Humour	**4. Fairness**
5. Kindness	**5. Humour**
Brianna	*Ginger*
1. Humour	**1. Humour**
2. Judgement	**2. Love**
3. Love	3. Honesty
4. Kindness	**4. Kindness**
5. Prudence	5. Hope
Helen	*Morgan*
1. Appreciation of beauty	**1. Gratitude**
2. Spirituality	2. Love
3. Kindness	**3. Spirituality**
4. Humility	**4. Kindness**
5. Love	5. Social intelligence
Mary	
1. Spirituality	
2. Zest	
3. Kindness	
4. Gratitude	
5. Creativity	
Harriet	
1. Spirituality	
2. Kindness	
3. Forgiveness	
4. Gratitude	
5. Fairness	

Note: Shared strengths are shown in bold type.

Table 16.3 Type of advice offered by mentors

Frequency of occurrence	Type of advice
29	Specific classroom activities
17	Relationship formation and maintenance
17	Creating a positive classroom (or course) atmosphere
12	Advice for self-care
10	Learn about yourself
9	Awareness of issues (e.g. cultural differences)

'course management'. For example, the mentor's advice, 'When calling on students who raise their hands, choose in a boy/girl pattern' (Fairness), was categorised as a classroom activity by one coder and classroom management by the other. The seven discrepancies were resolved by adding 'atmosphere' to the classroom management category, and reserving the 'classroom activities' category for exercises or activities related to a specific lesson. The rest of the codes were agreed upon by discussion, and multiple codes were applied in specific cases. Results for each category will be described briefly below.

The most frequent mentors' advice pertained to specific classroom activities that could be used by the emerging teachers (the strength associated with the advice is shown in parentheses). Examples include: 'Play games in class that make the students laugh at themselves and each other' (Humour); 'Help students identify things they are grateful for through journals or conversations with others' (Gratitude); and 'Encourage students to do one act of random kindness each week. They can journal or share verbally the experience, their feelings, etc.' (Kindness).

The second most frequently occurring category concerns using strengths in the formation and maintenance of relationships. Specific advice included: 'Ask about the students' weekend, anything fun or interesting that they did' (Humour); 'Be interested in your students as people and how they want to grow in the classroom' (Love); and 'Try to help your students if they need it in their personal lives if you think it's appropriate' (Kindness).

The third category concerns creating a positive classroom atmosphere. Examples of advice in this category include: 'Write the homework on the board at the end of every class and verify that each student has written it down and understands what is expected of them' (Prudence); 'Involve students in decision-making. Use affinity diagrams, voting tools, and other strategies to give students a say in classroom expectations and procedures, as well as consequences. Ask them what they think is fair' (Fairness); and 'Allow, encourage, and build in time for students to display beauty in their work' (Beauty).

The next two categories are more psychologically oriented and concern teacher self-care and learning about one's self as a teacher. An example of teacher self-care is, 'If you find your day gets too full with helping others (i.e. doing unexpected favours), begin to build in time during your day for this. Saying no has its place for sure, but if kindness is a virtue of yours, just be sure to schedule it in. You could plan to leave school 45 minutes after the bell, instead of 30, to allow for some time to help others' (Kindness). A second example of self-care is, 'When you're feeling down, remember your bigger picture. Keep a quote or piece of scripture nearby that reminds you of why you're doing what you're doing' (Spirituality). Additional advice related to learning about one's self as a teacher was captured in suggestions such as: 'Notice how long you speak in conversations with co-workers, administrators, and students. Seek to listen' (Humility); and 'Learn about yourself. When do you have your best boost of energy throughout the day? What energizes you? What brings you down? Are there ways you can change your classroom set up or daily schedule to maximize your zest?' (Zest).

The final category of mentor advice promotes awareness of issues, and given that these are language teachers, often the advice pertained to cultural issues. 'Realize that cultures treat information differently' (Judgement); 'Remind students that the world is very large and there are so many beliefs and opinions!!' (Prudence); and:

> When learning about a new region, culture, or time period, take a virtual field trip. Print out and distribute boarding passes, arrange student chairs in airplane rows, and 'take off' and 'land' using Google Earth. (If you leave from your local airport, you can zoom right in on the plane your class is 'boarding'!) A lot of places around the world will allow you to use the street view, so you can virtually wander down the streets of Mexico City or around the lighthouse on New Zealand's northern tip (Creativity).

After receiving the advice provided by the experienced mentors in one of their practice teaching classroom experiences, the emergent mentees responded to the seven items on the PASSS. Their responses address our third research question and best address the ways in which strengths are perceived and acted upon by the mentees.

RQ3: Do emergent teachers respond positively to the acted-upon advice provided by their mentors? If so, in what ways?

Table 16.4 presents the degree to which the five emergent teacher mentees endorsed PASSS items on a 5-point Likert scale from strongly agreeing to strongly disagreeing. Results demonstrate a high level of positivity from mentees towards the personalised, strengths-based advice they received. In fact, none of the mentees' responses entered the 'disagree' or 'strongly disagree' category. Responses fluctuated between the 'agree' and 'strongly agree' classifications with the exception of Items 6 and 7, wherein 20% and 40% (respectively) stated that they neither agreed nor disagreed to feeling heightened perseverance after using their mentors' advice and having altered the mentors' advice to fit the needs of the class.

Along with the numerical ratings above, the PASSS also provide space for respondents to describe their experiences. These commentaries provided further evidence for the positivity of mentees' experiences. Excerpts from each emergent teacher's commentary are provided to reflect the broader theme in each of their responses to each item.

(1) Satisfaction in relationships

The strongest positivity was evident in the question about relationship satisfaction. Four of the five mentees (80%) strongly agreed that their

Table 16.4 Percentages of emergent teacher mentees' responses to PASSS items

Using my signature strengths in the new ways suggested by my mentor-teacher:

	Strongly disagree	Disagree	Neither	Agree	Strongly agree
(1) Gave me more satisfaction in my relationships with my students	–	–	–	20%	80%*
(2) Strengthened my sense of well-being in my classroom	–	–	–	40%	60%
(3) Enhanced my sense of confidence in my abilities as a teacher	–	–	–	40%	60%
(4) Increased my resilience and buffered me from weaknesses I feel I have as a new teacher	–	–	–	60%	40%
(5) Improved my coping skills in relation to the stresses of the classroom	–	–	–	80%	20%
(6) Heightened my perseverance and ability to accomplish the goals I set for my students and for myself	–	–	20%	60%	20%
(7) I adapted my teacher-mentor's advice to make it a better fit for me	–	–	40%	40%	20%

Notes: *The sample size was five; items above are rank ordered according to strength of endorsement by the mentees.

mentors' advice gave them more satisfaction in their relationships with their students. Mentees commented that:

> (i)t was good to be able to embrace myself and my personality in my teaching. (Brianna)

> I do think after I allowed myself to fully embrace my strengths I have felt more like myself in the class … (Mary)

Both of these responses reflect a developing sense of authenticity as a teacher, which is a key component of the notion of signature strengths, reflecting a sense of being 'the real me' (Seligman, 2002). A sense of authenticity helps buffer job stress felt when teachers try to play a role that is expected of them, or cannot decide among the 'tyranny of the shoulds' they face (see Horney, 1950). Additional responses to this question featured a sense of bonding with students through the use of strengths.

> By implementing my mentor's advice, I felt that I related better to the students in the classroom. (Harriet)

> The lessons that I have felt were the most successful were the ones during which students and I bonded through laughter. (Shelley)

> Knowing [my students'] backgrounds, their interests, and their motivations helped me be a better teacher both relationally and academically. (Helen)

It is interesting that Helen suggests that the relationships with students help her better understand herself; humanistic scholars suggest that understanding oneself is a key to forming harmonious relationships (Oxford, 2016).

(2) Well-being in the classroom

The second most positive responses were obtained from the question that asked whether emergent teachers' sense of well-being was strengthened in their classrooms. In response, two of the respondents reinforced the theme of authenticity:

> I felt more comfortable being myself in the classroom, instead of trying to be like my coordinating teacher. (Brianna)

> Taking the signature strengths test and reflecting on my own virtues has helped me maintain a calm and happy mindset because I know that I possess qualities that will help me continue to develop into an effective educator. (Shelley)

In both cases, a sense of well-being is being justified on the basis of authentic development as a teacher. Along similar lines, Helen felt that 'my mentor teacher's advice reassured me that my strengths will be useful in building relationships'.

One outcome of the procedure used in this study seems to be developing understanding among the mentees of the importance of interpersonal relationships in teaching. In the process of becoming a teacher, social and emotional skills become critically important to the well-being, school performance, satisfaction and psychosocial development of emerging teachers, with effects that spill over into the quality of their professional and personal lives (Karatzias et al., 2002; Natvig et al., 2003; Petrides et al., 2004; Rask et al., 2002). As they develop a synergy between who they are and their technical skills, emergent teachers can benefit from the mentoring of more experienced teachers who can help them find applications of their unique pattern of strengths.

Additionally, in responding to the question of well-being, both Harriet and Mary mentioned specific strengths. Mary said that her mentor's advice made her look at her strengths differently, and used this as a perspective from which to reinterpret activities she was performing.

> I didn't see revising activities as just a task but as a way to show my strength of creativity. (Mary)

> Playing music before school and between classes was one way I could incorporate my appreciation for beauty in the classroom. It helped me feel more comfortable and at home in the classroom and the school in general. (Harriet)

Both Mary's and Harriet's comments show the potential impact of actively considering one's strengths to create new meaning and personal relevance in an activity. Perhaps this is a version of the sort of epiphany that Seligman

(2002) described for a signature strength, specifically in realising the benefit to well-being from novel applications of strengths. Harriet described the role of playing music before and between classes as helping her in various areas of her life – a ripple effect of activating signature strengths in the classroom that expand to school and home life (MacIntyre *et al.*, 2016).

(3) Confidence as a teacher

Emergent teachers' burgeoning confidence was strongly endorsed in the PASSS survey. Three of the five respondents did not provide further elaboration on this item because they said they had said what they wanted about confidence in previous questions. However, Helen described her building sense of confidence:

> Much of her [my mentor's] advice centers around relationships with students and with others because most of my strengths are in the relational realm. It is always intimidating standing in front of a new group of students. By being reassured that relational characteristics are important and can be used to educate students in more than just academic fields, I feel more confident in the fact that I will be able to make a difference in students' lives.

Helen also directly addressed the issue of using the mentor's advice in specific areas of her strengths. She felt 'reassured' that dealing with relationships is relevant to teaching and seems to reinforce her desire to have an impact on students' lives, not just their academic learning. This reassurance can help to sort out some of the conflicting advice emergent teachers might receive (Beijaard *et al.*, 2004). The mentor's advice was taken to extend beyond the classroom, as Mary suggested,

> Being a teacher won't just end at 4 everyday. I want to be the role model my students look up to as they see me working and challenging myself out of the classroom too. Morgan (her mentor) gave great advice for me to even work on bettering myself.

It is instructive to note that this comment came in response to a question about enhancing a sense of confidence in teaching abilities. Mary seems to be understanding the teacher as a role model for students, something that does not end when the school day ends. Mary further suggests that the mentor's advice is bettering her as a person, an idea she connected to her ability to be a teacher.

(4) Resilience

The item on the PASSS that dealt with mentees' resilience also included the notion of buffering them from the weaknesses they might feel as new teachers. In response to this question, all five emergent teachers mentioned a specific strength in conjunction with a piece of advice provided by the mentor that was especially helpful. For example, in responding to advice from her mentor on the importance of planning, Brianna drew upon her strengths of judgement and prudence: 'being aware of my judgment and prudence trains me to understand how important planning needs to be for me.' Strengths such as judgement and prudence can be associated with the teachers' sense of responsibility for students in conjunction with her position as a professional. Teachers make hundreds of judgements per day (Borko & Shavelson, 1990), so prudent judgement might be expected. Other strengths, however, seem less obviously applicable. For example, Shelley mentioned bravery:

> During my initial reflections, I considered how I would use bravery to advocate for my students. My mentor-teacher helped me to expand this idea by giving me ideas for instilling bravery in my students.

This advice seems to capture well the idea of using an emergent teacher's strength in a new way, specifically helping the mentee find ways to help her students find their own bravery. The mentor's advice included learning from brave heroes and applying bravery badges for students. There also was encouragement for the emergent teacher to find her own bravery as a teacher in the school, to '(b)e audacious in your advocacy, stand up for your kids and be fearless when colleagues or parents try to tear them down'.

Within the geographic region in which the study was conducted, spirituality plays a role in daily life for many. The mentors' advice included using spirituality to create a guide, drawing upon a sense of purpose for making decisions and interpreting events. Helen indicated that:

> The spirituality advice helped me to re-center and refocus myself, particularly after a lesson that didn't go as well as I had hoped, or when I felt unsure of my teaching capabilities.

Like spirituality, using the strength of forgiveness was suggested as a means of interpreting events. Harriet's mentor told her to own her mistakes and be the role model of forgiveness for her students. Harriet responded '... her advice gave me room to breathe, knowing that whatever happened, we would be able to learn something from the lesson, both teacher and student'.

Although some of the top strengths of the emergent teachers might not obviously be related to classroom teaching in all contexts (such as bravery or spirituality), the advice of mentors who share those strengths and can help emergent teachers use them in new ways appears to have been well received (see Mitchell *et al.*, 2015).

(5) Coping skills

The item that targeted coping strategies prompted insightful reflection on the part of two mentees. Brianna commented:

> There is no such thing as a perfect classroom, so being aware and accepting that things will happen and finding ways to cope is better than assuming the best always and not knowing what to do with something goes wrong.

Helen also found wisdom in her mentor's advice:

> Under several of my strengths, my mentor reminded me that it is okay to say no to things. As teachers, we carry enough weight that we don't need to, to say yes to everything that is placed in front of us. Oftentimes I can have the mentality that I need to do it all and have it all together. This causes the stress to build and distracts me from caring for the students that I am responsible for. The students in my classroom are my first priority. If I make a mistake, it's okay. Students can follow my example in how to react when mistakes are made.

With Helen's response, we see how multiple strengths can fit into a larger system. She refers to the stress of being expected to 'have it all together' and to agree to all the requests that come her way. Reflecting on her mentor's advice, Helen seems to acknowledge that her personal strengths provide a viable way of prioritising requests and deciding what can and what cannot be done. Both Helen and Brianna acknowledge that teachers will make mistakes and that there is no perfect classroom, but that teachers can and do cope with issues as they arise. For Helen, the act of coping with teaching issues is itself a teaching moment, one that she can use to model reacting to stress for her students.

(6) Perseverance

The item that dealt specifically with perseverance in the accomplishment of goals generated a response that showed professional maturity beyond the emergent teacher's experience. Brianna commented:

> My mentor helped me to enforce the idea that as a student teacher and new teacher, I need to worry about being respected and not being everyone's friend. In my first placement, I tried to make the students like me, and I quickly learned that it was a disaster for my classroom management skills. I was nervous for working with kindergarten because it is an age group I am unfamiliar with, so I put them liking me over me being a respectable teacher in their eyes and it was hard to come back from, so I now know how important it is to stick to my goals of the teacher I envision myself to be.

Kanno and Stuart (2011) described perseverance with teaching leading to a similar transition in a case study of one of their young language teachers, Amy, who was developing a greater outward confidence and authority to help manage student behaviour in the classroom.

(7) Adapting advice

The final question asked about the mentees' work to adapt the mentors' advice. This question generated less reaction than the above questions, and perhaps that is understandable for at least two reasons. First, simply, the mentees did not have a lot of time to work with the mentors' advice. The development of character strengths takes place over an extended period of time. The emergent teachers in the present study had only a few weeks to work with the information and advice from the mentors. The process of finding a teacher's own best practices takes more time than we made available to the mentees in the study. If a similar study were to be conducted in the future, it would be advisable to follow up on the adaptation of mentors' advice over a longer period of time. A second possible reason for little response to this question is that respondents had already offered the comments they wanted to make as part of earlier answers to the survey.

What We Learned about Strengths

The results of this study provide some interesting revelations about strengths as a potential focal point for connecting mentors and mentees. The process of generating advice based on matching of strengths seemed to be effective in targeting key elements of social and emotional intelligence, such as nurturing relationships, empathy, emotion perception, expression, and openness to novel experiences (Goleman, 1995; Mayer, 2000; Mayer et al., 2004; Salovey & Mayer, 1990). As such, even though the participants did not meet their mentors face to face, they were able to connect with each other in meaningful ways, focusing on personal strengths that mentor and mentee had in common in addition to enacting their roles as teachers (see Buchmann, 1986, 1993). The specific advice provided by mentors took aim at strengths and implicated key processes that have been linked to reducing teacher burnout, including finding one's own style within the profession and avoiding the 'tyranny of the shoulds' (Horney, 1950). Results show that this process appears to develop components of psychological capital, including better relationships, confidence and resiliency that the emergent teacher can call upon when needed (Luthans et al., 2007). These soft skills, the human side of being a teacher, are core competencies ultimately linked to conceptualisations of professional responsibility and accountability (Fullan et al., 2015). Falout and Murphey (this volume), in their chapter on job crafting, describe the ways in which language teachers informally create opportunities to make their work more meaningful. It is interesting that none of the teachers in their study mentioned job crafting being influenced by mentors, yet in the present study we see mentors advising emerging teachers on ways to adjust their work to suit their strengths, with positive results. This approach highlights that freedom for job crafting allows the person-in-the-role to capitalise on their configuration of strengths which can enhance positive emotion and energy (Seligman, 2002), as well as increase the meaningfulness of their work and teacher well-being (Wrzesniewski, 2016; Wrzesniewski & Dutton, 2001).

We also learned that strengths themselves are complex and malleable. Mentors offered advice that worked along multiple pathways and often drew upon more than one strength at a time. For example, one mentor suggested: 'Build a culture of forgiveness in your classroom. When you make a mistake, own it and ask for forgiveness. Show your students what to do when they mess up through your model' (Forgiveness). The advice can be coded into three categories. First, there is an element of self-care in owning mistakes and asking for forgiveness. Secondly, there is an element of classroom atmosphere in building a culture of forgiveness among students and their teacher. Finally, there is an element of forming stronger relationships in asking for and modelling forgiveness. These strategies draw upon multiple strengths at the same time. Although the procedure asks for participants to identify and use one specific strength in a new way, those strengths do not exist in isolation from each other; they can be conceptualised as a uniquely configured, dynamic network (see Biswas-Diener et al., 2011). Identifying and using one strength can involve other, related strengths that are implicated in the local situational context; it is a form of dynamic stability (Thelen, 2005), wherein strengths have consistency but they also change over time. Future research on the development of strengths might address their motivational qualities, as described by Seligman (2002), including a yearning to use them, a feeling of authenticity, and invigoration when using the strength. In this way, the development of strengths might be examined as a continuous (rather than a fixed) process, as part of a dynamic, motivational system (Larsen-Freeman, 2015).

Limitations

The level of detail in the advice mentors offered and the descriptions of the emergent teachers' reactions provides encouragement that strengths provide a fruitful way to guide mentorship. However, we must keep in mind the limitations of this research. The design of this study features an individual-level analysis, rather than group-level statistics. This approach allows for an in-depth look at mentoring strengths within the bounds of a specific relationship. The study design does not allow for generalisation, and the transferability of the advice from one context to another would require careful consideration of the individual's configuration of strengths and the teaching context. Yet, the approach of matching mentors and mentees based on strengths seems to be transferable and might be considered over a longer time frame or with multiple cycles of advice and feedback. Given the timespan of the study, it was not possible to evaluate the long-term implementation of the strengths by the emergent teachers. It would be very interesting to follow up this study with an investigation of the teachers' behaviour after a few years in the classroom, to see if the mentors continue to have an impact. The distribution of strengths obtained in the small sample tended to focus on the caring dimension of strengths (McGrath, 2015), and we would expect very different advice to emerge from constellations of strengths that emphasise other dimensions, such as self-control or inquisitiveness. All of our mentors and mentees shared kindness as a strength; none reported learning, leadership or teamwork among their top five strengths. It is not known whether the distribution of strengths among teachers at large so heavily favours aspects of caring, but our data certainly do emphasise character strengths in the relationships between language teachers and their mentors. In an area of pedagogy where culture, communication and self-presentation are central to the teaching process, it is worth asking about the alignment of character strengths between mentor and mentee (Eby *et al.*, 2013; Ensher & Murphy, 1997), a question that also might be applied to the relationships between teachers and students. This may be a productive area for future research in language teaching.

Summary and Conclusion

As chapters in this anthology demonstrate, the psychology of the language teacher is complex and well worth understanding in more depth. In the present study, our focus has been on applying character strengths that teachers have at the beginning of their careers, and the role of mentoring in developing those strengths. Emergent teachers in the present study shared strengths related to kindness, fairness and honesty, the same top three strengths as the general population. When mentors, sharing similar strengths with their mentees, offered advice to new teachers, they suggested specific classroom activities, ways to improve relationships and create positive atmosphere in the classroom, as well as techniques for self-care and learning about one's self as a teacher. The focus of this project has been on the reaction of emergent teachers to the advice provided by experienced mentors with whom they shared signature character strengths. Although the sample was small, mentees consistently reported that the advice they received was helpful. Mentees strongly agreed that mentor advice gave them more satisfying relationships with students and a sense of confidence and well-being in the classroom. Further, they agreed that their resiliency and coping skills increased, and they felt heightened perseverance in pursuit of their goals as a teacher.

Famed Greek writer, Nikos Kazantzakis, has been quoted as saying that, 'True teachers are those who use themselves as bridges over which they invite their students to cross; then, having facilitated their crossing, joyfully collapse, encouraging them to create their own' (Notable-quotes, 2016). The experienced teachers in this study created bridges through their mentorship of their shared-strengths mentees. The emergent teachers, with more questions than answers to their understanding of their growing professional identity, took up the wisdom provided to them and received the benefit of using their signature strengths in new ways. New teachers face conflicting emotions, but through positive strengths-based interventions can confront their fears and revel in their hopes while at the same time becoming reflective practitioners. Jackie's mentorship included a letter to Shelley which she shared with us for this project. In the letter, Jackie wrote: 'Shelley, I hope you find success in applying these values in your classroom. I've found that we're most effective when teaching the things about which we are passionate, so I'm confident that you'll do very well with your lessons. I look forward to hearing stories of both your successes and your struggles, as they combine to make us better at what we do. Best of luck to you!' This is what building bridges to the next generation of positive teachers is all about; this is mentorship.

Note

(1) We use the term 'emergent teacher' throughout our chapter in an attempt to label novice teachers positively, with the connotation that they are growing into their professional selves.

References

Abell, S.K., Dillon, D.R., Hopkins, C.J., McInerney, W.D. and O'Brien, D.G. (1995) 'Somebody to count on': Mentor/intern relationships in a beginning teacher internship program. *Teaching and Teacher Education* 11 (2), 173–188.

Asención Delaney, Y. (2012) Research on mentoring language teachers: Its role in language education. *Foreign Language Annals* 45 (S1), S184–S202.

Beijaard, D., Meijer, P. and Verloop, N. (2004) Reconsidering research on teachers' professional identity. *Teaching and Teacher Education* 20 (2), 107–128.

Biswas-Diener, R., Kashdan, T.B. and Minhas, G. (2011) A dynamic approach to psychological strength development and intervention. *Journal of Positive Psychology* 6 (2), 106–118.

Borko, H. and Shavelson, R.J. (1990) Teacher decision making. In B.F. Jones and L. Idol (eds) *Dimensions of Thinking and Cognitive Instruction* (pp. 311–346). Hillsdale, NJ: Lawrence Erlbaum.

Botvin, G.J., Baker, E., Dusenbury, L., Botvin, E.M. and Diaz, T. (1995) Long-term follow-up results of a randomized drug abuse prevention trial in a white middle-class population. *Journal of the American Medical Association* 273, 1106–1112.

Buchmann, M. (1986) Role over person: Morality and authenticity in teaching. *Teachers College Record* 87 (4), 527–543.

Buchmann, M. (1993) Role over reason: Morality and authenticity in teaching. In M. Buchmann and R.E. Floden (eds) *Detachment and Concern: Conversations on the Philosophy of Teaching and Teacher Education* (pp. 145–157). New York: Teachers College Press.

Bullough, R.V. Jr. (2005) Being and becoming a mentor: School-based teacher educators and teacher educator identity. *Teaching and Teacher Education* 21 (2), 143–155.

Clifton, D.O. and Harter, J.K. (2003) Strengths investment. In K.S. Cameron, J.E. Dutton and R.E. Quinn (eds) *Positive Organizational Scholarship* (pp. 111–121). San Francisco, CA: Berrett-Koehler.

Colby, A. and Damon, W. (1992) *Some Do Care: Contemporary Lives of Moral Commitment.* New York: Free Press.

Eby, L.T., Allen, T.D., Hoffman, B.J., *et al.* (2013) An interdisciplinary meta-analysis of the potential antecedents, correlates, and consequences of protégé perceptions of mentoring. *Psychological Bulletin* 139, 441–476.

Ensher, E.A. and Murphy, S.E. (1997) Effects of race, gender, perceived similarity and contact on mentor relationships. *Journal of Vocational Behavior* 50 (3), 460–481.

Flores, M.A. (2004) *The Early Years of Teaching: Issues of Learning, Development and Change*. Porto: Res-Editore.

Freeman, D. and Johnson, K. (1998) Reconceptualizing the knowledge-base of language teacher education. *TESOL Quarterly* 32 (3), 397–417.

Fullan, M., Rincon-Gallardo, S. and Hargreaves, A. (2015) Professional capital as accountability. *Education Policy Analysis Archives* 23 (15).

Goleman, D. (1995) *Emotional Intelligence*. New York: Bantam Books.

Gregersen, T. and MacIntyre, P.D. (2014) *Capitalizing on Language Learners' Individuality: From Premise to Practice*. Bristol: Multilingual Matters.

Gregersen, T., Hein, K., Talbot, K., Claman, S. and MacIntyre, P.D. (2015) Evaluating activities to create positive outcomes among language learners and teachers. *Studies in Second Language Learning and Teaching* 4 (2), 327–252.

Gregersen, T., MacIntyre, P.D. and Meza, M. (2016) Positive psychology exercises build social capital for language learners: Preliminary evidence. In P.D. MacIntyre, T. Gregersen and S. Mercer (eds) *Positive Psychology in SLA*. Bristol: Multilingual Matters.

Hargreaves, A. (2005) Educational change takes ages: Life, career and generational factors in teachers' emotional responses to educational change. *Teaching and Teacher Education* 21 (8), 967–983.

Hargreaves, A. and Fullan, M. (2012) *Professional Capital: Transforming Teaching in Every School*. New York: Teachers College Press.

He, Y. (2009) Strength-based mentoring in pre-service teacher education: A literature review. *Mentoring & Tutoring: Partnership in Learning* 17 (3), 263–275.

Hobson, A., Ashby, P., Malderez, A. and Tomlinson, P. (2009) Mentoring beginning teachers: What we know and what we don't. *Teacher and Teacher Education* 25 (1), 207–216.

Horney, K. (1950) *Neurosis and Human Growth*. New York: Norton.

Johnson, S., Berg, J. and Donaldson, M. (2005) *Who Stays in Teaching and Why: A Review of the Literature on Teacher Retention*. The Project on the Next Generation of Teachers. Cambridge, MA: Harvard Graduate School of Education.

Jonson, K.F. (2002) *Being an Effective Mentor: How to Help Beginning Teachers Succeed*. Thousand Oaks, CA: Corwin.

Kanno, Y. and Stuart, C. (2011) Learning to become a second language teacher: Identities-in-practice. *The Modern Language Journal* 95 (2), 236–252.

Karatzias, A., Power, K.G., Flemming, J., Lennan, F. and Swanson, V. (2002) The role of demographics, personality variables and school stress on predicting school satisfaction/dissatisfaction: Review of the literature and research findings. *Educational Psychology* 22 (1), 33–50.

Kelchtermans, G. (2005) Teachers' emotions in education reforms: Self-understanding, vulnerable commitment and micropolitical literacy. *Teaching and Teacher Education* 21 (8), 995–1006.

Kelchtermans, G. and Ballet, K. (2002) The micropolitics of teacher induction: A narrative biographical study on teacher socialization. *Teaching and Teacher Education* 18 (1), 105–120.

Larsen-Freeman, D. (2015) Ten lessons from CDST: What is on offer. In Z. Dörnyei, P.D. MacIntyre and A. Henry (eds) *Motivational Dynamics in Language Learning* (pp. 11–19). Bristol: Multilingual Matters.

Leaver, B.L. and Oxford, R. (2001) Mentoring in style: Using style information to enhance mentoring of foreign language teachers. In B. Rifkin (ed.) *Mentoring Foreign Language Teaching Assistants, Lecturers, and Adjunct Faculty* (pp. 55–88). Boston, MA: Heinle & Heinle/American Association of University Supervisors, Coordinators and Directors of Foreign Language Programs.

Lindgren, U. (2005) Experiences of beginning teachers in a school-based mentoring pro-gramme in Sweden. *Educational Studies* 31 (3), 251–263.

Luthans, F., Youssef, C.M. and Avolio, B.J. (2007) *Psychological Capital: Developing the Human Competitive Edge.* Oxford: Oxford University Press.

MacIntyre, P.D. and Mercer, S. (2014) Introducing positive psychology to SLA. *Studies in Second Language Learning and Teaching* 4 (2), 153–172.

MacIntyre, P.D., Gregersen, T. and Mercer, S. (2016) Introduction. In P.D. MacIntyre, T. Gregersen and S. Mercer (eds) *Positive Psychology in SLA* (pp. 1–9). Bristol: Multilingual Matters.

Malderez, A. and Bódoczky, C. (1999) *Mentor Courses: A Resource Book for Trainer-Trainers.* Cambridge: Cambridge University Press.

Malderez, A. and Wedell, M. (2007) *Teaching Teachers: Processes and Practices.* London: Continuum International.

Marable, M. and Raimondi, S. (2007) Teachers' perceptions of what was most (and least) supportive during their first year of teaching. *Mentoring and Tutoring: Partnership in Learning* 15 (1), 25–37.

Mayer, J.D. (2000) Emotion, intelligence, emotional intelligence. In J.P. Forgas (ed.) *The Handbook of Affect and Social Cognition* (pp. 410–431). Mahwah, NJ: Lawrence Erlbaum.

Mayer, J.D., Salovey, P. and Caruso, D.R. (2004) Emotional intelligence: Theory findings and implications. *Psychological Inquiry* 15 (3), 197–215.

McGrath, R.E. (2015) Integrating psychological and cultural perspectives on virtue: The hierarchical structure of character strengths. *Journal of Positive Psychology* 10 (5), 407–424.

Mitchell, M.E., Ebya, L.T. and Ragins, B.R. (2015) My mentor, my self: Antecedents and outcomes of perceived similarity in mentoring relationships. *Journal of Vocational Behavior* 89, 1–9.

Molenaar, P.C.M. and Campbell, C.G. (2009) The new person-specific paradigm in psy-chology. *Psychological Science* 18 (2), 112–117.

Mongrain, M. and Anselmo-Matthews, T. (2012) Do positive psychology exercises work? A replication of Seligman *et al.* (2005). *Journal of Clinical Psychology* 68 (4), 382–389.

Natvig, G.K., Albrektsen, G. and Qvarnstrøm, U. (2003) Associations between psycho-social factors and happiness among school adolescents. *International Journal of Nursing Practice* 9 (3), 166–175.

Nias, J. (1996) Thinking about feeling: The emotions in teaching. *Cambridge Journal of Education* 26 (3), 293–305.

Notable-Quotes (2016) Teaching quotes III: Quotes about teaching. See http://www.notable-quotes.com/t/teaching_quotes_iii.html

Olsen, B. (2010) *Teaching for Success: Developing your Teacher Identity in Today's Classroom.* Boulder, CO: Paradigm.

Oxford, R.L. (2016) Toward a psychology of well-being for language learners: The 'EMPATHICS' vision. In P.D. MacIntyre, T. Gregersen and S. Mercer (eds) *Positive Psychology in SLA* (pp. 10–90). Bristol: Multilingual Matters.

Park, N. (2004) Character strengths and positive youth development. *Annals of the American Academy of Political and Social Science* 591, 40–54.

Park, N. and Peterson, C. (2009) Character strengths: Research and practice. *Journal of College and Character* 10 (4).

Park, N., Peterson, C. and Seligman, M.E.P. (2004) Strengths of character and well-being. *Journal of Social and Clinical Psychology* 23 (5), 603–619.

Park, N., Peterson, C. and Seligman, M.E.P. (2006) Character strengths in fifty-four nations and the fifty US states. *Journal of Positive Psychology* 1 (3), 118–129.

Peterson, C. (2006) *A Primer in Positive Psychology.* Oxford: Oxford University Press.

Peterson, C. and Seligman, M.E.P. (2004) *Character Strengths and Virtues: A Classification and Handbook*. New York: Oxford University Press/Washington, DC: American Psychological Association.

Peterson, C., Park, N. and Seligman, M.E.P. (2006) Strengths of character and recovery. *Journal of Positive Psychology* 1 (1), 17–26.

Petrides, K.V., Frederickson, N. and Furnham, A. (2004) The role of trait emotional intelligence in academic performance and deviant behaviour at school. *Personality and Individual Differences* 36 (2), 277–293.

Pillen, M., Beijaard, D. and den Brok, P. (2013) Tensions in beginning teachers' professional identity development, accompanying feelings and coping strategies. *European Journal of Teacher Education* 36 (3), 240–260.

Rashid, T. (2015) Positive psychotherapy: A strength-based approach. *Journal of Positive Psychology* 10 (1), 25–40.

Rask, K., Ðstedt-Kurki, P., Tarkka, M.T. and Laippala, P. (2002) Relationships among adolescent subjective well-being, health behaviour and school satisfaction. *Journal of School Health* 72 (6), 243–249.

Richards, J.C. (2008) Second language teacher education today. *RELC Journal* 39, 158–177.

Salovey, P. and Mayer, J. (1990) Emotional intelligence. *Imagination, Cognition and Personality* 9 (3), 185–211.

Schön, D. (1983) *The Reflective Practitioner: How Professionals Think in Action*. New York: Basic Books.

Schön, D. (1987) *Educating the Reflective Practitioner*. San Francisco, CA: Jossey-Bass.

Schreiner, L.A., Hulme, E., Hetzel, R. and Lopez, S.J. (2009) Positive psychology on campus. In S.J. Lopez and C.R. Snyder (eds) *The Oxford Handbook of Positive Psychology* (pp. 569–578). Oxford: Oxford University Press.

Seligman, M.E.P. (2002) *Authentic Happiness: Using the New Positive Psychology to Realize your Potential for Lasting Fulfillment*. New York: Free Press.

Seligman, M.E.P., Steen, T.A., Park, N. and Peterson, C. (2005) Positive psychology progress: Empirical validation of interventions. *American Psychologist* 60 (5), 410–421.

Seligman, M.E.P., Rashid, T. and Parks, A. (2006) Positive psychotherapy. *American Psychologist* 61 (8), 774–778.

Sin, N.L. and Lyubomirsky, S. (2009) Enhancing well-being and alleviating depressive symptoms with positive psychology interventions: A practice-friendly meta-analysis. *Journal of Clinical Psychology* 65 (5), 467–487.

Smith, J. (2001) Modeling the social construction of knowledge in ELT teacher education. *ELT Journal* 55 (3), 221–227.

Smith, T.M. and Ingersoll, R.M. (2004) What are the effects of induction and mentoring on beginning teacher turnover? *American Educational Research Journal* 41 (3), 681–714.

Thelen, E. (2005) Dynamic systems theory and the complexity of change. *Psychoanalytic Dialogues* 15 (2), 255–283.

van Fleet, J.K. (1973) *The 22 Biggest Mistakes Managers Make and How to Correct Them*. West Nyack, NY: Parker Publishing.

VIA Institute on Character (2016) *The VIA Survey*. See http://www.viacharacter.org/www/Character-Strengths-Survey (accessed 19 December 2016).

Volkmann, M.J. and Anderson, M.A. (1998) Creating professional identity: Dilemmas and metaphors of a first-year chemistry teacher. *Science Education* 82 (3), 293–310.

Weissberg, R.P. and Greenberg, M.T. (1997) School and community competence-enhancement and prevention programs. In W. Damon (ed.) *Handbook of Child Psychology* (pp. 877–954). New York: Wiley.

Woodworth, R.J., O'Brien-Malone, A., Diamond, M.R. and Schüz, B. (2016) Happy days: Positive psychology interventions effects on affect in an N-of-1 trial. *International Journal of Clinical and Health Psychology* 16 (1), 21–29.

Wright, T. (2010) Second language teacher education: Review on recent research on practice. *Language Teaching* 43 (3), 259–296.

Wrzesniewski, A. (2016) How to build a better job. A. Wrzesniewski interviewed by S. Vedantam. *Hidden Brain: Conversation about Life's Unseen Patterns*. Podcast, 29 March. See http://www.npr.org/2016/03/28/471859161/how-to-build-a-better-job (accessed August 2016).

Wrzesniewski, A. and Dutton, J.E. (2001) Crafting a job: Revisioning employees as active crafters of their work. *Academy of Management Review* 26 (2) 179–201.

17 Psychological Insights from Third-age Teacher Educators: A Narrative, Multiple-case Study

Rebecca L. Oxford, Andrew D. Cohen and
Virginia G. Simmons

Ripeness is all.[1]
William Shakespeare

Older adult language learners, sometimes called lifelong or third-age language learners, have started to gain research attention (De Bot & Makoni, 2005; Gabryś-Barker, 2017; Gabryś-Barker *et al.*, 2016; Martinez, 2012; Thompson, 2016). This chapter also focuses on older adults. Specifically, it takes you on a tour through the land of *third-age teacher educators* (TATEs) in the foreign and second language field. This is likely to represent some of the first research on the topic, as the third-age concept does not seem to have been previously applied to studying teacher educators in our field or, indeed, elsewhere. In this chapter we discuss the third age as a concept, pointing out its strengths and some caveats. Then we present a narrative study of third-agers and come to some important conclusions.

Your Guides to the Third-age Teacher Educator Realm

We are participant-researchers for the study and your guides to the TATE realm. Like other third-agers, we are retirees, who participate actively and purposefully in work and projects, often experience well-being, manage our negative emotions well and feel innovative, creative and productive. However, we have other characteristics that not all third-agers have, such as strong extraversion, experience of living and travelling abroad and opportunities to learn from other cultures.

Rebecca, a newly minted 70-year-old, consults for TESOL projects, teaches adjunct graduate courses, writes, edits two book series and various books and travels globally. Andrew, 72, does much the same (without formal teaching or book series editing), enhanced by extensive interactions with grandchildren. Virginia (Ginny), 74, works full-time in Southeast Asia as a teacher educator, runs an international charitable organisation with Russian partners, travels widely and plans the next big adventure. We are not necessarily typical of language teacher educators of our age; we are probably more 'third-age' than most.

What is the Third Age?

TATE means third-age teacher educators in the language field. The term 'third age' describes relatively healthy 'young-old' people who have gone through the first age of life (education) and the second age (employment) and are now retired, while feeling energy, purpose and well-being.

Some see the third age as a concept, a life phase and a social status of an individual (Carr & Komp, 2011); others view it as a social construction and a cultural field (Gilleard & Higgs, 2011). Barnes (2011) described the third age as a paradox, a point when certain adults experience life and self with greater positivity in terms of identity, self-esteem, emotional stability, emotional regulation and subjective well-being, while some basic cognitive functions slowly decline. Lawrence-Lightfoot (2009) argued that the features of the third chapter (third age), which she outlined as passion, risk-taking and adventure, are available for those older people who perceive abundance, seek meaning and purpose and do not focus on failure. Not every retiree enters the third age or even wants to, although Barnes (2011: 1) called it 'the golden age of adulthood'.

A Few Caveats about the Third Age

Chronological ages presented for the third age vary. Examples are 50–75 (Lawrence-Lightfoot, 2009) or 70–84 (Smith, 2000). Moen (2011) raised concerns about the conceptual sequence of first–second–third ages, because this sequence is very lockstep and age-graded. Despite the caveats, we have found the third-age concept is very appropriate as a general description of this phase of our lives as teacher educators, as our narratives show.

Why is it Important to Understand Third-age Teacher Educators?

We believe that an understanding of TATEs is important for several reasons. First, compared to younger colleagues, TATEs have a longer history in the language field and a more extensive professional perspective. They can help sensitise younger colleagues to the historical and methodological dynamics of the field and to lessons learned from the past. Secondly, Shakespeare opined that 'ripeness is all' (see the epigraph), and TATEs can be 'ripe' in the best sense. 'Ripe' means *sufficiently advanced in preparation or aging; thoroughly matured, as by study or experience; fully developed in mind or body; ready or eager; seasoned, as in ripe judgment* (Free Dictionary, 2016). Thirdly, TATEs serve to influence language teachers, who in turn affect language learners, and thus these teacher educators affect communications around the world. Finally, TATEs have a passion for helping the language field, with or without pay.

Methodology

In this study, our aim was to systematically uncover the main characteristics of TATEs and to relate this new information to existing scientific knowledge about third-age people in general. In the first step, Rebecca, psychologist and applied linguist, created guiding questions (see the Appendix), in response to which we each wrote a narrative of about 15 pages.[2] Her current research interests overlap with many areas our study: personality types, emotions, emotional (affective) self-regulation, motivation, lifespan development, culture and languages. She and Andrew have long theorised and researched learning strategies and styles. He is a specialist in a vast range of linguistic areas, including pragmatics, i.e. the nexus of language and culture, and has taught applied linguistics for decades while learning 13 languages. Ginny specialised in special education, educational leadership and related areas before turning to the teaching of English as a second language and starting her new career overseas in her early seventies.

Working with the complete narratives, we used grounded theory analysis (Corbin & Strauss, 2007; Strauss & Corbin, 1998), in which the themes arose directly from the data and were not pre-established. The first stage of analysis was open coding, during which 46 initial themes arose, including some (e.g. multilevel education and future time perspective) that were not covered by the guiding questions. The second stage, axial coding, involved finding relationships across the 46 themes. This stage resulted in four central themes: (a) emotions and emotion regulation; (b) future time perspective; (c) psychological responses to physical and cognitive changes; and (d) self-concept, self-esteem and achievements. The results below include narrative segments illustrating the four central themes.

Results

Results are presented thematically below. For each theme, we present what the existing research says and then compare this with excerpts from our narratives.

Theme 1. Emotions and emotion regulation

We all try hard to handle our negative emotions well, experience positive emotions and savour good things.

What existing research says about Theme 1

Frederickson (2001, 2003, 2004) cited happiness, curiosity, interest, pleasure and joy as positive emotions. Seligman (2011: 17) added 'ecstasy, comfort, warmth'. Such positive emotions, argued Frederickson, broaden the individual's attention and build innovative thoughts, actions, skills and psychological resources (such as resilience) which are useful for the future. Positive emotions 'trigger upward spirals toward emotional well-being' (Frederickson & Joiner, 2002: 172) and have positive physical consequences (Waugh *et al.*, 2008). *How we relate to this research:* All three of us actively try to experience positive emotions and are aware of their power and importance.

Some psychologists have suggested *savouring*, i.e. noticing and appreciating the positive aspects of life, as a new model of positive experience (Bryant & Veroff, 2007) and as a set of activities for promoting happiness (Lyubomirsky, 2008; Peterson, 2006). Savouring is more than pleasure; it involves 'conscious attention to the experience of pleasure' (Bryant & Veroff, 2007: 5) of self and others. People can experience past savouring (reminiscence), present savouring, or future savouring (anticipation). *How we relate to this research:* We also believe in savouring and try to do it often. We are intrigued by its past, present and future forms, which were new to most of us.

Positive psychologists denigrate 'negative' emotions for narrowing our response options to survival behaviours (Frederickson, 2001, 2003, 2004), rather than broadening our options. When older adults face negative emotions, especially despair, in a productive way, they can attain integrity (Vaillant, 2002). Emotional intelligence and humour, a mature defence mechanism (Peterson, 2006), can help individuals transform negative emotions to a more positive state of mind (Goleman, 2005). *How we relate to this research:* Our narratives mention many emotion regulation strategies, such as Ginny's humour.

What we wrote about Theme 1

Narrative 17.1 Data extracts about positive emotions and savouring

Rebecca: *Talking about psychological factors with my language education colleagues and reading deeply in psychology give me joy. I experience wonder and happiness when my graduate students and I share a literary or artistic moment or when we talk about transformational education. Aside from work, positive emotions come from listening to music, writing poetry and being with my husband and our*

---

dog. I love to watch 'Sherlock' with Benedict Cumberbatch, 'Saturday Night Live,' and the humorously mind-bending British murder mystery series, 'Father Brown.' I love an exquisite film, even if it makes me cry. I dream about future trips (visiting Santorini!), but I truly savour current trips and past trips, like our crazy honeymoon in Siberia.

Andrew: *I tend to be upbeat much of the time. My family and friends bring me great happiness. I also enjoy having physical possessions that make my life more comfortable, like an adjustable bed and a reclining chair (where I sleep the last hour or two of every night). I have a fine step-through bicycle and an upright battery-assisted trike for my cycling. I have a highly functional desktop computer ... I have neat walking sticks for circling the lake. I have an excellent trumpet and guitar. So, my joys are both from being where I am now in my physical and spiritual life, having the accoutrements I have to enjoy this life, and doing things that give me joy. I also read the Marie Kondo (2014) book,* The Life-Changing Magic of Tidying Up, *and have put into practice a lot of her suggestions. For instance, my drawers now have homemade dividers which make it a lot easier for me to find just what I need from a particular drawer. It definitely gives me joy to be well organised.*

In terms of savouring, I enjoy that I can shape each day as I wish rather than having to rush off to teach. I get to pick and choose my instructional interactions carefully. Whereas my one meal with my spouse each day used to be supper, now we often have three meals together, which gives us a lot of visit time which is nurturing. I also prepare a fruit salad every morning with fresh California fruit. I see life lived best as a fruit salad, with lots of different items co-existing in the same bowl. Just as this makes the fruit eating experience more enjoyable, so having lots of variety in life (different people, different events, different languages, different countries and so forth) provides for an enriched experience each day.

Ginny: *I don't know if I am ever content. I always want a 'happening' for tomorrow and a plan for that happening. The planning is as exciting as the happening. Since I make up my mind that I will have a good time at whatever I am doing, most things bring me happiness and joy.*

I have to admit, what brings me the most joy is reflecting on some of the best moments. Best moments with children and grandchildren. Best moments with husband. Best moments with family and friends. Best moments with students. Reflection, yes, reflection. Savouring the past and savouring the planning for the future.

> ### Narrative 17.2 Data extracts about negative emotions and emotion regulation
>
> **Rebecca:** *Sometimes I feel anxious about health. What will happen when I get old? (I don't feel old yet.) Will I always be able to write? Can I still travel worldwide? Will I have much pain? I took heart from my sister-in-law, who wrote a note for my 70th birthday: 'These big numbers [like 70] are scary, but I truly believe that you are only as old as you feel, and the meanings of our ages are not what they were even one generation ago' (Christine S. Oxford, personal communication, 12 December 2016).*
>
> *Many negative emotions, such as tension, anger and sadness, crawled through my veins repeatedly during a lengthy presidential campaign. I often reminded myself of Martin Luther King, Jr.'s statement for us to respond to darkness with light, and to respond to hate with love. If I feel myself slipping into depression for any reason, I consider Mattieu Ricard's (2003) statement that happiness includes acceptance of both painful and pleasant emotions. Ricard makes me appreciate the value of sadness. I need to develop greater self-compassion along the way.*
>
> **Andrew:** *Although I have fear of what the future has in store for me in terms of my health, I mostly do not spend time worrying about it. My wife and I recently finished watching season #12 (2015–16) of* Grey's Anatomy (ABC, 2015), *the medical drama about surgeons in Seattle. This show has opened my eyes to a huge number of medical problems that are lurking out there. I maintain peace of mind by assuming these medical nightmares will not happen to me, at least not any time soon.*
>
> *I have had some short (one-two day) bouts of depression, generated in part I think by the fact that I have MS (multiple sclerosis), which has limited my mobility. A friend who is a psychoanalyst recommended that I read the Williams and Penman (2012) book,* Mindfulness: An Eight-Week Plan for Finding Peace in a Frantic World. *Consequently, I did many of the exercises in the book and found them helpful, especially the one about acknowledging any depressing thoughts and getting that they are just thoughts and nothing more. It worked to move me out of depression. I also seek help to be resilient and make wise decisions. The only major situation was in 1990–91 when the issue was whether to leave Israel over the threat of war with Iraq. I relied on input from my parents, from a first cousin and from a support group that I had been a member of for a decade in Israel. Input from these sources was valuable in the face of a family crisis that could have cost me my marriage. Ultimately, my wife agreed to the move back to the US for the sake of our marriage,*

although she truly wished to continue living in Jerusalem once the Gulf War was over.

Ginny: *I experience moments of fear, mostly about my husband's health or my health. How do I handle my fears? Well, sometimes I talk to others about it; sometimes I just let it pass with time. I can't dwell on it; I have too much to do.*

I might have an occasional depression, but not a deep depression. It is more like 'being down.' I have never taken any types of drugs for this. Most of the time I just get down and wallow around in it. When I can't stand it anymore, I put on my 'big girl panties' and deal with it. I am moody and more like a roller coaster with my ups and downs of emotions.

I also use humour to lighten things up. Here are some of many examples: The secret is to run around with people older than you are, and you will always be young. Also, as long as my mother is alive, my brother and I will always be young, so when she dies we are going to keep her alive with machines – just to preserve our youth.

Theme 2. Future time perspective

Theme 2 focuses on our relationship to the future.

What existing research says about Theme 2

Brothers *et al.* (2014) designed a questionnaire to represent three theoretical dimensions of future time perspective (FTP): future as open, future as limited and future as ambiguous. Compared with other age groups (18–39 and 40–59), older participants (60–93) viewed their futures as less open and more limited. However, when older adults identified *less* strongly with their actual age group (just as we three do while busily creating new possibilities around the world), they tended to score higher on having an open future. *How we relate to this research:* Compared to many older adults, as in the Brothers *et al.* (2014) study, we think of our futures as more open and full of possibilities.

What we wrote about Theme 2

Narrative 17.3 Data extracts about future time perspective

Rebecca: *I do not identify with most other people my age. Compared with most, I feel more full of possibilities for changing myself and the world. I plan to keep creating a legacy of empowerment, peace, love and communication. I am excited about sharing my peace activities*

(Oxford, 2013, 2014, 2017) in South America and the US for use in language education. I am co-editing a book series on transforming education and another on spirituality, religion and education, as well as publishing poetry. The future will be filled with such opportunities. I am grateful and excited.

Andrew: *An interesting question is just what I would like to contribute to the world in the next 10–25 years. For one thing, I will continue to post papers and PowerPoint presentations on the open-access website <https://z.umn.edu/adcohen> that I have maintained for many years – an idea that I got from my dear colleague Bonny Norton. I also have a book chapter that will appear on the topic of how to get published internationally. It will be in a new volume edited by Jim McKinley and Heath Rose, entitled,* Doing Research in Applied Linguistics: Realities, Dilemmas and Solutions *(Cohen, 2017). Part of my payback philosophy is to pass on to others the strategies that I have found valuable in getting published over the years. I also continue to answer as thoughtfully as possible every email inquiry that I receive from colleagues and graduate students regarding issues in applied linguistics research, about which I am considered an expert. I never just hit the delete button.*

Furthermore, I look forward to the eventual publication of my new book now in progress for Multilingual Matters, Learning Pragmatics from Native and Nonnative Teachers. *I realise that I need not be publishing any more books, but my philosophy is to keep publishing them as long as I have something new to say. While my health holds out, I look forward to continuing to give invited plenary talks at conferences around the globe.*

Ginny: *Let's talk about expectations for the future. I guess when I think about the world, I think about 'my' world, the people I meet, the influence on them and how this is passed to future generations. It is similar to the Adams saying about a teacher, 'a teacher affects eternity; he can never tell where his influence stops' (Adams, 1918: 300). I think about the knowledge I have gained and what is worth sharing.*

I want to continue teaching students and training teachers. I want to share my piece of global and cultural understanding with others. I have grown, I have changed and I have become a more complete human being because of my experiences. If others cannot have the same experiences, maybe they can learn something about them through me.

Theme 3. Psychological responses to physical and cognitive changes

We had a lot to say about this very difficult, challenging theme.

What existing research says about Theme 3

Most existing research on this theme was done on older people in general, not just third-agers. Active intellectual involvement, such as that of older university educators, can delay the onset of aging and age-related diseases (Kristjuhan & Taidre, 2010), as can consistent physical activity (Sigelman & Rider, 2012). *How we relate to this research:* Andrew's dedication to exercise will protect and strengthen him. We can be protected from cognitive ravages of aging when we engage in interesting events, meet new people, do research, study languages and immerse ourselves in cultures. When we delve into exciting plots on TV – delightful British murder mysteries or fascinating reruns of medical dramas (see earlier) – we feel our minds growing.

Older adults, not specifically third-agers, have many memory strategies (metamemory) and have less confidence in their memory skills than younger adults (Sigelman & Rider, 2012). *How we relate to this research:* Andrew and Rebecca know a lot about memory strategies because of research and teaching concerning learning strategies. Ginny's memory is very sharp, partly because of her deep interest in meeting and remembering many people and partly due to the university courses she taught. We all feel confident about using our memories. We seem to be unlike other older adults reported in existing research in that regard.

The selection, optimisation and compensation (SOC) framework helps us understand how to deal with cognitive or physical tasks (Sigelman & Rider, 2012). Selection refers to choosing tasks that are most important. Optimisation means doing those tasks building on strengths rather than weaknesses. Compensation means finding alternative ways, if necessary, to accomplish a task. *How we relate to this research:* Rebecca intentionally uses this framework. She started doing so at age five, when she had polio, although she did not know the terminology. For her it has been a mind-over-matter phenomenon and a survival requirement, unlinked to book learning. Now it is becoming useful for managing the rigours of aging.

Many third-agers have turned to the practice of mindfulness to become more centred in the present, thus lowering stress, gaining greater spiritual depth and reducing or preventing physical disease (Kabat-Zinn, 2013; Tolle, 2004). *How we relate to this research:* This is important to us too. Andrew's mention of mindfulness is under Theme 1 in relation to depression, and Rebecca brings up mindfulness in Theme 3 in relation to coping somehow with the physical challenges of aging.

Third-agers, some as early as age 65, encounter ageist stereotypes, such as: old/older people are unattractive, elderly, old, senior citizens, sick, weak, frail, dependent, decrepit, forgetful and incompetent (Mortimer & Moen, 2016; Sigelman & Rider, 2012). These social weapons are even more strongly aimed at fourth-agers[3] than at third-agers. Negative stereotypes, when internalised, become dangerous self-stereotypes and can harm self-esteem and physical health (see Theme 4). Reducing negative stereotypes about aging might reduce and even prevent age-related physical declines (Levy *et al.*, 2009). *How we relate to this research:* We try to avoid negative stereotypes and try not to internalise them. We feel very strongly about this and dislike these stereotypes intensely.

What we wrote about Theme 3

Narrative 17.4 Data extracts about psychological responses to physical and cognitive changes

Rebecca: *I faced death at age 5, when I contracted polio in a California epidemic. I became paralyzed and could not breathe or swallow. I had a metal breathing apparatus in my throat and a feeding tube from my nose to my stomach, and I lived in an oxygen tent. At 70, I wonder what will happen to me. I am experiencing loss of balance and slowness while walking, and I get help in carrying suitcases or driving long distances. It could be post-polio syndrome or something else. On the bright side, with an awareness of physical changes, I tend to focus on tasks that are important to me (especially my research on integrating peace activities into language education and on affective language learning strategies), optimise my efforts by using my strengths, and compensate for difficulties by finding new strategies. I have probably used this meta-strategy sequence for a long time, but I am much more intentional about it now.*

I have become less worried about what other people think about my body's functioning, for example, whether my walking 'looks' too slow or whether I seem graceful in a wheelchair. I love the statement by Victor Hugo that as his body declined, his mind grew and therefore old age brought a blossoming (in de Hennezel, 2008). My mind is as strong as ever. I would like to start using mindfulness techniques like meditation and breathing exercises. I want to become more mindful, thus being more spiritually centred and having less pain and stress.

Andrew: *My wife and I share what is going on with us, in sickness and health. Fortunately, we are mostly healthy, although I did acquire late-onset multiple sclerosis (MS) seven years ago, which has affected my balance. I now use walking sticks to help me keep my*

balance when I walk long distances. I play trumpet and Sabina plays piano, so we do duets together once a week or so. I also play lead trumpet in a community band and play guitar which enables me to lead singing at various family events. I guess it could be considered a gift that my disease came in a late-onset version and that I am in remission and consequently am not taking any medicines other than vitamin D. I am still able to travel to international conferences and to do consulting. Every so often, I am reminded that I have perhaps 20 years more to live and then the quality of those years depends greatly on the care that I take of myself. Hence, I never scrimp and save regarding my workout regime, my diet and my safety. Especially with my late-onset MS, I do everything possible to keep myself as healthy as possible and do my best not to fall.

Ginny: *I mentioned earlier having fears about my husband's health or my health. I think age does that and you realise that you have lost many of your physical attributes. I don't tolerate illness very well. I do not take any types of medicine except a vitamin when I remember it. I believe that if someone is sick, they should be over it in 3 days. Even my children will admit that when they were growing up, they were seldom sick because it just wasn't allowed in our family. Ten years ago my husband had an aortic dissection and it was probably the most tolerant I have ever been with illness. I can't focus on these fears.*

Theme 4. Self-concept, self-esteem and achievements

We believe age does not set any limit on our passion for our work, twist our self-concept or depress our self-esteem.

What existing research says about Theme 4

Self-concept. 'Self-concept is a complex construct consisting of different dimensions or selves, namely physical, social, familial, personal, academic, and many other situational ones' (Rubio, 2014: 43). Self-portraits define an individual's self-schemas, and a collection of self-schemas comprises that individual's overall self-concept. *How we relate to this research:* Self-schemas that pertain to all three of us might include 'I am intelligent, a world traveller, a family member, an artistic person.' Two of us overtly mention spiritual or religious aspects of our self-concepts.

Self-esteem. Self-esteem is the evaluative aspect of the self-concept, rated on a person's own high–low scale. Sigelman and Rider (2012) gave evidence that ageist stereotypes, when internalised, can be detrimental to self-esteem. Levy (2003) found that activating *positive* stereotypes of aging can boost cognitive task performance. *How we relate to this research:* Just hearing someone say an ageist stereotype can stimulate negative emotions. It can push our buttons, even if we do not internalise the statement. Therefore, we actively try to ignore all negative stereotypes (see Theme 3). We have rarely heard a positive stereotype of aging in our country, although some of us have heard such things in the Far East or Southeast Asia, suggesting a role for attending to cultural differences in aging studies and the well-being of TATEs.

What we wrote about Theme 4

Narrative 17.5 Data extracts about self-concept and self-esteem

Rebecca: *My self-concept has often included being a scholar and a language person. So far I have written, edited, or co-edited 14 books; published 250+ articles, chapters and book reviews; and edited or co-edited eight journal special issues. At 70, I travel the world, write books, and teach and it is a rich life.*

I see myself as a naturally gifted teacher and have won many teaching awards, as well as a lifetime achievement award (received when I was only in my 40s!) for research. I am a good mentor and my protégés give more to me than I can ever give to them. One TESOL student, Young, named her first baby after me in 1990. A current TESOL student asked her mother to send me a special necklace from Turkey; another, an American, often gives me little toys and sends special artwork and quirky stories. I hear from former students on Facebook all the time. These relationships with students are better than diamonds and gold. I feel covered with wave after wave of love, a great ocean of it. My career (most of the time, anyway) shined and sparkled. It even danced and did cartwheels. I was in charge but not really in charge; the universe was clearly intervening in my favour. Things were going so well for so long that I could not take full credit for it all, despite my philosophical allegiance to autonomy, agency and strategies. I was overjoyed to help students become better teachers and do excellent doctoral research. My books kept selling and I was continually promoted until I did not want to be promoted anymore. (My desire for further promotion waned after I had been Associate Dean of a 3000-student college for several years.) Despite the seeming glories of my career life, my personal life was often in some degree of chaos until I met my husband Clifford when I was 54. He had spent many years in Africa (he was also a cultural nomad) and had teaching experience. He was charming, sweet, spiritually inclined, intelligent and a good dancer. It was kismet. When we married, a newfound happiness visited our home and stayed. Cliff went to work teaching math to ESL students until retiring in 2006. I retired from the University of Maryland in 2008 so that we could move to Alabama to take care of my mother, who is now 93.

I see myself as a poet and to some degree a visual artist. I am happy that my poems and photographs are being published in journals and books. The cover of my next book bears one of my photographs, taken on a lake in Nepal. I am encouraged by the famous American folk artist Grandma Moses, who started painting at age 78 and did not stop until she died at 101. If she could do these artistic things, then I can, too. I want to be what I call an 'artist of life' in a broad sense (Oxford, 2013).

I am a devoted traveller. What about the physical dimension of my traveller self-concept and the level of self-esteem related to it? Now that I am older I experience greater stiffness, weakness, pain and awkwardness than many other people when travelling. Because of long distances, I have opted for wheelchairs in airports. I take pride that with sheer inner will, passion and hope I survived as a child and I rejoice with anything my body can do, but I admit that I have a sense of low self-esteem about physical weakness now.

Positive stereotypes of aging are the exception rather than the rule. Perhaps the rise of sexy, intelligent television journalists like Wolf Blitzer and Tom Brokaw and actors like Isabelle Hubbert, Robert Redford, Jane Fonda and Meryl Streep will change negative attitudes. I am concerned that older men are accepted as attractive, while most older women, quite unlike Isabelle, Jane and Meryl, are not. There is still a lot of prejudice toward older women in our society. I feel it.

Andrew's narrative includes: his education at Harvard and Stanford; many colourful events; descriptions of the role-modelling of his talented parents, including his mother, who dreamt of being on the Supreme Court; lists of numerous well-known colleagues and specific accomplishments in teaching, research and publication; portrayals of wide travels; and family responses to historical situations, such as the looming threats of violence from Saddam Hussein. His story reflects a range of self-concept portraits (e.g. in learning, teaching, researching, playing music and squash, trying to get Arabs to join his Education Network in Israel, returning in the nick of time to the US, travelling to far-flung sabbatical locations). It also displays a strong combination of competence and worthiness, reflecting highly positive self-esteem. Unfortunately, there is no room for the whole story here, so we will reduce the comments and present only certain illustrative scenes.

Andrew: *My zeal to have Mexican-American children be proud of their language and cultural heritage got me in touch with my hypocrisy since I couldn't speak my language of heritage, Hebrew, and wasn't conversant in Jewish culture. So when my wife wanted to live in Israel, I agreed. So in 1975 we left Los Angeles for Israel and a professorial position in language education at the Hebrew University. The experience bolstered my self-concept since I learned my heritage language and experienced the meaning of being a secular Jew in Israel. I taught there for 17 years – in Hebrew after the first year. I developed Arabic language skills at a language centre where I also gave talks to Hebrew and Arabic learners on strategies for successful learning.*

In 1990, when Saddam Hussein invaded Kuwait, it scared my child-of-Holocaust-survivor spouse so much that she fled Israel with our son and went to live temporarily with her brother's family in the US. Consequently, I accepted a position at the University of Minnesota, where I was to be a faculty member in Second Language Studies for 22 years, until my retirement in 2013. During that period, I received two awards which boosted my self-concept. The first was to receive the Scholar of the College award for 2002–2005 from the College of Liberal Arts. This coveted award is given to just three faculty members each year. The second was the Distinguished Scholarship and Service Award for 2006 from the American Association for Applied Linguistics.

In retirement, I continue to give talks at conferences around the world; write articles, chapters and books; review journal articles and book proposals; and respond regularly to queries from graduate students and colleagues. I also study Mandarin (my 13th language, now in my fifth year). It supports my self-esteem to continue professional activities. Where does the motivation come from to continue to do this? I continue to have a fascination for the field of applied linguistics and research in the field and it pleases me to receive acknowledgements from my colleagues for my academic contributions. In fact, I have written or edited 17 books, over 220 articles or chapters and various online courses and manuals. I have presented my research in 33 countries located on six of the seven continents of the world (North America, South America, Europe, Asia, Oceania and Africa), and have lived in five of these continents, in some cases, like South America and Europe, for anywhere from one to sixteen years.

Where does such a high level of energy and motivation come from that sets me apart from some, if not many, applied linguists? What aspects of my personality or background (aside from my parents and my education) help to explain my achievements? Back in 1975, I took a personal growth course and then subsequent courses and seminars. This personal growth work made me careful about my commitments in life. As an outgrowth of the program, I resumed my trumpeting and competitive squash, which I had given up out of a perceived lack of time. I also chose research studies more carefully, created a time-management system, which ensured time for academic writing as well as a rich non-academic life (family time, hobbies and physical exercise).

To keep my late-onset MS under control, I work out at my local YMCA every other day and walk around a 3.5-mile lake once a week. I practice my trumpet and play in a community band, interact regularly with our two local grandsons and participate actively in a men's book club I created. My wife and I also created a film club with seven couples. This and various other activities are the outgrowth of our participation in a local synagogue. All these wonderful activities contribute to my self-esteem.

One of the nice things about being retired, and also a reason why my professional writing takes place at a more relaxed pace than in the past, is that I have family duties that I take seriously, mostly involving our five grandchildren in Florida and California. It gives me pleasure to play the guitar or trumpet for the grandchildren, to take them to a children's theme park or play centre, or to make up stories that amuse them, such as a continuing one about hapless George who keeps getting fired from every new job. Also, I love to engage them in meaningful discussions about topics such as eclipses and language learning.

By joining a reform temple in Oakland, CA, my wife and I have greatly expanded our social networks. We are part of a regular group of perhaps 50 congregants who conduct a lay-led service once a month at the synagogue. I formed a men's book club, we have formed a film club, we joined a friendship club, I play trumpet in a local band and we participate in other networks as well. By returning to Northern California, we are back in regular contact with a married couple that we used to hang out with in our graduate student years. This brings me joy. My wife is my major sounding board and we always have long, involved conversations whenever needed.

Ginny's response concerns her self-perception as a fine teacher, her experiences in educational administration at district and state levels, her Russian connections, her managerial skills in creating a Russia–West Virginia (WV) organisation and the constant expansion of that organisation over 77 trips to Russia.

Ginny: *When it comes to DOING something, I just study it and then decide to do it. I don't think about 'me' at this time. Since I never give up, the task is always completed. It is never the thought, 'I can do it' it is only 'I will do it.' When I decided I wanted to become an English language teacher and travel overseas, one of my friends told me it was hopeless. I was too old and she had friends that had tried and were always eliminated because of their age. The thought went through my head, 'I will get a job and do what I want to do. Your friend didn't try hard enough.' I did <u>not</u> think, 'I am a great teacher and will be able to do better than your friend.' My thought process included trying hard and succeeding.*

Teaching is a great art and teaching skills must be learned and perfected through a continuum of change. I believe that I am a great teacher and teacher trainer because of my willingness to learn and change. Acquisition of these skills and knowledge demands a commitment. The commitment demands an inner strength gained from a strong self-esteem.

In addition to having a family, I taught elementary education, special education (learning disability, gifted and all other types), adult basic education and technology across two states. I was married when I received my BSc, had small children during the work on each Master's Degree and was 40+ when I left home with two children and relocated in another state to receive my doctorate. Each success in being a change agent bred more success. Each success increased my self-confidence in my ability and intuition, heightened my self-esteem and enriched my self-concept. I was fortunate to be a part of many educational programs and as a leader, I was able to analyse and synthesise information and create a change in focus for the future.

I retired in 2014 and left with my husband and grandson to teach in Kazan, Russia. My relationship with Russia actually began many years ago and it changed my life, resulting in 77 trips to that country to date. Glasnost opened the door for travel and a West Virginia (WV) 'teacher in space' finalist led a group to Russia. On her return, she asked me to talk to a group of Russians about gifted education, because under Communism they could not have such a programme. It was an astounding interaction. Driving home, I decided that if the Russians wanted to see gifted education in action, I would organise it. I asked the Governor's permission to invite two Russian students and a Russian educator to come to a summer honours academy in West Virginia. That summer the snowball began rolling.

We organised the first trip of official representatives to Russia for the end of December 1992. I was 50 years old, well educated and had achieved a respectable lifestyle but had rarely travelled internationally. As a representative of the WV Department of Education, I organised the trip for 25. During this first trip, we created, a 501c3 [charitable] organisation that focused on creating global understanding in the areas of education, community, culture and business. This organisation is still very active and I have remained President since its inception. During this development, I never said, 'Can I do this?' The statement was, 'It needs to be done.' Never was the focus on me or my abilities; the focus was on achievement – outside of me.

In 2015 I returned from Russia and left for Battambang, Cambodia, where I teach as an English Language Fellow funded by the US Department of State. I don't like it, I LOVE it. Living in Battambang, Cambodia is like growing up in Boomer Bottom, but the people speak Khmer instead of English. It is safe, it is friendly and it is an easy, relaxed and simple lifestyle. It is amazing that since we have moved here we have no experience of 'culture shock' even though the living conditions are quite different than what we just left. I believe that growing up in Boomer Bottom, living on teachers' salaries for much of our lives and generally living from pay check to pay check has taught me to be resourceful, adaptable, creative and flexible. I had read about a better life, exotic adventures and luxury and I wanted them. I could not always buy them, so I created them. I learned to work extra for extra money; I learned crafts and skills to help any endeavour. These creative and adaptable skills produced success that then allowed me to go a little further with the next level. Living in Cambodia, I remember how we lived and what we did. It is not really like stepping back in time; it is a refresher course and reminds me of the things that have made me the person of strength that I have become, a person who is self-confident and very self-aware.

Synthesis

Theme 1. Emotions and emotion regulation

Emotions powerfully influence us, but, at this age, we seem to have excellent emotion regulation strategies. Our strategies for sustaining positive emotions and managing negative ones include: seeking and expressing beauty, intentionally looking for meaning, using mindfulness and savouring.

Theme 2. Future time perspective

Unlike some other older people, we see the future as open and offering abundant opportunities, and this attitude brings such opportunities towards us.

Theme 3. Psychological responses to physical and cognitive changes

Cognitive declines have not occurred, but physical changes are happening: Andrew's late-onset MS, Rebecca's imbalance and weakness and Ginny's husband's health issues. Andrew uses mindfulness practice and long walks, Rebecca physically compensates and Ginny rejects illness outright. We accept physical change, overtly challenge ageist physical stereotypes and stay productive and connected with others.

Theme 4. Self-concept, self-esteem and achievements

This theme emphasised our rich self-concepts as teacher educators, public speakers, administrators, writers, spouses, family members and so on – fertile ground for high self-esteem and achievement. However, self-esteem is not equally high in all areas for each person. We thoroughly reject negative ageist stereotyping and self-stereotyping. It would be wonderful to encounter more positive stereotypes of aging as we hope we might inspire.

Conclusions

In this study we used narratives to analyse ourselves as TATEs in the language field. Our narratives showed that we: have good emotional regulation much of the time; have very strong FTPs and are open to new, fluid possibilities (unlike many of our age, reportedly); notice our physical changes but address them in diverse ways among the three of us; do not think about cognitive changes; and deny ageist stereotypes that might get in the way of our self-esteem. We are fierce with excitement and energy. This chapter has discussed our metaphorical 'ripeness' in relation to our narratives, which are contextualised by prior research and organised by the four emergent themes. We view our life stage not as a ragged shuffling towards death but instead as a phase of great vibrancy, emotional richness and increasing wisdom, even though we experience some physical signs of aging.

Due to our natural self-awareness, further stimulated by participation in this intensive study, we might not be typical of people our age, or even of other TATEs. Our self-awareness and our study participation have allowed us to explain ourselves cogently, we hope. We believe that our thoughts about the four themes might well enlighten others who are interested in third-agers or specifically in TATEs. We each bring our own perspectives and individual personalities, as well as a shared compassion, and we want to contribute to a greater understanding of TATEs and third-agers.

We feel the population of third-age teachers and teacher educators have important contributions to make and are worthy of a larger body of research. We invite others to collaborate with us in conducting further research on TATEs (and also on older language teachers). Mutual understanding of older and younger professionals in our field will contribute to a culture of greater acceptance and appreciation that has ramifications for language teacher education as well as for language teaching and learning.

We three, the participant-researchers in this study, will keep contributing our ripeness – our wisdom, knowledge, ideas, experience and sincerity in language teacher education and other areas – to all who can benefit, within the boundaries of our time and energy. As we continue our lives, work and interpersonal relationships, we can become a little more 'ripe' and a bit more focused, more loving and more giving. 'To every thing there is a season, and a time to every purpose under heaven' (King James Bible Online, 2016: Ecclesiastes 3:1), and we cherish this season of ripeness.

Appendix: A Selection of Our Guiding Questions

How old are you now? Where were you born, and where did you live while growing up? What was the short history of your family of origin? What have been some features of your marriage? What is the greatest achievement in your personal life so far, and why?

What have been the main elements and achievements of your career to date? What are you doing now in your post-retirement work and family life? What makes you keep going in your career when you no longer have to do so?

What do you make of this immense outpouring of energy, activity and motivation? Is it typical in the education or language field? Do you have a lot of friends or colleagues who are like yourself in energy, activity and motivation? Have you ever been called a 'superman' or 'superwoman'? Where do the energy and motivation come from, and what aspects of your personality or background help to explain this phenomenon?

You seem to be a person with autonomy, which consists of having the capability to take responsibility for your life, being willing to do so, and taking action in that direction. Could you share an example of your current-day autonomy? Does your autonomy relate to your self-esteem and, if so, how? How would you describe yourself [self-concept], and how do you see your self-esteem? While you are in this stage of your life, do you experience socio-emotional selectivity? [Note: Results for this last question were not reported here due to complexity.]

What do you think about the concept of the 'third age' that is sweeping Europe, Australia and elsewhere? You have formally retired and are over 50, but you keep on working in various ways. Does the 'third age' concept seem meaningful to your life? Are you currently involved or have you previously been involved in any older-adult learning opportunities or organisations, and if so, what was it like? Are you teaching or have you previously taught in any older-adult learning organisations, and if so, what was it like? Would you ever do so?

What brings you joy, contentment or happiness? Do you ever experience fear when thinking about the future? If so, what is this fear about, and how do you handle it? Do you ever experience depression? If so, is your depression situational, genetic or both? How do you handle it? Please describe a recent situation in which you have been resilient when facing difficulties or adversity. What personal (e.g. personality, intelligence) or social (e.g. family, friends, situation) 'protective factors' helped you be resilient and why?

You have been quite a traveller. In the past, where have you travelled and when? What countries were the most meaningful to you? Are you travelling or living overseas now, and if so, how do you like it and why? Where do you hope to go next? Do you hope or expect that your spouse or family will go with you?

How do other people view you and your current professional and charitable contributions? Do you have a lot of friends, colleagues or family members who are like yourself in energy, activity and motivation?

What do you hope to give to the world in the next 10–25 years? How has your realisation of the limited amount of time remaining (unfortunately, we all have a circumscribed number of decades left) affected your aspirations?

Note to the reader

You are very welcome to use or adapt these guiding questions for research purposes. If you conduct research on third-age teacher educators, Rebecca L. Oxford (rebeccaoxford@gmail.com) would appreciate hearing from you about your guiding questions, research design, results and implications. Internationally sharing and compiling future research on third-age teacher educators is a good idea, we believe. It is valuable for researchers interested in third-age teacher educators and third-age language learners to actively share information with one another.

Notes

(1) About the epigraph: it is from Shakespeare, W. (1914), *King Lear*, Act V, Scene 2, lines 13–15. Oxford: Oxford Shakespeare. It was written in 1605 or 1606. 'Ripeness Is All' was once the main title of our chapter. Interestingly, long after we wrote the chapter, Rebecca discovered that George Vaillant's (2002) book, *Aging Well*, contains a chapter entitled 'Ripeness Is All: Social and Emotional Maturation'.
(2) Rebecca's own narrative is more research-tinged (certainly not research-based, as it remains very personal), reflecting nearly 40 years of teaching and researching in teacher education and psychology (e.g. developmental, educational, positive, existential and abnormal psychology). In psychology the term *abnormal*, despite its pejorative sound, is still (unfortunately) used to refer to 'different from the norm'.
(3) The Berlin Aging Study identified the fourth age as age 85–100+ (Smith, 2000), although age parameters of the fourth age are usually left vague.

References

ABC (American Broadcasting Company) (2015) *Grey's Anatomy, Season 12*. See http://abc. go.com/shows/greys-anatomy/episode-guide/season-12 (accessed 13 November 2016).

Adams, H. (1918) *The Education of Henry Adams: A Biography*. Boston, MA: Massachusetts Historical Society.

Barnes, S. (2011) Third age: Golden years of adulthood. San Diego State University Interwork Institute, San Diego, CA. See http://calbooming.sdsu.edu/documents/ TheThirdAge.pdf.

Brothers, A., Chiu, H. and Diehl, M. (2014) Measuring future time perspective across adulthood: Development and evaluation of a brief multidimensional questionnaire. *Gerontologist* 54 (6), 1075–1088.

Bryant, F. and Veroff, J. (2007) *Savoring: A New Model of Positive Experience*. Mahwah, NJ: Lawrence Erlbaum.

Carr, D.C. and Komp, K. (2011) *Gerontology in the Era of the Third Age: Implications and Next Steps*. New York: Springer.

Cohen, A.D. (2016) Andrew D. Cohen website. See https://z.umn.edu/adcohen (accessed 12 November 2016).

Cohen, A.D. (2017) Afterword: Strategies for getting the study published. In J. McKinley and H. Rose (eds) *Doing Research in Applied Linguistics: Realities, Dilemmas and Solutions* (pp. 253–257). Abingdon and New York: Routledge.

Corbin, J. and Strauss, A. (2007) *Basics of Qualitative Research* (3rd edn). Thousand Oaks, CA: Sage.

De Bot, K. and Makoni, S. (2005) *Language and Aging in Multilingual Contexts*. Clevedon: Multilingual Matters.

de Hennezel, M. (2008) *The Warmth of the Heart Prevents Your Body from Rusting: A French Guide for a Long Life, Well-Lived*. New York: Penguin.

Frederickson, B.L. (2001) The role of positive emotions in positive psychology: The broaden-and-build theory of positive emotions. *American Psychologist* 56 (3), 218–226.

Frederickson, B.L. (2003) The value of positive emotions: The emerging science of positive psychology looks into why it's good to feel good. *American Scientist* 91 (4), 330–335.

Frederickson, B.L. (2004) The broaden-and-build theory of positive emotions. *Philosophical Transactions of the Royal Society of London (Biological Sciences)* 359, 1367–1377.

Frederickson, B.L. and Joiner, T. (2002) Positive emotions trigger upward spirals toward emotional well-being. *Psychological Science* 13 (2), 172–175.

Free Dictionary (2016) Ripe. See http://www.thefreedictionary.com/ripe (accessed 8 July 2016).

Gabryś-Barker, D. (ed.) (2017) *Life-long Learning: The Age Factor in Second/Foreign Language Acquisition and Learning*. Bristol: Multilingual Matters.

Gabryś-Barker, D., Wojtaszek, A. and Gałajda, D. (organisers) (2016) *International Conference on Foreign/Second Language Acquisition. Theme: Life-Long Learning: The Age Factor in Second/Foreign Language Acquisition and Learning*. Szczyrk, Poland, 19–21 May.

Gilleard, C. and Higgs, P. (2011) The third age as a cultural field. In D.C. Carr and K. Komp (eds) *Gerontology in the Era of the Third Age: Implications and Next Steps* (pp. 33–50). New York: Springer.

Goleman, D. (2005) *Emotional Intelligence: Why It Can Matter More Than IQ* (2nd edn). New York: Bantam Books.

Kabat-Zinn, J. (2013) *Full Catastrophe Living: Using the Wisdom of Your Body and Mind to Face Stress, Pain, and Illness*. New York: Bantam Dell.

King James Bible Online (2016) Ecclesiastes 3:1. See http://www.kingjamesbibleonline. org/Ecclesiastes-3-1/.

Kondo, M. (2014) *The Life-Changing Magic of Tidying Up: The Japanese Art of Decluttering and Organizing.* Berkeley, CA: Ten Speed Press.

Kristjuhan, Ü. and Taidre, E. (2010) Postponed aging in university teachers. *Rejuvenation Research* 13 (2–3), 353–355.

Lawrence-Lightfoot, S. (2009) *The Third Chapter: Passion, Risk, and Adventure in the 25 Years after 50.* New York: Farrar, Straus & Giroux.

Levy, B.R. (2003) Mind matters: Cognitive and physical effects of aging self-stereotypes. *Journal of Gerontology: Psychological Sciences and Social Sciences* 58 (4), 203–211.

Levy, B.R., Zonderman, A.B., Slade, M.D. and Ferrucci, L. (2009) Age stereotypes held earlier in life predict cardiovascular events in later life. *Psychological Science* 20 (3), 296–298.

Lyubomirsky, S. (2008) *The How of Happiness: A New Approach to Getting the Life You Want.* New York: Penguin.

Martinez, E. (2012) A focus on specific learning and teaching methods for older adult foreign language learners. *International Journal of Aging and Society 2 (4),* 103–111.

Moen, P. (2011) A life-course approach to the third age. In D.C. Carr and K. Komp (eds) *Gerontology in the Era of the Third Age: Implications and Next Steps* (pp. 13–32). New York: Springer.

Mortimer, J.T. and Moen, P. (2016) The changing social construction of age and the life course: Precarious identity and enactment of 'early' and 'encore' stages of adulthood. In M.J. Shanahan, J.T. Mortimer and M.K. Johnson (eds) *Handbook of the Life Course, Vol. 2* (pp. 111–130). New York: Springer.

Oxford, R.L. (2013) *The Language of Peace: Communicating to Create Harmony.* Charlotte, NC: Information Age.

Oxford, R.L. (ed.) (2014) *Understanding Peace Cultures.* Charlotte, NC: Information Age.

Oxford, R. (2017) Peace through understanding: Peace activities as innovations in language teacher education. In T. Gregersen and P.D. MacIntyre (eds) *Exploring Innovations in Language Teacher Education: Transformational Theory and Practice.* New York: Springer.

Peterson, C. (2006) *A Primer in Positive Psychology.* New York: Oxford University Press.

Ricard, M. (2003) *Happiness: A Guide to Developing Life's Most Important Skill* (trans. J. Browner). New York: Little, Brown.

Rubio, F.D. (2014) Self-esteem and self-concept in foreign language learning. In S. Mercer and M. Williams (eds) *Multiple Perspectives on the Self in SLA* (pp. 41–58). Bristol: Multilingual Matters.

Seligman, M.E.P. (2011) *Flourish: A Visionary New Understanding of Happiness and Well-being.* New York: Atria/Simon & Schuster.

Shakespeare, W. (1914) *King Lear.* Oxford: Oxford Shakespeare.

Sigelman, C.K. and Rider, E.A. (2012) *Life-span Human Development.* Belmont, CA: Wadsworth.

Smith, J. (2000) The Fourth Age: A period of psychological mortality? Max Planck Institute for Human Development, Berlin. See http://www.demogr.mpg.de/Papers/workshops/010730_paper01.pdf.

Strauss, A. and Corbin, J. (1998) *Basics of Qualitative Research: Techniques and Procedures for Developing Grounded Theory* (2nd edn). Thousand Oaks, CA: Sage.

Thompson, C. (2016) *Losing my Voice and Finding Another.* Frankfurt am Main: Brandes & Apsel Verlag.

Tolle, E. (2004) *The Power of Now: A Guide to Spiritual Enlightenment.* Novato, CA: New World Library.

Vaillant, G. (2002) *Aging Well: Surprising Guideposts to a Happier Life from the Landmark Harvard Study of Adult Development.* New York: Little, Brown.

Waugh, C.E., Tugade, M.M. and Fredrickson, B.L. (2008) *Psychophysiology of stress and resilience.* In B. Lukey and V. Tepe (eds) *Biobehavioral Resilience to Stress* (pp. 117–138). Boca Raton, FL: CRC Press.

Williams, M. and Penman, D. (2012) *Mindfulness: An Eight-Week Plan for Finding Peace in a Frantic World.* New York: Rodale.

18 Exploring Language Teacher Psychology: A Case Study from a Holistic Perspective

Mehvish Saleem

In language learning psychology research the focus has primarily been on the psychology of the language learner. However, a stakeholder that has been somewhat neglected and is pivotal to explore is the teacher. Indeed, Mercer *et al.* (2016: 215) argue that 'teacher psychology is equally if not more important than learner psychology', and some recent publications (e.g. Hiver & Dörnyei, 2017; Kubanyiova, 2012) as well as this book also demonstrate that a teacher-centred approach within the field of 'psychology of language learning' merits further attention. A gap in our understanding of language teacher psychology (LTP) concerns a preference for investigating psychological constructs as isolated and decontextualised entities. However, researchers have recently advocated more holistic and situated approaches into psychologies generally (Barcelos, 2015; Mercer, 2014). The study reported in this chapter aims to exemplify how an integrated view might generate helpful insights into LTP.

Research on Language Teacher Psychology

Despite the fact that some areas of LTP have been widely examined, work on other aspects still remains relatively in its infancy. Some of the well-established domains of enquiry in teacher psychology in SLA include cognitions and identity. Various constructs have been examined in these areas, a comprehensive overview of which can be seen in Borg (2006) and Cheung *et al.* (2015), respectively (see also Mercer & Kostoulas, this volume). However, as Mercer *et al.* (2016) argue, apart from these notable exceptions, empirical work on LTP is on the whole considerably less developed and has some clear gaps when compared to research on learner psychology. Within psychological research in SLA it is being increasingly recognised that earlier conceptualisations of individuals' psychology may have been rather oversimplified (Dörnyei, 2010). Earlier studies have tended to break down psychological processes into their constituent components and discretely examine specific variables, such as self-efficacy, beliefs and emotions, etc., with a view to studying their impact on teaching (Chacón, 2005; Mousavi, 2007). While this line of research has advanced our knowledge in respect of specific factors in SLA and the kind of outcomes they may lead to, a key limitation of such a view is that it obscures the relationships among diverse psychological processes and tells us little about how psychological components interrelate. Indeed, Carter and Sealey (2000: 11) argue that 'reducing each to merely a manifestation of the other (...) necessarily results in a theory which is unable to capture the complex relations between them'. Mercer *et al.* (2012) also point out that such discrete treatment of psychological constructs contributes towards a fragmented view of individuals' psychology. More recently, researchers have recognised the importance of taking an integrated view to complement and extend earlier work (Barcelos, 2015; Kubanyiova, 2012; Mercer, 2014). In this study I argue for research on teacher psychology from a holistic perspective, in order to bring together understandings from diverse psychological components and examine how they connect with each other.

A second key dimension of psychology that needs consideration is how it can be understood in contextualised terms. Traditionally, context has been viewed as a static and external variable, which has been theorised to influence mental processes but over which individuals have no control (Ushioda, 2009). Recently, however, researchers have acknowledged that a meaningful investigation of individuals' psychology requires a deeper understanding of the situated nature of psychological processes and the reciprocal relationships between the individual and their social contexts (see, for example, Kalaja *et al.*, 2015; Ushioda, 2009). These relationships are described as dynamically evolving and bi-directional by Ushioda (2015: 48), who also argues that individuals 'are not simply located in particular contexts, but inseparably constitute part of these contexts'. In a similar vein, Mercer (2016) describes the interaction of individual and context as parts of a single system. In keeping with these views, in this study I will consider context (including temporal and situational) as an inherent part of teachers' mental lives, defining as well as being defined by their experiences, and suggest that we need to explore the complexity of teachers' psychology in context. This is especially interesting to explore, considering that contexts can help frame teachers' mental lives as well as be shaped by their experiences.

Thus, based on the consideration of the literature, in this chapter I propose an exploration of LTP from a holistic perspective. A detailed discussion of the study is as follows.

The Study

This study aims at understanding LTP by empirically exploring the psychology of an individual teacher in context. While acknowledging the inseparability of individual and context, as suggested above, pragmatic and epistemological considerations mean that it is necessary to define boundaries in order to study any individual's psychology. Defining a case in this way, however, does not preclude a holistic understanding that highlights the contextualised and situated nature of psychology. To that end, this study will endeavour to generate a descriptive understanding of the bounded system of a person and their psychology in context. For the purpose of this study, teacher psychology will be defined as an amalgam of diverse components which are interrelated and socially situated. Teacher psychology is understood as being an integrated whole with the context because it forms an inseparable part of a teacher's lived experiences. Taking a holistic view on teachers' psychology is useful in providing a broader picture and generating fresh insights as to how psychological constructs might function together. It is also phenomenologically valid as it enables understanding of how teachers make meaning in their mental lives.

To achieve these aims a qualitative case study was considered appropriate mainly because it can enable in-depth, holistic and contextualised understandings of a single bounded case (Yin, 2014), and thus provide 'full and thorough knowledge of the particular' (Stake, 2000: 22). While 'the search for particularity competes with the search for generalizability' (Stake, 2003: 140), it is important to note that this case study is instrumental in nature in the sense that it aims to generalise to a theoretical proposition and generate useful insights about LTP, rather than generalise to a population (Yin, 2014). Given that my aim in this study is to examine teacher psychology as a situated and integrated whole, I argue that case study design can also enable me to explore the 'complexity, embedded character, and specificity' of an individual's psychology (Gillham, 2000: 6) as well as to 'preserve the wholeness, unity and integrity of the case' (Punch, 2013: 122).

Participant and context

This study was conducted in a tertiary-level setting in southern Pakistan. Data were generated with a male ESL teacher over a period of three months. The participant voluntarily agreed to take part in this research after being informed about the study's aims, the data generation procedures and the intended data use. The teacher participant was selected for three reasons: first, his willingness and reliability to commit for a prolonged period was important to generate data for the duration of the study; secondly, his relatively extensive teaching experience in diverse teaching contexts was expected to enable rich insights into his professional experiences as well as well as into the contextual realities; lastly, the nature of my relationship with the participant, a former co-worker, enabled me to build rapport, gain an insider's perspective probing deeper into teacher's psychological experiences, and look at nuances in his responses. To ensure that my relationship with the participant does not influence data generation and lead to impression management, I used an open-ended approach rather than presupposing or predicting events and experiences. Similarly, the analysis relied on inductive, data-driven methods, in order to ensure that the findings were mainly shaped by the information that Alex provided, rather than any presuppositions and prior knowledge I had about the context. To ensure anonymity and confidentiality, the participant was assigned a pseudonym and other identifying markers in the data were referred to in general, non-specific terms.

This case study participant, Alex (pseudonym), was in his early forties at the outset of this study and had 17 years of teaching experience. Alex is originally from the northwestern region of Pakistan, where he received his early education. He speaks multiple languages. He completed his Bachelor's degree in social sciences and then continued his Master's degree in English literature at a state university in southern Pakistan. Alex started his teaching career as a secondary school teacher and, at the time of this study, he was working as a full-time faculty member at a university. He had been working at that university for 13 years with his role at the time being an assistant professor. His major job responsibilities included teaching and conducting research. He was also academically engaged in pursuing a PhD.

Methods

Data were generated using multiple research tools during the summer term of 2014, which lasted for 11 weeks. Three non-participant classroom observations and audio-video recordings (hence, COR1–3), semi-structured and stimulated recall interviews (I1–I3 and SR1–SR3, respectively) and nine weekly diaries (TD1–9) were employed in order to elicit the participant's ongoing experiences, while an autobiographical narrative (TA) was used to generate data on his retrospective experiences. The use of multiple methods enabled rich and holistic insights on the connections of participant's diverse psychological experiences and contexts and also represented a '"true" fix on a situation by combining different ways of looking at it or different findings' (Silverman, 2010: 277).

The use of semi-structured interviews enabled detailed understandings of the teacher's psychology, which would not have been possible through other methods in isolation (e.g. self-report questionnaires). For the interviews a reference guide was prepared in advance. However, some probing questions based on the participant's responses were also included during the interviews. The interviews, which were audio-video recorded, lasted between 50 and 90 minutes. In order to understand the participant's psychology in context, non-participant classroom recordings and observations were used. The observations spread over a period of 10 weeks, each lasting between 80 minutes and two hours. These were conducted at mutually convenient but sensibly spaced time intervals (i.e. at the beginning, middle and towards the end of the semester) and in ways intended to minimise the effects of the researcher's presence and any distraction that the participant might feel. Each observation was followed by a stimulated recall session to enable the participant to converse about his experience in regard to the observed events. Although the participant was not always available immediately after the observations, the time between the event observed and the recall interview was no longer than two days. Each recall interview lasted between 35 and 90 minutes. All interviews were conducted using both English and Urdu to enable the participant to freely reflect on his experiences. In the narrative that follows, Urdu quotations are italicised and their translation is provided in square brackets. For the autobiographical narrative and weekly diaries, which were written in English, the participant was provided with a set of guiding questions with emphasis on detailed reflections. On a weekly basis, the participant reflected on his ongoing experiences in the diary templates sent to him via email and returned the completed diaries at the end of each week.

Analysis

In order to enable holistic and situated insights into Alex's psychology as a teacher I employed an inductive coding approach, which made use of the methodological rigour of grounded theory (Charmaz, 2014), but additionally built on insights from the literature as a broad analytical framework around which emerging themes were scaffolded. For the analysis, first, a working representation of verbal data was produced, wherein all interviews were transcribed verbatim. Then the transcribed data, weekly diaries and teacher autobiography were digitalised for analysis using ATLAS.ti. Data analysis began with line-by-line coding, which identified the teacher's diverse cognitions, emotions, motivation and behaviours and information on contextual dimensions. Through a process of coding and re-coding, some of the initial codes were reviewed, collapsed or merged until themes or clusters of psychological experiences were formed. The analysis then focused on making sense of the connections between these psychological experiences. Throughout the coding process, analytical memos were used to analyse the complex nature of the data and raise theoretical questions about the complexity manifested in the data. Then, in light of the literature, I considered the data and revisited the memos to describe how this teacher's psychology and contexts form a complex whole. The individual themes were integrated around the theoretically emerging concept of psychological connectedness, which forms the Findings section of this paper.

Findings

In this section I will show how a holistic perspective can be useful in understanding how different aspects of Alex's psychology and contexts connect. In order to illustrate Alex's psychological connectedness I examine three broad themes which appear to be salient in his data. For Alex, these key themes are: emotional control, inspirational role and mentorship role.

Emotional control

The first theme refers to a characteristic that Alex strongly believes one should possess as a teacher, which is 'emotional control'. Throughout his data he expresses his general belief that it important for teachers to 'robe your emotions' (I1), a statement that echoes Buchmann (1993). For example, he explains that he feels teachers should have a sort of a protective shield. As he says, 'an educational person (...) should be able to curb his instincts; should be able to control his emotions. Your emotions could be a wild horse. It could get you into trouble' (I2). According to him, teachers should have 'a sense of detachment [and should not] get emotionally involved' (I1). His belief serves as an 'ought-to' frame of how he thinks a teacher ought to feel and act in respect to regulating and suppressing their emotions.

Not only does Alex believe this about teachers generally, but he also believes he is able to exhibit this behaviour himself. For example, he talks about not showing his emotions to his students and reports having 'a robotic sort of an approach to teaching where I am actually angry, but I do not show that anger' (I2). Here it appears that his belief leads him to engage in 'emotional labour' (King, 2016; see also King & Ng, this volume) in interacting with learners in his class. Emotional labour can be understood as managing one's emotions in order to comply with the social norms that accompany a professional role. For example, he reports on his own behaviours as being 'mechanical (...). You make me angry (...) and I need to go and take that class, it is not that I am going to take my anger to that class' (I1). Indeed, the classroom observation and recording data show that he regulates his negative emotional and behavioural response, for instance, when his students perform poorly on an in-class descriptive writing task (COR2). Later, in a stimulated recall interview, he reflects on how he actually felt and what he wanted to do when this incident took place, reporting, 'I felt like pulling my hair' (SR2), although the classroom recording data suggest that he did not display any frustration in class. This suggests that the learners' poor performance, as a contextual factor, can trigger his negative feelings; however, his belief that teachers should regulate emotions then mediates his emotional and behavioural responses, leading him to suppress his true feelings in his actual interactions with the learners.

Interestingly, Alex emphasises teachers' emotional control, not because he believes teachers' emotionally loaded responses might negatively affect his learners, but because he believes it can have negative influences on teachers themselves. Speaking of his emotional regulation, he goes on to interpret his students' belief, and reports that they might think, 'Alex Parangian *he~ , jaldi tap jae~ge*' [*Alex is a Parangian (fictional ethnicity), he will be easily annoyed*] (I1). This is interesting because he suggests that he personally feels this is how his students view him. What is not certain is whether this interpretive belief actually emerges from his perception of how his students view him or some other cultural stereotypes. Generally in Pakistani culture, the ethnic group indexed here with the fictional name 'Parangian' is considered to be impulsive and short-tempered and so it could be possible that he interprets his students' view of his ethnic background to be his vulnerable side. Thus, his personal belief that teachers should hide or 'robe' emotions (I1) or have 'a robotic sort of an approach' (I2) also possibly emerges from culturally shaped perceptions.

Another possible interpretation concerning his belief about teachers' emotional control could be drawn from how he talks about his childhood experiences as a learner. In one of his semi-structured interviews, he reflects upon how he and his classmates made fun of their teacher, who lost his cool upon being teased by one of Alex's classmates.

> Teacher *ke saat essa hota he (...) hamaare ek* teacher *the (...)* class *me vo* board *pe kuch likh raha tha aur piichhe se kisi ne awaz nikaal di. vo nahi pakaR saka ke kis ne avaz nikaali he lekin* we took him for a ride. *issi tarha~ log aap ko* as a teacher *bhi* use *karte he~ aur* as a boss *bhi* use *karte he~ . tu ye hota he.* [*This is what happens with a teacher. One of my teachers was writing on the board and a student teased him. The teacher could find out who did it, but we took him for a ride. This is how people use you as a teacher and as a boss. This is what happens*]. (I1)

Here he suggests that this is what he experienced with his own teacher and how he, along with his other classmates, exploited his teacher's perceived emotional weakness. Perhaps his perceptions about his own experiences as a learner are a source of his beliefs that teachers generally should supress their emotions. He explains,

> I grew up going to a government school and we used to take our teachers for a ride knowing and playing on their weaknesses. (...) So, go to your work place, but do not carry your emotions with you. Keep your heart at home. (I2)

It could possibly be that because of the way Alex perceives his experiences as a learner, he does not want to go through the same experience as a teacher, and so he has come to believe that a teacher 'should be able to control his emotions' (I2).

Inspirational role

The second theme in Alex's data concerns his belief that a teacher should have an 'inspirational role'. He explains that he feels that it is important for a teacher to be someone whom students look up to as a 'source of inspiration' (TA). His belief that teachers generally should transmit positivity or be able to inspire or motivate learners appears to combine with his belief that he is able to act as an inspiration for his learners. For example, when discussing his past as a school teacher, he reports that:

> When I was teaching this class eight, there were twenty-five students, all girls and I do not know why uhm they were inspired by me. Maybe I was a young guy. I mean I was not that young, twenty-six or twenty-seven and these girls were kids. And I was a six feet two inches uhm I felt like Gulliver. So, I inspired those girls. (I1)

In the excerpt, Alex reports on his perception of his physical appearance, and also the implicit belief that his height had inspired his students and the more general view that he perceives himself as someone who positively influences his learners. The strength of his belief about the role of a teacher's physique in inspiring learners can also be seen in how he believes that teachers 'who are concerned about the fact that they are short (...) should not be teacher[s]' (I1).

Importantly, descriptions of his inspirational role are exclusively reported within the context of a school in connection with a group of rather young learners. In his self-report data there is not a single instance where he describes his inspirational role with respect to the specific group of adult learners he taught at the time of this study, which suggests that the particularities of the context could change the interactions of his psychology and might call forth a different manifestation of his inspirational role. In this sense, it is possible that his view of his inspirational role as a teacher varies depending on the group of learners he interacts with, and thus hints at the dynamic nature of his psychology.

Another set of beliefs held by Alex about the ways teachers can inspire learners can be seen in an extract where he discusses the role of passion in teaching. Reflecting on his past experiences as a student, he points out that:

> Looking back as my days as a student I realize one thing that there is much more to teaching then just merely going to the class and delivering a particular lecture. I strongly feel that a teacher should carry a certain amount of passion to [their] classroom without which a teacher would be just a deliverer of a certain topic. (TA)

In this extract Alex connects his belief that teachers should be passionate back to his experiences as a learner. Although this belief apparently contradicts his previous statements about robotic teaching, it is possible that his emphasis on teachers' emotional control refers only to negative emotions and excludes positive emotions. As he explains: 'Happiness *tu dekhaata hu~ [I do show my happiness]'* (I1). What the extract also seems to suggest is Alex's beliefs that teachers should come up with teaching strategies that inspire, rather than simply deliver a lecture.

Examples of how Alex enacted his inspirational role through appropriate teaching strategies was observed in the classroom and also recorded in his personal reflections on his teaching practices. The classroom observation and recording show that, on one occasion, he incorporated an unplanned outside class task (e.g. observing a painting) as a reference frame for a descriptive writing task (COR2), in order to inspire his learners to write. Later, he reflected on this strategy saying, '*vo* partition *vali* picture *bohat* inspiring *he. [That picture on partition is very inspiring].* You know that picture tells you a million stories and you can use that picture for a variety of activities' (SR3). It could be that he feels his use of such teaching strategies serve as an enactment of his inspirational role.

Speaking of his experiences in other contexts, Alex also appears to equate his inspirational role as a teacher with how he views himself in the sports domain, showing how domain boundaries are subjective and permeable:

> I: So, knowing that you were not a good student back then and that now you are a good teacher who can inspire his learners, how does that make you feel?
> A: I take pride in it because I have also played cricket at the professional level. The whole team looks up to you and so you have to do something and you do it and you get a pad [sic] on your back at the end of the day; that is where the motivation comes from. So, the same goes for the teacher as well. (I1)

The excerpt illustrates how Alex's belief about his perceived inspirational role makes him feel proud. Moreover, the way he expresses his beliefs that, as a professional player, the whole team looked up to him and that 'the same goes for the teacher as well' perhaps suggests that he perceives his role in different contexts or domains in similar ways. In fact, the strength of this schema is such that he even represents his sports background as one where he, not the coach, instructed the other players. This shows how his psychological experiences of different contexts and domains interrelate, and thus suggests the socially situated and connected nature of his psychology. This has important implications for research and is an example of the importance of holistic perspectives to accommodate subjective domain interconnections (see also Mercer, 2011).

Interestingly, Alex not only believes himself to be positively influencing or inspiring his learners, but believes he is inspired by them too, which suggests the existence of reciprocal relationships between teacher and learner psychology. For example, he reports:

> And the other thing that I would like to give credit to myself is that I get inspiration from my students. Like if I tell them something and I see that

okay they have picked it up and they are using it, even that little thing can inspire me. (I1)

Instances of how context influences Alex can also be seen in his more specific beliefs concerning the group of learners he taught during this study. For example, he reflects on his weekly experiences as: 'Obviously, I felt more motivated and encouraged by the progress made by my students so far' (TD6). Clearly, his perception of his learners' progress triggers his positive feelings and motivation and thus shows how his interpretation of his experiences and relationship with his learners plays a significant role in shaping his ongoing psychology. It reinforces the understanding of the connections between teacher and learner psychologies, with teachers also drawing motivation from their experiences with their learners (Frenzel *et al.*, 2009; Gregersen & MacIntyre, 2015; Tardy & Snyder, 2004).

Mentorship role

A final theme in the data, closely connected to Alex's beliefs about inspiring learners, concerns a teacher's potential to mentor or coach learners. The importance of mentorship is emphasised in Alex's general beliefs about teachers. For example, he reportedly considers that teachers involved in coaching should be 'able to go down to the level of the students' (I1). He expresses similar beliefs in relation to himself as well. For instance, he assigns himself the role of a 'coach' and a 'guide' (I1) and reports that this self-assigned role makes him feel positive. As he elaborates, 'I mean I used to take extra pleasure in that [i.e. mentoring]' (I1). This suggests that his cognitions combine with his affect, and that his psychological well-being is connected to the meaningfulness he assigns to his professional role, a theme that is also explored by Falout and Murphey (this volume).

Moreover, perhaps the way he attributes to himself the role of a coach or a guide triggers his motivation, stimulating a behavioural response of fostering learning and providing guidance to his learners. This is particularly evident in the classroom data, for instance, when he steps forward, in response to the needs of his learners or the environment, to guide the weaker students of his class in solving a crossword puzzle (COR1). Later, he reflects on his classroom behaviour, saying:

> … when they are stuck, you give them a word and they are there. (…) another group who did not have any idea about what is going on. So, then you will have to sit at least for the first time and do it with them … (SR1)

Alex reports that he guides his learners during in-class tasks by actually sitting with them and helping them do the task. Similar enactments of his supportive role also appear in the data, when he sits with two of his weaker students to support and guide them as they struggle to complete an in-class descriptive writing task (COR2), and in respect to another task, when he states that he sits with his learners in order to help them 'do a paragraph or an essay' (SR1). Clearly, these examples show that his beliefs about his positive role as a teacher align with his classroom practices and thus suggest that he interprets his experiences and interactions with learners as positively influencing the learners.

However, there are instances in his data where his beliefs about a teacher's mentorship role appear to contradict his reported practices. This is evident, for instance, when he recalls his teaching experience in the first lecture, reporting, 'People are not sure why they are asked to use T.H.E., 'the', 'a' or 'an'. So, more importantly we need to tell them about it. But that is about it, I am not going to go back to it' (SR1). The excerpt shows his belief that teachers 'need to tell them about it'; however, it seems that he also has expectations of just how much support he is willing to provide to his pupils in this instance. This belief could be interpreted as contradicting his belief that a teacher should be able to offer guidance and 'go down to the level of the student' (SR1). Perhaps this contradiction arises from his specific language-related beliefs. He explains that '... grammar is something (...) I mean at the Bachelor's level (...), it is not something that you should do with them (...). I never do grammar with my students at this level at least' (SR1). Another possible interpretation could stem from his beliefs about what he perceives as the aims of language teaching in tertiary settings (e.g. 'at the Bachelor's level', 'at this level'), in which he does not see this lower level of language problems as falling within his remit. These instances suggest that his beliefs and practices reflecting his mentorship role vary in diverse areas of the language and teaching role. At first, it would seem that it is possible to hold contradictory beliefs and practices, yet from a holistic, situated view it can be seen how different roles and linguistic domains could change the interactions and patterns in his psychology. In other words, he may view his role as a teacher in ways that vary according to tasks, language areas, learners and contexts suggestive of the dynamism of his psychology.

Once again, in his mentorship role, he makes connections to his experiences as a sportsman. For example, he states: 'So, teaching is again something which uhm I connect it to my days as a sportsman because even when I was playing I was very supportive of others; would guide them and coach them' (I1). Indeed, the way he views himself supporting others not only in the teaching domain but even in the sports domain again indicates how he connects different contexts or domains as relevant from his perspective. Moreover, it is interesting to note that, in the domain of sports, the way he views himself as a coach is a role that is not formally assigned to him; rather, he self-attributes this role. He states,

> ... during the games when I used to see people who have taken my advice and worked on it and they are you know reaping its benefit so, I think (...) that is how I would say that I am a natural teacher or natural coach for that matter. (I1)

Alex perceives other people as having benefited because of his advice and actions, attributing their success to the role he has played. Once again, it shows how his perceptions of others are also important in the construction of his own psychology and how he relates to them. Indeed, the social context in which he is situated is inherently part of contributing to shaping his psychology. It is a good illustration of how his psychology is socially situated and connected to others in his social world.

Discussion

In this study, I have chosen to examine the data from a holistic perspective, discussing salient themes and considering the interconnectedness of various dimensions of Alex's psychology and its socially situated nature against the backdrop of each specific theme. The findings illustrate the value of taking a holistic perspective to examining teacher psychology in respect to two key areas: the multicomponential and interconnected nature of Alex's psychology; and the socially situated and thus dynamic nature of his psychology.

The first insight gained from a holistic perspective is the indication in the data of the multicomponential nature of Alex's psychology, which is constituted by a complex web of cognitions, affect, motives and behaviours, each of which could be regarded as a complex dynamic system (see, for example, Feryok, 2010). The dense interrelationships between these connections make it difficult, if not impossible, to meaningfully separate components from each other. Adopting an analytical approach that looks into themes is able to show how diverse psychological components and contexts come together and form a complex whole in respect to certain emergent individual themes. For example, we can see in the data, when the learners perform poorly, how Alex's affective and behavioural responses are mediated by his belief about the importance of teachers regulating their own emotions. The interconnected nature of teachers' psychology illustrated in this study supports the value of taking a holistic perspective, as argued in other recent studies (Barcelos, 2015; Kubanyiova, 2012).

Secondly, Alex's data exemplify well the socially situated and connected nature of his psychology and the permeable cross-domain boundaries of his psychology. For instance, Alex's psychological experiences which are relevant to his description of his professional roles as a teacher (e.g. emotional control, mentoring) form an inextricable part of the social contexts with which he interacts (e.g. teaching, learning and sports). The data hint at the bi-directional relations between teacher and learner psychologies, such as when he reports drawing inspiration from his learners, while in turn being a source of inspiration for them. These interconnections across individuals' psychology are suggestive of the social and potentially relational nature of human psychology. Taking a holistic approach to capture relationships between learner and teacher psychology and their social contexts can allow for conceptualisation of an individual's psychology in more situated and relational terms. In this study, the findings suggest that the boundaries of a teacher's psychology are rather open. So, for instance, Alex was not only inspired by learners, but also believed he inspired them. Obviously, exploring the learners' perspectives and their psychologies simultaneously might usefully complement our understanding of how people's psychologies and contexts interconnect (cf. Sampson, 2016). This relational interpersonal dimension of psychology lends support to findings from other studies which also showed a perceived link between learner and teacher psychology (Frenzel *et al.*, 2009; Gregersen & MacIntyre, 2015), and suggests that a person's psychological system can be thought of as being an open system which is connected to other people's psychologies and contexts. Only in theoretical terms can we perhaps meaningfully 'bound' a person's psychology.

In respect to domain boundaries, the data showed how Alex's psychology stretched across typically distinct domains (e.g. language teaching and sports). In this study, the boundaries separating these domains seemed to be rather blurry, as cognitions and feelings appeared to permeate boundaries having relevance across domains. Some examples of this include when he compared his current role as a university lecturer with previous roles in sports or when Alex invoked his childhood learning experiences to define his perceptions of how teachers should behave in his current context. Such articulation of the connections of psychology across different contexts, temporal and contextual domains, suggests the permeability of domain boundaries in psychology and the importance of holistic perspectives in revealing an individual's subjective understanding of domains (see also Mercer, 2011). The permeability of boundaries makes it difficult to neatly draw sharp distinctions in terms of personal and professional domains, which seems to reflect findings elsewhere about the phenomenological experience of teacher lives (Day & Gu, 2014).

Moreover, Alex's data illustrate how the dense web of interconnections that constitutes this teacher's psychology appears to be dynamic across diverse situations. In this respect, the findings show stability in terms of how he interprets his professional role as a teacher (e.g. mentoring) across different contexts or domains (e.g. teaching and sports). However, the data also indicate that Alex's psychology can be thought of as changing across situations. This is evident, for instance, when he seemed to view his mentorship role in defined ways that vary depending on language areas, learners and contexts (e.g. avoiding teaching grammatical rules at the Bachelor's level), or when he reflects upon his inspirational role explicitly in relation to his past teaching experience in the context of a school, with a group of young learners but not with respect to his present context of adult learners, which perhaps suggests that his view of his inspirational role may vary across diverse teaching contexts or groups of learners. These findings suggest that it can be analytically helpful to consider teacher psychology as being dynamic; the ways in which a teacher's psychology interacts with diverse contexts is likely to change the interactions and patterns in their psychology (Henry, 2015).

Conclusion

The findings from the analysis of this teacher's psychology highlighted the potential offered by a holistic perspective in illustrating the connected and situated nature of psychology. While researchers might argue that these holistic explanations provide a subjective viewpoint of the individual and may not represent their lived experiences accurately, I believe that looking at teacher psychology from a holistic perspective has value in the sense that it provides a framework to generate an integrated and situated, rather than a reductionist and de-contextualised understanding of teachers' psychological lived experiences and lives. A holistic stance also points to the potential for conceptualising teacher psychology as a complex dynamic system. The findings from this study imply some features of complex systems theory (e.g. multicomponentiality and open systems including contexts), which may offer a useful avenue for future research aiming to be explicitly informed by this perspective.

The research findings also have implications for language teacher education. Teacher education and professional development programmes typically focus on developing instructional strategies and pedagogical skills. However, such programmes could be expanded to incorporate an awareness of teachers' psychology, helping trainees to appreciate the possible influences on their personal and professional lives and how to regulate this effectively to ensure positive professional well-being (Durr et al., 2014). One idea could be for teacher development programmes to include activities (e.g. psychological reflections), which enable teachers to make sense of the connections between their personal and professional psychological experiences, recognise the emerging patterns of their psychology and consider how these can shape their practices (Mercer et al., 2016). This would be particularly useful in identifying positive psychological patterns and ways of being as these ensure future language teachers thrive and flourish in their professional roles (Castle & Buckler, 2009).

References

Barcelos, A.M.F. (2015) Unveiling the relationship between beliefs, emotions and identities. *Studies in Second Language Learning and Teaching* 5 (2), 301–325.

Borg, S. (2006) *Teacher Cognition and Language Education: Research and Practice.* London: Continuum.

Buchman, M. (1993) Role over person: Morality and authenticity in teaching. In M. Buchman and R.E. Floden (eds) *Detachment and Concern: Conversations in the Philosophy of Teaching and Teacher Education* (pp. 145–157). New York: Cassell.

Carter, B. and Sealey, A. (2000) Language, structure and agency: What can realist social theory offer to sociolinguistics? *Journal of Sociolinguistics* 4 (1), 3–20.

Castle, P. and Buckler, S. (2009) *How to Be a Successful Teacher.* London: Sage.

Chacón, C.T. (2005) Teachers' perceived efficacy among English as a foreign language teachers in middle schools in Venezuela. *Teaching and Teacher Education* 21 (3), 257–272.

Charmaz, K. (2014) *Constructing Grounded Theory: A Practical Guide through Qualitative Analysis.* London: Sage.

Cheung, Y.L., Said, S.B. and Park, K. (2015) *Advances and Current Trends in Language Teacher Identity Research.* Abingdon: Routledge.

Day, C. and Gu, Q. (2014) *Resilient Teachers, Resilient Schools: Building and Sustaining Quality in Testing Times.* London: Routledge.

Dörnyei, Z. (2010) The relationship between language aptitude and language learning motivation: Individual differences from a dynamic systems perspective. In E. Macaro (ed.) *Continuum Companion to Second Language Acquisition* (pp. 247–267). London: Continuum.

Durr, T., Chang, M.-L. and Carson, R.L. (2014) Curbing teacher burnout: The transactional factors of teacher efficacy and emotion management. In P. Richardson, S.A. Karabenick and H.M.G. Watt (eds) *Teacher Motivation: Theory and Practice* (pp. 198–213). New York: Routledge.

Feryok, A. (2010) Language teacher cognitions: Complex dynamic systems? *System* 38, 427–436.

Frenzel, A.C., Goetz, T., Lüdtke, O., Pekrun, R. and Sutton, R. (2009) Emotional transmission in the classroom: Exploring the relationship between teacher and student enjoyment. *Journal of Educational Psychology* 101, 705–716.

Gillham, B. (2000) *Case Study Research Methods.* London: Continuum.

Gregersen, T. and MacIntyre, P.D. (2015) 'I can see a little bit of you in myself': A dynamic systems approach to the inner dialogue between teacher and learner selves. In Z. Dörnyei, P.D. MacIntyre and A. Henry (eds) *Motivational Dynamics in Language Learning* (pp. 260–284). Bristol: Multilingual Matters.

Henry, A. (2015) The dynamics of possible selves. In Z. Dörnyei, P.D. MacIntyre and A. Henry (eds) *Motivational Dynamics in Language Learning* (pp. 83–94). Bristol: Multilingual Matters.

Hiver, P. and Dörnyei, Z. (2017) Language teacher immunity: A double-edged sword. *Applied Linguistics* 38 (3), 405–423.

Kalaja, P., Barcelos, A.M.F., Aro, M. and Ruohotie-Lyhty, M. (2015) *Beliefs, Agency and Identity in Foreign Language Learning and Teaching.* Basingstoke: Palgrave Macmillan.

King, J. (2016) 'It's time, put on a smile, it's time!': The emotional labour of second language teaching within a Japanese university. In C. Gkonou, D. Tatzl and S. Mercer (eds) *New Directions in Language Learning Psychology* (pp. 97–112). Cham: Springer.

Kubanyiova, M. (2012) *Teacher Development in Action: Understanding Language Teachers' Conceptual Change.* Basingstoke: Palgrave Macmillan.

Mercer, S. (2011) *Towards an Understanding of Language Learner Self-Concept.* Dordrecht: Springer.

Mercer, S. (2014) Re-imagining the self as a network of relationships. In K. Csizér and M. Magid (eds) *The Impact of Self-concept on Language Learning* (pp. 51–72). Bristol: Multilingual Matters.

Mercer, S. (2016) The contexts within me: L2 self as a complex dynamic system. In J. King (ed.) *The Dynamic Interplay between Context and the Language Learner* (pp. 11–28). Basingstoke: Palgrave Macmillan.

Mercer, S., Ryan, S. and Williams, M. (eds) (2012) *Psychology for Language Learning: Insights from Research, Theory and Practice.* Basingstoke: Palgrave MacMillan.

Mercer, S., Oberdorfer, P. and Saleem, M. (2016) Helping language teachers to thrive: Using positive psychology to promote teachers' professional well-being. In D. Gabryś-Barker and D. Gałajda (eds) *Positive Psychology Perspectives on Foreign Language Learning and Teaching, Second Language Learning and Teaching* (pp. 213–229). Cham: Springer.

Mousavi, E.S. (2007) Exploring 'teacher stress' in non-native and native teachers of EFL. *English Language Teacher Education and Development* 10, 33–41.

Punch, K.F. (2013) *Introduction to Social Research: Quantitative and Qualitative Approaches*. London: Sage.

Sampson, R.J. (2016) EFL teacher motivation *in-situ*: Co-adaptive processes, openness and relational motivation over interacting timescales. *Studies in Second Language Learning and Teaching* 6 (2), 293–318.

Silverman, D. (2010) *Doing Qualitative Research: A Practical Handbook*. London: Sage.

Stake, R.E. (2000) The case study method in social inquiry. In R. Gomm, M. Hammersley and P. Foster (eds) *Case Study Method* (pp. 19–26). London: Sage.

Stake, R.E. (2003) Case studies. In N.K. Denzin and Y.S. Lincoln (eds) *Strategies of Qualitative Inquiry* (pp. 134–164). Thousand Oaks, CA: Sage.

Tardy, C.M. and Snyder, B. (2004) 'That's why I do it': Flow and EFL teachers' practices. *ELT Journal* 58 (2), 118–128.

Ushioda, E. (2009) A person-in-context relational view of emergent motivation, self and identity. In Z. Dörnyei and E. Ushioda (eds) *Motivation, Language Identity and the L2 Self* (pp. 215–228). Bristol: Multilingual Matters.

Ushioda, E. (2015) Context and dynamic systems theory. In Z. Dörnyei, P.D. MacIntyre and A. Henry (eds) *Motivational Dynamics in Language Learning* (pp. 47–54). Bristol: Multilingual Matters.

Yin, R.K. (2014) *Case Study Research: Design and Methods*. Thousand Oaks, CA: Sage.

19 Conclusion: Lessons Learned, Promising Perspectives

Achilleas Kostoulas and Sarah Mercer

In this final chapter, we would like to reflect on the chapters that we have had the privilege of editing in this collection, consider the lessons we have learned from working with our colleagues, and propose what we consider to be promising perspectives for the future of the field of language teacher psychology.

Lesson 1: There is a Need for Research into Language Teacher Psychology

Many of the contributions in this collection raise awareness of the needs and challenges that language teachers face in their professional roles. While some of these issues are shared by teachers regardless of discipline, there is also evidence of dimensions that are specific to language education, which typically involves moving between languages, cultures and identities. For example, in Chapter 6, Li and De Costa discuss the problems facing Chinese teachers of English who had been trained in the UK in negotiating their teaching identities, roles and expectations when they began their teaching careers in China. By drawing attention to the ways discrepancies between the two settings are perceived, the authors point out the unique challenges language teachers face in constructing their identities. Similarly, Wyatt (Chapter 8) reminds us that teacher self-efficacy beliefs 'intersect with language proficiency'. He reflects on the possible implications for the well-being of language teachers whose proficiency is still developing, and alerts us to the fact that the ongoing debates about the role of native speakers in language education can impact the self-efficacy beliefs of language teachers.

Another area of interest concerns the challenges associated with transitions between different stages in language educators' careers, which appear to be associated with cognitive and affective changes. One frequently examined transition is when teachers move from their initial teacher education into the school system, and this remains a key area for researchers to understand. For example, in this collection, Kalaja and Mäntylä in Chapter 3 report on early-stage teachers who experienced a shift in the perceptions of their roles and their expectations. The chapters by Li and De Costa (Chapter 6) and Sahakyan et al. (Chapter 4) focus on the transitions to understandings that were more closely grounded in local circumstance and feasibility compared with their educational training. Transitions later in the career, which might involve taking on new professional roles such as becoming a teacher trainer (as reported in Kostoulas & Lämmerer, Chapter 15) or working from new perspectives in the third age (Oxford et al., Chapter 17), also bring along their own psychological challenges. However, to date, these kinds of transitions remain woefully under-researched.

The chapters that make up this volume offer a number of useful starting points for further explorations into the psychology of language teachers. Given increasing awareness of the psychological dimensions of language teacher well-being and the impact of this on teachers' ability to teach to the best of their abilities (Albrecht, 2006; Corcoran & Tormey, 2012; Furrer et al., 2014), we now need more research to understand language teacher psychology per se, but also empirically informed interventions that can help to empower and support teachers, such as those suggested in Chapter 13 by Falout and Murphey and in Chapter 16 by Gregersen and MacIntyre. Perhaps most importantly, a focus on teacher psychology would serve to highlight the value and importance of language teachers and their criticality for effective language teaching. At a time when the teaching profession finds itself under sustained scrutiny and sometimes hostile public discourse, we believe that the academic community can, and indeed should, signal the importance of teachers, not just because if teachers feel valued, this will have a knock-on effect into practice (Bajorek et al., 2014), but also because of a fundamental belief in their value as professionals and people in their own right.

Lesson 2: There Exists a Vibrant Fertile Landscape for Future Growth

Perhaps the most obvious lesson to be learned from this collection is that the landscape for research into teacher psychology that exists in SLA is possibly not as barren as the relative paucity of existing research might at first suggest. The receptiveness of a major publisher to the proposal that eventually developed into this collection, and the reception that this project received from potential contributors suggest that there is awareness of a niche that has yet to be fully empirically addressed. Preparing this collection has given us insights into how researchers across SLA are increasingly investing their time in and dedicating their scholarship to the study of diverse aspects of language teacher psychology. Connecting these independently pursued research strands is likely to provide momentum to the field's attempts to better understand the psychology of language teachers, and to ensure that teachers as key stakeholders are given at least equal attention to learners in our research into the psychology surrounding language learning and teaching processes.

Another development, which we consider especially encouraging, concerns the recent growth of positive psychology in the field of SLA (e.g. MacIntyre *et al.*, 2016). Alongside existent work on teacher identity and cognitions, this promises to become potentially one of the core areas of research in language teacher psychology. This welcome development is showcased in a number of chapters in this collection designed to promote the well-being of teachers, such as Gregersen and MacIntyre (Chapter 16), who explicitly draw on the Values In Action Inventory of Strengths (Peterson & Seligman, 2004), as well as Falout and Murphey (Chapter 13), who report on a 'job crafting' (Wrzesniewski & Dutton, 2001) intervention. By ensuring that our understanding of language teacher psychology explores teacher flourishing and not only deficit, problem-oriented views, the field is well positioned to create a balanced and comprehensive understanding of teacher psychology. Furthermore, positive psychology interventions are often closely connected to the immediate practical needs of language teachers, and this link between academic research and practical concerns is especially welcome.

Taking a broader look at the field, we can draw on work that already exists beyond SLA in the general, social and educational psychology. Examples of how language teacher psychology can build on existing scholarship can be found in the chapters on teacher self-efficacy beliefs (Wyatt, Chapter 8), language teacher identity (Li & De Costa, Chapter 6; Varghese, Chapter 5) or language teacher agency (White, Chapter 12). Similarly, the chapters by King and Ng (Chapter 9) and Hiver *et al.* (Chapter 2) demonstrate how an understanding of language teacher motivation can capitalise on the rich corpus of motivation research in general teacher education. Similarly, in their discussion of resilience in Chapter 15, Kostoulas and Lämmerer provide us with another example of how constructs can be adapted to the specific domain of language teacher psychology, and in Chapter 14 Hiver shows how existing conceptualisations can be extended by putting forward new constructs such as language teacher immunity. As the field of language teacher psychology continues to develop and generate domain-specific theory as appropriate, we feel that this interdisciplinary porosity can be expanded further. Not only do we in SLA benefit from drawing on psychological disciplines, but we have much to offer those feeder disciplines in return as we work on constructs in ways unique to the relevant needs and profile of our specific domain.

Lesson 3: The Field is Marked by Methodological and Theoretical Diversity

Another source of optimism we can see from the collection of papers concerns the potential for a diverse range of methodological approaches – something we think marks out the interdisciplinary area of language teacher psychology advantageously compared to traditional psychology paradigms. Within this short collection alone, there are empirical studies employing more traditional survey studies (e.g. Dewaele & Mercer, Chapter 11), narrative studies (e.g. Oxford *et al.*, Chapter 17), case studies (e.g. Kostoulas & Lämmerer, Chapter 15) and mixed methods approaches (e.g. Gkonou & Mercer, Chapter 10). Alongside these more established research traditions, there is also research that has employed more novel, innovative approaches. One example of such methodological innovation is provided in Chapter 3, where Kalaja and Mäntylä report on a multimodal analysis which combined verbal and visual data. Also, in Chapter 18 Saleem approaches thematic analysis from a holistic perspective in order to generate a situated understanding of a language teacher's psychology. It was interesting to note that, although this was not explicitly invoked, many chapters in this volume used reflection as part of their research methodology. Knowing the value of personal reflection for well-being (Siegel, 2007), this suggests a useful practical dimension for empirical work as well as interventions focusing on teachers.

Related to the multitude of methodological approaches is also the theoretical diversity evinced in these papers – something we greatly appreciate. As noted earlier in this chapter, multiple contributions to the volume are inspired or informed by positive psychology. Other authors, such as Sahakyan *et al.* (Chapter 4) and Kalaja and Mäntylä (Chapter 3), draw on possible selves theory (Dörnyei, 2005; Markus & Nurius, 1986), whereas the contributions by Varghese (Chapter 5) and Li and De Costa (Chapter 6) are grounded in sociocultural theory. The increasing trend to use relational, holistic and complexity-inspired theoretical perspectives is also in evidence in this collection. In Chapter 10 Gkonou and Mercer explicitly evoke a relational perspective in order to describe the beliefs and practices of language teachers. Similarly, Feryok's conceptualisation of language teacher cognitions as an emergent phenomenon in Chapter 7 draws directly from the conceptual toolkit of complexity theory. The same applies, to different degrees, to the construct of language teacher immunity put forward by Hiver in Chapter 14, the complexity-informed description of resilience by Kostoulas and Lämmerer (Chapter 15), and Saleem's holistic description of a teacher's psychology (Chapter 18).

Promising Perspective: The Broad Vista of Yet-to-be-explored Territory

As we take stock, we note that there remains a pressing need for more research, and that there is evidence of vibrant activity from which such research might emerge and adequate diversity that would help future research to develop unconstrained from restrictive theoretical and methodological bias. In the final section of this chapter we now offer a number of suggestions regarding what directions such work might take.

This collection has presented some relatively familiar constructs, such as identity, cognitions and motivation, and it has shown how they might be further developed and built on as we continue to construct deeper and more nuanced understandings of language teacher psychology. Equally importantly, the collection has extended the field by introducing a range of less frequently researched constructs. In Chapter 10 Gkonou and Mercer explore the role of emotional and social intelligence in connection to the beliefs and practices of language teachers; in Chapter 11 Dewaele and Mercer discuss the role of teacher attitudes; in Chapter 13 Falout and Murphey explore the relevance of job crafting; in Chapter 16 Gregersen and MacIntyre draw on signature strengths from positive psychology; and in Chapter 14 by Hiver and Chapter 15 by Kostoulas and Lämmerer the immunity and resilience of language teachers is investigated. These initial explorations into teacher psychology provide us with a starting point for defining the field. We expect that future research will likely engage with these themes in greater depth and additional constructs will become the focus of further empirical work. For example, the concept of flow in relation to language teaching promises to be a fertile area for future work (cf. Tardy & Snyder, 2004). As the research agenda expands, it promises to be exciting to see how our understandings of the constructs may develop in terms of their potentially domain-specific character, as well as possible interconnections between constructs.

The other key vista to be explored is a broader range of SLA teacher populations. While pre-service teachers will likely remain a key population to work with, we also need to better understand the psychology of in-service teachers at different stages of their careers, all the way up to and into retirement. The study by Oxford et al. (Chapter 17), which reports on the psychological experiences of third-age educators, is expected to be seminal in this regard. Future work in this direction is expected to add to the rich descriptions that the authors have provided, and perhaps enable comparisons with the experiences of third-age educators in different settings around the world. Another group of teachers who have not received much empirical attention to date are teacher educators. In Chapter 15 Kostoulas and Lämmerer present a case study of the resilience of such a teacher, and it will be important to appreciate how this group of teachers and their psychologies develop and how this affects their approaches to working with pre-service and also in-service teachers. Expanding the focus of enquiry to include these other language teacher populations is important as we seek to appreciate the psychological conditions facing all types of teachers across their career trajectories and in a range of settings.

In principle, it is important to underscore the value of *all* the teachers who make up the language teaching and learning community.

Finally, we expect future work in language teacher psychology to expand in order to encompass a much more expansive range of language teaching contexts. For example, in respect to English language teachers, the global spread of the language has meant that English is now taught in a very diverse range of geographical and cultural contexts, where the relations between local and global cultures are not always uncomplicated and, as Li and De Costa show in Chapter 6, this situation also impacts the psychology of language teachers. Similarly, Wyatt points out in Chapter 8 that there are effects on language teacher self-efficacy related to the marginalisation of languages other than English, and the concomitant possible devaluation of the professional role of the professionals who teach these languages. There is clearly a need for more empirical work that will shed light on how these shifting linguistic balances are experienced in diverse settings, and how these perceptions impact language teachers' psychology. Future work on language teaching psychology must ensure that it encompasses the experiences of teachers of a range of foreign and second languages, not just English. Moreover, there is much scope for work that could investigate the diverse institutions where language teaching takes place. In addition to primary, secondary and tertiary education, language learning increasingly takes place in 'non-traditional' settings (e.g. very young learners, informal settings, online communities, digital learning environments, refugee integration programmes), all of which are associated with differing and varying teacher roles, functions, expectations and identities. Studies that will generate in-depth, situated understandings of the psychology of language teachers in connection with all these diverse settings will be important in contributing towards an ecologically informed and more comprehensive theory of language teacher psychology.

Final Words

Part of our motivation for putting together this volume has been to generate a greater interest in and awareness of language teacher psychology in the community at large – both in empirical and practical terms. We hope that this collection may be able to contribute in some small part to that endeavour. As editors, we have drawn considerable pleasure and inspiration from engaging with the perspectives contained in the chapters that make up this collection. We hope that you, too, will find the content of this volume to be stimulating and that it inspires you for your own work, whether in language education research or in the practice of language teaching. There remains much work to be done but with a solid base to build on and promising perspectives ahead, there is reason to be optimistic about the future of this exciting and critically important field of enquiry.

References

Albrecht, K. (2006) *Social Intelligence: The New Science of Success*. San Francisco, CA: Jossey-Bass.

Bajorek, Z., Gulliford, J. and Taskila, T. (2014) *Healthy Teachers, Higher Marks? Establishing a Link between Teacher Health and Wellbeing, and Student Outcomes*. London: The Work Foundation. See https://www.educationsupportpartnership.org. uk/sites/default/files/resources/healthy_teachers_higher_marks_report_0.pdf

Corcoran, R.P. and Tormey, R. (2012) How emotionally intelligent are pre-service teachers? *Teaching and Teacher Education* 28 (5), 750–759.

Dörnyei, Z. (2005) *The Psychology of the Language Learner: Individual Differences in Second Language Acquisition*. Mahwah, NJ: Lawrence Erlbaum.

Furrer, C.J., Skinner, E.A. and Pitzer, J.R. (2014) The influence of teacher and peer relationships on students' classroom engagement and everyday motivational resilience. *National Society for the Study of Education* 113 (1), 101–123.

MacIntyre, P.D., Gregersen, T. and Mercer, S. (eds) (2016) *Positive Psychology in SLA*. Bristol: Multilingual Matters.

Markus, H. and Nurius, P. (1986) Possible selves. *American Psychologist* 41 (9), 954–969.

Peterson, C. and Seligman, M.E.P. (2004) *Character Strengths and Virtues: A Classification and Handbook*. New York: Oxford University Press.

Siegel, D.J. (2007) *The Mindful Brain: Reflection and Attunement in the Cultivation of Well-being*. New York: Norton.

Tardy, C.M. and Snyder, B. (2004) 'That's why I do it': Flow and EFL teachers' practices. *ELT Journal* 58 (2), 118–128.

Wrzesniewski, A. and Dutton, J.E. (2001) Crafting a job: Revisioning employees as active crafters of their work. *Academy of Management Review* 26 (2), 179–201.

Index